Forbidden Prayer

To the memory of my father
To my mother

Forbidden Prayer

Church Censorship and Devotional Literature in Renaissance Italy

GIORGIO CARAVALE

Università di Roma Tre, Italy

Translated by

PETER DAWSON

ASHGATE

Italian original edition: L'orazione proibita. Censura ecclesiastica e letteratura devozionale nella prima età moderna, © 2003, Firenze, Olschki.

Published by
Ashgate Publishing Limited
Wey Court East
Union Road
Farnham
Surrey, GU9 7PT
England

Ashgate Publishing Company
Suite 420
101 Cherry Street
Burlington
VT 05401-4405
USA

www.ashgate.com

British Library Cataloguing in Publication Data
Caravale, Giorgio.
Forbidden prayer : church censorship and devotional literature in Renaissance Italy. – (Catholic Christendom, 1300–1700)
1. Devotional literature – Censorship – Italy – History – 16th century. 2. Devotional literature – Censorship – Italy – History – 17th century. 3. Catholic Church – Prayers and devotions – Censorship – Italy – History – 16th century. 4. Catholic Church – Prayers and devotions – Censorship – Italy – History – 17th century. 5. Catholic Church – Doctrines – History – Modern period, 1500– 6. Censorship (Canon law – History – 16th century. 7. Censorship (Canon law – History – 17th century. 8. Italy – Church history – 16th century. 9. Italy – Church history – 17th century.
I. Title II. Series
264'.02'00945'09031-dc22

Library of Congress Cataloging-in-publication Data
Caravale, Giorgio.
Forbidden prayer : church censorship and devotional literature in Renaissance Italy / Giorgio Caravale.
p. cm. – (Catholic christendom, 1300–1700)
Includes bibliographical references and index.
ISBN 978-1-4094-2988-3 (hardcover : alk. paper) – ISBN 978-1-4094-3992-9 (ebook)
1. Censorship – Religious aspects – Christianity – History. 2. Devotional literature – Censorship. 3. Devotional literature – Publishing. 4. Italy – Church history – 16th century. 5. Italy – Church history – 17th century. I. Title.
BR115.C38C395 2011
242'.8024509031–dc23

2011029465

ISBN 9781409429883 (hbk)
ISBN 9781409439929 (ebk)

Printed and bound in Great Britain by the MPG Books Group, UK

Contents

Foreword

The aim of this book is to describe the attempt made by the Congregations of the Inquisition and the Index during the sixteenth century and the early decades of the seventeenth to purify certain devotional texts written in vernacular Italian, eliminating any heterodox elements or encrustations of superstition that they might contain and imposing strict uniformity in all liturgical and devotional practices. More specifically, a series of works will be considered whose subject is religious but not necessarily theological or liturgic, intended to maintain or increase the devotion of the faithful, whether lay persons or ecclesiastics;[1] treatises and even simple little devotional works over which the ecclesiastic organs entrusted with the task of keeping a watchful eye on Roman orthodoxy exercised their authority, either preventing the circulation of those parts of writings they deemed most harmful or surgically removing them. The subject of prayer, the leitmotiv of the entire work, makes it possible both to trace the evolution over the decades of the contents and forms of this type of spiritual or pious literature and to analyze at the same time the development of ecclesiastic censoring strategies with regard to this important sector of contemporary book production.

The attempt by Rome to impose rigid uniformity in the liturgic and devotional practices of the faithful was triggered by the gradual spreading of Protestant doctrines throughout the Italian peninsula and by the subsequent condemnation in the Index in 1559 of several texts devoted to prayer. In these works the compilers of the Pauline Index discerned – or believed they had discerned – clear evidence of heterodoxy, occasionally somewhat arbitrarily likening to the message of the Reformers examples of an inward spiritual religiosity that sank its roots in a rich medieval tradition that continued to flourish in the late fifteenth century and the early decades of the sixteenth. The battle engaged against the peril of Protestantism was to continue, albeit with less pressing urgency, into the

---

1 In addition to G. De Luca's classic work, *Introduzione alla storia della pietà*, Rome, Edizioni di Storia e Letteratura, 1962, see E. Barbieri's recent paper, *Tradition and change in the spiritual literature of the Cinquecento*, in *Church, Censorship and Culture in early modern Italy*, ed. by G. Fragnito, Cambridge, Cambridge University Press, 2001, pp. 111–33, published in fuller form in Id. – D. Zardin, *Libri, biblioteche e cultura nell'Italia del Cinque e Seicento*, Milan, Vita e Pensiero, 2002, pp. 3–61. For a general introduction to the topic, U. Rozzo's *Linee per una storia dell'editoria religiosa in Italia (1465–1600)*, Udine, Forum, 1993, continues to be fundamental, while a more recent work is *Il libro religioso*, also edited by Rozzo and by Rudj Gorian, Milan, S. Bonnard, 2002.

decades that followed, engaging fields of doctrine that were relatively remote. Mystic treatises on the subject of prayer were censured, even by a process of significant self-censorship, often as the result of the fact that the defenders of Roman orthodoxy, with some exaggeration, likened the question of the mystic expropriation of human will (and the consequent total abandonment to the will of God) to the Lutheran doctrine of the bondage of the will.

It was only after setting up a first sturdy bulwark against Lutheran infiltrations, with the Index of 1559, that the Church authorities committed themselves to the work of purifying prayer and liturgy from the superstitious and apocryphal encrustations that had sedimented over the centuries. This process drew vigor from the reformist demands still present in the Roman Curia, but certainly owed much to the insistent Protestant criticism of the external manifestation of Catholic religious practices. In other words, the process fulfilled, on the one hand, a broader program of inner reform of the Church and of a precise restoration of ecclesiastic tradition and, on the other, the need to subtract certain arguments from Protestant polemics.

In actual fact, the project of redefining and purifying the Church's orthodox patrimony and the related re-establishment of an inward, intimist dimension of religion, which the head-on opposition in the early part of the century had unilaterally attributed to the Protestant enemy, was destined to gradually lose strength, with the setting of the sun on the generations of ecclesiastics who had themselves promoted the project and especially with the gradual disappearance of the Protestant menace.

The conquest and the social and religious control of the uneducated faithful masses very soon became the primary objective of ecclesiastic action. In the last two decades of the sixteenth century the censor's alarm at the most disparate cultural and religious expressions of the universe of the 'unlettered' grew at a rate that was inversely proportional to the attention paid by the organs of repression in Rome to the devotional style of mystic prayer which – intended to conduct 'nuns and gentlewomen' to the very threshold of impeccability – distinguished itself by its innately elitist attitude.

The control of the religiosity of the 'simple' became the strategic priority of the Church of the Counter-Reformation, and the fight against using the vernacular became the symbol and instrument of that priority. As part of an offensive aimed at imposing ecclesiastic mediation as the sole channel for cultural production and enjoyment, many texts which in recent decades had satisfied the devotion of the 'simple', introducing them to an inner, intimist religiosity, were taken out of circulation. In this context, the fight against superstition lost much of its meaning and effectiveness. The need to involve the faithful on the emotional plane, the firm intention to arouse the interest of the great mass of the faithful, together with the widespread conviction that the specter of heresy had finally been driven out of Italy, turned the elements of superstition targeted by the project for the purification of the patrimony of orthodoxy into useful instruments of control in the hands of the ecclesiastic hierarchy. The devotional armamentarium, which until the earliest years of the seventeenth century had been the object of a process of censorship not lacking in historical perspective and philological exactitude, was exploited in order to stir the imagination and the emotions of the faithful, as part of a cultural design that now totally renounced the encouragement of the faithful believers' sense of individual responsibility and their power of discernment. Compared to the lucid and pugnacious declarations of war on any kind of intermingling of the sacred and the profane pronounced by the ranks of the Tridentines, this was a significant reversal of intent.[2]

In the absence of any strict regulation or action designed or intended to counteract all forms of superstition, the ambitious project of creating liturgic and devotional uniformity turned out to be wishful thinking. In addition to the not uncommon obstacles related to the difficulty of operating the machinery of repression, plus cases of localized resistance, there was also the ambiguous attitude of the Church hierarchies, which formally continued to propound rigid rules of prescription and prohibition when they themselves belied and disregarded those selfsame rules, bending them in order to achieve their higher objective of conquering the masses. The decree of 1601 on litanies and prayers – though initially designed with slightly different intentions – soon became not only the symbol of the failure of the project of uniformity but also the symbol of an increasingly more precisely defined ecclesiastic strategy, inasmuch as it provided for a dual system of rules which governed the recitation of litanies in public but also allowed ample scope for 'unofficial' liturgic and devotional practices in private. These concessions had the effect of slackening the censor's hostility to 'superstitions', formally recognizing the existence of a gap between the official rule and actual custom.[3] This was a renunciation by the Roman authorities of any attempt to fill an ever-more manifest hiatus between doctrine and religious practice – a renunciation that was also a strategy, one in which it is perhaps possible to discern far off the deep split between official religion and the conscience of those who keep the

[2] The unsuccessful Catholic battle for the separation between the sacred and the profane was also dealt with by P. Burke, *Popular culture in early modern Europe*, New York, Harper & Row, 1978, chapter 8.

[3] On these issues see now also G. Fragnito, *Proibito capire. La Chiesa e il volgare nella prima età moderna*, Bologna, Il Mulino, 2005, pp. 232–59.

faith, which today is a characteristic feature of the relationship between the Church and the laity.[4]

The viewpoint chosen for conducting this research is that of the internal activity of Church departments in Rome. The analysis therefore focuses mainly on the directives and policies of censorship drawn up within the two congregations, on the general guidelines of censorship of the authorities in Rome, and on the presumable underlying ideological reasoning. A careful reading of the epistulary correspondence between the local offices and the central congregations, i.e. a study of censorship documents sent from peripheral areas and arriving on the cardinals' tables in Rome, has in certain cases made it possible to analyze the way these directives of the central authorities were received at local level and to provide, as far as possible, a complete survey of their individual progress. The manifest and deliberate downsizing of the role of the bishops is partially justified not only by the method of research, i.e. the selection of sources, but also by the sharing of the view that:

> the bishops of Trent did not have the task of leading the people along the ways of righteousness and teaching them which ways were illicit. Religion's negative pedagogy was put in the hands of the Inquisition, which had to decide what was right and proper and what was dubious or decidedly heretical in the life of society and in people's thoughts; which books one was permitted to read; the people with whom one could have dealings […]; *which devotions were permitted and which were not.*[5]

---

[4] In this regard I think the most effective definition is that expressed by the Catholic philosopher Pietro Prini, who used the term 'submerged schism' (*Lo scisma sommerso. Il messaggio cristiano, la società moderna e la Chiesa cattolica*, Milan, Garzanti, 1999).

[5] A. Prosperi, *Il Concilio di Trento: una introduzione storica*, Turin, Einaudi, 2001, p. 152 (emphasis added). See also Id., *Tribunali della coscienza. Inquisitori, confessori, missionari,*Turin, Einaudi, 1996, pp. 370–71. There is a substantial collection of synodal documents on the theme of superstition edited by C. Corrain and P. Zampini, *Documenti etnografici e folkloristici nei sinodi diocesani italiani*, Bologna, Forni editore, 1970; however, as Prosperi points out (ibid., p. 370, footnote 6), one should bear in mind that these must have been recommendations rather than peremptory orders.

Note to the English Edition

The translation of this book was sponsored by a grant from the Commissione Nazionale per la Promozione della Cultura Italiana all'estero (National Commission for the Promotion of Italian Culture Abroad), part of the Italian Ministry of Foreign Affairs.

My thanks go to the members of the Commission and to the translator of the book, Peter Dawson, for his receptiveness and for the professional quality of his work. Tom Gray and Ann Allen of the Ashgate publishing house were my invaluable guides throughout the lengthy editing process that accompanied publication. It was a pleasure to work with them. The assistance of Francesca Borgo was fundamental to my finding an appropriate cover illustration. Compared to the Italian edition (Florence, Olschki, 2003), the bibliography has been updated only when absolutely necessary, while some of long textual citations that previously appeared in the footnotes have been cut, thus leaving more space for the original Italian or Latin versions of passages which in the text have been translated into English. Finally, in a few rare cases, footnote content has been moved into the text. The text itself has been amended with only minor adjustments.

G. C.

PART I
Inner Devotion, Lutheranism, and Church Censorship in the First Half of the Sixteenth Century

CHAPTER 1

The *Pater Noster* from Savonarola to Seripando

In 1513, in the *Libellus a Leonem X*, Pietro (Vincenzo) Querini and Paolo (Tommaso) Giustiniani placed the question of the relationship between *religio* and *superstitio* – for the first time in clear and precise manner – at the center of an articulated project to reform Church customs.[1] After a lucid contextualization of the concept of superstition[2] and lengthy discussion of certain improper uses of Christian ceremonies that caused them to lose their original meaning, the two Camaldolese hermits used their attentive diagnosis to produce two orders of 'therapy'.

On the one hand, once it had been established that the use of magic and divinatory practices of pagan origin was fueled by 'ignorance of languages' ('*ignoranza delle lingue*'), the only possible remedy was to translate into the vernacular at least those parts of the Bible that were read aloud in church during the liturgy:[3] only in this way could the involvement of the faithful in religious ceremonies be taken to be an active role of participation in, and understanding of, the mysteries celebrated, preventing the inevitable detachment due to failure to comprehend the liturgical texts from fueling their fantasies.

On the other hand, in view of the infinite and uncontrollable *varietas* of superstitious practices, or of such practices so to be considered, the only solution to the problem that might restore to the Church a renewed and purified concept of *religio* was a forceful reiteration of the principle of ecclesiastic authority in matters of religious ceremony and practice.

---

1 J.B. Mittarelli and A. Costadoni, *Annales Camaldulenses Ordinis Sancti Benedicti quibus plura interseruntur tum ceteras Italico-monasticas res, tum historiam ecclesiasticam remque diplomaticam illus*, Venetiis, Pasquali Giambattista, 1755–1773, tome IX, Venetiis 1773, ff. 612–719. There is a recent Italian translation: *Lettera al Papa. Paolo Giustiniani e Pietro Quirini a Leone X*, edited by G. Bianchini, presentation by F. Cardini, Modena, Artioli, 1995.

2 The definition offered, as we shall see, was to continue to be surprisingly in tune with the times throughout the course of the century and beyond: 'Whensoever an expedient shall claim to procure good health by virtue of its qualities, then it is to be considered superstition and therefore evil and criminal' ('Quicquid aliud, quam quod secundum naturam suam sanitatem induce valeat, tenetur it superstitiosum, et proinde impium ac criminosum, esse': ibid., ff. 685–6).

3 *Annales Camaldulenses*, f. 683.

The two Venetians' suggestion to Pope Leo X sounded somewhat peremptory. Only the ceremonies and practices solemnly established by the Holy Church were considered right and proper, all others were to be condemned: 'You shall declare that all forms of ceremonies not established by the Holy Church are worship of the Devil'.[4] Thus, not only: 'shall you condemn, first of all by public edict, all prayers promising this or that grace or healing or consolation or escape from accidents, thanks to rubrics',[5] but 'you shall not allow any prayer to be recited or written that has not been established by the Church, or by the Holy Doctors approved by the Church'.[6] The same approach was to be made to the psalms, sacred images, votive statues, and to all manner of representations, whether pagan or Christian.[7] Everything that was not explicitly approved by the ecclesiastic authorities had to be vigorously and tenaciously opposed. If the ceremonies of old were synonymous with orthodoxy, 'the making of new rites and ceremonies' ('*fare riti et cerimonie nuove*') thus became a sure synonym of heterodox preferences.[8]

While in the sixteenth century this latter therapy was destined to become the cardinal principle of ecclesiastic and inquisitorial strategy in liturgic and devotional matters,[9] the proposal to translate the Holy Scripture into the vernacular as an antidote to the 'ignorance of languages' ('*ignoranza delle lingue*') met with decidedly less good fortune, as we shall see.[10]

---

[4] 'ea omnia cerimoniarum genera, quae a sancta Ecclesia instituita non sint, diabolicas esse observationes declarabis' (ibid., p. 687).

[5] 'illas omnes [orationes] praecipue manifesto edicto condemnabis, quae propriis titulis, seu rubricis hanc aut illam sanitatis, aut consolationis gratiam, aut infortunii liberationem promittunt' (ibid.). The two authors particularly criticized certain 'miraculous' forms of prayer directed to the saints, without however calling into question the principle of the intercession of the Holy Souls: 'They recite prayers to particular Saints for particular diseases as if the Saints in Heaven, each and every one, had been allotted the care of a particular part of the human body. Whence the discontinuance of the custom of invoking the Lord and Father of all creatures, who alone can cure all infirmities'. (ibid.)

[6] 'nullas orationes neque deferri, neque scribi neque dici consenties, nisi quae a sancta Ecclesia, a sanctis ab Ecclesia approbatis doctoribus sunt institutae.' (ibid.).

[7] Ibid., f. 688.

[8] Cf. A. Prosperi, 'Intellettuali e Chiesa all'inizio dell'età moderna', *Storia d'Italia*, Annali, *Intellettuali e potere*, C. Vivanti (ed.), Turin, Einaudi, 1981, pp. 159–252, in particular p. 176; and Id., 'Il monaco Teodoro: note su un processo fiorentino del 1515', *Critica storica*, XII, 1975, p. 91.

[9] Cf. below, chapter II.

[10] The different fate of these two therapies recommended by Querini and Giustiniani provides us with evidence of the fragility (or at least the ambivalence) of historiographic categories, like that concerning the Catholic Reformation, to which the *Libellus* was frequently attributed. If, on the one hand, the first of the two therapies was to establish itself in the course of the sixteenth century as the kingpin of Counter-Reformation ecclesiastic politics in matters

The need (implicit in this last request advanced by Querini and Giustiniani) for a more deeply felt, more inward participation of the faithful in acts of devotion, as opposed to the formalistic, ostentatious practices that seemed to prevail in the Catholic world in the late fifteenth and early sixteenth centuries, came from afar.[11]

In the early 1490s Girolamo Savonarola[12] had devoted two little spiritual works to the subject of prayer, namely the *Sermone dell'oratione* ('Sermon on Prayer')[13] and the *Trattato in difensione e commendazione*

related to liturgic texts, on the other hand the second was totally thwarted by the steadily increasing affirmation of the vernacular/heresy equation after Lutheran doctrines began to filter down through the Italian peninsula: on the one hand, therefore, we have a statement of principle that was to prove to be very fruitful in the process of the construction of that particular ideology and, on the other, a testimony of the 'Catholic reformation' succumbing to the dominant Counter-Reformation ideology. Cf. on these issues, G. Fragnito, *Gasparo Contarini. Un magistrato veneziano al servizio della Cristianità*, Florence, Olschki, 1988, p. 221 et seqq.; on the confluence of many typical instances of the 'Catholic Reformation' in the 'mystique' of the Inquisition, cf. P. Simoncelli, 'Inquisizione romana e Riforma in Italia', *Rivista storica italiana*, C (1988), pp. 3–125. On the concept of the 'Catholic Reformation', cf. the classic work by H. Jedin, *Riforma cattolica o Controriforma? Tentativo di chiarimento dei concetti con riflessioni sul Concilio di Trento*, Brescia, Morcelliana, 1987 (IV edn; I edn 1957). On these topics, see now O'Malley, *Trent and all that. Renaming Catholicism in the Early Modern Era*, Cambridge, Ma., Harvard University Press, 2000.

11 Since the thirteenth century, first Franciscan and then Dominican spirituality – with all due differences deriving from the differing traditions – had placed the theme of inward prayer at the heart of religious discourse. Taking their example from St Francis, both St Clare and St Anthony had located 'the foundation of contemplative life in the spirit of prayer', while St Bonaventure had indicated the practice of 'perfect prayer' as an indispensable stage of the mystical ascent toward God. In the fourteenth century, developing Thomas Aquinas' concept of the spirit – especially with Domenico Cavalca – Dominican tradition viewed the activity of mental prayer as the essence of the contemplative practice of mystic asceticism; later, Catherine of Siena pronounced humble, continuous, faithful, and disinterested prayer to be 'the instrument through which the soul acquires all virtue', asserting the superiority of mental prayer over vocal prayer. Thus, by way of the great spiritual thinkers of the fifteenth century, such as St Anthony and Ludovico Barbo, the theme of mental prayer reached the start of the sixteenth century, finding in Savonarola the last follower of a rich medieval tradition. For a first approach to these topics, cf. M. Petrocchi, *Storia della spiritualità italiana*, vol. I, *Il Duecento, il Trecento e il Quattrocento*, Rome, Edizioni di Storia e Letteratura, 1978. See also G. Getto, *Letteratura religiosa dal Duecento al Novecento*, Florence, Sansoni, 1967, to be integrated with Id., *Letteratura religiosa del Trecento*, Florence, Sansoni, 1967.

12 There is an extensive bibliography concerning this well-known Dominican preacher; here we note only the critical review by C. Vasoli, 'Da un centenario all'altro. Bilancio degli studi savonaroliani', *Una città e il suo profeta. Firenze di fronte al Savonarola*. Proceedings of the National Convention (Florence, 10–13 December 1998), edited by G.C. Garfagnini, Florence, Edizioni del Galluzzo (Savonarola e la Toscana, 15), 2001, pp. 3–35. For Savonarola's relationship with the Inquisition and censorship, cf. below, note 41.

13 The *Trattato o vero sermone dell'orazione*, Florence Miscomini, 20 October 1492, was republished in G. Savonarola, *Operette spirituali*, edited by M. Ferrara, vol. I, Rome, Angelo Belardetti editore, 1976, pp. 189–224, cf. also the critical note on pp. 395–407. The

dell'orazione mentale ('Treatise in defense and praise of mental prayer').[14] For Savonarola too the initial stimulus was a criticism, made more explicitly than in the writings of Querini and Giustiniani, of the outward ceremonies and devotional practices performed by the faithful in observance of the precepts of the Church of Rome.

Recognizing that vocal prayer, as merely a practice for its own sake, was the symbol of this sterile devotionalism, Savonarola railed against the mechanical reciting of paternosters and psalms:

> This we see by direct experience: many men and women, reputed to be devout in spirit, have persevered for many years in vocal prayer and nonetheless they are the same as they were before. We see them to be lacking in spirit, lacking in discernment, lovers of earthly things, sensual in their living; always ready to chatter away, mostly about other people's business, making fun of others, mocking the simple and pure of heart; they have no compunction for their sins; they are partisans of churchmen of various orders; vainglorious, envious, and haughty, and harder of heart than their fellow men; they have a beam in their own eye yet seek the mote in the eye of others.[15]

In other words, such people 'believe that divine worship consists only of singing psalms and saying words, and they cannot imagine that any prayers can exist other than the vocal sort, as they have never tried anything spiritual'.[16] External ceremonies, according to Savonarola, since the origin of the 'primitive Church' ('*la primitiva Chiesa*'), have instead

---

citations are taken from this edition. On Savonarola's *Sermone and Trattato* (cf. following note), cf. M. Petrocchi, *Storia della spiritualità italiana*, vol. I, pp. 117 et sqq. and A.J. Schutte, *Printed Italian vernacular religious books 1465–1550. A finding list*, Geneva, Droz, 1983, pp. 339–40 and 342–3.

14 The *Trattato in difensione e commendazione dell'orazione mentale*, Florence Miscomini, 1492, is in G. Savonarola, *Operette spirituali*, vol. I, pp. 157–85, critical note on pp. 385–94. The citations are taken from this edition.

15 'Questo vediamo per esperienzia chiara: che molti uomini e donne, domandati spirituali, sono perseverati molti anni nella orazione vocale e in queste cerimonie esteriore, e nientedimeno sono quel medesimo che prima. Noi gli veggiamo essere senza spirito, senza gusto, amatori delle cose terrene, sensuali nel vivere; cicalono volentieri e massimamente de' fatti d'altri, e fannosi beffe dell'altri, dileggiando li semplici e retti di core; non si compungono de' loro peccati; partigiani de' religiosi di diversi ordini; vanagloriosi, invidiosi e superbi, e più duri di core che tutti gli altri uomini; portano loro la trave nell'occhio e vanno guardando la festuca del compagno' (G. Savonarola, *Trattato in difensione e commendazione dell'oratione*, pp. 184–5).

16 'credono ch' el divino culto non stia in altro se non in cantare salmi e dire parole, e non possono pensare che altre orazioni si possino fare se non queste vocale, non avendo mai provato cose spirituali' (ibid., p. 161).

had the sole function of helping infirm Christians to reduce the distance that separates them from God:

> the greater the infirmity of faith that the Holy Spirit [...] sees in Christian people, the more it multiplies the ceremonies of the Church, so that, occupied in such matters, in some manner they take delight in things divine.[17]

> The Church's state of health had been declining over the centuries, 'the corruption of the times' ('*corruzione de' tempi*') was such that 'now, being totally deprived of spirit, ceremonies are to them of little or almost no use, just as, when a sick man is deprived of his bodily power, no medicine can do him any good'.[18] It is, therefore, necessary to return to the sound principles that inspired the 'early Church', always remembering that 'God seeks from us inner worship, without excessive ceremony'.[19]

Had Savonarola's pronouncements gone so far as to challenge the role of religious intermediation that the Church of Rome had thought fit to assign itself, i.e. a role it had played for centuries and centuries, the implicitly radical content of these last words might have alarmed the church hierarchy. However, Savonarola had no intention of proclaiming the utter uselessness of outward ceremonies: they were to resume their original function of being a devotional stimulus, a halfway point on man's progress toward God:

> Christians, both laymen and clergy, must – according to their individual capacities and in the measure granted to them by grace of the Holy Ghost – turn to mental prayer. They must not however for that reason condemn vocal prayer, which is necessary and useful insofar as it also serves for the purpose of mental prayer.'[20]

In other words, the Dominican preacher believed that vocal prayer was 'subordinate to mental [prayer];'[21] it must create the condition 'whereby

[17] 'lo Spirito Santo [...] quanto più ha visto gravar la infirmità del spirito nel populo cristiano, tanto più ha fatto multiplicare le cerimonie della Chiesa, acciocché, occupato in quelle, in qualche modo si diletti delle cose divine' (ibid., p. 177).

[18] 'ora, essendo mancato tutto el spirito, le cerimonie sieno loro poco utile o quasi nulla, così come quando all'infermo è mancata la virtù naturale non giovono più le medicine' (ibid.).

[19] 'Dio cerca da noi el culto interiore senza tante cerimonie' (ibid., p. 176).

[20] 'Gli cristiani così religiosi come laici si debbono transferire, quanto possono e quanto gli è concesso dalla grazia dello Spirito Santo, alle orazioni mentali, non condennando però per questo la orazione vocale, la quale è tanto necessaria e utile quanto la deserve alla orazione della mente' (ibid., p. 160).

[21] 'ordinata alla [orazione] mentale' (ibid., p. 171).

a man shall raise his mind to God and become alight with divine love and holy contemplation';[22] the moment a man reaches this state of 'ascesis' ('*ascesi*'), words no longer serve any purpose and indeed often hinder communication with God.[23]

Thus, having introduced distinctions between the different levels of 'attention' ('*attenzione*') that could be achieved during vocal prayer (up to the same level as that of mental prayer), Savonarola ended up pronouncing a judgment that was diametrically opposite to that soon to be advanced by Querini and Giustiniani on the question of 'ignorance of languages' being the main cause of popular superstition. While the two Camaldolese held that people who did not understand what they read could not pray properly, Savonarola maintained that the criterion of the value of prayer was its inward nature: attention to the actual words, in his opinion, was relegated to the level of a pleonastic corollary. The first two forms of attention considered by the Dominican, i.e. attention paid to correct pronunciation of words and to their literal meaning, had a mainly negative connotation. On the one hand, there were 'scrupulous people' (*gli 'scrupolosi'*) who 'take their time to enunciate their words and are very careful to not leave out the smallest part of their oration'[24] – such people, according to the author of the *Treatise*, did not attain the real purpose of prayer because 'they divert their minds from God and their attention wanders'.[25] On the other hand, 'concentration' (*la 'concentrazione'*) on the meaning of the words was 'not wholly to be lauded'[26] 'since it occupies the mind in many matters because of the diverse meanings of the words that are said in vocal prayer':[27] 'it is more like repeating a lesson than praying'.[28]

The third and last form of attention was directed toward God alone. Only those who, also through vocal prayer, succeed in elevating their mind 'above itself' (*sopra di sé*), and thus in forgetting 'all things human and themselves',[29] will be able to remain 'with all their heart's affection [...]

[22] 'acciochè l'uomo levi la mente a Dio e s'accenda del divino amore e delle sante contemplazioni' (ibid.).

[23] *Trattato o vero sermone*, p. 218. See also *Trattato in difensione e commendazione dell'oratione*, p. 172.

[24] 'attendono ad esplicare ben le parole e sono molto intenti a non lasciare alcuna particula della loro orazione' (ibid., p. 167).

[25] 'desviano la loro mente da Dio e continuamente sono vaghi' (ibid.).

[26] 'non è al tutto laudata' (ibid.).

[27] 'perché fa discorrere la mente in molte cose per la varietà delle sentenzie d'esse parole che si dicono nella orazione vocale' (ibid.).

[28] Assomiglia più ad 'uno studiare che orare' (ibid.).

[29] 'tutte le cose umane e se medesima' (ibid.).

fixed on Him [God]';[30] they will then be able to recite correctly the words of prayer and fully understand its meaning, even though this will be a conditioned reflex of the 'state' ('*stato*') reached. 'Even the ignorant' (*etiam gli ignoranti*) could achieve this level of attention, even those 'who do not understand what they are saying, yet proffer the words of the psalms and prayers with all reverence to God, with whom in their mind they are at one'.[31] For

> although such people do not understand, they sometimes find more joy and more solace in the psalmody of the Church than those who are educated, but not because of the words, which they do not understand, but because in their mind they are at one with God.[32]

Savonarola's final 'judgment' (*sentenza*) was very clear: 'And yet, without words, it is possible to raise one's mind to God and to pray'.[33] To Savonarola's way of thinking, the understanding of the words – on which, within a few years or so, the two authors of the *Libellus* were to focus their attention – was neither a necessary nor a sufficient condition for a sincere and fruitful act of worship. The question of inward dialogue concerned the worshipper's capacity to raise his mind on high.

Despite reaching different conclusions on this important issue, the basic diagnosis they started from (Querini and Giustiniani on the one side, Savonarola on the other) was identical, i.e. a highly critical attitude towards any mechanical adherence to devotional forms advocated by the Church, and the necessity of the worshipper's total emotional and rational absorption during prayer and acts of devotion.

It should be clear from these brief introductory remarks that neither of these two positions, despite their critical stance, strayed beyond the confines of orthodox Catholicism.[34] The whole matter was more a call to

---

30 'con tutto lo affetto del suo core [...] fisso dinanzi a lui [Dio]' (ibid.).

31 'e' quali non intendono quello che dicono, ma proferiscono le parole de' salmi e dell'altre orazioni con riverenzia a Dio, al qual sono uniti con la mente' (ibid.).

32 'benché non intendino, hanno alcuna volta più gusto e più consolazione nella salmodia della Chiesa che non hanno e' dotti, non per le parole, le quali loro intendono, ma per la unione della mente con Dio' (ibid., p. 168).

33 'E però, senza parole si può elevare la mente a Dio e fare orazione' (ibid.).

34 It is clear, for example, that in the *Libellus* the call to use the vernacular – motivated by the intention of raising worshippers' ability to understand prayers – was not due to any subversive religious message, of which there was not the slightest trace. For while it is certainly true that basically it reflected a pessimistic analysis of Church morals and certainly implied criticism of the *mœurs* of the Church hierarchy, the context was one of absolute orthodoxy in which, as we suggested above, the final objective was the reaffirmation of the principle of the unique and exclusive nature of the *magisterium* of the Church.

order, something that might annoy some leading figures in the hierarchy in Rome but could not be regarded *per se* as a danger to Catholic doctrine or Catholic institutions.

A similar judgment can be passed on the *Espositione sul Paternoster* ('Exposition on the Lord's Prayer'), published in Florence by the Dominican monk in 1494, two years after the two sermons on prayer.[35] This was the Italian translation of a Latin manuscript version that appeared six years later.[36] As the Proem clearly states, the *Espositione* was, with regard to the question of the various levels of 'attention', merely a concrete 'application' of his thinking to the Paternoster, by far the best-known prayer of the time. There were four levels at which prayer affected the faithful: reading, meditation, praying itself, and contemplation.[37] This line of argument, as was manifest in Savonarola's two previous works, did not exclude a clear statement of the instrumentally necessary function of outward acts: the Church sacraments, the lauds, i.e. everything concerning ceremonies, are disposed *ad interiora mentis aedificanda* ('to construct the inner mind').[38] Apart from the Spanish Indices of 1559 and 1583, which condemned the Spanish translation of Savonarola's short work *Exposicion sobre el Pater noster* ('Exposition on the Lord's Prayer'),[39] these three minor pieces were never expressly mentioned in the Roman Indices. Yet this kind of

---

[35] *Espositione sopra il Pater noster*, Florence, 1494; cf. also A.J. Schutte, *Printed English Vernacular Religious Books 1465–1550*, pp. 338–9.

[36] *Expositio orationis dominicae*, Florence, Antonio Tubini, 1500, also in G. Savonarola, *Operette spirituali*, pp. 225–77; cf. also critical note on pp. 409–26. Ferrara informs us that the manuscript version dates from 1484 (ibid., p. 411); see also U. Rozzo, 'La cultura italiana nelle edizioni lionesi di S. Gryphe (1531–1541)', *La Bibliofilia*, XC, 1988, pp. 161–95, in particular p. 188). On this 'operetta' by Savonarola, cf. also A. Prosperi, 'Les commentaires du Pater noster entre XV et XVI siècles', *Aux origines du catéchisme en France*, Paris, Desclée, 1989, pp. 87–105, in particular p. 89.

[37] St Bonaventure devised the celebrated subdivision of the three 'ways to perfection' into the perfective, the illuminative, and the unitive; each stage, he said, corresponded to a 'means' by which a believer can pass to the next stage: by 'meditation', he attains peace following the perfective way; by 'prayer' he reaches the torch of wisdom and truth ('illuminative way'), and by 'contemplation' he cleaves to God by virtue of His love ('unitive way'). St Bonaventure also specified three things that were indispensable for a prayer to be perfect: one's thoughts must be turned in a state of repentance towards all human suffering, one must render thanks, and one's attention must be directed solely to the object of one's prayer; cf. M. Petrocchi, *Storia della spiritualità italiana*, I, pp. 19–21.

[38] *Expositio*, p. 228.

[39] *Index des livres interdits*, directeur J.M. De Bujanda, Centre d'Études de la Renaissance, Éditions de l'Université de Sherbrooke- Libraire Droz, Sherbrooke-Genève, vols I–X, 1985–1996, vol. V, *Index de l'Inquisition espagnole, 1551, 1554, 1559*, 1984, p. 477 and vol. VI, *Index de l'Inquisition espagnole, 1583, 1584*, p. 594. The two Spanish indices included the *Dominicae precationis explanatio* (on which cf. below): *Index*, vol. V, p. 347 and vol. VI, p. 515.

publication – which Savonarola had inaugurated – was to be very much the object of attention in mid-sixteenth-century Indices.[40] The 1559 Roman Index and, later on, the Tridentine Index banned several of Savonarola's *Sermoni* (*Sermons*) and Prediche (*Preachings*) – in the one Index, condemned to absolute prohibition, in the other *quamdiu expurgantur* –[41] in addition to *Dominicae precationis explicatio, impressa Lugduni, per Gryphium, et alios* ('Explanation of the Lord's Prayer, printed in Lyons by Grifo and others'),[42] and an anonymous *Espositione dell'oratione del Signore in volgare, composta per un padre non nominato* ('Exposition of the Lord's Prayer in the vernacular, composed for an unnamed Father').[43] The first of these was the famous edition published and printed in Lyons 'possibly prior to 1530 and subsequently – by the year 1546 – reprinted there at least 15 times'; this edition included Savonarola's comments on the psalms, plus the anonymous *Precationis explanatio e Alia Dominicae orationis expositio* ('Explanation of prayer and further exposition of the Lord's Prayer').[44] In the second case the generalizing nature of the language prevents any certain identification. However, it is certainly possible to

---

40 For a general view of this type of literature, see A. PROSPERI, *Les commentaires du Pater noster*.

41 *Index des livres interdits*, vol. VIII, *Index de Rome 1557, 1559, 1564. Les premiers index romains et l'index du Concile de Trente*, ed. J.M. De Bujanda, Sherbrooke-Geneva, Centre d'Études de la Renaissance-Librairie Droz, 1990, pp. 501–5. For the censorship of Savonarola's works, cf. the essay by G. FRAGNITO, 'La censura ecclesiastica e Girolamo Savonarola', *Rivista di Storia e Letteratura Religiosa*, XXXV, 1999, pp. 501–29, and U. ROZZO, 'Savonarola nell'Indice dei libri proibiti', in *Girolamo Savonarola: da Ferrara all'Europa*, Proceedings of the International Conference, Ferrara, 30 March–3 April 1998, G. Fragnito and M. Miegge (eds), Florence, Sismel-Edizioni del Galluzzo (Savonarola e la Toscana, 14), 2001, pp. 239–68. On Girolamo Savonarola and his clashes with the Inquisition, cf. M. FIRPO – P. SIMONCELLI, 'I processi inquisitoriali contro Savonarola (1558) e Carnesecchi (1566–67): una proposta di interpretazione', *Rivista di storia e letteratura religiosa*, XVII, 1982, pp. 200–52; R. KLEIN, *Il processo di Savonarola*, preface by A. PROSPERI, Ferrara, Corbo, 1998; and *I processi di Girolamo Savonarola (1498)*, I.G. Rao, P. Viti, R.M. Zaccaria (eds), Florence, Edizioni del Galluzzo (Savonarola e la Toscana, 13), 2001.

42 *Index des livres interdits*, vol. VIII, pp. 484–5, 638, 660. Savonarola's paper had already been condemned in the 1549 and 1554 Venetian Indices. Cf. *Index des livres interdits*, vol. III, *Index de Venise, 1549, et de Venise et Milan, 1554*, Sherbrooke-Genève, 1987, pp. 182, 333; cf. also U. ROZZO, 'La cultura italiana nelle edizioni lionesi di S. Gryphe (1531–1541)', pp. 188–92.

43 This work figured in the Venice Indices as early as 1549 and 1554 (*Index des livres interdits*, vol. III, respectively pp. 203–4 and 271) and also remained in the unpromulgated 1590 and 1593 Indices (ibid., vol. IX, p. 433). Regarding the Pauline and Tridentine Indices, see *Index des livres interdits*, vol. VIII, pp. 258–9.

44 With regard to *Dominicae precationis explanatio*, Mario Ferrara uses some persuasive reasoning to confute Schnitzer's attribution of the work to Savonarola (*Operette spirituali*, vol. I, pp. 417–19). In Ugo Rozzo's reconsideration of this Lyons edition of Gryphe, he appears to accept Ferrara's position by not excluding a '*callida iunctura*' regarding the

report a change in the general climate which, though having no direct effect on Savonarola's cited works, did nonetheless put the spotlight on that sort of writing. Why this change in attitude? What might it lead to? Without a doubt, one of the plainest of all reasons for this interest was the popularity of the translation into the vernacular of Luther's commentary on the same prayer.[45] Following the publication of this short text, the genre inaugurated by Savonarola – if for no other reason than the common topic considered and the similar publishing style – aroused deep suspicion and therefore made it liable to censorship.

For it was indeed true that Luther's commentary proposed afresh many of Savonarola's arguments, but placing them in a context which from the doctrinal point of view could be defined as heterodox.[46] The starting point of Luther's argument was (as in the case of Savonarola) his manifest disapproval of certain devotional customs that were very

---

'attempt to pass the whole book off as a work by the celebrated monk' (U. Rozzo, 'La cultura italiana nelle edizioni lionesi', p. 188; for the quotation in the text see ibid.).

45 M. Luther, *An Exposition of the Lord's Prayer for Simple Laymen*, in Id., *Luther's Works*, American Edition, Saint Louis, Concordia Pub. House – Philadelphia, Fortress Press, 1955– , vol. 42, *Devotional Writings*, I, ed. by Martin. O. Dietrich, pp. 19–81. For an Italian edition, see M. Luther, *Il 'Padre nostro' spiegato nella lingua volgare ai semplici laici*, Id., *Scritti religiosi*, V. Vinay (ed.), Turin, Utet, 1967, pp. 205–78. The text was republished separately in 1982, again edited by Valdo Vinay and published by Claudiana (M. Luther, *Il Padre nostro spiegato ai semplici laici*, Turin, 1982). For the extent to which the text was known in Italy, see S. Seidel Menchi, 'Le traduzioni italiane di Lutero nella prima metà del Cinquecento', *Rinascimento*, XVII, 1977, pp. 31–108, in particular pp. 40 et seqq. An introduction to the subject of prayer in the age of the Reformation can be found in the fundamental essay by A. Prosperi, 'Penitenza e Riforma', *Storia d'Europa*, vol. IV, *L'età moderna. Secoli XVI–XVIII, M. Aymard* (ed.), Turin, Einaudi, 1995, pp. 183–257, in particular pp. 210–29.

46 Regarding the doctrinal (and political) nexus between Savonarola and Luther, first formulated by contemporary Catholic controversialists (in particular by Ambrogio Catarino Politi), see the following: D. Cantimori, 'Incontri italo-germanici nell'età della Riforma', 'Rivista di studi germanici', III, 1938, pp. 63–89, now in Id., *Umanesimo e religione nel Rinascimento*, Turin, Einaudi, 1975, pp. 112–41, in particular p. 118; P. Simoncelli, *Evangelismo italiano del Cinquecento. Questione religiosa e nicodemismo politico*, Rome, Istituto Storico Italiano per l'età moderna e contemporanea, 1979, pp. 1 et sqq.; and Id., 'Preludi e primi echi di Lutero a Firenze', *Storia e politica, XXII* (1983), phase IV, pp. 674–744; L. Lazzerini, *Nessuno è innocente. Le tre morti di Pietro Pagolo Boscoli*, Florence, Olschki, 2002; and G. Caravale, *Sulle tracce dell'eresia. Ambrogio Catarino Politi (1483–1553)*, Florence, Olschki, 2007. The relationship between Savonarola's way of thinking and that of Luther was also considered by M. Firpo, *Gli affreschi di Pontormo a San Lorenzo. Eresia, politica e cultura nella Firenze di Cosimo I*, Turin, Einaudi, 1997, pp. 339 et seqq., who drew attention to the tension between Cosimo I and Rome and to the alliance stipulated between the friars of St Mark and the Roman Curia as a function of their anti-Medici bias; he also stressed 'Savonarolism's early Counter-Reformation effects', moving in a different direction from that of the nexus between religious heterodoxy and political dissidence devised by Simoncelli.

popular with the Catholics. 'Sham oral prayer', which was defined as a 'mouth's thoughtless mumbling and chattering',[47] was compared to 'spiritual prayer', that 'prayer [which] reflects the heart's innermost desires, its sighing and yearning'.[48] The different 'qualitative' value of the two manners of praying was visible in the effect they had on the devout: 'the former makes hypocrites and gives a false sense of security; the latter makes saints and respectful children of God'.[49] On the one hand, a sterile, empty outward act that makes the faithful falsely 'sure of themselves,' so that 'such prayers are concerned more with our honor than with God's';[50] on the other, an inward practice that permits true contact between man and God. It was a head-on clash between two opposing forces, but one that Luther immediately toned down, possibly because when the document was drawn up, the break with the Church of Rome was not yet complete. Before proceeding to an examination of the 'seven petitions' contained in the text of the prayer, Luther felt he had to make it clear that he did not reject the armamentarium of the Church of Rome in its entirety, or 'St Bridget's Fifteen Prayers, rosaries, the crown prayers, the Psalter, etc.'.[51] Luther hastily clarified his intentions, adding, 'I do not condemn words or the spoken prayer, nor should anyone spurn them. On the contrary, they are to be accepted as an especially great gift of God"[52] It was just that he thought that too much trust was placed in such prayers. Luther was thus reproposing Savonarola's idea of oral prayer as a necessary instrument serving as a preliminary to mental prayer, as a midway step preceding 'meditation of the heart': 'Such oral prayers are to be valued only insofar as they spur and move the soul to reflect on the meaning and the desires conveyed by the words.'[53] They are to be condemned only when 'the words are not employed for their fruitful purpose, namely, to move the heart, but are only mumbled and muttered with the mouth, on the false assumption that this is all that is necessary"[54] Luther's attempted compromise, however, went even further. After establishing oral prayer's instrumental but therefore necessary character, he proceeded to make a further distinction by recognizing the value – in the name of the sacred principle of obedience – of the prayers of 'priests and monks" Prayers recited merely 'for the sake of riches, honor, and praise' were absolutely

47 M. Luther, *An Exposition of the Lord's Prayer for Simple Laymen*, p. 20.

48 Ibid.

49 Ibid.

50 Ibid., p. 21.

51 Ibid., p. 22.

52 Ibid., p. 25.

53 Ibid., pp. 20–21.

54 Ibid., pp. 25–6.

to be avoided.[55] However, the prayers 'sung or read by priests and monks, [or those] imposed by penance or by vows',[56] nevertheless also have a beneficial effect (despite the lack of real participation by the worshipper) for the simple reason that the prayers are repeated in conformity with the principle of obedience:[57] 'Even a prayer that is spoken with the mouth and without devotion (with a sense of obedience) becomes fruitful and irritates the devil.'[58] Obedience, therefore, took on a value that was even higher than that of a close relationship with God.

This 'conciliatory' attitude was, however, in actual fact, roundly belied by the work itself. If anyone skimmed through the pages of the 'exposition' of 'the seven petitions' contained in the Lord's Prayer, the basic nucleus of Lutheran doctrine was clear for all to see, i.e. the worthlessness of human works and the exaltation of God's saving grace. Each part of the Lord's Prayer was given a strictly predestinationist interpretation, the main features of which were the constant reminder of man's misery and an unfailing call to throw oneself on God's mercy in accordance with an established pattern that required a call to self-denigration followed by an invocation exalting the power of God.[59]

Apart from these unquestionably heterodox doctrinal arguments, there then appeared an element that was long to be identified as one of the most

---

55 Ibid., p. 20.

56 Ibid.

57 This, as we all know, is a central pivot of Lutheran doctrinal thought, and a principle that subsequently became very important in combined political and doctrinal developments. A first approach to these considerations is to be found in R.H. Murray, *The political consequences of the Reformation*, New York, Roussel and Roussel, 1960 (I edn 1926); L. Firpo, 'Il pensiero politico del Rinascimento e della Controriforma', *Grande Antologia Filosofica*, vol. X, Milan, Marzorati, 1964, pp. 179–803; S.E. Ozment, *The Reformation in the Cities. The Appeal of Protestantism to Sixteenth-Century Germany and Switzerland*, New Haven-London, Yale University Press, 1975; H.A. Oberman, *Masters of the Reformation. The Emergence of a New Intellectual Climate in Europe*, Cambridge, New York, Cambridge University Press, 1981.

58 M. Luther, *An Exposition of the Lord's Prayer for Simple Laymen*, p. 20.

59 Each of the seven questions therefore produces, according to Luther, two effects: it humbles man and it raises him up. It humbles him because it makes him reflect on his misery, it raises him up because it makes him reflect on the greatness of God. Luther interprets the words 'Hallowed be thy name', for example, in the following terms: 'I confess and am sorry that I have dishonoured your name so often and that in my arrogance I still defile your name by honoring my own. Therefore, help me by your grace so that I and my name become nothing, so that only you and your name and honor may live in me' (ibid., p. 35). The words 'Thy Kingdom come' were interpreted as a message of humiliation because they oblige man to openly confess that 'God's Kingdom has not yet come to us' (ibid., p. 37). Likewise, 'Thy will be done on earth, as in heaven', constituted first and foremost a signal of our accusing ourselves 'with our own words, declaring that we are disobedient to God and do not do his will. For if we really did his will, this petition would not be necessary' (ibid., p. 42).

redoubtable threats to the devotional and liturgic system of the Catholic Church, i.e. the affirmation of the Paternoster's superiority over all other prayers. The Lutheran call to regard as 'untrustworthy' 'all other prayers that do not understand and express the content and meaning of this one'[60] was an attack on the very foundations of the Catholic Church, which did indeed look upon the Paternoster as an important prayer but still one to be used in the same way as many others. In other words, the insistence on one prayer was potentially destructive for a system that was based on the rigidly controlled recitation of a considerable number of prayers, each of which had its allotted moment during the day.[61] Christ's invitation to the faithful 'to pray without ceasing' was certainly not, the German heresiarch added, merely a suggestion that they should continually turn the pages of devotional books or endlessly recite Paternosters and Ave Marias – in other words that the faithful should fill their days with continual acts of outward devotion; it was intended to be taken as an exhortation not to interrupt inward spiritual prayer even during their daily working activities, to keep God constantly in the forefront of their thoughts.[62]

From that moment on, for the Catholic authorities, exhortation to 'spiritual' and 'mental' prayer and insistence on the Paternoster as the one fruitful prayer became evident symptoms of a message that was dangerous both doctrinally and socially. Conversely, through a mechanism that is not too hard to understand, the numerous 'Expositions of the Lord's Prayer' published in those years continued to use this invitation to mental praying and the Lord's Prayer in order to spread positions reflecting various degrees of hostility towards the Church of Rome.[63]

---

60 Ibid., p. 21. Luther firmly believed that the Paternoster was the only truly necessary prayer because 'every absolution, all needs, all blessings, and all men's requirements for body and soul, for life and beyond, are abundantly contained in that prayer' (ibid., p. 22). Luther believed that the absolute quality of this prayer was demonstrated by the fact that even a simple but faithful repetition of it by heart could be of benefit to a man, although he might not fully understand the literal and allegorical meaning of the individual words: 'All who are heavy-laden, and even those who do not know the meaning of these words, may well pray this prayer. In fact, I regard it to be the best prayer, for then the heart says more than the lips' (ibid., p. 23).

61 O. Niccoli, *La vita religiosa nell'Italia moderna*, Rome, Carocci, 1998, pp. 13 et seqq; and A. Prosperi, 'Preghiere di eretici: Stancaro, Curione e il Pater noster', *Querdenken. Dissens und Toleranz im Kandel der Geschichte*. Festschrift zum 65. Geburtstag von Hans R. Guggisberg, herausgegeben von M. Erbe, H. Fuglister, K. Furrer, A. Staehelin, R. Wecker und C. Windler, Palatium Verlag im J & J Verlag, Mannheim, 1996, pp. 203–21, in particular p. 205.

62 M. Luther, *An Exposition of the Lord's Prayer for Simple Laymen*, p. 24. Because, Luther explained, 'prayer is nothing else than the lifting up of the heart or mind to God' (ibid., p. 25).

63 A. Prosperi, 'Les commentaires du Pater noster', p. 101.

The most significant work in this new vein that Savonarola opened up was an anonymous *Espositione utilima sopra il Pater noster* ('Most useful exposition of the Lord's Prayer'), attributed by Adriano Prosperi to the Mantuan Hebraist Francesco Stancaro.[64] It was not the only anonymous 'espositione' of the sort, but it may well be that the censors in charge of drawing up the Index of forbidden books in the mid-sixteenth century had precisely this writing in mind when they chose to ban the *Espositione dell'oratione del Signore in volgare, composta per un padre non nominato* ('Exposition of the Lord's Prayer in the vernacular, composed for an unnamed Father').[65]

The *Espositione utilima* took up the same tone and topics as Luther in his commentary on the Paternoster. As this was one of Stancaro's last published writings in the vernacular before he fled from Italy,[66] the message contained in the brief preface 'to the reader',[67] in which the writer declares that the work he is publishing reached him from an undefined source, is likely to have been – as has already been observed – a 'rhetorical device to deny any personal responsibility':[68] it may have been the twofold stratagem (anonymity and false authorial attribution) of a man who had become fully aware of the change in the political climate that could now be felt and who would soon have to admit, even in his heart of hearts, the futility (and impracticality) of such fine subtleties – and indeed, in the end, he chose to leave Italy in all secrecy.

Stancaro was beginning to find the Nicodemite[69] habit rather too tight for his liking, as may be deduced from reading his comments on the 'new' category of men accused of contributing to the devaluation of the real

---

64 A. Prosperi, 'Preghiere di eretici', pp. 207–8. On Francesco Stancaro, see F. Ruffini, *Francesco Stancaro. Contributo alla storia della Riforma in Italia*, Roma, 1935; and Th. Wotschke, 'Francesco Stancaro. Ein Beitrag zur Reformationgeschichte des Ostens', Altpreussische Monatsschrift, XLVII, 1910, pp. 465–98, 570–613. Cf. also the entry 'Stancaro, Francesco', J. Tedeschi, *The Italian Reformation of the Sixteenth Century and the Diffusion of Renaissance Culture. A Bibliography of the Secondary Literature (ca. 1750–1996)*, compiled by J. Tedeschi in association with James M. Lattis, Historical Introduction by M. Firpo, pp. 470–72.

65 Cf. also above.

66 A. Prosperi, 'Preghiere di eretici', p. 207.

67 *Espositione utilima sopra il Pater noster, con duoi devotissimi trattati, uno in che modo Dio esaudisce le orationi nostre, l'altro di penitentia*, Venice, 1539, c. 565v.

68 P. Simoncelli, *Evangelismo italiano del Cinquecento. Questione religiosa e nicodemismo politico*, Rome, Istituto storico italiano per l'età moderna e contemporanea, 1979, p. 101.

69 A. Rotondò, 'Atteggiamenti della vita morale italiana del Cinquecento. La pratica nicodemitica', *Rivista storica italiana*, LXXIX, 1967, pp. 991–1030. Regarding Nicodemism there is a vast bibliography based largely on Delio Cantimori's groundbreaking studies; here it will suffice to refer to the entry 'Nicodemism', J. Tedeschi, *The Italian Reformation of the Sixteenth Century*, pp. 969–72.

meaning of prayer: for in addition to his harsh invective against those who behaved like 'gentiles, [...] who believed that God could be contented only by those who recited interminable prayers',[70] and who thought that the more psalms they recited, the greater their benefit would be,[71] Stancaro pointed his finger at the 'Pharisaic hypocrisy'.[72] Those who, following the ancient custom of the Pharisees, prayed openly 'in the public square and at street corners' (*ne le piaze, et ne li cantoni*) and in fact 'prayed only where was a multitude of people' (*non oravano se non in luogo dove era frequentia di gente*) so that they would be 'thought to be good Christians and praised by those who were indeed good Christians'[73] and did not pray for the 'praise and glory of the Father, and for the good of our neighbor',[74] were to be despised at least as much as those who prayed at excessive length and parrot-fashion.

The remedy to all this, according to Stancaro, was an intimistic withdrawal into oneself, the creation of one's own private sphere, out of the public eye, but not necessarily in conflict with one's fellow man. Stancaro, like Luther, had no desire to disown outward practices: 'The Lord has not condemned failure to pray publicly in church', he wrote;[75] in holy places one should 'thank God for benefits received'[76] with prayers and praises shared with the other 'brethren' (*frategli*).[77] True prayer was something different, he said; it was 'a speaking to God';[78] it was 'our heart and our spirit addressing the Almighty',[79] 'an ardent and eager colloquy of the heart with God',[80] a private and personal prayer, a process of inward collection of one's thoughts that required physical (or at least mental) isolation from public life, as well as a profound detachment from all things terrestrial:[81]

70 'Gentili, [...] che pensavano Iddio non esaudire, se non quegli che facessino longhissime orationi' (*Esposizione utilima*, cc. 568r–v).

71 Ibid., c. 573v.

72 'hipocresia pharisaica' (ibid., cc. 566v–567r).

73 Solamente per essere 'tenuti boni christiani, et laudati da quegli' (ibid., cc. 567v–568r.)

74 'Per laude e gloria del padre, et per utilità del prossimo' (ibid., c. 568v).

75 'Non ha dannato il Signore che non si faccia oratione pubblicamente ne la chiesa' (ibid., c. 570r).

76 'si ringratia Dio de li benefici recevuti' (ibid., c. 572v).

77 Ibid., cc. 569v–570r.

78 'Un parlare con Dio' (ibid., c. 570v).

79 'il parlare del cuore, et del animo nostro indirizzato a lui' (ibid., c. 571r).

80 'uno ardente et desideroso colloquio di animo con Dio' (ibid., cc. 571v–572r).

81 'Prayer requires that a man's mind shall be vacant and devoid of all other manner of cogitation, and distracted from all worldly pursuits so that he may speak to God without impediment and with the greatest of devotion' ('A la oratione si richiede la mente humana essere vacua et aliena da ogni altra cogitatione, et abstratta da le occupationi mondane, acciò con ardentissimo affetto senza impedimento parli con Dio;' ibid., cc. 573r–v).

> Verily Christ teaches us that when we pray we enter a room, close the door, and in secret pray to the Father and with these words we learn to flee ambition; and if we succeed in fleeing it with all our heart and soul and if we pray to the Father not in false holiness but to commit ourselves entirely to God, then shall we have rightly prayed in the closed room, even though we were in the midst of a great throng of people.[82]

The same passage from the Gospel,[83] taken here as an example of Stancaro's intimistic self-withdrawal, was destined a few years later – in a political and religious context that no longer permitted any of the slight margins of maneuver still possible in the 1530s – to have clearly Nicodemitic implications.[84]

However, over and beyond the significant modifications undergone by the call to mental prayer and the references in the Scriptures – modifications reflecting the changing political and religious set-up of the various historic Italian States – it maintained throughout an attitude that was hostile to the Church of Rome or at least was interpreted as being so by the Roman ecclesiastical authorities.

This can be seen in the fact that the further one proceeds in one's reading of Stancaro's *Espositione utilima*, the clearer the imprint of Protestant doctrine becomes, as also its close affinity with the Lutheran Paternoster. The call to justification by faith alone (and the concomitant devaluation of man's works) is a recurring feature of the text. After stating that 'we must pray in faith, trusting in the satisfaction of God *alone*',[85] Stancaro begins his 'explanation' of the phrases that one by one make up the Lord's Prayer and, with reference to the invocation 'Our Father, which art in Heaven', proposes Luther's interpretation almost word for word:[86]

> They are but a few words but they contain a most ample commemoration of God's goodness towards us, by which the eternal and heavenly Father has taken

[82] 'Così ci insegna Christo che orando entriamo in camera, et chiusa la porta secretamente oriamo al padre, per queste parole siamo insegnati a fuggire l'ambinone, la quale se con tutto il petto la fugiremo et oraremo al padre non per simulata santità, ma per commettersi in tutto a Dio, rettamente haveremo orato ne la camera serrata, se bene fussimo in una gran moltitudine di gente' (ibid., cc. 572r–v).

[83] The passage is taken from the Gospel of St Matthew (Matt. 7). The passage about the 'closet' is also present in Savonarola (see *Operette spirituali*, p. 230).

[84] See below, chapter 2.

[85] 'bisogna orare in fede, confidandosi ne la satisfattione de solo Christo' (*Espositione utilima*, c. 575v).

[86] M. Luther, *An Exposition of the Lord's Prayer for Simple Laymen*, pp. 22–6.

us wretched and wicked sinners as his adoptive sons and made us heirs to His heavenly land through His one and only begotten son our Brother Jesus Christ.[87]

A few lines further on he closely follows Luther's explanation of the invocations 'Thy Kingdom come' and 'Thy will be done', which he says jointly present a rigid opposition between 'sinful flesh' and the saving grace of God:

> Let His Kingdom come [...] but while we strive to achieve this work, the flesh is unwilling and contrary, and again draws us away from the freedom of grace into the slavery of sin, and perforce we are obliged to ask this third question. Thy will be done etc. [...] For this reason [i.e., the realization of God's will] our flesh so violently calls us away from Thee our King.[88]

To dispel any possible remaining doubt about Luther's influence on this writing, here is one of the clearest and most deliberate devaluations of free will:

> Give us Thy Holy Spirit, so that my will, which is so evil and unfaithful, so full of wicked feelings, so full of hatred and malice and rancor toward my neighbor, so full of self-love, may be refashioned as Thou wilt.[89]

---

87 'Sono poche parole ma conteneno una amplissima commemoratione de la divina bontà verso di noi, per la quale lo eterno et celeste padre, noi miseri et scelerati peccatori, ne ha accettato per suoi figliuoli adottivi et fatti heredi de la celeste patria, mediante il suo figliuolo unigenito et nostro fratello Iesu Christo' (*Espositione utilima*, c. 575).

88 'Che venga il regno suo [...] ma mentre che ci sforziamo di far questo negocio, la carne ne è contraria et obsta, et di novo ne tira in drieto da questa libertà de la grafia, ne la servitù del peccato, essa necessità consequente-mente ne spinge a questa tertia dimanda. Sia fatta la volontà tua etc. [...] Di qua [ossia, dalla realizzazione della volontà divina] la carne nostra troppo violentemente ci revoca da te Re nostro' (ibid., cc. 587r–v).

89 'Donaci il spirito tuo santo, che la volontà mia prava et piena de infedeltà, piena di pravi affetti, piena di odio e malevolentia et rancore verso il prossimo, piena de l'amor proprio, sia reformata secondo il voler tuo' (ibid., c. 588v). In his attempt to explain the 'substance' of the divine will, Stancaro again follows Luther's text closely: 'Thy will is first that we know you as our God and heavenly Father, and that above all things we love you with all our soul and with all our heart, with all our strength, and then that we love our neighbor as we do ourselves, Thy will is that we soon heed Thy commands and abstain from all our vices and sins not out of fear of Hell but out of filial love alone'. ('La volontà tua è che primieramente te conosciamo per nostro Dio, et padre celeste, et che sopra ogni cosa te amiamo con tutta l'anima, con tutto il cuore, con tutte le force nostre, poi che amiamo il prossimo nostro come noi medesimo, la volontà tua è che brevemente di cuore facciamo tutti li toi comandamenti, et che si absteniamo da tutti li vini et peccati non per paura del inferno, ma per solo amor tuo filiale;' ibid., cc. 588v–589r). For the corresponding passage by Luther, cf. *An Exposition of the Lord's Prayer for Simple Laymen*, pp. 43 and 48.

At this point, as if by some consolidated automatic process (in the Protestant way of thinking), this devaluation of the human will was followed by a condemnation of the Pelagian heresy, presented by the author as the only real alternative to the Lutheran doctrine. To reach this condemnation Stancaro made use of the explanation of the precept 'And forgive us our trespasses, as we forgive those who trespass against us',[90] which he explained in the following way: 'Our condonation is not the cause of God's remitting our sins but is a sign and a subject of divine forgiveness'.[91] Anyone convinced of the contrary, Stancaro went on, would be guilty of the 'Pelagian heresy' (*heresia pelagiana*): 'Beyond this point the source of good works would be not God but we ourselves, and this is the Pelagian heresy condemned by the Holy Mother Church'.[92] Then, casting doubt on two basic principles of the entire doctrinal and ecclesiologic set-up of the Church of Rome, i.e., fear of a specific punishment as a deterrent against sin,[93] and – as we also saw in Luther –[94] the rigid division of the liturgic moments during the day of the faithful,[95] Stancaro in the end saved very little of Roman orthodoxy. The references to the 'Holy Mother Church' (which significantly were omitted in the 1547 edition following his flight),[96] as also to outward practices like fasting and abstinence, testify to the disquiet of a man deeply torn between instinctive support of Luther's position and a sincere and illusory loyalty to the Church of Rome (which it would be impossible for him to maintain much longer), yet detract nothing from the work's clearly heterodox content.

The literary tradition reflected in Stancaro's *Espositione* offers further examples of the de facto overlapping of the call to inward faith and devotional behavior exercised in the practice of mental prayer (a call often accompanied, as said, by the claim of the Paternoster's 'supremacy'

---

[90] 'Et remette a noi li nostri debiti come noi li rimettiamo alli nostri debitori' (ibid., c. 595v).

[91] 'La condonatione nostra non è causa che Dio ci rimetta li peccati nostri, ma è segno et argumento de la divina remissione' (ibid, c. 599r).

[92] 'Oltra di questo il principio del bene operare non saria da Dio, ma da noi, et questa è la heresia pelagiana dannata dala santa madre chiesia' (ibid.). The Pelagian heresy was not however the only one to which Stancaro devoted his attention. Commenting on the 'daily bread' referred to in the Lord's Prayer, he warns against the inherent perils of the Anabaptist heresy (ibid., cc. 594r–v).

[93] '[T]hy will', says Stancaro, 'is that [...] we abstain from all sins and vices not out of fear of Hell but only because of our filial love for Thee' ('[L]a volontà tua è che [...] si absteniamo da tutti li vitii et peccati non per paura del inferno, ma per solo amor tuo filiale;' ibid., c. 589r).

[94] Cf. above.

[95] 'Thou canst pray at any hour in any place' (ibid., c. 575v).

[96] See A. Prosperi, 'Preghiere di eretici', p. 209 and note 18.

above other prayers) and heterodox doctrinal elements. Antonio Brucioli's Calvinistic work *Pia espositione ne dieci preceti, nel Symbolo apostolico, et nella oratione dominica, dove si ha quello che ci comandi Iddio, quello che si debbe credere, et come si debba orare* (*Devout exposition in ten precepts, in the apostolic Symbol and in the Lord's Prayer, containing what God commands us, what we must believe, and how we must pray*) was clearly heretic,[97] a somewhat unoriginal piece of writing that faithfully reproduced whole passages of Calvin's *Institutio* translated into the vernacular. This treatise, in addition to its reiterations of the 'bondage of the will' ('*servo arbitrio*') to which man was inexorably condemned[98] (and to the corresponding invocations of a 'sure and certain' salvation obtained solely with the help of faith),[99] declared that the Lord's Prayer was not only 'the most powerful and the most effective of all the prayers that have ever come upon this earth' but was also the only one to have real value and effect before God:

> The Father does not grant the prayer that the Son did not command, for the Father knows the meaning and the words of his Son; nor does He accept those things that human invention devised but only those things that the wisdom of Christ proclaims.[100]

Equally threatening for the devotional set-up of the Catholic faith was the existence of texts of clearly Erasmian inspiration which, in opposition to Savonarola-style anti-intellectualism, insisted on word-for-word understanding of the Gospel text. Here it will be sufficient to mention Giovanni Pico della Mirandola,[101] the author of a *Breve et*

---

97 Venetia, per Francesco Brucioli et frategli, 1542. The Calvinist origin of this work printed by Brucioli, which except for some points is a word-for-word reproduction of whole passages of Calvin's *Institutio christianae religionis*, was pointed out many years ago by T. Bozza, 'Calvino in Italia', *Miscellanea in memoria di Georgio Cernetti*, Turin, Bottega d'Erasmo, 1973, pp. 409–41, in particular pp. 411–19. On Brucioli, in addition to G. Spini's classic work *Tra Rinascimento e Riforma. Antonio Brucioli*, Florence, La Nuova Italia, 1940, cf. the bibliographic entry *Brucioli, Antonio*, in J. Tedeschi, *The Italian Reformation*, pp. 143–7.

98 *Pia espositione*, c. 2r–v; Bozza omits this passage.

99 Ibid., cc. 25v–26r; my emphasis. Bozza's comparison stops at the introductory papers and the 'Commento al Symbolo apostolico' ('Comment on the apostolic Symbol').

100 'Il padre non esaudisce la oratione che non dettò il figliuolo, per che il padre conosce i sensi, e parole del suo figliuolo, né riceve quelle cose che si usurpò la inventione humana, ma quelle cose che espone la sapientia di Christo' (Pia espositione, c. 72v). For the passage quoted above in the text ('più prestante, et la più efficace di tutte le altre orationi che mai sieno venute in terra'), cf. ibid.

101 On this writer, see M.T. Fumagalli Beonio Brocchieri's volume, *Pico della Mirandola*, Milan, Piemme, 1998, and the bibliography therein; see also the volume edited by Patrizia Castelli cited in the next footnote.

acuta dichiaratione sopra il Pater nostro, in which, before beginning his 'exposition' of the Lord's Prayer,[102] he declared outright that intense personal meditation must be based on the literal understanding of the text of the Gospel, and especially on the exclusive model of prayer that is offered by Christ in the pages of the Gospel itself.[103] Here too, side by side with the Erasmian-style invitation to practice religious tolerance expressed by Pico in the passage where he urges the faithful to 'pray for the Jews, for the Turks, for the heretics, and for all Christians',[104] there are numerous statements which from the doctrinal point of view were compromising, such as when he writes that 'it is an absolute certainty that we are not saved because of our merits but only by God's mercy'.[105]

It is therefore hardly surprising that in the late 1540s the equation between the exaltation of the Lord's Prayer and the presence of heretic doctrines was almost complete. It is revealing that as early as 1547, when Brucioli's work was reprinted, its Venetian publishers (Alessandro Brucioli and Brothers) – perhaps in an attempt to escape the ever stricter censorship

---

102 *Breve et acuta dichiaratione sopra il Pater nostro del signor Giovanni Pico della Mirandola*, s.d., s.l. (I cite from the copy kept in the Vatican Apostolic Library, R.I.V. 1919, int. 8); 1523 is the date appearing on the volume edited by Girolamo Regino cited by A. PROSPERI, 'Les commentaires', p. 98 and footnote 29, p. 104. On this text cf. above at ID., 'Celio Secondo Curione e gli autori italiani: da Pico al "Beneficio di Cristo"', *Giovanni e Gianfrancesco Pico. L'opera e la fortuna di due studenti ferraresi*, P. Castelli (ed.), Florence, Olschki, 1998, pp. 163–85, in particular pp. 167 et sqq.

103 Ibid., c. 79.

104 'pregare per i giudei, per gli turchi, per gli heretici, et per tutti gli christiani' (ibid., c. 77; cf. also A. PROSPERI, 'Preghiere di eretici', p. 220).

105 'è cosa certa che noi non ci salviamo per i meriti nostri, ma per la sola misericordia di Dio' (ibid. c. 89). Also reflecting this Erasmian tradition are the *Espositione dell'oratione domenicale* (1525) by Pellegrino Moretto, regarding which cf. A. PROSPERI, 'Les commentaires du Pater noster', p. 99 and ID., 'Penitenza e Riforma', p. 221. See also the orthodox and anonymous *Interpretatione della Oratione dominica, ebraica, greca et Latina*, Venice 1522, on which cf. A. PROSPERI, 'Les commentaires', p. 94, and ID., 'Preghiere di eretici', pp. 217–18. A very interesting question, but lying beyond the scope of the present work, is raised by another text mentioned by Prosperi, namely *De inventoribus rerum* by Polydore Vergil, who added the Lord's Prayer in the appendix as an example of the invention of Christian prayers ('Preghiere di eretici', p. 217 and footnote 43); the Roman censorship of the work (see ibid.) is very likely linked at least in part to the presence of the Lord's Prayer, also in view of the fact that Lauro's Italian translation, printed in Venice by Giolito in 1543, immediately proclaimed in its title that it contained an 'exposition of the Lord's Prayer': *De la origine e de gl'inventori de le leggi, con la espositione del Pater nostro* (ibid.); for more general information on this, see A. STEGMANN, 'Le 'De inventoribus rei christianae' de Polydor Virgil ou l'érasmisme critique', *Colloquia erasmiana turonensia*, ed. by the Centre d'études supérieures de la Renaissance de Tours, De Pétrarque à Descartes, 24, vol. I, Paris, 1972, pp. 313–21, and more recently *Beginnings and discoveries. Polydore Vergil's De inventoribus rerum*, an unabridged translation and edition with introduction, notes and glossary by Beno Weiss and Louis C. Pérez, Nieuwkoop, De Graaf Publishers, 1997.

network in the Venice area – opted to omit precisely the part devoted to prayer.[106] Even more significant was the action of the Inquisitors in Friuli, who – a few years before the compilers of the Indices of Forbidden Books condemned not only the treatises by Luther and by Calvin on the value of prayer but also the anonymous *Espositione dell'oratione del Signore in volgare* –[107] ordered the transcription in their records of the following testimony of a friar from Udine as evidence of his unequivocal 'corruption of spirit' ('*corruzione di spirito*'):

> I held only the Paternoster in high esteem. When I went to church I would kneel before the sacrament and there with my bare Paternoster I would pray to Jesus Christ to pray to the Heavenly Father for me, for I would hear nothing of the intercession of the saints. To Him alone would I confess my sins with open heart, only in Him did I hope they might be remitted, and when sometimes I approached the priest, I would say, 'Father, I have sinned greatly and offended the majesty of God in the Ten Commandments of the Law, the seven deadly sins, the five senses of the body, and the three theological virtues; I have neglected to devote great care to works of bodily or spiritual mercy. And yet I believed and I believe in one God, and in His Son our Lord Jesus Christ who was conceived by the Holy Ghost and then born to the Virgin Mary; and in whatever other way or manner I may have offended her divine majesty, with all my soul I declare the fault to be mine. Ideo precor (Therefore I beseech).' Such was the confession that I made at that time and even though it was he who absolved me, I believed I had been absolved by the mighty hand of God because mental confession always came before. This state of affairs lasted from 1548, about St Sebastian's Day, until 1555 on the eve of Assumption Day in August.[108]

---

[106] T. Bozza, 'Calvino in Italia', p. 419.

[107] Cf. above, p. 9. For the works of Luther and Calvin the respective references are to *Simplex et aptissimus orandi modus* (condemned in the Roman Indices of 1559 and 1564, cf. *Index de livres interdits*, vol. VIII, p. 682) and *La forma delle preghiere ecclesiastiche*, condemned in the Roman Indices of 1559, 1564 (*Index des livres interdits*, vol. VIII, pp. 472–3 and 592–3) and of 1590 and 1593 (ibid., vol. IX, p. 434).

[108] 'Non facea stima d'altro che del Pater noster. Quando io andava alla chiesa mi inginochiava inanti al sacramento et ivi col nudo Pater noster pregava il signor Giesù Christo che pregasse il Padre celeste per me, né per cosa alcuna volevo sentir la intercession de' santi. Solo a lui rimetteva di core li miei peccati, solo in lui speravo la remission di quelli, et quando alle volte mi appresentavo al sacerdote, dicea: 'Padre, io ho peccato grandemente et offeso la maestà divina nelli 10 comandamenti della lege, nei sette peccati mortali, nei cinque sentimenti del corpo, nelle tre virtù theologali; non mi son dato troppo all'opere della misericordia corporali né spirituali. Ho creduto però et credo a un solo Iddio et nel suo Figliuolo signor nostro Giesù Christo, ch'el sia concetto di Spirito Santo, et anchora nato di Maria vergine, et a tutto 'l resto de questi 12 articoli della santa fede et in ogni altro modo et via che io havesse offesa la sua divina maestà, l'anima mia et il prossimo mio, con tutto 'l core dico la colpa mia. Ideo precor'. Tal era la confessione ch'io facevo all'hora et ancorché egli mi assolvesse, lenivo d'esser stato assolto dalla potente man d'Iddio, percioché sempre precedeva la confession mentale. Questa cosa durò [dal] 1548 attorno s. Sebastiano sino 1555 alla vigilia della

This prayer – one that was prescribed in the most widely used catechetical texts in the early years of the sixteenth century and continued in the 1520s to be strongly recommended by the ecclesiastic hierarchies –[109] had thus become the symbol of the threatening and all-pervading heresy of the Lutherans. 'This heresy started with the Paternoster and will end with pikes and muskets' ('*Questa heresia comincia dal Pater noster e finisce nella picca et nel archibuso*'), Alvise Lippomano wrote to Cardinal Marcello Cervini in 1547.[110] This declaration was all the more weighty and significant because it came from a churchman who a mere six years before had dedicated to the Lord's Prayer an impassioned *Espositione volgare*[111]

Assonta d'agosto' (Udine, Archivio Arcivescovile, 'Confessione di fra Vincenzo da Udene della vita tenuta in Spilimbergo 1548 sino al 1555…', cc. 3v–4r, in G. MICCOLI, 'La storia religiosa', *Storia d'Italia, Dalla caduta dell'Impero romano al secolo XVIII*, vol. II, Turin, Einaudi, pp. 431–1079, cited passage p. 1042). Reading the Inquisition records it is in any case clear that the teaching of the Lord's Prayer as the only truly Christian prayer, as opposed to all other forms of prayer and devotion, was a common practice among philo-Protestants in Venice ('the Paternoster is more popular than the Ave Maria'; cf. F. AMBROSINI, *Storie di patrizi e di eresia nella Venezia del '500*, Milan, Franco Angeli, 1999, pp. 195–6 and footnote 95; J. MARTIN, 'Out of the Shadow: Heretical and Catholic Women in Renaissance Venice', *Journal of Family History*, 10, 1985, pp. 21–33, p. 23, in Lucca ('Nor do they want any prayer to be said other than the Paternoster and they prohibit the Avemaria': cf. M. BERENGO, *Nobili e mercanti nella Lucca del Cinquecento*, Turin, Einaudi, 1974, I edn 1965, pp. 407–8 and footnote 1; and S. ADORNI BRACCESI, *Una 'città infetta.' La repubblica di Lucca nella crisi religiosa del Cinquecento*, Florence, Olschki, 1994, p. 125), in Siena (V. MARCHETTI, *Gruppi ereticali senesi del Cinquecento*, Florence, Nuova Italia, 1975, p. 75), and in Bologna ('Because I worship at St Stephen's Church and I have been there often out of devotion and I go there almost every morning to get indulgences [...], sometimes my husband says to me when he sees me going to that church so often, 'Do you not think, Isabella, that you had better stay at home and say your prayers [...]? [...] and sometimes he would say [...]: 'A Paternoster said with all one's heart is worth more than saying a rosary:' G. DALL'OLIO, *Eretici e inquisitori nella Bologna del Cinquecento*, Bologna, Istituto per la storia di Bologna, 1999, p. 343 footnote 83). More generally, the attention the Inquisitors paid to the topic of prayer is also evidenced by a lawsuit brought in 1543 against one Girolamo Rinaldi, an artisan, who used to direct the collective prayers of a group of lay people who met together to recite the Office of Our Lady. He had, however reformulated the pronouncement of absolution in Christocentric terms (cf. S. SEIDEL MENCHI, *Erasmo in Italia, 1520–1580*, Turin, Bollati Boringhieri, 1987, pp. 73–4).

109 In 1521, in his work *Opus Noviter editum pro sacerdotibus curam animarum habentibus* ('Work newly published for priests who have souls in their care'), Milan, 1521, Filippo Sauli, the Bishop of Brugnato, stressed that it was the duty of curates to ascertain how familiar the members of their flock were with the Paternoster; cf. A. PROSPERI, *Les commentaires du Pater noster*, pp. 97–8 and footnote 28, p. 104.

110 Letter from Bologna, 16 November 1547, cited by A. PROSPERI, *Preghiere di eretici*, p. 216, edited by G. BUSCHBELL, *Reformation und Inquisition in Italien um die Mitte des XVI Jahrhunderts*, Padeborn, 1910, pp. 289–90 and by M. FIRPO-D. MARCATTO, *Il processo inquisitoriale del cardinal Giovanni Morone*, vol. II, t. 1, Rome, 1984, pp. 247–8.

111 *Espositioni volgari del Reverendo M. Luigi Lippomano vescovo di Modone, et coadiutore di Bergamo, sopra il Simbolo Apostolico cioè il Credo, sopra il Pater nostro, et*

in which – even if he could almost see the shadow of Roman censorship beginning to loom over this semi-literary semi-religious genre –[112] he had striven for the 'profitable advantage of all poor but devout persons, and principally those who will not or cannot learn the Holy Scripture or who do not fully understand it', explaining

> in the vulgar tongue the Apostolic Symbol, the Paternoster, and the two precepts of Charity, which three things constitute what for us is to be believed, desired, and done in this world, for if a man observes them in their entirety he may without a doubt call himself a perfect Christian, and gain the immortal glory of eternal life.[113]

Ten years were to pass, with three Indices of Forbidden Books (two in Venice in 1549 and 1554 and one in Rome in 1559), before the Roman authorities initiated a process of reappropriation of the Lord's Prayer. It was only in 1559 – significantly the same year as the promulgation of the strictest Roman Index of all – that the Archbishop of Salerno, Girolamo Seripando, was able to consider dedicating a complete cycle of sermons to the Paternoster.[114] However, Catholic treatise writing was to continue to

---

sopra i due precetti della charità, nelle quali tre cose consiste ciò che si dee dal buon christiano credere, desiderare, et operare in questo mondo. Opera catholica et utilissima ad ogni Cristiano ('Expositions in the vulgar tongue by the Reverend Monsignor Luigi Lippomano, Bishop of Modone and Co-Adjutor of Bergamo, regarding the Apostolic Symbol, that is to say, the Credo; regarding the Paternoster, and regarding the two precepts of charity. Which three things constitute what a good Christian must believe, desire, and do in this world. Catholic work of extreme utility to all good Christians'), Venetia, apud Hieronimum Scotum, 1541.

112 The style used by the author of the dedication of the work, rather than being that of the conventional formula, seems that of an artful *captatio benevolentiae* (ibid., c. A2r–v).

113 'a profittevole utilità di tutte le divote e povere persone, et massimamente di quelle, che non vogliono, o non possono studiare la sacra scrittura, overo così bene non la intendono', esponendo 'in lingua volgare il Simbolo Apostolico, il Pater nostro, et i dua precetti della Charità, nelle quali tre cose consiste ciò che si dee da noi credere, desiderare, et operare in questo mondo, et osservandole l'huomo intieramente, senza dubbio si può chiamare perfetto Christiano, et acquistare la gloria immortale di vita eterna' (ibid., c. A2r). This work is notable for the skill with which it combines a strong appeal to the inward quality of devotion with clear references to the outward aspects of Catholic devotion; cf., for example, the frequent references to the 'fasting and alms-giving' (*al 'digiuno et all'elemosina'*) that must accompany every single act of prayer (ibid., 84v), and the insistent references to the value of auricular confession (ibid., c. 114v).

114 It would in fact appear to be no chance matter that the Lord's Prayer question was taken up, on the Catholic side, by a leading figure of the Augustine order who had long frequented *spirituali* circles. Seripando certainly ended up within the ranks of pure orthodoxy, from which indeed he may never have strayed; yet his sermons continued to ring with violent invective against the apparent outward superficiality of some members of the clergy: cf. R.M. Abbondanza Blasi, *Tra evangelismo e riforma cattolica. Le prediche sul Paternoster di Girolamo Seripando*, introduction by G. De Rosa, Rome, Carocci, 1999,

reflect the effects of this unnatural assimilation (heresy/Lord's Prayer), and the consequent censorship, until the end of the century.[115]

p. 85; the *Appendix* contains the unabridged text of the sermons on the Lord's Prayer (ibid., pp. 99–317). On this subject, see also F.C. CESAREO, 'Penitential Sermons in Renaissance Italy. Girolamo Seripando and the *Pater Noster*', *The Catholic Historical Review*, 83 (1997), pp. 1–19. For more general reading on Seripando, in addition to H. JEDIN, *Girolamo Seripando, Sein Leben und Denken im Geisteskampf des 16. Jahrhunderts*, 2 vols, Würzburg, Rita-Verlag, 1937–38, cf. the Proceedings of the Conference on *Girolamo Seripando e la Chiesa del suo tempo nel V centenario della nascita* (held in Salerno, 14–16 October 1994), A. Cestaro (ed.), Edizioni di Storia e Letteratura, 1997 and M. CASSESE, Girolamo Seripando e i vescovi meridionali (1535–1563), 2 tomes, Naples, Editoriale Scientifica, 2002.

115 Cf. below, ch. 8.

CHAPTER 2

Mental Prayer and the *Spirituali*

The 'heresy' of mental prayer was widespread among not only the working classes and members of the local clergy[1] but also the upper echelons of the hierarchy. The most emblematic case is surely that of Cardinal Federico Fregoso. One of Fregoso's works, entitled *Pio et christianissimo trattato della oratione* ('Pious and most Christian treatise on prayer') and printed somewhat significantly only in 1542, i.e. after his death,[2] was targeted in a two-pronged attack by the Church of Rome in the mid-1550s: on the one hand, as we have seen, there was the exacerbation of the battle against the Lutheran (and Erasmian) appeal to inward devotion; and, on the other, there was the settling of old scores within the Roman Church itself, which saw the victory of the Carafian party over the *spirituali* group of which Fregoso had been a leading figure.[3] Together with the anonymous treatise

[1] Local churchmen found themselves involved in numerous Inquisition trials. A priest from Modena, Giovanni Bertari, was obliged to recant in public, in obedience to a ruling issued by a court in Rome that bore the signature of Girolamo Meandro, for criticizing the contemporary practice of prolonged, mechanical vocal prayer. Bertari believed it was necessary to understand the words of recited prayers (see S. Seidel Menchi, *Erasmo in Italia*, pp. 74–5, and for other testimonies of criticisms of various Catholic devotional practices cf. ibid., pp. 103 et seqq.).

[2] On the death of Fregoso, which occurred in 1541, cf. G. Brunelli, *sub voce*, in *Dizionario biografico degli italiani* (hereafter DBI), vol. L, Rome, Istituto dell'Enciclopedia Italiana, 1998, pp. 396–9, in particular p. 399; and P. Simoncelli, *Evangelismo italiano del Cinquecento*, p. 113. As far as I can ascertain, there is no documentary evidence to support the hypothesis advanced by Pier Paolo Vergerio that he was poisoned ['Fregoso, who was made a Cardinal and soon afterwards poisoned (a matter of public knowledge, as is rumoured of another exceptional gentleman, M. Gasparo Contarena)'; 'Fregoso, il qual fu fatto Cardinale e non molto doppo avelenato (come è publica fama, si come è ancor fama di quell'altro singolar gentile huomo di M. Gasparo Contareno):' *A gl'Inquisitori che sono per l'Italia. Del Catalogo di libri eretici, stampato in Roma nell'Anno presente.* MDLIX, c. 28r]. On Fregoso, besides Brunelli, see also M. Firpo, *Il processo inquisitoriale del cardinal Giovanni Morone,* vol. I, *Il Compendium,* Rome, Istituto storico italiano per l'età moderna e contemporanea, 1985, pp. 281–2.

[3] On this point, but also more in general on the fluctuating fortunes of the Italian *spirituali*, we may note, in addition to the already cited work by P. Simoncelli, *Evangelismo italiano del Cinquecento*, cit., the works of G. Fragnito, 'Evangelismo e intransigenti nei difficili equilibri del pontificato farnesiano', *Rivista di storia e letteratura religiosa*, XXV, 1989, pp. 20–47, and of M. Firpo, *Tra alumbrados e 'spirituali'. Studi su Juan de Valdés e il valdesianesimo nella crisi religiosa del '500 italiano*, Florence, Olschki, 1990; Id., *Inquisizione romana e Controriforma. Studi sul cardinal Giovanni Morone e il suo processo d'eresia*, Bologna, Il Mulino, 1992; Id., *Riforma protestante ed eresie nell'Italia del Cinquecento*,

Della giustificazione, della fede e delle opera ('On Justification, faith and works')[4] and the *Praefatio in Epistolam D. Pauli ad Romanos* ('Preface to St Paul's Epistle to the Romans'),[5] his heartfelt exaltation of mental prayer was condemned by the Index of Paul IV.[6] Fregoso's *Pio et christianissimo trattato* contained a systematic presentation of many of the arguments advanced in the literature up to that point in time regarding treatises of the sort that approved of the principle of spiritualist-type inward devotion, providing a number of incisive in-depth analyses. The author criticized the mechanical, repetitive recitation of prayers by the faithful (a totally useless practice that might indeed even do more harm than good)[7] and flatly opposed the false promises of superstitious prayers, which deluded sinners into believing themselves to be free of 'evil' ('*male*') simply because they had repeated aloud the text of a prayer;[8] discussion ranged from whether a church was privileged as a place of worship[9] to severe condemnation of the Catholic practice of saying prayers to saints and the Virgin Mary.[10] In a manner that was by then well established, Fregoso compared the sterile practices of outward devotion with the virtues of inward acts of devotion and intimate dialogue with God. Prayer had to be directed to God alone and one of its features should be its brevity:[11] the evangelic precept that

---

Rome-Bari, Laterza, 1993; Id., *Dal sacco di Roma all'Inquisizione. Studi su Juan de Valdes e la Riforma italiana*, Alessandria, edizioni dell'Orso, 1998.

4 The work was recently attributed to Fregoso by Valerio Marchetti, who announced he had come upon the manuscript text (no copy of the edition thought to have been printed in Venice in 1543 has ever been found). Marchetti has declared his intention to produce a critical edition but to date this has not appeared (see S. Seidel Menchi, *Erasmo in Italia*, p. 165 and footnote 102 pp. 406–7): Marchetti's attribution, if confirmed, could put an end to the *querelle* that began immediately after the death of Fregoso, with Vergerio's insinuations (*A gl'Inquisitori che sono per l'Italia. Del Catalogo di libri eretici, stampato in Roma nel l'Anno presente,* MDLIX, c. 28r–v). On the book's banning, cf. *Index des livres interdits,* vol. VIII, p. 763.

5 *Index des livres interdits*, vol. VIII, p. 763.

6 The work *Pio et christianissimo trattato della oratione, il quale dimostra come si debbe orare et quali debbeno essere le nostre preci a Iddio per conseguire la eterna salute et* felicità (Venice, Gabriel Giolito de' Ferrari, 1542) was condemned in the Venetian Index in 1554 (*Index des livres interdits*, vol. III, pp. 273–4), the Roman Index in 1559, and the Tridentine Index in 1564 (*Index des livres interdits*, vol. VIII, pp. 469–70).

7 *Pio et christianissimo trattato della oratione*, cc. XLVIv–XLVIIr and ibid., c. XVIv–XVIIr.

8 Ibid., c. XXIIIr.

9 'The place where one prays is of no importance, for true worship lies in adoration and raising of the spirit and in truth and purity of heart' ('Il luogo dell'oratione essere di nulla importantia, ma la vera adoratione consistere nell'affetto e sollevatione dello spirito e nella verità e purità del cuore'; ibid., c. XIr).

10 Ibid., c. XXIr.

11 'No one but He can help us or grant the favors we ask' ('Nessun altro che lui ci possa aiutare né concederne le gratie addimandate'; ibid., v. XXv).

we must 'pray without ceasing' was not to be interpreted as an invitation to the uninterrupted reciting of rosaries or telling of beads but rather in the spiritualistic sense, i.e., as an unbroken conjoining of thought and heart with God.[12] For while not denying the benefits, including material benefits, which – according to 'the Book of Judges in the times of the law of old' ('*il libro de i giudici nel tempo della legge antica*') but also 'in our own age' ('*nell'età nostra*')[13] – 'the praying of holy men'[14] succeeded in obtaining from God's good will,[15] Fregoso stressed that 'the sweetness and gentleness' (*dolcezza et soavità*) deriving from mental union with God was superior to any other form of benefit arising out of devotion.[16] In this context, the invitation to 'shun the vainglory of the Pharisees' (*fuggire la vanagloria dei Pharisei*), who prayed openly in public in order to gain people's approval, and the corresponding call to close the 'door' of one's room and pray 'secretly' (*secretamente*) in the 'closet of one's heart' (*nel cubicolo del cuor*)[17] could still be treated – within the limits then imposed on religious movement and freedom – as an anti-Nicodemite message, in a sense that is well exemplified by the refusal of any split between public and private morality, as we may read a few lines below: 'We hold that is not right to reason with God [...] or to have one thing in one's heart and another in one's tongue [...], for, if it is blameworthy when reasoning with men who are worth less than we, how much the more hateful will it be when speaking to God?'[18]

Fregoso was thus picking up Erasmian and Lutheran topics and reworking them with new arguments in light of the particular social and religious context of Italy. Fregoso even took up a stand on the delicate issue of the understanding of words, whereby he reached a sort of compromise between Lutheran anti-intellectualism and the Humanist philologism of Erasmus. On the one hand, the influence of Erasmus led him to pay particular attention to the meaning of words, urging the devout believer to consider with great care the individual parts of a prayer: 'Examine

[12] 'The doctrine of Jesus Christ teaches us that 'much prayer' does not simply consist in many words but rather in good thoughts and appropriate wishes in loving and venerating God with fear and awe' ('la dottrina di Giesù Christo ci insegna che la molta oratione non consiste nelle molte parole, ma nelle cogitationi buone nelli giusti desideri nell'amare e venerare Dio con timore e tremore'; ibid., c. XVIr).

[13] Ibid., c. VIIIv.

[14] 'l'oratione di santi uomini' (ibid., c. XVIIIr).

[15] Ibid., c. VIIIr–v.

[16] Ibid., c. VIIIv.

[17] Ibid., c. XIv.

[18] 'Noi tenemo che non sia per niente lecito nel ragionare con Dio [...] havere una cosa nel cuore et l'altra nella lingua [...] il che se è biasimevole usare ragionando con gl'huomini etiam a noi inferiori, quanto sarà più detestabile usarlo nel parlare con Dio?' (ibid., c. XLVIv).

diligently all parts of the prayer so that there is no possible cause for it to displease the Almighty, who never grows weary of listening to our requests and satisfying them'.[19] On the other hand, in a manner that is only apparently contradictory, he ended up subordinating the importance of understanding individual words to the absolute value of mental prayer.[20]

However, it was elsewhere that the Roman Church's greatest perils had to be sought. As in *Della giustificazione* (*On Justification*), so also in *Pio et christianissimo trattato della oratione,* Fregoso – though never explicitly denying the doctrine of retribution for works done – was unable to mask his heterodox leanings. For example, when discussing how to prepare for prayer and the kind of questions to put to God, Fregoso reminded the reader that man – 'most vile dust' (*vilissima polvere*)[21] – must not present himself before the Heavenly Father 'to seek a reward for his good works, almost as if collecting a debt, but [...] he must know himself and confess that he is an iniquitous sinner that dare not raise his eyes to Heaven',[22] and above all he must take care not to question the principle of the impossibility of derogating from divine grace: 'In all his questions and thanksgivings and observations he must ensure that there is no word that might derogate from the Grace of God'.[23] The exaltation of God's salvific grace (always complementary to the degradation of human arbitrium) is also given some space a few paragraphs further on: 'We must beg God at every instance to multiply and increase all virtues for without His grace we are unable by ourselves to conceive of anything good'.[24]

19 'Con ogni diligentia essaminare tutte le parti della sua oratione acciò che per qual si voglia causa non restasse indegnata verso d'essa anima la soprema bontà che mai si stracca d'ascoltare le nostre dimande et essaudirle' (ibid., c. XXIIIv).

20 Ibid., c. XLVr.

21 Ibid., c. XLVIr.

22 Per 'domandare premio delle sue buone opere, quasi come che a riscuotere un debito, [...] ma si conosca e confessi peccatore] pien[o] d'iniquità intanto che non

[a]rdisca levare gl'occhi al cielo' (ibid., c. XXVIv).

23 'in tutte le dimande sue e ringratiamenti e osservationi, avvertisca che non vi sia alcuna parola che possa derogare alla gratia di Dio' (ibid.).

24 'A Dio si domandi con ogni instantia la moltiplicatione e l'acrescimento di tutte le virtù perché senza la gratia sua noi non siamo sufficienti pure a pensare alcuna cosa buona da noi medesimi' (ibid., cc. XLIIIr–v). A little further on, the declaration of the total absence of human arbitrium was to some extent attenuated by the addition of a more orthodox 'without His help' (*senza l'aiuto suo*): 'And we above all must beseech Him to multiply the three divine virtues [...] faith, hope, and charity, because without His help we can neither believe Him nor have perfect hope in Him' ('E massime devono pregarlo si degni moltiplicare quelle tre divine virtù [...] la fede, la speranza e la carità perché senza l'aiuto suo noi no' 1 possiamo né credere né in lui sperare perfettamente'; ibid., c. XLIIIv).

The text's Lutheran inspiration was made unequivocally clear by the way 'God's will' (*volontà divina*) was emphasized[25] and by Fregoso's remarks on the invocation "deliver us from evil" in the Lord's Prayer, remarks that are faithfully transposed from Luther's own comment on the prayer. For while it is true that Luther had stressed the fact that the request to be saved from 'evil' did not come until the end of the prayer, and therefore after recognition of man's total incapacity and wretchedness and after repeated requests to the Supreme Father to illuminate man with His saving grace, we find Cardinal Fregoso writing in the following terms:

> Not only must we pray that He grant us these virtues but much more importantly we must pray that He watch over us and free us from all sin, just as Jesus Christ taught us to pray to our Father and to make this plea at the end of our prayer and of all the requests we have made.[26]

In light of these observations, the specific emphasis – in a context that otherwise would not have required a specific reference to the question – on the 'benefit of Christ' (*beneficio di Cristo*) takes on a particular color. Finding himself under the obligation to provide an explanation why some requests made in prayer are granted while others are not, Fregoso referred to the impossibility of understanding the mysteries of God and His judgments. In a very few cases, the Cardinal asserted, God had revealed these mysteries to man, the most significant case being that of the death of Christ on the cross. God's decision not to grant the prayer of the crucified Christ, who begged to be saved, found its explanation in God's desire to sacrifice His son for the salvation of mankind, thus showing His infinite mercy:

> And what shall we say of Christ's prayer, when He begged His father to pass to Him the cup of His suffering and His prayer was not granted, surely such a worthy prayer, proffered by Christ's divine person with such insistence and feeling that the sweat turned into blood and ran down His face, in many respects deserved – above all the others combined together – to be granted, and

25 'In all your petitions and pleas, your intention is nearly always a sort of general protest so that His will shall always be done, for it is always right and always good, and is always useful to us in the most necessary and most important part, although we may not be aware thereof' ('In tutte le tue petitioni e domande tu intendi sempre quasi come un general protesto, che sempre sia adempita la volontà sua la quale sempre è giusta sempre è buona, e a noi sempre è utile nella parte più necessaria e di maggior importanza se bene forse da noi non fosse conosciuto'; ibid., c. XLIv).

26 'non solo dovemo pregarlo che ci conceda queste virtù, ma molto più che ci guardi e liberi da ogni peccato, si come Giesù Christo ci insegnava che dovessimo orare il patre nostro, ponendo questa domanda per conchiusione della nostra oratione, e di tutte le nostre petitioni' (ibid., c. XLIIIIr).

yet it was opposed by the mercy of God, who ruled cruelly against the flesh of His own Son so that he might be all the more merciful to those who were already damned.[27]

The eloquent silence surrounding the question of retribution for works done was in any case no longer sufficient to conceal the text's Protestant doctrinal imprint. Fregoso's position was considerably aggravated still further by his harsh attitude toward the leaders of the Church, who in his opinion were guilty of not combating popular superstition and indeed even of fomenting it. Going well beyond generic attacks on 'mechanical praying' (*preghiera meccanica*) and devotional formalism, Fregoso inveighed against 'the highest reaches of the Roman hierarchy' (*le parti più alte*), and even explicitly accused the 'pinnacle of the church' (*pinnacolo del tempio*) of 'corruption' (*corruttela*), with an unmistakable reference to the Supreme Pontiff himself:

> This corruption [...] first infected the lowest ranks of the populace, which are most inclined to accept these vain superstitions, and then rose to the highest parts. This most evil tempter then entered the holy city and ascended even to the pinnacle of the temple, from where it tempts and perturbs all things, distracting wretched foolish souls from worship and adoration of the Creator.[28]

Fregoso's harsh attack on the Church of Rome did not spare even strict Catholic dogmatism, which – albeit indirectly and with some subtlety (the theme of the paragraph in question was always the impossibility of knowing God's will) – was seriously doubted:

> God's judgments are a bottomless and unfathomable abyss, but even so we may ponder them provided we do so with moderation and sobriety, for it is rash foolishness to speak of them in decisive and resolute terms.[29]

---

27 'Ma che vogliamo dire dell'oratione di Giesù Christo quando pregava il padre suo che passasse da lui il Calice della sua passione e non potè essere esaudita, certo che questa tale così degna oratione è dalla divina persona di Christo offerta con tanta instantia et affettione che 'l sudore convertito in sangue gli cadeva dalla faccia, meritava sopra tutte l'altre unite insieme essere per molti rispetti essaudita se la sola misericordia di Dio non si fosse opposta il quale verso la carne del figliuolo suo volse parere crudele per essere tanto più misericordioso alle già condannate anime della natura humana' (ibid., c. XIXv–XXr).

28 'Questa corruttela [...] primieramente ha occupato la plebe più infima come quella che è sempre più inclinata a ricevere queste vane superstitioni e poi è ancho salita alle parti più alte et è entrato questo pessimo tentatore nella città santa, et è asceso infino al pinacolo del tempio e de lì tenta e perturba ogni cosa rimuovendo le misere e sciocche anime dal culto e adoratione del creatore' (ibid., c. XXIv).

29 'Li giudici di Dio sono uno infinito abisso e imperscrutabile, e benché ragionare se ne possa parimente se si fa con modestia e sobrietà, temeraria sciocchezza certo è parlare diffinitamente e con determinatione' (ibid., c. XIXr).

Fregoso could not escape condemnation. The text, as already said, was included in the Venetian Index and the compilers of the first Roman Index in 1559 did not hesitate a moment before reissuing the ban on it. As has been amply documented, the 1559 Index contained the most drastic condemnation hitherto pronounced of vernacular versions of the Bible as well as severe restrictions even on reading the Latin text.[30] Thus, the discovery in Fregoso's writings of repeated appeals for direct reading of the holy text – a practice recommended as the best method for preparing the way to mental prayer, and particularly useful in the case of 'simpletons and idiots' (*semplici et idioti*)[31] – would therefore have appeared to be not only an additional reason for banning the work but also a manifest confirmation of the heresy/sacred text link currently being postulated.

Little effect was therefore achieved by the absolutely orthodox remedies recommended by Fregoso for those who wished to flee 'the memory of sensual pleasures, whether experienced or desired' (*memoria de i piaceri sensuali o havuti o assiderati*), and 'the care for riches' (*sollecitudine delle ricchezze*). For this purpose the author, following the best orthodox Catholic tradition, prescribed two cures, one of the body and one of the spirit:

> Fasting, to tame the provocation of greed, and almsgiving, to slake the insatiable thirst of avarice, which like two stanchions support prayer so that it shall lean neither right nor left.[32]

Equally ineffective and belated was the pedagogic and doctrinal theory included at the end of the treatise in which – with reference to the faith/works done relationship – he foreshadowed a dual level (esoteric and exoteric) of indoctrination. It is likely that he was seeking to forestall the accusation that he had not expressly declared his support of free will and of retribution for works done, implying that those who were steadfast in their faith needed no clarification with regard to dogmas with which they were perfectly familiar. Fregoso made a careful distinction between 'those who are infirm of faith and indeed scarcely believe at all'[33] and 'those who are faithful and firmly believe in the afterlife and in a recompense for

---

30 *Index des livres interdits*, vol. VIII, pp. 25–50; G. Fragnito, *La Bibbia al rogo. La censura ecclesiastica e i volgarizzamenti della Scrittura (1471–1605)*, Bologna, Il Mulino, 1997, pp. 75 et seqq.

31 Ibid., c. XXVv. Cf. also ibid., c. XXXVIIv.

32 'il digiuno per domare l'insolentia della carne, e la limosina per estinguere l'insatiabil sete dell'avaritia i quali come due puntelli sostengono la oratione che non inclini né a destra né a sinistra' (ibid., c. XXXv).

33 'coloro che sono infermi nella fede né molto credono' (ibid., c. XXXVIr).

works done'.[34] While the infirm of faith have to be indoctrinated about the recompense for works done and about free will, as also about the importance that these two elements are destined to have at the moment of passing to the afterlife,[35] the firm believers, who do not need to be 'enlightened' about this, should content themselves with having complete trust in God's infinite mercy and 'liberality' (*liberalità*) and avoid being preoccupied in their prayers about the 'health of the soul' (*salute dell'anima*).[36] Fregoso therefore proposed a theory possessing many levels of interpretation. While Catholic readers may have taken this as a sufficiently plausible justification for his silence – construed as a sign of approval – with regard to the orthodox version of the relationship between faith and works done, he may have wished to urge spiritual readers to continue to have faith – in the manner of Nicodemus – only in God's merciful grace.

The attempts to achieve some sort of compromise were unsuccessful. After the turn of the mid-century there was no longer any room even for subtle simulatory or dissimulatory distinctions.[37]

As he compiled his text, Fregoso could glimpse threats looming on the horizon. Reading between the lines, in certain autobiographic references one can sense his preoccupation in his allusions to the hostile atmosphere that he felt developing around him. 'We must also pray for our enemies [...] forgiving them for their insults',[38] he wrote, *à propos* the contents of 'correct' prayer; and again, a little further on:

> We must conjoin [...] [the plea] for patience in the face of the world's adversities and [...] for patience and tolerance of not only the major insults of fortune but

---

[34] 'quelli che sono fedeli, e fermamente credono la vita futura, e la retribuzione delle opere' (ibid., c. XXXVIv).

[35] Ibid., c. XLr.

[36] Ibid., c. XLVr.v.

[37] In this context of ferocious hostility to the enemy, appeals to tolerance in the manner of Erasmus or more precisely of Pico della Mirandola (cf. above, pp. 19–20), such as we see in the following example, did not meet the approval of the Inquisitors: 'Nor must we abandon the non-believers, the Jews, and the heretics but we must pray that God will enlighten them with His truth, imitating our Mother Church, which prays and intercedes not only for His children but also for His enemies, and this is the universal prayer that Jesus Christ taught when He desired us to invoke Our Father as the universal father who is common to us all' ('Né si deve per niente abbandonare gl'infedeli, i Giudei e gli heretici pregando Dio li voglia illuminare della verità sua imitando la Chiesa madre nostra, che ora et intercede non solo per gli suoi figlioli, ma anchora per gli suoi nemici, e questa tale universale oratione insegnava Giesù Christo quando voleva che invocassimo il padre nostro, come padre universale e commune a tutti'; ibid., c. XLv).

[38] 'Si deve etiam fare oratione per li nostri nemici [...] perdonandoli le ingiurie' (ibid., c. XLIr).

also the minor ones which, like straw or dry twigs, catch fire more easily and then receive all the violence of the heat from the larger pieces of wood.[39]

The gradual tightening-up in the religious and political world and the resultant narrowing of the room for maneuvering which until then the *spirituali* had enjoyed eventually led to the approval, on 13 January 1547 during the sixth session of the Council of Trent, of the decree on justification.[40] The only way to save Cardinal Fregoso's writings from their actual fate would have been a subtle process of 'adjustment', as in the case of Crispoldi, or by accompanying the work with explicit declarations of orthodox faith, as Porzio did. Tullio Crispoldi wrote several short devotional works in the 1530s on the subject of prayer and religious devotion in which – probably as a precautionary measure of self-defense – he employed the strategy of anonymity.[41] He spent part of his priesthood as a guest of Bishop Giberti in Verona,[42] divided 'between evangelism and the Counter-Reformation', as can be seen in his writings, which reveal an ambiguous swaying between potentially heterodox positions and assuredly orthodox positions that was undoubtedly the product of his complex personality and his religious training but also of the frontier position occupied by the group of *spirituali* he mixed with.

If on the one hand, for example, he defended the doctrine of the intercession of the saints, on the other he presented (in the first of his works) a collection of incentives selected for the purpose of a manner of devotion based entirely on the inner inspiration that is directed by the Holy Spirit,

---

[39] 'si deve [...] congiungere [...] [la domanda] della patientia nelle avversità del mondo, e [...] la patientia e tollerantia delle ingiurie non solo delle grandi, ma etiam delle picciole, le quali come paglia o minuti stecchi più facilemente s'accendono e ricevono il fuoco dell'ira che vi fanno le legne grosse' (ibid., c. XLIIIr).

[40] The text of this decree is in *Conciliorum Oecumenicorum Decreta,* edited by G. Alberigo, G.A. Dossetti, P.-P. Joannou, C. Leonardi, and P. Prodi, Bologna, Istituto per le Scienze religiose, 1973, pp. 671–81, and in *Concilium Tridentinum. Diariorum, Auctorum, Epistolarum, Tractatuum nova collectio,* Freiburg, Brisgoviae, B. Herder, vol. V, 1911, pp. 791–9. An adequate first analysis of the decree can be found in H. Jedin, *Storia del Concilio di Trento,* vol. II, Brescia, Morcelliana, 1962, pp. 354–6.

[41] In chronological order Crispoldi published *Le Meditationi sopra il Pater noster* (Sept. 1534), *Meditationi dechiarative del Paternostro* (Dec. 1534), *De la Ave Maria et del Credo* (1535), and *Oratione sopra il Pater noster* (1540) (cf. A. Prosperi, *Les commentaires du Pater noster*, pp. 99–100).

[42] On Crispoldi, see F. Petrucci, *sub voce*, in DBI, vol. 30 (1984), pp. 820–22; A. Prosperi, *Tra evangelismo e controriforma. Giovan Matteo Giberti, 1495–1543,* Rome, Edizioni di Storia e Letteratura, 1969, *ad indicem;* C. Ginzburg and A. Prosperi, *Giochi di pazienza. Un seminario sul 'Beneficio di Cristo',* Turin, Einaudi, 1975, *ad indicem*; P. Simoncelli, *Evangelismo italiano, ad indicem*; M. Firpo, 'Il "Beneficio di Cristo" e il Concilio di Trento', p. 62; and Id., *Il processo inquisitoriale del cardinal Giovanni Morone*, vol. I, pp. 343–4. But see now the recent work by P. Salvetto, *Tullio Crispoldi nella crisi religiosa del Cinquecento. Le difficili 'pratiche del viver christiano'*, Brescia, Morcelliana, 2009.

describing prayer as a gesture of encouragement and excitement of the soul and rejecting the Catholic idea that prayer itself was a meritorious act in the eyes of God. A recurrent feature of many of his writings is therefore the alternation of statements related to the defense of the doctrine of meritorious works and others that say completely the opposite, linked to the exaltation of the gratuitousness of divine justification.[43] With regard to *De Ave Maria*, for instance, Crispoldi uses various arguments to defend the propriety of prayers that implore the saints 'to pray for us' (*affinché preghino per noi*) so that 'we may learn the path they trod in order that this may be an inducement for us too to enter within'[44] and then explains to his readers that man's good works are 'nothing by themselves, but are of value only because they are performed out of faith.'[45]

However, over and above these difficult attempts to reconcile mutually conflicting doctrinal positions, the security of this Veronese priest, when he found himself deprived of Giberti's religious authority on the latter's death in 1543, depended during the decades to come on a subtle process that required the rewriting of certain compromising passages in his works.[46]

Those who lacked the natural propensity for doctrinal compromise, or for self-censorious action as in the case of Crispoldi himself, still had to have recourse – if they wished to continue to treat the subject of inward prayer – to explicit and repeated declarations of orthodox faith. Such was the case of the humanist Simone Porzio,[47] the author of a work entitled

43 Cf., A. PROSPERI, *Les commentaires,* pp. 100–101.

44 'possiamo imparare la strada che hanno tenuta loro, et ne siano uno incitamento ad intrarvi' (T. CRISPOLDI, *De Ave Maria,* s.l., s.d, c. 371v).

45 'un niente da sé, ma solo vagliano perché le facemo sotto questa fede' (ibid, cc. 379v–380r, cf. also C. GINZBURG and A. PROSPERI, *Giochi di pazienza*, pp. 17 et sqq.). Statements like the following are typical of the attempted doctrinal compromise proposed by Crispoldi: 'The more we perform our actions out of faith, the more they are worth and the more they are accepted by God, because they are performed in the knowledge that in themselves they are nothing but are of value only because they are performed out of faith, that is to say, that our Blessed Lord, for the merits of His Son, makes us worthy to perform these works to His glory, and benignly forgives us for all the sins which we commit because of our weaknesses and because we do not perform these acts in the manner that most suits our worthiness' ('Le opere nostre bone tanto vagliono et tanto sono accettate da Dio, quanto sono fatte in fede, perché si fanno con questa cognitione che elle siano un niente da se, ma solo vagliano perché le facemo sotto questa fede, cioè che Dio benedetto per li meriti del suo figliuolo fa degni di fare quelle tali opere a sua gloria, et tutto quello che per nostra fragilità vi peccamo su, et non le facemo con tutti quelli modi che si convengono a tanta nostra dignatione, esso benignamente lo ne perdona'; ibid., c. 380v).

46 See C. GINZBURG and A. PROSPERI, *Giochi di pazienza*, p. 22.

47 On Porzio, cf. *Filosofia, filologia, biologia: itinerari dell'aristotelismo cinquecentesco,* D. Facca and G. Zanier (eds), Rome, Edizioni dell'Ateneo, 1992; P. ZAMBELLI, *L'Apprendista stregone. Astrologia, cabala e arte lulliana in Pico della Mirandola e seguaci,* Venice, Marsilio, 1995, p. 210; EAD., 'Scienza, filosofia, religione nella Toscana di Cosimo I',

Modo di orare christianamente con la espositione del Paternoster ('How a Christian prays, with an exposition of the Lord's Prayer'), following Giovan Battista Gelli's translation into the local Florentine dialect,[48] a work that, starting from its very title, clearly showed the influence of Erasmian thinking.[49] It was only after taking great pains to underline in most orotund terms the merits of good works that Porzio eventually began to turn his thoughts to the value of mental prayer – i.e. it was only after clearly stating that we are 'sons and heirs of the Supreme Father [not] only by our love and by our intentions, but also by effects and by works'[50] that the author felt free to move on to what were by then the traditional criticisms (in this particular literary genre) directed at 'Hypocrites, who love to pray in the Synagogues, and at the street corners so that others may see them'[51] and at worshippers who pronounce interminable prayers 'stitching together great multitudes of words'.[52] His concluding statement was that true devotion comes when 'through prayer and oration we enter into communion with God.'[53]

Statements related to the *spirituali* genre survived only if followed by another statement asserting the exact opposite, which thus constituted the denial of the foregoing assertion. So, for example, after taking a stand against prayers addressed to saints ('prayers should be said only to God'),[54] he immediately toned down the controversy by referring to the intercessory power of the 'angelic souls' (*anime angeliche*):

Florence and Venice: comparisons and relations. Acts of two Conferences at Villa I Tatti in 1976–1977, organized by Sergio Bertelli, Nicolai Rubinstein, and Craig Hugh Smyth, vol. 2: *Il Cinquecento*, Florence, La Nuova Italia, 1980, pp. 1–52; A. De Gaetano, *Giambattista Gelli and the Florentine Academy*, Florence, La Nuova Italia, 1976. More recently, cf. E. Del Soldato, 'La preghiera di un alessandrinista: i commenti al Pater noster di Simone Porzio', *Rinascimento*, XLVI, 2006, pp. 53–71.

48 On Gelli, besides De Gaetano's work cited in the previous footnote, cf. P. Simoncelli, *La lingua di Adamo. Guillaume Postel tra accademici e fuoriusciti fiorentini*, Florence, Olschki, 1984, *ad indicem*, and M. Firpo, *Gli affreschi di Pontormo a San Lorenzo. Eresia, politica e cultura nella Firenze di Cosimo I*, Turin, Einaudi, 1997, *ad indicem*.

49 *Modo di orare christianamente con la espositione del Pater noster, fatta da M. Simone Portio Napoletano. Tradotto in lingua Fiorentina, da Giovan Batista Gelli*, Florence, apud Lorenzo Torrentino, MDLI; the Latin edition, to the best of my knowledge, was first published only the following year: S. Porzio, *Formae orandi christianae, enarratio. Eiusdem in Euangelium Diui Ioannis scholion*, Florence, apud Laurentium Torrentinum, 1552.

50 'figliuoli et heredi del sommo Padre [non] solamente con l'affetto et con l'intentione, ma anchora con gli effetti et con l'opere' (S. Porzio, *Modo di orare*, c. 14).

51 'Hypocriti, i quali amano di orare ne le Sinagoghe, et ne cantoni de le piazze, acciochè gli huomini gli vegghino' (ibid., c. 16).

52 'accozzando insieme grande moltitudine di parole' (ibid.).

53 'ci congiugniamo mediante la oratione et preci con Dio' (ibid., c. 15).

54 'questa debbe darsi solo a Dio' (ibid., c. 22).

> To the doubt whether we should use this kind of prayer when we honor the saints, [...] the answer is that for us this is the only true way to worship God, and is called *latria*, or adoration; for the fact is that we pray to the saints not so that they may, of their own volition, perform a deed that benefits us but so that they should beseech God to act on our behalf in relation to the matter on the basis of their merits and their virtue.[55]

Similarly, before extolling the private, inward sphere of prayer, Porzio felt obliged to point out that public prayer also had its own particular function and its own basic value:

> And even if you pray in public, but do so for the general good and to set others a good example, seeking only the glory of God and to be helped by Him, and not mere reputation and honor among other men, it will be as if you were praying in private, since the Lord God is ever present and well disposed to those who invoke Him.[56]

Thus, both private and public prayers received God's blessing: 'For surely certain forms of prayer, both public and private, [...] much please the Lord'.[57]

It is therefore clear that the altered religious conditions imposed a different code of expression. In this respect it is important to emphasize that the precept expressed in the Gospels to pray in 'the most secret part of your closet' (*la parte più secreta della camera*) was applied some ten or twenty years after the previous literary versions with a totally opposite meaning. While in Savonarola, Luther, and Stancaro[58] this practice – always accompanied by the almost exclusive appeal to the supreme value of inward prayer – was perceived as a clear call to flee the 'duplicity' of heart and tongue, in Porzio's work – preceded by a proclamation declaring the propriety of public prayer and followed, as we shall shortly see, by a

---

[55] '[A] questo dubio, se quando noi honoriamo i santi, noi dobbiamo usare questa sorte di prece [...] si debbe rispondere, che questa debbe darsi solo a Dio ottimo et grandissimo, essendo ella appresso a nostri quel solo et vero culto di Dio chiamato latria, il quale si conviene solamente a lui; imperò che noi honoriamo et preghiamo i santi, non perché ci faccino bene alcuno in virtù loro propria, ma lo impetrino per noi da Dio mediante i loro meriti, et i loro preghi' (ibid., 22–3).

[56] 'Et se pure tu orerai in publico, ma per il bene commune, et per dar buono essempio a gli altri, cercando solamente la gloria, et lo aiuto di Dio, et non la reputatione et l'honor de gli huomini, et sarà come se tu orassi in ascosto imperò che il Signore è sempre presso et favorevole a quelli che lo chiamano' (ibid., c. 131).

[57] 'Et certamente che sono certe orationi tanto publiche, quanto private, [...] le quali sono molto grate a Dio' (ibid., c. 32).

[58] Cf. above, ch. 1.

sublimation of the distinction between the public and the private world – it took on what were evidently Nicodemite connotations.[59] If we read the passage in question in the light of historical knowledge of the political and religious climate of the early 1550s, there can be no doubt about its real meaning:

> And this manner of praying, which Our Savior described to us with the simile of the closet, requires that when you desire to pray, you go into your room, where He previously taught you it was wrong to pray in public, and now demonstrates the place that should be chosen; and so says: When you pray, that is, when you wish to honor God in due and proper fashion, which is what this word means to the Greeks [...], when you pray, that is, when you resolve to perform this act, go into your room, into the most secret part of your house: and there, where you normally store your treasures and your most valued possessions, you must say your prayer, which is far more precious than any other treasure you possess, and our Master means in this place, the safest and most secret place, and here you place your heart. And when you manage to rid yourself of worldly temptations and no longer allow yourself to be attracted and lured away by the pleasures of the flesh but instead refrain from satisfying its desires, denying and belittling yourself, then you will walk wholly in the right spirit and will seek God with all your heart, which then will not be divided but entirely directed towards the Almighty.[60]

A few lines further on, as we have already seen, comes the punctual codification – with its sublimating effect – of the theorized distinction between public and private. This is done by means of an explicit reference to the text in the Gospels:

> As we read in St Luke, when he says that Christ taught by day in the temple but by night left it to climb the mount, whence by day he taught openly as a

[59] See P. Simoncelli, *Evangelismo italiano*, p. 365.

[60] 'Et questo modo di orare disegnandoci il Salvator nostro con la similitudine de la camera dice. Quando tu vuoi orare entra dentro a la tua camera, dove havendoci insegnato primeramente come non si debbe orare in publico, dimostra hora qual sia il luogo che si debbe eleggere; Onde dice. Quando tu ori, cioè quando tu desideri honorare debitamente et convenientemente Dio, che così significa appresso a Greci questa parola [...]. Quando tu ori cioè, quando tu deliberi far tal cosa, entra dentro a la tua camera cioè, ne la più secreta parte de la casa tua; et dove tu sei solito et consueto di ascondere, et riporre i tuoi tesori, et le tue cose più pretiose, riponi anchora l'oratione tua, la quale è di gran lunga più pretiosa di qual si voglia altro tesoro, et vuole significare in questo luogo il maestro nostro, il tuo più sicuro et secreto luogo, et quivi riponi il cuore tuo. Onde quando tu ti libererai da le perturbationi del mondo, et non ti lascerai allettare, et tirare da le lusinghe de la carne, né adempierai i suoi desideri, ma abnegherai et abbasserai te medesimo, allhora tu camminerai totalmente in ispirilo, et cercherai Dio con tutto il cuore, il quale non sarà allhora diviso, ma tutto rivolto a Dio' (S. Porzio, *Modo di orare*, cc. 28–9).

> minister of the people in the temple, while by night he prayed for himself and for others; and not only should priests imitate this sort of life but they should also strive with all their might to attain *such perfection*.[61]

At certain moments, it is true, Porzio seemed unable to blot out his original Protestant convictions entirely and he indulged in impassioned exaltations of faith, explaining that 'all good works are the fruits of faith' (*tutte le opere buone sieno frutti della fede*) and that 'it is certainly a work of faith to believe in Him who was sent by the supreme Father, and this firm and steady faith makes us what we are and orders and advises us with all the strength of our spirit to love and honor the Lord'.[62] The conclusion of the treatise, however, brought the subject back once again to the realm of solid orthodoxy (apart from an uncontrolled final fling that once again allows us to glimpse the confused and chaotic state of his thinking).[63] The manifest defense of man's free will accompanied a restatement of the principal function of praying by the faithful, prayer being interpreted not only as a means by which to approach God and remember one's sins but also as an instrument to 'ingratiate' (*ingraziarsi*) the Almighty Father in view of the final judgment:

> God does not order you to pray to Him so that you may make your desire known to Him but so that you may adapt it and make it familiar to him, thanks to the frequency of your prayers so that you humble yourself, remember your sins, and recall having offended him. Because, in addition, although God knew *ab aeterno* that by His grace and the good use of your free will you shall beseech and you shall merit heaven, He did not preordain your destiny with the result that your power of decision and choice was left free.[64]

---

61 'come scrive Luca dicendo che Christo insegnava il dì nel tempio, et la notte usciva di quello, et andava a stare nel monte, onde insegnava come publico ministro palesemente nel tempio il giorno, et la notte orava et pregava per sé et per gli altri; la qual sorte di vita debbono non solamente imitare i sacerdoti, ma ingegnarsi con ogni diligenza il più che possono di condursi *a tal perfettione*' (ibid., c. 35; my emphasis).

62 'è certamente l'opera della fede, credere in colui il quale è stato mandato da il sommo padre, et questa fede essendo ferma et stabile in Dio è quella che ci rende tali, et che ordina noi stessi et consiglia tutte le forze dell'animo nostro a la dilettione et all'amore di Dio' (ibid.).

63 To some extent the concluding words minimized what had been said about the value of prayer: 'And although He may still grant you Paradise even without your prayers and without your virtues, He nevertheless desires these good movements of the mind' ('Et se bene egli può anchora darti il Cielo senza le tue orationi, et senza i tuoi preghi, egli vuole niente di manco questi tali buoni movimenti de lo animo'; ibid., c. 40).

64 'Dio non ti comanda che tu lo preghi perché tu gli facci noto il desiderio tuo, ma perché tu lo pieghi et rendatelo familiare, con la frequenza delle orationi, perché tu ti humilii, et perché tu ti riduca spesso a memoria i tuoi peccati, et ricorditi di haverlo offeso. Perché se bene oltra di questo dio conobbe ab eterno, che mediante la gratia sua, et il buono uso del libero arbitrio tuo, tu impetrerai et meriterai il Cielo, egli non ti predestinò però di tal

If one considers the various crypto-Reformation allusions and orthodox statements of this humanist, his appeals to mental prayer, and his attacks on the vanity of outward signs of devotion, one cannot help observing that the entire treatise is permeated with a tone of asceticism which, though never becoming a key structure of the discourse, occasionally becomes apparent and leaves slender but clearly discernible signs of its presence: a presence that suggests a final reflection. As Porzio wrote:

> Through the prayers we say to God [...] we certainly separate ourselves from the things of this earth and go towards those of Heaven, and we are drawn by our brethren toward our Father who is not terrestrial but divine by virtue of the affection and desire of our mind; and in the end He teaches us the way and the manner for us to return to a state of grace in ourselves and with which we can induce our senses to heed the call of reason and be obedient to Him, through fasting; so it is therefore that the absence of affections and the elimination of human passion, if annulled by us, will allow us to re-create a new man who is not only dear to God but also friendly and benevolent to other men.[65]

This ascetic vein was well tempered by a humanistic type of intellectualism which, insisting on the primary role of the rational element,[66] kept it remote from the total abandonment to the will of God, which the defenders of Catholic orthodoxy learned to recognize as the most insidious element of the mystic contemplative tradition: so long as it remained imprisoned, and well controlled, in the complexities of humanistic rationalism, its invitation to 'self-denial' (*abnegazione*) as the way 'to walk totally in spirit' (*camminare totalmente in ispirito*) and to seek 'God with all one's heart' (*Dio con tutto il cuore*)[67] would not therefore preoccupy the authorities of the Roman Inquisition. The theorization of

---

maniera che non ti lasciassi la podestà de lo arbitrio, et de lo eleggere libera' (ibid., c. 40). On *Espositione del pater*, in the appendix to *Modo di orare*, see the remarks made by P. SIMONCELLI, p. 367 and footnote 173.

65 '[Mediante la oratione et le preci con Dio [...] noi certamente ci partiamo da le cose terrene et andiamo alle celesti, et siamo tirati da fratelli al Padre nostro non terreno, ma divino secondo lo affetto et il desiderio della mente nostra; et ci insegna finalmente la via et il modo, per il quale noi possiamo ritornare in gratia con noi stessi, et col quale noi possiamo indurre il senso a seguitare la ragione, et ad essergli obbediente con questo digiuno; conciò sia cosa che un mancamento degli affetti, et uno spogliarsi de le passioni humane, le quali essendo discacciate da noi, faranno che noi riedificheremo un nuovo huomo, non solamente caro a Dio, ma amico et benevolo anchora a gl'altri huomini' (S. PORZIO, *Modo di orare*, cc. 15–16).

66 In the framework of a complex theorization of the relationship between praying and contemplation, we read: 'Using *reason*, we conceive and represent Him [God] in our mind in three ways' ('Noi ce lo [Dio] proponiamo et rappresentiamo nell'animo con la ragione in tre maniere'; ibid., c. 20).

67 Ibid., c. 29.

mental prayer as an instrument to reach 'divine union' (*divina unione*) with God through the deprivation of all personal affections and earthly goods, the total annihilation of one's will, and profound self-hatred had been systematically expounded in quite a different manner in the writings of authors such as Battista da Crema and Serafino da Fermo, certainly arousing greater apprehension among the defenders of Roman orthodoxy.

CHAPTER 3

Serafino da Fermo and Lorenzo Davidico

The manifestations of the contemplative religiosity which, in the wake of the beghard tradition of the Free Spirit,[1] presented a foretaste of many features of the seventeenth-century tradition of 'quiet prayer' (*orazione di quiete*),[2] were unaffected – apart from a few exceptions[3] – by the action of Roman censorship, and re-emerged right in the middle of the 'century of the baroque.'[4] In Spain in the first half of the sixteenth century the Inquisition authorities were confronted with the parallel development of Protestant movements and the beliefs of the *Alumbrados*,[5] and it was therefore possible to attack either of these manifestations of heresy indiscriminately. But things went differently in Italy, for ever since the fourteenth century Italian mysticism had developed – except for a few exceptions such as the aforementioned beghard heresy – within the framework of Catholic orthodoxy. When Protestant doctrines began to spread throughout Italy, this tradition offered, among other things, an

---

1 On this, see the classic study by R. GUARNIERI, *Il movimento del Libero Spirito. Testi e documenti*, in *Archivio Italiano per la Storia della Pietà*, vol. IV, Rome, Edizioni di storia e letteratura, 1965, pp. 351–708; and also, more recently, EAD., 'Prefazione storica', to Margherita Porete, *Lo specchio delle anime semplici*, Rome, Edizioni San Paolo, 1994, pp. 7–54.

2 For a first approach, see M. PETROCCHI, *Il Quietismo italiano del Seicento*, Rome, Edizioni di storia e letteratura, 1948; R. DE MAIO, 'Il problema del quietismo napoletano', *Rivista storica italiana*, LXXXI, 1969, pp. 721–44; G.V. SIGNOROTTO, *Inquisitori e mistici nel Seicento italiano. L'eresia di Santa Pelagia*, Bologna, Il Mulino, 1989, and *L'eresia dei perfetti. Inquisizione romana ed esperienze mistiche nel Seicento italiano*, Rome, Edizioni di storia e letteratura, 2003.

3 Cf. below, chapter 7.

4 P. SIMONCELLI, 'Il "Dialogo dell'unione spirituale di Dio con l'anima" tra alumbradismo spagnolo e prequietismo italiano', *Annuario dell'Istituto storico italiano per l'età moderna e contemporanea*, XXLX–XXX, 1977–78, Rome, 1979, pp. 565–601, in particular pp. 599–600.

5 See B. LLORCA, *Die Spanische Inquisitation und die "Alumbrados" (1509–1667)*, Berlin-Bonn, Ferd. Dummlers Verlag, 1934; J.E. LONGHURST, *Erasmus and the Spanish Inquisition: The Case of Juan de Valdés*, Albuquerque, The University of New Mexico Press, 1950; *Reforma española y Reforma luterana. Afinitades y diferencias a la luz de los misticos españoles (1517–1536)*, Madrid, Fundación Universitaria Española, 1975; *Inquisición española y mentalitad inquisitorial*, Barcelona Ariel, ed. Angel Alcalà, 1984; and also the classic study by M. BATAILLON, *Erasmo y España. Estudios sobre la historia espiritual del siglo XVI*, Mexico-Buenos Aires, Fondo de cultura economica, 1966 (II edn).

important contribution to orthodoxy's defense against Lutheran thinking.[6] As a result of this development it was therefore much more difficult for the Roman authorities, distracted as they were by the danger of Lutheranism, to establish precisely where, in the sixteenth and subsequent centuries, the uncertain boundary between orthodoxy and heterodoxy actually lay: in any case, an indiscriminate 'mystic hunt' would have been harmful as regards the fight against Lutheranism, which – at least until the 1570s – continued to be the primary objective of the ecclesiastic hierarchies.

This is the background against which the sixteenth-century work *Trattato utilissimo et necessario della mentale oratione* ('Most useful and necessary treatise on mental prayer')[7] by Serafino da Fermo should be read.[8] This publication, though containing many of the features which during the seventeenth-century attack on quietism caused the reaction of the Church authorities, at the time succeeded in passing through the Roman censorship unscathed (the work was however condemned in Spain, where it was placed several times on the Index).[9] This treatise, it should be immediately said, was explicitly ascetic-mystic and radical in its spiritualistic implications, as were the writings of Serafino's master, Battista da Crema, whose writings were condemned by the Holy Office in 1552 and placed on the Index in 1559.[10]

Like other documents we have considered, this one by Serafino da Fermo was prompted by the bleak realization of the spreading of the empty devotionalism of mere words. Also in this treatise 'the hypocrites and the superstitious' (*hypocriti et superstitiosi*) who pray to the Lord 'by voice alone and bare ceremonies'[11] constitute a negative term of

---

[6] On the orthodox mystic tradition, cf. G. Getto, *Letteratura religiosa dal Due al Novecento*, pp. 159 et seqq.; and on Battista's and Serafino's anti-Lutheranism, cf. L. Bogliolo, *Battista da Crema. Nuovi studi sopra la sua vita, i suoi scritti, la sua dottrina*, Turin, Società Editrice Internazionale, 1952.

[7] *Trattato utilissimo et necessario della mentale oratione, et come acquistar si possi, del Reverendo padre Don Seraphino da Fermo Can. Regulare et predicatore rarissimo.* In Venetia, Comin da Trino, 1541.

[8] On Serafino da Fermo, see G. Feyles, *Serafino da Fermo canonico regolare lateranense (1496–1540). La vita, le opere, la dottrina spirituale*, Turin, Società Editrice Internazionale, 1942.

[9] His work *Obras espirituales* was banned both by the Spanish Index of 1559 (*Index des livres interdits*, vol. V, pp. 539–41) and in that of 1583 (*Index des livres interdits*, vol. VI, p. 632). In Italy only his *Apologia di fra Battista da Crema* was placed on the Roman Index of 1559 and on that of 1564 (*Index des livres interdits*, vol. VIII, pp. 677–8).

[10] *Index des livres interdits*, vol. VIII, pp. 379–80.

[11] 'con sola voce et ignude cerimonie' (*Trattato utilissimo et necessario della mentale oratione*, c. 2v). 'Many [...] strive to say many offices and prayers, and are always muttering as they go their way, and often, to satisfy their appetite, they neglect works of charity and become haughty, [...] but their heart is not intent on what they are saying for their lips remain

comparison used by the author to exalt prayer coming from the 'heart', 'in spirit and truth' (*in spirito et veritade*).[12] However, his train of thought led him on in hitherto unexplored directions. The ultimate goal of his impassioned exposition was, as Serafino made clear from the outset, 'mental union' (*mentale unione*) with God. For him, mental prayer was thus not just inward prayer, an intimate conversation with God, as up to this point we have grown accustomed to seeing it treated. Instead, prayer was 'the ardent longing for God' (*l'ardente desiderio di Dio*), the means by which man could achieve 'perfect union' (*perfetta unione*) with the prime object of his desire. The entire treatise is dominated by this mystic upward tension, and its tormented development is well summed up in the metaphor of the

> ascent of a high mountain, which at first is scabrous and slippery, gradually becomes less steep, and finishes in a most pleasant and fertile meadow, to climb up to which whoever so wishes must relinquish every weight, be of good spirit, employ all industry, and proceed in order, starting at the bottom up to the top.[13]

According to the method of division devised by Savonarola – or rather by Bonaventura – four levels are involved in the ascent to the top of the 'mountain'. The first is the 'Lesson' (*lettione*),[14] the second is 'Meditation'

---

dry as they move them, and they allow their mind to wander in various idle thoughts' ('Molti [...] si sforzano dire molti ufficii, et orationi, et sempre vanno brontolando, et spesso lasciano per sodisfare al proprio appetito, le opre della charità, et diventano sdegnosi, [...] non hanno però il cuore intento a quel che dicono, ma solamente moveno l'asciutte labbra, lasciando la mente in diversi pensieri otiosamente discorrere'; ibid., cc. 10r–v).

12 Ibid., c. 3r–v.

13 'salimento d'un alto monte, che nel principio è scabroso, et lubrico, et pian piano diventando men difficultoso, finisce in un campo affienissimo, et fertilissimo, al qual chi vole ascendere, convien che disponga ogni peso, et facci buon animo, et adoperi ogni industria, et preceda per ordine cominciando dal basso infino alla cima' (ibid., c. 17r).

14 'Regarding this aspect, I have already said that among all books you must choose only those that lead you to domination of your passions, and also beware that curiosity does not spur you to the desire for knowledge, for that would bring not union and mortification but distraction and the excitation of *amour propre*' ('Di quella ho già detto che debbi sceglier tra gli altri libri sol quelli che alla perfetta vittoria delle tue passioni ti conducono, in questo sia svegliato, che la curiosità non ti traporti al desiderio di sapere, perché non riportaresti unione, et mortificatione, ma distrattione, et fomento dell'amor propio;' ibid., c. 60v).

(*meditatione*),[15] the third 'Mental Prayer' (*mentale orazione*),[16] and the fourth 'Contemplation' (*contemplazione*).[17] As a believer makes his way along this scale, he passes from the condition of a 'beginner' (*incipiente*) to that of one who is 'proficient' (*proficiente*), finally reaching a state of 'perfection' (*perfezione*):

> [1] In prayer you will be a *beginner* when, with your love of God and your love of the world vying within you, you feel great resistance when you raise your mind to God, as if you desired to lift a great weight off the ground, and although you may sometimes enjoy some light, that will immediately turn to naught and you will return to your habitual heaviness of heart. [2] But when your diffidence ceases, as you gain more of the familiarity that begins to develop in the colloquium with God, and when you no longer proceed with such doubtful spirit but rather, almost with a sense of certainty, you seek to obtain that which you now pray for, and without difficulty you are able to continue this inward practice, and tolerate the secret silence, then you will be able to say you are *proficient* in prayer, but be careful lest the peril of tepid belief return and draw you back again. [3] *perfect* prayer is all fire, ever burning in the heart, and shining so brightly in the intellect that it lets us know of every slightest sin, and

---

[15] 'When the mind by its own is ruminating that which it has gathered in the pasture of the lesson, and here it is in your interest to have sufficient patience to withstand the importunate thoughts that will come to torment you, reducing the spirit to the first object, every time that it flees, that in the end you will be victorious' ('Quando per se stessa la mente va ruminando quel che nel pascolo della lettione ha raccolto, et quivi ti conviene haver patientia di sopportare gli importuni pensieri, che in quel tempo ti molestaranno, riducendo tante volte l'animo al primo oggetto, quante volte fugge, che all'ultimo restarai vincitore'; ibid., c. 60 v.).

[16] 'Mental prayer is no more than an elevation of the mind toward God, without the din of words, and in prayer you will find, at one moment, fatigue and, at another, delight, depending how faithfully you have practiced it – nevertheless, jaculatory prayers are extremely useful and, being very short, they must be very frequent in every place and in every action, for the more frequent they are, the less fatigue they cause, just as a candle lights more readily when it has just been extinguished and still preserves some of its former heat' ('non è altro che una elevation di mente in Dio, senza strepito di parola, et in questa se ritrova hor fatica, hor diletto, secondo che più fidelmente sarà da te essercitata, però molto sono utili l'orationi giaculatorie, le quali debbono come sono brevissime, esser anchor frequentissime in ogni luoco, et operatione, et quanto più saranno frequenti, tanto meno haranno di fatica, come la candela più leggiermente s'accende quando di fresco è smorzata, et anchor mantiene un poco del caldo passato'; ibid., cc. 60v–61r).

[17] 'This (sc. contemplation) is so purified by excess of love that the soul is transformed into God and can be said to be more in God than in itself, yet it is moved without difficulty by God rather than by itself. This level is attained after great efforts and total victory over oneself' ('Questa è per eccessivo amore, tanto purgata, che l'anima in Dio trasforma, et più si può dir esser in Dio, che in se stessa, però senza difficultà più tosto è mossa da Dio, che da se si mova, a questo grado non si perviene se non dopo molte fatiche, et piena vittoria di se stesso'; ibid., c. 61r).

in the end brings oblivion to all outward things of the world and carries the soul off above itself into the abyss of divine obscurity.[18]

The first phase appears to be the most difficult to overcome: 'All industry must be employed to curb the imagination, lest it stray in idle thoughts',[19] in other words the objective must be 'to achieve victory over the passions, and evil desires'.[20] Only by cutting away such terrestrial 'impediments' (*impedimenti*)[21] will the true believer be able to approach the state of mental union with God. 'Those who load themselves with many burdens, that is to say, with many terrestrial occupations, fruitless arguments, and sensual pleasures'[22] have no chance of reaching the summit of the mountain.

If one is to get rid of these 'ties' (*lacci*), one must concentrate one's thoughts on 'painful objects' (*oggetti penosi*),[23] catalyse one's 'memory' on the recollection of 'evil',[24] 'gather together in the mind [...] all the damage that is received from sin', ensuring that 'the will can desire nothing but evil'.[25] 'If [...] you persevere in this study', Serafino went on, 'you will become a changed man, because this meditation will bring your soul to scorn the world, to flee sin, to fear the pain of suffering, and to love virtue.'[26]

Only in this way, following Christ's example and reflecting on 'the fallacy of the world, the brevity of time, the nearness of death, and the

---

18 '[1] sarai nell'oratione *incipiente,* quando combattendo in te dall'una parte l'amor d'Iddio, dall'altra del mondo sentirai molta resistentia in sollevar la mente a Dio, come se un grave peso volesti alzare da terra, et se pur qualche volta gustarai un poco di luce, subito andarà in niente, et tornarai alla solita gravezza. [2] Ma quando mancare la diffidentia per la dimistichezza, che nel divin colloquio nasce, et già non più con l'animo così dubbioso, ma quasi certo andarai d'impetrar quel che orando domandi, et senza difficultà potrai continuar l'interior essercitio, et tollerare il secreto silentio, potrai dire esser *proficiente* nell'oratione, et guardati che '1 pericolo della tepidità non ti conduca ritornare indietro. [3] ^*perfetta* oratione è tutta di fuoco sempre arde nel cuore, et luce nell'intelletto talmente, che fa conoscere ogni minimo peccato, et ultimamente induce oblivione di tutte le cose esteriori, et rapisce l'anima sopra di se stessa nell'abisso della divina caligine' (ibid., cc. 72r–v; my emphasis).

19 'Tutta l'industria deve esser collocata nel raffrenar l'imaginatione, che in otiosi pensieri non discorra' (ibid., cc. 62r–v).

20 'riaver vittoria delle passioni, et desiderii cattivi' (ibid., c. 62v).

21 Ibid., c. 20r.

22 'quelli che di molti pesi si carigano, cioè di terrene occupationi, d'infruttuosi ragionamenti, de diletti sensuali' (ibid., c. 18r).

23 Ibid., c. 31r.

24 Ibid., c. 71v.

25 'raccogliere nella mente tutto il danno che dal peccato se riceve', facendo sì che 'la volontà non potrà voler altro che male' (ibid., cc. 71r–v).

26 'se in questo studio [...] tu perseveri [...] diventerai un altro huomo tramutato, perché l'animo tuo per tal meditatione sarà indulto al dispreggio del mondo, alla fuga del peccato, al timor delle pene, et amor della vertù' (ibid., c. 32r).

danger of hell',[27] will a man be able to curb 'his vain cogitations and, by making fresh resolutions, change his life for the better'.[28]

From this point of view, the acts of devotion recommended by the ecclesiastic authorities, 'such as fasts, vigils, and bodily hardships, as also poverty, chastity, and obedience',[29] are a 'commendable' (*lodevole*) instrument placed by the Church in human hands 'because they remove impediments to prayer with their importune agitations, which disturb our minds like the winds of a tempest,'[30] and 'lead us to perfect prayer'.[31] Thus, up to this point, Serafino da Fermo remained within the consolidated ranks of Catholic orthodoxy.[32]

At this juncture the disciple of Battista da Crema advanced further along the successive phases of the mystic ascent to the top of the mountain. By dint of practicing 'holy hatred' (*santo odio*) of his own person, the true believer reaches the second phase of his 'ascent' (*ascesa*), passing from the state of a 'beginner' (*incipienza*) to that of 'proficiency' (*proficienza*). Only by showing willingness, as Serafino wrote, 'to be cast down for his sake into all evil, be it temporal or eternal, and thus to hate yourself with infinite hatred', [33] will a man succeed in loving God 'infinitely' (*infinitamente*) as he deserves.[34]

This is the moment when man's soul unites with God. By divine mediation (and in this way alone) he regains – as if by some sort of conditioned reflex – trust in himself and the rest of mankind:

> Then will you truly love God and since true love can be found only in Him, you will again love yourself, and your neighbor, and in this way holy hatred will

---

[27] 'la fallacia del mondo, la brevità del tempo, la vicinanza della morte, il pericolo dell'inferno' (ibid., c. 37r).

[28] 'le infruttuose cogitationi, et facendo spesso novi proponimenti tramutare in meglio la vita sua' (ibid.).

[29] Ibid., c. 9v.

[30] 'perché ci tolgono gli impedimenti di orare con le importune agitationi, che conturbano la mente nostra come venti tempestosi' (ibid.)

[31] 'ci conducono all'oration perfetta' (ibid.). Cf. also his reflections on the necessary function of jaculatory prayers (ibid., cc. 38r–v), which are, however, accompanied by a critical comment on the emptiness of certain ways of praying (ibid., c. 62r).

[32] It was hardly likely that Serafino's anti-intellectualism (see in particular ibid., c. 54r and cc. 57r–v) would in any way preoccupy an ecclesiastic organization that was about to launch a violent attack on reading the Bible in the vernacular (regarding which, cf. G. FRAGNITO, *La Bibbia al rogo*, *passim*).

[33] 'esser disposto per amor suo in ogni male, così temporale, come eterno esser precipitato, et così infinitamente odiar te stesso' (ibid., c. 50r).

[34] Ibid.

bring you to holy love, just as your disordered love of yourself brought you to lose God and yourself and all things of value.[35]

By giving up his will utterly and unequivocally to that of God (Serafino defines it the 'annulment' of human will), man attains, thanks to prayer, a condition of 'deification' (*deificazione*):

Prayer raises man above the things of this world and lets him converse in Heaven with the angels, and finally unite with the infinite majesty and ineffably become deified, and act like God, for he who prays in spirit and in truth is not moved to do so by himself or by his own will but by the spirit that dwells within them.[36]

When a man reaches this 'deifying' (*deificante*) stage, he not only 'acquires what sinning has caused him to lose'[37] but also reaches a state of 'perfection' in which each 'part of our soul' (from the part said 'carnal' to the 'irascible' and the 'rational') finds real 'peace':

And if we seek real peace, [our mind] has no other way but prayer, and this brings us into the presence of God, where the part of us said to be carnal rediscovers goodness, which is its true object, and once satiated it rests. So ends the work of the irascible, since beyond any possible contradiction it is in God in a state of perfect enjoyment, and the rational, contemplating the first truth, strives to know no more.[38]

Thus, having reached the third and final stage of the mystic ascent, defined the 'perfect prayer' (*oratione perfetta*), Serafino must have distinctly perceived the risk of action by the Inquisition. Despite having faithfully trodden in his master's footsteps (as regards both content and language), Serafino chose not to venture down the slippery path of the mystic effects resulting from the achievement of this state of 'perfection'. Although he had initially suggested

---

35 'Allhora veramente amarai Dio, et perché non si ritrova vero amor se non in lui, amarai anchor te stesso, et il prossimo tuo, così il santo odio t'indurrà al santo amore, come l'amor disordinato di te stesso t'induceva [a] perder Dio e te stesso et ogni bene' (ibid., c. 50v).

36 'L'oratione è quella che fa ascendere l'huomo alle cose sopramondane, et conversar in cielo con gli angeli, et finalmente congiongersi alla infinita maiestà, et in uno ineffabile modo deificarsi, et operare come Iddio perhò che colui che ora in spirito e veritade, non si move da sé, né dal proprio volere, ma secondo il spirito che habita in esso' (ibid., cc. 3v–4r).

37 's'acquista quel, che peccando havea perduto' (ibid., c. 14v).

38 'Et se vuole acquetarsi [la mente nostra] non ha altro mezzo che la oratione, la qual ci conduce a Dio, dove la parte nostra detta concupiscibile ritrova il bene, quale è suo vero oggetto, et satiata se riposa, così cessa l'opra dell'irascibile, essendo in Dio fuor d'ogni contrario, in godimento perfetto, et la rationale contemplando la prima verità più oltre non s'affatica in sapere' (ibid., cc. 21r–v).

he had acquired 'a certain degree of confidence that he was one of the elect'[39] (where the word *certain* was deliberately ambiguous, in a state of perfect equilibrium between a 'heretic' affirmation of the certainty of salvation and the diametrically opposite interpretation of an attempt to diminish the statement's clarity), Serafino preferred to hide behind an explicit declaration of deliberate anonymity,[40] avoiding the danger of making any insidious claims about the state of impeccability and the total freedom of those who were 'perfect',[41] claims that were to prove decisive in the conviction of Battista da Crema.[42] As the albeit scarce documentation available for this first half of the sixteenth century shows, the decisive element in the Holy Office's condemnation of the Dominican monk in 1552[43] was his sense of the absolute certainty of his faith (and impeccability), which was an essential component of a believer's attainment of the state of 'perfection', a sense that permeated all his writings. The Inquisitors must have viewed this as a fresh interpretation of beghard elements,[44] the effects of which

---

39 'certa fidanza di essere nel numero degli eletti' (ibid., c. 5v).

40 Ibid., cc. 124r–v.

41 Serafino too had spoken about 'freedom', without, however, attributing to it the central role it had for Battista da Crema – he relegated it to the answer to one of the 'doubts' he had raised in the appendix to his treatise (ibid., cc. 117v–118r).

42 On Battista da Crema, see L. BOGLIOLO, *Battista da Crema*; O. PREMOLI, *Storia dei Barnabiti nel Cinquecento,* Rome, Desclée & C, 1913, *passim*; M. FIRPO, *Nel labirinto del mondo. Lorenzo Davidico tra santi, eretici, inquisitori*, Florence, Olschki, 1992, pp. 18–48; E. BONORA, *I conflitti della Controriforma. Santità e obbedienza nell'esperienza religiosa dei primi barnabiti*, Florence, Le Lettere, 1998, in particular pp. 103 et seqq. Although Battista da Crema never devoted a specific work to the topic of prayer, this can be said to have been the leitmotiv of his entire *œuvre*; cf. L. BOGLIOLO, *Battista da Crema*, pp. 61–3.

43 The Holy Office's condemnation (on which in addition to E. BONORA, *I conflitti della Controriforma*, p. 145, see also S. PAGANO, 'La condanna delle opere di fra' Battista da Crema. Tre inedite Censure del Sant'Offizio e della Congregazione dell'Indice', *Barnabiti Studi*, 14, 1997, pp. 221–310, in particular, pp. 238 et seqq.) was followed by the ban on his works pronounced by the Roman Index of 1559 and in that of 1564 (*quamdiu expurgantur*), cf. *Index des livres interdits*, vol. VIII, pp. 379–80.

44 Twenty years before the College of Cardinals showed any interest in the writings of Battista da Crema, Gian Pietro Carafa, one day to become Pope Paul IV, had perceived in the teaching of this Dominican monk a dangerous reproposal of the characteristic features of medieval beghardism. In a letter to Battista written in 1531, the Neapolitan prelate 'demonstrated that he had realized that the monk's disobedience to his superiors was no chance happening but the reflection of a solidly argued doctrinal position, based on which the institution was not granted any right of control over an individual's religious experience' (E. Bonora, *I conflitti della Controriforma*, p. 146). As Elena Bonora explains, Carafa had fully realized that 'the reckless pursuit of temptation [...] led to the annulment of individual will, and this for Battista was the root of all evil. [...] By advancing this mystic interpretation, i.e. the union of human and divine will achieved through the total suppression of the former, man's actions were placed beyond any possible judgment, since his compliance with the will of God came to be stronger than any objective standard of evaluation' (ibid., p. 145). A papal breve issued by Paul III soon afterward, in 1536, directed against the 'conventicles' in

dangerously coincided with the Lutheran concept of salvation by faith alone.[45]

The impunity allowed to Serafino da Fermo's treatise thus confirmed what up to this point might have been reasonable to suspect, i.e. that the exaltation of mental prayer (even with its recently bold mystic interpretations) did not per se perturb the Inquisition authorities. Mental prayer was strongly opposed only inasmuch as it soon became associated with the heresies of Lutheran doctrine.

For the purposes of our argument, the vicissitudes of *Monte d'oratione*,[46] a work by Lorenzo Davidico, another of Battista da Crema's disciples, are rather like the squaring of the circle. Despite prolonged and repeated attempts to incriminate him,[47] the Inquisition authorities could find no trace of heresy in his writings. Despite his spending several spells in prison, and despite his repeated escapes, the treatise (as also all his vast number of publications)[48] was untouched by the censorship of the Church – a process that must have been meticulous and, in his case, not entirely unprejudiced.

It may be useful to devote a few more pages to the writings of this ambiguous popularizer of the work of the Dominican master, trying to focus on the ways in which the mystic aspect of prayer succeeded in penetrating the strict canons of Catholic orthodoxy. Whereas Serafino da Fermo was saved by a prudent silence with regard to the more delicate stages in the mystic ascent to God, in the case of Davidico it was his repeated and exaggerated declarations of orthodoxy and his violent (though not particularly original) attacks on the Lutheran heresy that procured for him not only 'absolution' for his writings but also the glories of Counter-Reformation spirituality.

Milan that were 'inspired' by the work of Battista da Crema, provided confirmation of what was by then a consolidated link between beghard heresy (Free Spirit) and the Dominican's mystic doctrine: describing the claimed origins of these 'sects', the breve used the following unequivocal terms 'multae haereses ab Ecclesia damnatae, praesertim beguinarum et pauperum de Lugduno nuncupatae' ('many heresies condemned by the Church, in particular those said by Beguines and paupers in Lyons'; ibid., pp. 189 et seqq., in particular p. 191).

45 In light of these considerations it appears legitimate to argue that the treatise could scarcely be accused of pelagianism, as has been authoritatively stated (cf. M. Petrocchi, 'Pelagianesimo di Battista da Crema', *Rivista di storia della Chiesa in Italia*, VIII, 1954, pp. 418–22).

46 *Monte d'oratione composto per il reverendo sacerdote M. Lorenzo Davidico Predicatore fidelissimo*. In Rome, per i tipografi Valerio e Luigi Dorico, l'anno del Giubileo, 1550.

47 On Davidico and his ups and downs with the Inquisition, see M. Firpo, *Nel labirinto del mondo*, op. cit., vol. I - D. Marcatto, *Il processo inquisitoriale di Lorenzo Davidico (1555–1560). Edizione critica,* vol. II, Florence, Olschki, 1992.

48 See the bibliography of his works presented by Massimo Firpo in the appendix to his volume entitled *Nel labirinto del mondo,* pp. 237–58.

Many pages in Davidico's text are taken up by what had by then become the ritual accusations leveled against the empty devotionalism of believers who customarily prayed 'without any mental attention',[49] but the heart of the work is a chaotic but impassioned defense of Catholic devotional practice, threatened by hard Lutheran criticism. First, Davidico was in favor of the liturgic division of the time devoted to prayer, as assimilated by the Catholic church from ecclesiastic tradition:

> Now if the Apostles established with David certain fixed times for prayer, should we too not continue to imitate them, since we are above all encouraged in this practice by the Holy Church, which being guided by the Holy Spirit cannot err? Also, before Martin Luther, what did people do in the churches of Germany? Of course they did what true men of religion and ecclesiastics do in Italy, and with admirable fervor.[50]

Second, inspired by the same principle, Davidico championed the doctrine of the intercession of saints, a doctrine that had been radically challenged by the Protestant heresy:

> We must not pray only for ourselves, but also humbly invoke the saints, because they do pray for us, notwithstanding some modern heretics preach the opposite [...] If the arguments and reasonings of the Lutherans were indeed of any value, the Saints would have been wrong to pray for others, and the Church, from the times of the Apostles until the present day, would have erred, invoking the Saints to intervene on our behalf, if they do not pray. And although God alone beatifies and bestows grace, it is His custom to achieve this effect using second causes, which is what the Saints' intercessions are in this particular context.[51]

---

[49] 'senza mental attenzione' (*Monte d'oratione*, c. 7r–8r, 15v, 16r). Regarding the traditional opposition between mental prayer and vocal prayer, cf. cc. 11v, 15r, 19r and 20v; regarding jaculatory prayer and 'holy' prayer, see ibid., cc. 16v–17r.

[50] 'Hor se li Apostoli con David havevano alcuni tempi statuti per l'oratione non li dovemo ancora noi havere ad imitatione di quelli massime essendo indulti a tal pio essercitio dalla Chiesa santa, la quale per essere retta dal Spirito santo non può errare? Oltra di questo avante Martino Luthero che si faceva nelle chiese di Germania? Certo quello che fanno li veri religiosi et ecclesiastici in Italia, e con mirabile fervore' (ibid., c. 35r).

[51] 'Non dovemo solamente orare per noi istessi, ma ancora invocar li Santi humilmente, peroché orano per noi, benché alcuni moderni heretici vadino predicando il contrario [...]. Se le ragioni et argomenti de lutherani valessono, adunque hariano fatto male li Santi pregando per altri, saria la Chiesa stata in errore dalli Apostoli in qua invocando i Santi a intercedere per noi, se non pregano. E benché Dio solo beatifichi e infonda le gratie, pur suole fare tale effetto mediante le seconde cause, quale a nostro proposito sono le intercessioni de Santi' (ibid., cc. 31v–32r).

Apart from these features, which provide a measure of his orthodoxy, the mystic content of Davidico's writing lacked all suggestion of subversive spiritualistic feeling and therefore appeared to be much less dangerous than even the supposedly orthodox Serafino da Fermo. Davidico's beliefs were in any case presented in an extremely fragmentary manner, immersed in a flood of words that flowed from his pen but left no clear trace on the paper. It is only with extreme difficulty that one succeeds in reconstructing – and even then not too clearly – his version of the mystic 'ascent of the mountain' (*ascesa del monte*).[52]

If at times the language used by Davidico seems to closely recall that of his master Battista da Crema, this mystic afflatus is often immediately belied by the presence of diametrically opposite tones. Thus, for example, we read at one moment that prayer is a 'delightful bond' (*dilettevole laccio*) thanks to which we can 'overcome temptations, increase our merits, root out our passions, procure the light and spirit and fire of truth, and gain better knowledge of the will of God,'[53] while a few lines later we find him saying that

> prayer should be used to guard the heart, the mouth, and all our senses, to pray to God not only for oneself but also for the Church, for the Sovereign Pontiff (whose authority on earth is a wonder to be seen), and for the union of the faithful, and to accompany a life of goodness.[54]

---

[52] Below is a short example of the general pattern that emerges if we put together the various elements scattered here and there throughout the text: 'Only by focusing on one's sins' ('concentrandosi sui propri peccati'; ibid. c. 20v), and thus by reaching the point where one distrusts 'one's own virtue' ('d'ogni propria virtude'; ibid. c. 18v), 'by becoming, for Christ's sake, the servant man of all – at least inwardly' ('facendosi per Christo l'uomo servo – interiormente almeno – de tutti'; c. 7v), by making the 'soul [...] accuse itself' ('che l'anima accusi se stessa'; 9r), and above all by practicing 'the true imitation of Christ' ('la vera imitatione di Christo'; c. 7v), only by these steps can a man aspire to 'total extirpation of all vices' ('totale estirpatione di tutti li vitii'; ibid.). This stage once having been reached, a man can attain a state of expropriation of his will in which he has 'true dominion over his mind, which is free of multitudes of cogitations, fantasies, and ideas' ('un vero dominio sopra la tua mente libera dalla multiplicità delle cogitationi, fantasie, imaginationi'; c. 6r) and excludes 'any other thought' ('ogni altro pensiero'; c. 6v). At this point, 'stripped of his will' ('spogliato d'ogni volontà'; c.18v) and robed in 'the sweet will of God' ('dolce volontà di Dio'; c. 20v), man can win 'true freedom of the Spirit' ('vera libertà del Spirito'; ibid., c. 7v) through 'spiritual and celestial nuptials' ('nozze spirituale e celeste'; c. 21r), i.e. by 'spiritual union with Him' ('spirituale unione con quello'; cc. 6r–v).

[53] 'a vincere le tentationi, ad augumentar li meriti, a estirpare le proprie passioni, a impetrar lume, spirito et fuoco di verità, et a venire in maggior cognitione della volontà di Dio' (ibid., c. 18v).

[54] 'con l'oratione bisognarla custodire il cuore, la bocca e tutti i nostri sensi, pregar Dio non solamente per se stesso, ma ancora per la chiesa, per il sommo Pontefice (la cui autorità è mirabile in terra), e per la unione delli fideli, et accompagnare la buona vita' (ibid., c. 6v).

In some cases the attempted compromise between conflicting lines of thought leads to paradoxical results, as, for example, when seeking to reconcile careful orthodoxy and mystic fervor all in one sentence, he writes:

> The way to pray is to do it without a way, as if intoxicated and madly in love, the place to do it is every place, especially in the Church according to Catholic rite and the time to do it is without interruption, if that is possible.[55]

The only common denominator among these confused and overlapping messages would appear to be the aim to gain the favor at one and the same time of all his potential readers or other interested parties, i.e. the followers of his master Brother Battista,[56] on the one hand, and the inflexible defenders of the Catholic faith, on the other.[57]

The result probably outdid the author's wildest hopes. Within a few years, his 'watered down' version of Battista's mystic message became a solid model of Counter-Reformation devotional practice.[58]

---

[55] 'Il modo di far oratione è farla senza modo, come inebriati et impazziti di amore, il loco è farla in ogni loco, massime in Chiesa secondo il rito de catolici, et il tempo è farla senza intermissione se è possibile' (ibid., c. 19r).

[56] In this respect there is a mystic high point when Davidico describes 'spiritual nuptials' (*nozze spirituali*): men feel 'inflamed with heavenly fire, they think in prayer and begin to meditate, they pray and contemplate what they like, with great delight and inner enjoyment [...] sometimes they are so raised toward God that when called they do not hear, when stung they feel no pain [...] because they have been dispossessed of themselves, because they do not seek, in a state of rapture, the taste of contemplation, consolations, and sweetness for their own pleasure' ('infiammati di quello celeste fuoco, pensano in la oratione si mettono a meditare, orano et contemplano quello che li piace, con gran delettatione et gusto interiore [...] alle volte sono così elevati in Dio che chiamati non sentono, e che punti non si dogliono [...] perché sono disproprietati di se stessi, perché non cercano rapti, il sapore della contemplatione, le consolationi et dolcezze interiori per suo contento;' ibid., c. 13r).

[57] The desire to be accepted by the Catholic authorities, toward whom he nurtured an ambiguous feeling of attraction and suspicion mingled with ill-guided personal ambitions, was ever present. Clear evidence of this can be seen in two cases: first, his censorious scrupulousness when he attacks 'sonnets, bawdy songs, and madrigals' (*sonetti, canzoni lascive et madrigali*'; ibid., c. 37r) and other 'tales and jests' (*fiabe et rise*) by suspect 'songsters' (*cantori*) not authorized by the strict directives of the Inquisition (ibid.), and, second, with a sudden change of direction, when in the final part of the work he relates all the benefits previously attributed to the practice of mental prayer to the more orthodox principle of obedience, which thus becomes the code with which to read the entire treatise (ibid. c. 26v and 31r).

[58] M. Firpo, *Nel labirinto del mondo*, p. 67.

CHAPTER 4

Pier Paolo Vergerio and the Antidevotional Controversy

This description of early sixteenth-century devotional modules cannot close without mentioning the best-known Italian opponent of Catholic devotionalism: the Bishop of Capodistria, Pier Paolo Vergerio.

Vergerio fled from Italy in 1549 after being accused of supporting Lutheran doctrines. He was one of the most prolific and aggressive of all sixteenth-century European polemicists.[1] Once he reached safer shores, he began a tireless activity as an author of pamphlets[2] devoting himself, among other things, to a systematic and mordant criticism of devotional practices that were widespread throughout Italy. In those same years he showed his sensitivity to the topic of prayer by having a small collection of prayers printed in 1549, some written by himself, which were introduced by a short *Oratione de' perseguitati et fuorusciti per lo evangelio et per Giesù Christo* ('Prayer of exiles and the persecuted for the Gospels and for Jesus Christ')[3] and by editing an anonymous *Forma delle publiche orationi, et della confessione, et assolutione, la qual si usa nella chiesa de forestierai, che è nuovamente stata instituita in Londra (per gratia di Dio) con l'autorità et consentimento del Re* ['Form of public prayers and of confession and absolution that is used in the strangers' church which has lately been established in London (by God's grace) with the King's authority and consent'] without any indication of date or place but probably attributable to the

---

1 *Pier Paolo Vergerio il Giovane. Un polemista attraverso l'Europa del Cinquecento*, edited by U. Rozzo, Atti del Convegno Internazionale di Studi (Cividale del Friuli, 15–16 Oct. 1998), Udine, Forum, 2000. On Vergerio's Italian period, see also A.J. Schutte, *Pier Paolo Vergerio. The Making of an Italian Reformer*, Geneva, Librairie Droz, 1977; and S. Peyronel Rambaldi, *Dai Paesi Bassi all'Italia. 'Il sommario della Sacra Scrittura. Un libro proibito nella società italiana del Cinquecento*, Florence, Olschki, 1997, pp. 162–84.

2 On his prolific publishing activity during these years (more than forty works in four years, not counting the works of others and translations which he edited) a fundamental text is an essay by S. Cavazza, 'Pier Paolo Vergerio nei Grigioni e in Valtellina (1549–1553): attività editoriale e polemica religiosa', in *Riforma e società nei Grigioni. Valtellina e Valchiavenna tra '500 e '600*, edited by A. Pastore, Milan, Franco Angeli, 1991, pp. 33–62.

3 S. Cavazza, 'Pier Paolo Vergerio', p. 42; F. Hubert, *Vergerios publizistische Tätigkeit nebst einer bibliographischen Übersicbt*, Göttingen, Vandenhoeck & Ruprecht, 1893, n. 22, pp. 269–70.

two-year period 1549–1550,[4] i.e. the years when the same printing house of Poschiavo also produced Giulio da Milano's heretical *Meditatione sul Pater Noster* ('Meditation on Lord's Prayer').[5] But what interested him most was to unmask the idolatry contained in certain outward forms of devotion of Catholic inspiration.

The nucleus of this activity consists of six short works written entirely in vernacular Italian in the early 1550s, works in which, thanks to his profound knowledge of Italian religious practice, Vergerio amused himself by taking to pieces the most widespread customs and devotional texts that were popular in the first half of the sixteenth century.[6]

---

[4] In the dedication 'To Ministers, and preachers of the churches of the distinguished Grisoni gentlemen, good health and peace in Jesus Christ' ('a Ministri, et predicatori delle chiese di magnifici signori Grisoni, salute et pace in Iesu Christo'), Vergerio said he had received this text from England but he did not specify the author's name. The British Library catalogue where this text is conserved attributes it with some doubt to Ochino or Vermigli, both of whom sojourned in the England of Edward VI in those two years (in 1550 Vergerio had himself dedicated a pamphlet *Al serenissimo re d'Inghilterra Edoardo Sesto de' portamenti di papa Giulio III*, cf. S. Cavazza, 'Pier Paolo Vergerio', pp. 41–2); the king's influence is in fact clear in the text where the anonymous author invokes upon himself the protection of God (ibid., cc. A6r–v). The frequent references to the doctrine of *Beneficio di Cristo* clearly characterize it as a work of the Reformation and one might even go so far as to attribute the text to the preacher of Siena. Regarding Ochino and Vermigli, we refer readers to the respective bibliographical entries in *The Italian Reformation*, (ed.) J. Tedeschi, pp. 361–78 and pp. 536–53; more generally, regarding the community of Italian exiles in England, see the fundamental essay by L. Firpo, 'La Chiesa italiana di Londra nel Cinquecento e i suoi rapporti con Ginevra', in *Ginevra e l'Italia.* Raccolta di studi promossa dalla Facoltà Valdese di Teologia di Roma, (eds) D. Cantimori, L. Firpo, G. Spini, F. Venturi, V. Vinay, Florence, Sansoni, 1959, pp. 309–412, now in Id., *Scritti sulla Riforma in Italia*, Naples, Prismi, 1996, pp. 117–94. See also the recent volume by A.M. Overell, *Italian Reform and English Reformations, c.1535–c.1585*, Aldershot, Ashgate, 2008.

[5] *Esortatione alli dispersi per Italia di Giulio da Milano. Vi è aggiunta una Meditatione sopra del Paternoster*, printed at Trent in 1549 [the indication 'at Trent' is false, as S. Cavazza, 'Pier Paolo Vergerio', p. 36, has correctly pointed out]. The existence of this first edition of the *Esortatione* was discovered and announced for the first time by E. Ronsford, 'Nuove opere sconosciute di Giulio da Milano', *Bollettino della Società di Studi Valdesi*, n. 138 (1975), pp. 55–8; the edition was also considered by U. Rozzo, 'L'Esortazione al martirio di Giulio da Milano', *Riforma e società nei Grigioni*, pp. 63–88, who is also the author of other studies on Della Rovere and his works: Id., 'Sugli scritti di Giulio da Milano', *Bollettino della Società di Studi Valdesi*, n. 134 (1973), pp. 69–85; Id., 'Incontri di Giulio da Milano: Ortensio Lando', Ibid., n. 140 (1976), pp. 77–108; Id., 'Le Prediche veneziane di Giulio da Milano (1541)', Ibid., n. 152 (1983), pp. 3–30.

[6] F. Hubert, *Vergerios publizistische Tätigkeit nebst einer bibliographischen Übersicht*, pp. 273, 275, 283, 287, 291, 296 [respectively works n. 27 *(Discorsi sopra i Fioretti di San Francesco, ne quali della sua vita, e delle sue stigmate si ragiona*, s.d., s.l.), n. 36 *(A quegli Venerabili Padri Dominicani che difendono il Rosario per cosa buona*, Basle, 1550), n. 67 *(Operetta nuova del Vergerio, nella quale si dimostrano le vere ragioni che hanno mosso i Romani Pontefici ad instituir le belle cerimonie della Settimana Santa*, Tiguri apud

The subjects touched on by Vergerio in these writings cover a wide part of the life of a devout Catholic: his idolatrous worship of statues and images, his attendance at 'false' Masses, his celebration of Holy Week, his observance of widespread devotional practices like the rosary, and his reading of short 'superstitious' works such as *I Fioretti di San Francesco* and *I Miracoli della Madonna*.[7]

As is known, Vergerio's entire works were condemned by the Roman Index in 1559, as also by that of Trent.[8] It is our current purpose to conduct a brief study of the contents of some of these short works in order to make an in-depth analysis of the motivations behind their condemnation (an analysis which will inevitably reflect the clearly Protestant slant of the text) and to attempt to contextualize the writings in the process of re-defining devotional models which the Church initiated from around the mid-century.

For example, starting with the first of these two points, in what is the most celebrated of these short works of his, *Discorsi sopra i Fioretti di San Francesco, ne quali della sua vita, e delle sue stigmate si ragiona*,[9] Vergerio censured the 'unholy vulgarities' (*cosacce impie*)[10] in the *Fioretti di San Francesco* from an exclusively Lutheran point of view. One of the favorite

Andream Gesnerum F. Rodolphum Vuissenbachium MDLII), n. 79 *(Ludovico Rasoro alla Abbadessa del Monasterio di Santa Giustina di Venetia, sopra un libro intitolato Luce di Fede*, stampato nuovamente in Milano per Giovanni Antonio da Borgo in laude della Messa MDLIII), n. 93 (*Della camera, et Statua della Madonna chiamata di Loretto, la quale è stata nuovamente difesa da Fra Leandro Alberti Bolognese, e da Papa Giulio III*. Con un solenne privilegio approvata. Nello anno MDLIII), n. 104 (*Che cosa sieno le XXX Messe chiamate di San Gregorio e quando prima incominciarono ad usarsi...*, nello anno MDLV)]. To these short works must be added the many critical references to devotional literature contained in his writings dedicated to the catalogues (relative to Venice in 1549, to Milan in 1554, and to Rome in 1559) of prohibited books: *Il catalogo de libri, li quali nuovamente nel mese di maggio nell'anno presente MDXLVIII sono stati condannati e scomunicati per heretici da Giovan Della Casa legato di Venetia e d'alcuni frati. É aggiunto sopra il medesimo catalogo un iudicio, et discorso del Vergerio*, Zurich, Christoph Froschauer, 1549 [where for example, Vergerio wrote the following words referring to the *Fioretti della Bibbia*: 'Where, besides infinite totally false doctrines and most vile tales taken – I say – word for word from *Metamorphoses* – and they are told, as if they were true things that happened in the times of the Old and the New Testaments' ('Ove, oltre infinite falsissime dottrine e marcissime favole tolte – dico – de parola in parola fuor del *Metamorfosi* – e si narrano come verità occorse nel tempo del Vecchio e del Nuovo Testamento)'; cited by G. FRAGNITO, *La Bibbia al rogo*, p. 312, note 117]; *Catalogo dell'Arcimboldo arcivescovo di Melano. Con una risposta fattagli in nome d'una parte di quei valenti huomini*, Tübingen, Morhard, 1554; *A gl'Inquisitori che sono per l'Italia. Del catalogo di libri eretici stampato in Roma nell'anno presente MDLLX*, Tübingen, s.t. 1560.

7 Cf. previous note.

8 *Index des livres interdits*, vol. VIII, p. 519. However, the Venice Index had in 1554 already included him among the condemned authors (cf. ibid., vol. III, p. 367).

9 For the full title, cf. above.

10 P.P. VERGERIO, *Discorsi sopra i Fioretti*, c. C2r.

targets of his polemic spirit was the recurrent assimilation that was presented in the work between the powers and qualities of St Francis and those of the Son of God: 'In the sixth chapter', Vergerio wrote for example,

> there is a most terrible thing, for it is said that St Francis was another Christ given to the world to save people and that God the Father desired to make Him in many of His deeds just like His son [...] By our Lady, this is one of the strangest things that all the devils in Hell can say, it is a horrendous blasphemy.[11]

It is true, Vergerio went on, illustrating his opinion on the matter, that 'God gives to all he chooses the same spirit that Jesus Christ had, Paul says so,'[12] but this is certainly not the interpretation intended by the author of the *Fioretti*, who instead seeks wrongly to attribute to St Francis a salvific power that only Jesus Christ possesses:

> The author of the book does not mean it in this way, but he will tell you clearly that since Christ with His virtues and His blood saved the chosen few, in the same way St Francis with his virtues and his stigmata came to save the people and get them out of Purgatory and into Paradise, which is horrendous.[13]

It is 'horrendous' above all because 'the power and the eternal virtue of the blood of the Son of God are totally denied'.[14] Vergerio's objection was that if one were to allow, even only for a moment, that someone else besides Christ had the power to save people's souls from their sins, granting them eternal life, the universality of the 'benefit of Christ' would be intolerably reduced. As Vergerio asserted:

> The passion and the death of Jesus Christ, incarnated in the Virgin Mary, were more than sufficient to gain the salvation of a hundred thousand million

---

11 'Nel sesto capitolo c'è una cosa terribilissima, si dice, che san Francesco fu un altro Christo dato al mondo per salute delle genti, et che Dio padre lo volle far in molti atti conforme, et simile a suo figliuolo [...] Madonna questa è una delle più strane cose che possano dire tutti i Diavoli dello inferno, ella è una bestemia horrenda' (ibid., c. C3v). Vergerio censured similar thoughts expressed in two other passages; cf. ibid., c. E6r and cc. E3v–E4r.

12 'in tutti quelli che sono degli eletti Dio manda di quello istesso spirito, che havea Giesù Christo, lo dice Paulo' (ibid., cc. C3v–C4r).

13 'L'autore del libro non la intende per questo verso, ma vi dirà chiaro che sicome Christo con i suoi meriti, e col suo sangue salvò gli eletti, così san Francesco con i suoi meriti et con le sue stigmate venne a salvar la gente, et cavarla fuor del Purgatorio, et metterla in Paradiso, la quale è una cosa horrenda' (ibid., cc. C4r–v).

14 'si niega affatto la efficatia, et la virtù eterna del sangue del figliuolo di Dio' (ibid., c. E6r). This 'scandalous' aspect had already been commented on by Vergerio in *Il Catalogo de libri*, c. K5r.

worlds, [...] and it is not necessary to repeat that sacrifice in other persons and that eternal Host but only to preach it with great attention and manifest it as He commanded us to do.[15]

For those who were slow on the uptake, Vergerio used language that was even more explicit:

But it takes more than that to be united with the Heavenly Father, it takes spirit, which it is His pleasure to give us, and those who have no spirit and have no living faith will become thin and waste away as they please, for there will be little fruit.[16]

Such eloquent exaltations of the principle of justification by faith alone could not leave the authorities in Rome indifferent, busily engaged as they were in the struggle against Protestantism.

But while the Roman censors were quick to realize that Vergerio's pungent spirit reflected the influence of Luther's harsh attacks on the Church of Rome's 'idolatry' and 'superstition', they must also have noticed the elements of Lutheran doctrine present in the *Fioretti di San Francesco*. Vergerio himself had seized the opportunity to point out and praise passages reflecting Protestant beliefs, thus indirectly facilitating the Roman censors' task. The passage, for example, from which the attentive Protestant polemicist would have liked to eliminate the 'impious' (*empia*) expression 'open your mouth and I will cack into it' (*apri la bocca ch'io li cacherò dentro*), contained a clear exaltation of predestination and of the certainty of salvation through faith alone. The story in the *Fioretti* told of a Demon that attempted to draw 'Brother Ruffino', a poor monk into temptation, by persuading him he was not among those predestined to salvation; only the decisive intervention of St Francis could drive out the Demon and 'confirm in all grace and sureness of salvation' (*confirmato in gratia et sicurtà della sua salute*) the hapless Ruffino:

'This chapter speaks of a certain Brother Ruffino, who was tempted by the Demon of predestination, and therefore he was melancholy because the Demon had put it in his heart that he was not among those predestined to eternal life; the Demon is very crafty knows full well how important it is for a Christian

---

[15] 'La passione, et morte di Giesù Christo, incarnato di Maria Vergine, fu sofficientissima per acquistar salute a cento millia migliara et millioni de mondi, [...] et non bisogna più rinovare in altre persone quel sacrificio, et quella hostia sempiterna, ma solo bisogna attendere a predicarla, et manifestarla si come esso ci ha comandato che havessimo a fare' (ibid., cc. E5v–E6r).

[16] 'Ma ci vuol altro a dover stare unito col celeste Padre, ci vuole spirito che a lui piaccia di donarci, et chi non lo ha, et non ha la fede viva potrà ben smagrirsi, e macerarsi quanto vuole, che vi sarà poco frutto' (ibid., C4v–5Cr).

> to be sure he is predestined to be one of the chosen, and desiring to take this weapon and shield out of the poor monk's hands, at a certain moment he appeared to him in the form of a crucifix and said to him you are not predestined to eternal life [...] and do not believe the son of Pietro Bernardo if he tells you the opposite, and do not even ask him this for neither he nor anyone else knows, except for me, the Son of God [...]. St Francis [...] tells him not to believe the words of the crucifix, because the Devil is in it, and not to consent to him or believe him when he tries to make you believe that you are not predestined, but when the Devil comes again to tempt you, answer him so, open your mouth (forgive me, I say in all reverence, if the author of the book himself prefers not to say it), and I will cack into it, and legend has it that this is what what Ruffino did, [...] and the Devil went away [...] and the monk was left full of joy and sweetness of spirit, and was as if wholly absorbed in God (it is said) and from that moment on he was so convinced of the grace and sureness of his salvation that he became quite another man and would have spent all his time, day and night, in prayer, contemplating things divine if he had been so permitted, for which reason St Francis said of him that Brother Ruffino was canonized by God in his lifetime'.[17]

Vergerio had not let the passage escape his attention, commenting that apart from the 'indignity of those five words [..] the rest seems fine to me, and I am sure it is if the Demon continually strives to strip us of our trust in God and of our certainty of the remission of our sins'.[18] Likewise Vergerio had not omitted to draw attention to another passage that must have perturbed orthodox readers of the *Fioretti* at least as much as it filled the exile from Rome with satisfaction:

---

[17] 'In questo capitolo si parla di un fra Ruffino, et si dice che egli era tentato dal Demonio della predestinatione, et però stava maninconico, perché questo Demonio li volea pur mettere in cuore che esso non era de predestinati a vita eterna; il demonio che è astutissimo sa ben esso quanto importa al Christiano, che egli sia securo della sua elettione et predestinatione, et però egli volea levare questa arma, et scudo di mano a quel povero frate, et una volta gli apparve in forma di crocifisso, et disseli tu non sei de predestinati a vita eterna [...] et non credere al figliuolo di Pietro Bernardo, né se lui ti dicesse il contrario, et ancho non lo domandare di questa cosa, però che lui né altri non lo sa. Salvo che io che son figliuolo di Dio. [...] san Francesco [...] li disse non creder alle parole di quel crocifisso, perché vi era il Diavolo dentro et non consentire, et non li credere quando ti vuol dar ad intendere, che tu non sei predestinato, ma quando il Demonio verrà più a tentarti di questo, rispondeli, apri la bocca (perdonatemi dico io con riverentia, se l'auttore del libro non lo vuol dire) che io li cacherò dentro, et segue la legenda a dire che fra Rufino così fece, [...] et il diavolo andò via [...] et il frate restò pieno di allegrezza, et dolcezza di spirito, et era come absorto in Dio (così dice) et dall'hora inanzi fu così confermato in gratia et securtà della sua salute, che tutto diventò mutato in un altro huomo, et sarebbe stato il dì et la notte in oratione a contemplare le cose divine chi lo havesse lasciato, onde dicea san Francesco di lui che frate Ruffino era in questa vita canonizzato da Dio'; ibid., cc. D2r–D3r).

[18] 'indegnità di quelle quattro parole [...] a me il resto par bello et credo certo che così sia, che il Demonio sempre si fatichi di spogliarci della confidentia di Dio et della certezza della remissione de peccati' (ibid., c. D3r).

In chapter XLIII there are ten golden words – would there were many of these – which tell of Brother Matthew, who is speaking to a monk. Now this monk, because of the greatness of his sins, was sure he would be damned, and he was in great despair, but the other says to him, do you not remember that God's mercy is greater than all the sins in the world? And that Christ our Saviour, to redeem us, paid an infinite price, and therefore be of good hope that for sure you are saved.[19]

The *Fioretti di San Francesco* do not appear in any of the sixteenth-century Indexes. They are, however, among the most frequently cited titles on locally compiled lists of banned books at the turn of the century in observance of the instructions of the Clementine Index.[20] The discovery of these Lutheran passages very likely prompted the confiscation of this short work; however, the presence on these lists of the *Fioretti* would not be fully comprehensible without considering another factor. In light of what we know about the censorship activities of the ecclesiastic authorities in the second half of the sixteenth century, the purpose of which among other things was to root out any superstitious elements in the devotional literature of the time,[21] it would appear to be justified to hypothesize that many of the 'superstitious' passages highlighted in Vergerio's analysis had aroused the attention of the censors in Rome. While Vergerio's condemnation of the bodily penitence suffered by St Francis – as also his violent invective against the comparison of the powers of the *poverello d'Assisi*, i.e. 'the poor little one of Assisi', to those of the Son of God[22] – was perhaps rather too obviously related to the doctrinally heterodox positions of this polemicist from Capodistria to be viewed unbiasedly by

---

19 'Nel XLIIII capitolo, vi sono diece parolette d'oro, o ne fussero molte di queste, vi si introduce un fra Mattheo che parla con un frate, il quale per la grandezza de suoi peccati se tenea esser dannato, et stava in gran malinconia, et dice, non ti ricordi tu che la misericordia di Dio eccede tutti i peccati del mondo? Et che Christo benedetto nostro salvatore pagò per ricomprarci un infinito pretio, et però habbi buona speranza che per certo tu sei salvato' (ibid., c. D7r).

20 Archivio della Congregazione per la dottrina della fede – Archive of the Congregation for the Doctrine of the Faith, formerly the Holy Office (henceforth ACDF), Index, series XVIII, one volume, c. 38v (*Index librorum qui in Indicem Romanum sunt suspensi vel prohibiti, qui asservantur in Conventu S. Iohannis ad Carbonariam. Per P. Magistrum Cherubinum Veronensem Augustinum Theologum Curiae Archiepiscopensis Neapolitanae in loco clave clauso de mandato Illustrissimi et Reverendissimi Cardinalis Gesualdi donec de loco convenienti in palatio Archiepiscop. Provideatur*); c. 48v (*Lista di libri prohibiti et sospesi che si trovano nell'Inquisitione di Ancona*); c. 62r (*Libri prohibiti et suspensi qui habentur in sancto offitio Veronae*); c. 79r (4 copies, in *Nota de libri abruciati mandata dal Vicario di Montepulciano a 27 d'ottobre*, cf. c. 79v). On the importance and the context in which these censorship lists were drawn up, cf. below, chapter 10.

21 Cf. below, chapter 5.

22 Cf. above.

the Inquisitors,[23] certain 'foolish statements' (*ineptie*) and 'falsehoods' (*falsità*) that he remarked on must instead have contributed in no small way to the development of critical awareness among the Catholics. An attentive reader could not fail to notice expressions like 'Open your mouth [..] and I will cack into it' (*apri la bocca che io li cacherò dentro*)[24] or 'superstitious' and 'fabulous' stories like one about St Francis, who 'set to talking about God with such fiery passion that all of the fire and all of a forest that grew close by began to burn, and people ran this way and that to put out the fire',[25] or one about Brother Simon, who, while 'in contemplation' (*in contemplatione*) and 'at prayer' (*in orazione*), 'did not feel a burning coal that fell on his bare foot',[26] while in contrast he was once inordinately annoyed by some harmless crows that he had roughly chased away.[27] In addition to these descriptions there was the 'horrid story' (*horribile historia*) written by Vergerio himself at the end of the work. To give substance to his attacks on the truth of St Francis' stigmata – about which, according to Vergerio, there was no evidence other than that provided by the usual source, i.e. Ruffino – he described to his readers a case of false sanctity fabricated purely for profit:

> In the year MDVII, in the town of Berne, four friars of the Observant Order of St Dominic, Giovanni Veter, Stefano Theologo, Francesco Ulschi, and Heinrich Steinecrer, noticing that Franciscan friars were held in higher esteem, had a greater following, and received more alms than they did, resolved that they too should have a saint with stigmata and the wounds of Jesus Christ, and as among their number in the monastery there was a friar who was an idiot, a simple fellow called Benedict, they chose him as the fittest person for the purpose of their deception. First of all, one of the four, the one who confessed him, began telling him he was on the way to becoming a great saint, [..]. Then, the next night the rascals made him drink some water that people call allopathic, which makes them sleep very soundly, and become stupefied and almost lose all their senses, [..] and with a stout nail they made wounds in his hands and his feet, and a fifth with a knife in his side, so when the luckless fellow awoke he found himself with the wounds and covered in blood.[28]

---

23 Cf. the passage in P.P. Vergerio, *Discorsi sopra i Fioretti*, cc. C3r–v.

24 Ibid., c. D2v.

25 'si messe a parlar di Dio tanto infocatamente, che tutto quel fuoco, et tutta una selva che era vicina cominciò ardere, et da ogni banda le persone correvano per ismorzar il fuoco' (ibid., cc. C6v–C7r).

26 'non sentiva un carbone ardente che li fosse posto sul pie' nudo' (ibid., c. D5r).

27 Ibid.

28 'Nel anno MDVII nella città di Berna quatto frati dell'ordine di san Dominico di osservantia, Giovanni Veter, Stefano Bosshorst Theologo, Francesco Ulschi, Heinrico Steinecrer, vedendo che i frati di san Francesco erano in maggior credito, et haveano più

Naturally, the Italian exile's purpose in telling this story was to question the saints' power of intercession. He concluded the tale by putting into the mouth of 'poor Brother Benedict' the following incontestable words: 'I believe for certain that just as I was deceived so too that poor woman, St Catherine of Siena, who was persuaded by certain monks that she had stigmata, was deceived'.[29] However, tales like this and 'superstitions' like those reported by Vergerio in his little works had the merit of drawing to the attention of the Church hierarchy the delicate issue of the uncontrolled degeneration that this kind of literature could bring with it, thus contributing to consolidate positions that had already made their mark among Catholic believers. The objective of the polemicist from Capodistria was to demonstrate that 'foolish statements' and falsehoods of the sort were anything but rare in the popular devotional literature of the time. It was not difficult for Vergerio to single out and expose to public ridicule the 'stupidities' (*gofferie*), the 'invented stories' (*fabule*), and the 'foul lies, concocted to deceive people' (*bugie marze, fatte per ingannare li popoli*), which fill such works: in the widely read *Miracoli della Madonna* ('Miracles of Our Lady'):

> Then there is another book', Vergerio wrote in his *Catalogo*, 'which publicly, and in the shops, and under the same porchways is sold, and it is called the *Miracles of Our Lady*. [...] It does not bear the author's name, which should be present when stories are written and miracles are described, but whatever the case, the author was a fool, a scoundrel, an ignoramus, a heathen. He imagined he could see a kingdom where a widow Queen or Duchess was left with a young son, and she ruled all as she pleased, and the son took little or no interest but was obedient to his mother and left everything to her. And the

concorso et più elemosine, che essi non haveano, si deliberarono di voler anchora essi haver un santo con le stigmate, et con le piaghe di Giesù Christo, et havendo nel monasterio loro un frate idiota, et semplice chiamato Benedetto elessero lui per soggetto buonissimo, sopra il quale si havesse a fare la barrarla, et prima uno de quatto, che lo confessava li cominciò a dare ad intendere che egli era sulla via di divenire un gran santo, [...] Poi nella sera seguente que gaglioffi li diedero a berre di quell'acqua chiamata da alcun allopiata, la quale fa dormire così forte, et stupire et quasi perdere tutti i sentimenti, [...] et con un buon chiodo li fecero le piaghe nelle mani, et ne piedi, et la quinta, con un coltello nel costato lo infelice svegliandosi si trovò con le ferite, e tutto sangue' (ibid., cc. E8r–F1r).

29 'io credo certo che così come sono stato ingannato io, così sia stata ingannata quella povera Donna di santa Caterina di Siena, alla quale ho inteso che certi frati diedero ad intendere che ella havea le stigmate' (ibid., c. E2r). It may be useful to point out at this point how for example Vergerio's *Delle statue et imagini*, punctually condemned by the authorities in Rome, contained elements that were clearly Lutheran in inspiration. One example will suffice: the passage where the author invited his dedicatee, the Abbess of St Giustina's Monastery in Venice, to forsake her monastic life – a passage in which the Lutheran elements are accompanied by the traditional invective directed against the devotional set-up of the Church of Rome (*Delle statue et imagini*, cc. C2v–C3r).

> author wrote and declared that so it was in the Kingdom of Heaven where our Lady rules and does all acts of grace and all justice, and that Jesus Christ is obedient and silent to all that she desires to do, like a son, and she did not heed it when her son was insulted, so long as she was held in the honor and esteem of the people. And here he tells a whole series of miracles, there is even this one, that Our Lady, to conceal the fault of a Nun who was faithful to her and was the Sacristan and had run away with a gentleman, dressed herself in the clothes of a Sacristan and performed her duties until she returned home. Is this not a fine occupation that the author gives to this most Holy Virgin mother of our Lord Jesus Christ, to dress and, as it were, to hold by hand and watch over a Nun who goes off to enjoy the pleasures of the flesh, what horrible things are these?;[30]

in *Madonna chiamata di Loreto* ('Our Lady of Loreto'), with regard to the legend of the origin of the birthplace of Christ:

> According to one of these books, after the death of Christ the Apostles consecrated the room where the angel came to deliver his message to the Virgin Mary, and they turned it into a church, and this is not true for the Apostles never consecrated that church or any other, they waited to do what they were commanded to do, and they went about preaching, and spreading the good tidings of Christ, and being guided by the Holy Spirit they knew full well that after Christ's coming to this world there was no longer any need for temples to be dedicated with water mixed with ash and wine and salt or to observe Jewish ceremonies. [...] I know that in that house, or church, they perform each year endless acts of idolatry, and that is the reason why in Christendom many other similar churches are tolerated and defended as well as miraculous figures (they

30 'Vi è poi un altro libro – aveva scritto Vergerio nel suo *Catalogo* – il quale pubicamente, et nelle boteghe, e sotto i medesimi portici si vende, il quale si chiama i miracoli della Madonna. [...] É senza il nome dello auttore, et sarebbe necessario che vi fosse dove si scrivono historie, et si narrano miracoli, ma sia stato chi si voglia, egli è stato un goffo, un ribaldo, un ignorante, un impio. Egli si è imaginato di vedere un regno, nel quale sia restata una Regina o Duchessa vedoa con un pupillo, et questa governi ogni cosa secondo la sua voluntà, et che il figliuolo non s'impacci né molto, né poco, ma stia soggetto alla madre, et lasci far a lei. Et tale costui ha scritto et depinto che sia il regno del cielo dove la Madonna governi, et faccia tutte le gratie, et tutte le iusticie, et che Giesù Christo sia obediente, et tacito a tutto quello, che a lei piace di fare come un pupillo, et che anche quella non tenghi conto, se il figliuolo è vituperato, pure che ella si veda in honore, et credito delle persone. Et quivi narra una frotta de miracoli, li più strani, et più scempi, et mal composti, et più dishonesti, et impii che mai siano stati scritti, vi è fino questo, che la madonna per coprire il fallo di una Monaca sua devota, la quale era Sacristana, et era fuggita via con un gentil'huomo, si vestì da Sacristana, et servì per lei, fino che ella tornasse a casa. Non è questo un bel affido, che colui dà alla santissima vergine madre del nostro signor Giesù Christo, di mantellare, et come tener mano, o far la guardia ad una Monaca, la quale vada a darsi piacere, che cose horribili sono queste?'; *Catalogo de libri*, cc. K3v–K4r). Then, a few years later he returned with passion to the same text; *Catalogo del Arcimboldo*, c. G3r).

say), which are nothing more than pagan. And what pen, what tongue, could ever fully tell the great offence done to God and to Christ by these lies and by these false apparitions?;[31]

in examples of the *Rosario della Madonna* ('Rosary of Our lady'):

There is another one called the Rosary, full of villainies, lies, and heresies, and lustful words and shameful acts of dishonesty. Here it is told that Our Lady worshiped the image of her Son, and she went on a pilgrimage, visiting the places where Christ was born, where he had fasted, where he had been taken, scourged, crucified, buried. And all these are rotten lies, invented to deceive ordinary people. There is a description of Our Lady's obsequies, and it is said that the cross was borne before her, and there were lighted candles, and she was given incense, and St Peter had his cope around him. And this too is done to get these people to observe such ceremonies, fooleries, and irreligious acts which for some time now have been seen to be done by miserly priests and monks. But there is worse in this rosary for it says that Our Lady went to the cell of a monk, Alan of the Rock, from Britain, and married him, giving him a ring and a favor made of her own fair hair, and then she gave him her fine breasts to suck, and with these caresses and delights sent him to preach the rosary, what do you think of that, o legate, o monks? Why do you allow this vile and treacherous book full of such licentiousness to fall into the hands of good Christians and why do you let the monks of St Dominic read it after Vespers in public churches to his devotees, both men and women?;[32]

---

31 'Ne è uno di questi libri, il quale dice, che doppo la morte di Christo gli Apostoli consacrarono quella camera, nella quale l'angelo entrò a fare l'ambasciata alla vergine Maria, et la fecero diventare una chiesa, et non è vero, che gli Apostoli consacrassero mai né quella, né altra chiesa di muro, essi attendevano a far quello, che era lor comandato, et andavano predicando, et portando attorno le buone novelle di Christo, et essendo amaestrati dallo spirito santo sapevano molto bene, che doppo la venuta di Christo in terra non bisognava più far le dedicationi de tempii con certe acque mescolate con cenere, vino, et sale, et usar cerimonie Iudaiche. [...] Io so che in quella casa, o chiesa si fanno ogni anno infinite idolatrie, et poi quella è cagione, che nel Christianesmo si tolerino et si difendano molte altre simili chiese, et figure miracolose (come dicono) che sono un mero paganesmo. Et qual penna, qual lingua potrebbe mai narrar a pieno le grandi offese, che si fanno a Dio, et a Christo per il mezzo di quelle buggie, et di quelle false apparitioni?;' *Catalogo de' libri*, cc. K2v–K3r). The work by Vergerio, entitled *Della camera et Statua della Madonna chiamata di Loreto*, was specifically dedicated to this short writing (cf. above).

32 'Ve ne è anche un altro chiamato il Rosario pieno di gofferie, di falsità di heresie, et di molte lascivie, et dishonestà vergognose. Quivi si narra, che la Madonna adorava la imagine di suo figliuolo, et che ella andava in peregrinaggio, visitando quei luochi dove Christo era nato, dove havea fatto il ieiunio, dove era stato preso, flagellato, crocifisso, sepolto. Et tutte sono buggie marze, fatte per ingannare i popoli. Quivi sono descritte le essequie della Madonna, et si dice, che fu portata la croce avanti, et vi furono delle candele accese, et le fu dato lo incenso, et che S. Pietro havea il piviale atorno. Et anche questo è fatto per stabilire la gente in quelle cerimonie, frascherie, et impietà le quali da certo tempo in qua sono state trovate da preti, et da frati avari. Ma vi è di peggio in questo rosario, vi è che la Madonna andò alla cella di un frate Alanno dalla rupe di Britania, et lo sposò con uno annello et (come si dice) con un favor

and even in some unknown *Prediche di San Vincenzo* ('Sermons of St Vincent').[33]

In light of these considerations it does not therefore appear to be a merely a coincidence if we find many of these short works among the edicts of condemnation issued by Inquisition bishops in the late sixteenth and early seventeenth centuries; in particular, a list appearing in 1614 of censured devotional works contains the title of a book called *Luce di Fede* ('Light of Faith'),[34] to which Vergerio had dedicated one of his six anti-devotional works, entitled *Alla Abbadessa del Monasterio, ... sopra il libro Luce di Fede* ('To the Abbess of the Monastery, ... on the book Light of Faith').[35] The philological principle behind Vergerio's criticism, a principle which in *Discorsi sopra i Fioretti* had been used only partially (moreover still remaining closely linked to his Lutheran point of view), emerged here more explicitly and more decisively. In the Proem to the Reader, Vergerio pronounced his indictment:

> Of all the arts and stratagems used by the Papacy to give credit to his inventions that go against the Word of God, and to make them seem right and proper, and not human inventions but genuine doctrines of Jesus Christ, there was one that he induced his superstitious creatures to compose, and had books printed in different languages in which he recounted idolatries and falsehoods, adding that these had been mentioned and indeed praised by St John, St Matthew, St Mark, St Luke, St Paul, and also the learned men of ancient times, and you know full well that when poor and ignorant people buy such books, they read them with great pleasure, devouring them whole, and seeing in them a representation of the authority of the Evangelists (need one say more?) and of the most learned men of culture, they drink it all down and believe every word of it, with the result that subsequently they firmly believe that anyone pronouncing an opposing view is a heretic.[36]

---

fatto de suoi capelli biondi, et poi lo basciò, et poi li diede a lattare le sue belle mamelle, et con queste carezze, et dilitie lo mandò a predicare il rosario, che vi pare o legato, o frati? Perché lasciate che questo libraccio traditor con tante ribalderie che egli ha dentro vada per le mani de popoli Christiani et che li frati di San Domenico doppo il vespero nelle publiche chiese lo leggano a suoi devoti, et alle sue devote?'; *Catalogo de libri*, cc. K4r–v).

33 *Catalogo de libri*, c. K4v.

34 This consists of a list drawn up by the Inquisitor of Bologna (see below, chapter 10).

35 Cf. above.

36 'Tra le altre arti e astutie che ha usato il papato per metter le sue inventioni contrarie alla parola di Dio in credito, e farle tener per buone, e cose non humane, ma per proprie dottrine di Iesu Christo, questa n'è stata una, che egli dalle sue creature superstitiose ha fatto comporre, e stampare de libri nelle lingue de popoli, e narrarvi dentro le marze idolatrie, e falsità e poi aggiungere che di esse ne habbia parlato, et le habbia lodate san Giovanni, san Mattheo, san Marco, san Luca, san Paolo, e poi anche gli antichi dottori, e ben sapete che la povera gente ignorante havendosi comperati tali libri, e con desiderio letti, e devorati, e veggendovi dentro allegata la autorità degli Evangelisti (che si può dir di più?) e de dottori più famosi, se le han

In particular, referring specifically to the publication he had at hand (*Luce di fede*), he manifested his sense of shock at the way it equated – in terms of 'value' (*valore*) and of 'utility to the soul' (*utilità alle anime*) – the 'passion and death of the Son of God' (*passione e morte del figliuol de Dio*) and the ceremony of Mass for believers.[37]

Over and above his Lutheran doctrinal prejudice against the 'effectiveness' (*efficacia*) of the Eucharist that Catholics believed in, it is interesting here to note that his criticism was directed mainly at the instrumental use of scriptural and patristic references that were arbitrarily brought in to support the argument in question (which was already in any case 'scandalous'):

> This Popery falsely cited three of the Evangelists, as well as St Paul, and also Chrisostomos, Augustine, Jerome, and others, stating that all of these celebrated Mass, which today is considered to be something good, and indeed that Mass, whether one said it or simply heard it, was as valuable and as useful to the soul as were the passion and death of the Son of God.[38]

When Vergerio declared with such philological precision that it was necessary to model devotional practices on accurate and documented biblical, evangelical, or patristic references,[39] he consistently made efforts

bevute, e saldamente credute, di maniera che poscia han voluto tenere per heretici tutti quei, che ne hanno sentito parlar in contrario' (*Alla Abbadessa del monasterio*, c. A2r).

[37] In his *Catalogo del Arcimboldo*, Vergerio made the same point using other terms: 'There is another, called light of faith, which asserts four or possibly six times that every time one of your wretched priests or sacrificers goes up to the altar and says this Mass of yours, it is as if Christ God's Son came down from Heaven just as He came down one thousand five hundred and fifty years ago and as if, taking human flesh again, He were once again crucified and died on the Cross' ('Ve ne è un altro chiamato luce di fede ove si afferma ben quatto, o sei volte, che qualunque fiata un di cotesti vostri sciagurati pretazzuoli o sacrificuli va all'altare, et dice cotesta vostra messa, tanto è né più né meno come se Christo figliuol di Dio smontasse come egli smontò da cielo già mille cinquecento cinquanta anni et presa carne humana fosse di nuovo veramente crocifisso, et morto sulla croce'; *Catalogo del Arcimboldo arcivescovo di Melano*, cc. G3r–v).

[38] 'Esso papesmo ha fatto falsamente allegare tre degli evangelisti, e anche san Paolo, e insieme Chrisostomo, Augustino, Girolamo, e degli altri affermando che tutti questi insieme habbiano tenuta la messa che hoggidi si usa per cosa buona, anzi che habbian detto di tanto valore, e di tanta utilità alle anime esser la messa a cui la dice overo l'ascolta di quanta è la propria passione, e morte del figliuol di Dio' (*Alla Abbadessa del monasterio*, cc. A2r–v).

[39] 'What passage either in the Gospel or in the Acts of the Holy Apostles can they bring forward to show that the Holy Spirit desired this to be done? And I say more, which successor of the Apostles or the ancient Fathers (one that genuinely apostolic) ever used it?' he wrote peremptorily with regard to 'the Holy Week ceremonies' ['Qual luogo o dell'Evangelio over degli atti de santi apostoli sapranno addurre il quale dimostri, che lo spirito santo habbia voluto, che ella si faccia? Et più dico, qual successore degli apostoli, o qual degli antichi padri (che sia stato veramente apostolico) la usò giamai?'; P.P. VERGERIO, *Operetta nuova del Vergerio, nella qual si dimostrano le vere ragioni, che hanno mosso i Romani Pontefici*

to ensure that the references were reliable and verifiable by anyone, even by the 'simplest of people' (*semplici*). This was his intention when he listed the 'virtues of the Holy Mass' (*virtù della santa messa*) quoted from a pamphlet inserted in the appendix of the volume *Luce di fede*, pointing out that none of the references to St John Chrisostomos, St Augustine, or St Gregory was in the slightest way truthful.

The discovery of a copy of this little treatise on the 'virtues of the Holy Mass' (which had already appeared as the appendix to *Luce di fede*) in a volume of Inquisition papers kept in the Archive of the Congregation for the doctrine of the faith (formerly the Holy Office)[40] would appear to provide further support for our hypothesis of an indirect influence of Vergerio's writings on the action of the Roman censors.[41] This would not in any case be the first instance of the Catholic authorities acknowledging Vergerio's criticisms.[42]

A more careful examination of the evolution of practices and censorship ideology in the second half of the century with regard to this type of literature will further clarify this working hypothesis.

---

ad instituir le belle cerimonie della settimana santa, Tiguri, apud Andream Gesnerum F. et Rodolphum Vuissenbachium MDLII, c. A3r].

40 A printed copy of the treatise *Le virtù, et le utilità che acquistano quelli che ascoltano la Santa Messa. Raccolte da diversi Santi Dottori, per il R. Don Fabio Napolitano*, in Napoli, e ristampato in Messina, per Pietro Brea, 1594, is to be found in a volume of the *Protocolli* of the Congregation of the Index: it was evidently seen by one or more members of the Congregation in the course of their work (ACDF, Index, Protocolli O, cc. 596r–599r).

41 In the same way it is legitimate to hypothesize that the invective directed at the ecclesiastic liturgic texts (among which Vergerio included not only the *Pontificale* and the book *Rituum ecclesiasticorum, sive sacrarum cerimoniarum sacrosanctae Romanae Ecclesiae libri tres*, but also the *Missale romano*, 'for there is not indeed in all the world another book containing so many heresies and blasphemies') which warmly supported the 'superstitious' worship of crosses and statutes (P.P. Vergerio, *A gl'Inquisitori che sono per l'Italia*, c 22r; Id., *Delle statue et imagini*, in the year 1553, cc. A4r–v) cannot have gone unnoticed at a time when the Roman authorities were dealing with the delicate question of the reform of liturgic texts (cf. above, chapter 5).

42 In one of the introductory essays in the eighth volume of the work he edited, De Bujanda writes that 'Pier Paolo Vergerio's critical remarks in his forgeries of the Indexes are sometimes maintained by the censors' (*Index des livres interdits*, vol. VIII, p. 36).

PART II
Superstitious Prayer and Mystic Prayer: Church Censorship from the Index of Paul IV to that of Clementine

CHAPTER 5

Towards Renewed Inwardness

The Index issued by Paul IV in 1559, as foreshadowed in the previous chapter, represented a significant turning-point in the relationship between church hierarchies and devotional literature.[1] The harsh sentence passed on heterodox devotional writings had made it possible to initiate a process of reappropriation of the subject of mental prayer, as also of the Lord's Prayer, by representatives of Roman Counter-Reformation culture. From that moment on – and even more so after the conclusion of the Council of Trent – it became possible to slacken the careful watch of the external enemy, but only to a certain extent, and begin a project of internal consolidation of the orthodox heritage. Clear evidence of this process is the gradual but irreversible shifting of the attention of the censors in Rome away from the writings of Luther's followers and other heresiarchs towards the works of Catholic writers.[2]

Dealing with the inward consolidation of Roman orthodoxy meant, in those times, both redefining the rules of dogma and discipline and, also because of the heterodox criticism it had received, revising the entire liturgic and devotional system, i.e. the total mass of rites and prayers that marked out the daily religious practices both of ecclesiastics and of ordinary believers.

The Roman Index of 1559, and in particular the part entitled *Instructio circa Indicem librorum prohibitorum* attached to it – a document printed in February 1559 by the Congregation of the Holy Office to combat the difficulties encountered by the Inquisitors in the application of the generic indications regarding censorship in the Index[3] – presented a preliminary draft of what would eventually constitute the Church of Rome's guidelines on liturgic and devotional matters. The determined attack launched by the

---

1 For an overall view of sixteenth-century church censorship (and in general in the modern age) starting from the Index of Paul IV, a fundamental work is A. ROTONDÒ, 'La censura ecclesiastica e la cultura', *Storia d'Italia*, vol. V, tome II, Turin, Einaudi, 1974, pp. 1397–1492. Cf. also M. INFELISE, *I libri proibiti*, Rome-Bari, Laterza, 1999.

2 P. SIMONCELLI, 'Documenti interni alla Congregazione dell'Indice 1571–1590. Logica e ideologia dell'intervento censorio', *Annuario dell'Istituto storico italiano per l'età moderna e contemporanea*, XXXV–XXXV, 1983–84, pp. 189–215.

3 *Index des livres interdits*, vol. VIII, pp. 39–50, in particular pp. 46–9; text of the *Instructio* on pp. 100–104; G. FRAGNITO, *La Bibbia al rogo*, p. 93.

Index against the use of the vernacular for 'holy things',[4] a practice that since the 1530s had become inseparably associated with the spread of the Lutheran heresy,[5] was not to remain limited to the text of the Bible alone. The *Instructio*'s ban on reading in the vernacular extended to divine offices (*uffici divini*) and the prayer of the hours: 'All divine offices in the vulgar tongue included among the Hours of the Blessed Virgin, or in any other way printed or written, are prohibited to all. [...] The same applies to the Prayers of the Hours, which are customarily sung in Latin in the churches, should they have been translated into the vulgar tongue'.[6]

However, the *Instructio* did not limit itself to explaining and clarifying prohibitions that were already present in the Pauline Index. On the one hand, it identified the source, or rather one of the sources, of devotional superstition, laying the foundations for the bitter struggle against this type of deviation in the years to come; on the other, it marked the first step

---

[4] It is certainly no chance matter that in the 'only universal Index prepared by the Roman Inquisition' (G. Fragnito, *La Bibbia al rogo*, p. 83), the Index which more than any other had as its main and possibly only aim the struggle against Protestant heresy contained the clearest condemnation of reading the Bible in the vernacular to be found in any Index, whether ecclesiastic or civil: 'Bibles written in the vulgar tongue, be it German, French, Spanish, Italian, English, or Flemish, etc. cannot be printed, read, or possessed without permission of the Holy Office of the Roman Inquisition' ('Biblia omnia vulgari idiomate, Germanico, Gallico, Hispanico, Italico, Anglico sive Flandrico, etc. conscripta nullatenus vel imprimi vel legi vel teneri possint absque licentia sacri Officii S. Ro. Inquisitionis'; *Index des livres interdits*, vol. VIII, p. 325; G. Fragnito, *La Bibbia al rogo*, p. 85). The condemnation of the complete text was accompanied by a specific prohibition: 'New Testament books in the vulgar tongue cannot in any circumstances be printed or possessed without the written permission of the Holy Office of the Roman Inquisition'. ('Novi Testamenti libri vulgari idiomate conscripti sine licentia in scriptis habita ab Officio Sanctae Rom. et universalis Inquisitionis nullatenus vel imprimi vel teneri possint'; *Index des livres interdits*, vol. VIII, p. 331, and G. Fragnito, *La Bibbia al rogo*, p. 85).

[5] One of the first testimonies of the vernacular/heresy nexus can be found in the opinion expressed by the Papal nuncio in Venice, Girolamo Aleandro, concerning the display of St Paul's *Epistole* by the Dominican Brother Zaccaria da Fivizzano, in 1532: 'Holy doctrine is not something to be put in the hands of the people or of ignorant persons, especially as we know that Luther's heresy multiplied and spread in Germany in that precise way' ('La dottrina sacra non è subietto da mettere in mani dil vulgo et di persone idiote, massime sappiando che la heresia lutherana è pullulata e cresciuta in Alemagna solo per questa via'; F. Gaeta, *Un nunzio pontificio a Venezia nel Cinquecento. Girolamo Aleandro*, Venice-Rome, Istituto per la collaborazione culturale 1960, pp. 118–19; O. Niccoli, *Prophecy and People in Renaissance Italy,* Princeton, Princeton University Press, 1990, pp. 119–20; first Italian edition: *Profeti e popolo nell'Italia del Rinascimento*, Rome-Bari, Laterza, 1987; G. Fragnito, *La Bibbia al rogo*, p. 70).

[6] 'Missae omnes vulgari idiomate inter horas beatae virginis insertae, sive quomodocunque aliter impressae vel conscriptae penitus interdictae sunt. [...] Idem censetur de horariis precibus, quae in Ecclesiis latinae decantari solent, si in vulgarem linguam conversae deprehendantur.' (*Index des livres interdits*, vol. VIII, p. 104).

in a process of precise philological recovery of the traditional ecclesiastic heritage, which hitherto had been 'mortgaged' by the Lutheran heresy, with its claims to some kind of hermeneutic exclusive right over holy texts and the patristic tradition.

With regard to the first of the two points, the Pauline Index maintained that the superstitious use of prayers by devout Catholics originated in the 'rubrics' located in the appendix or at the beginning of the actual prayers. Thus it was not so much the content of the prayers that drew the Inquisitors' censorial attentions as the particular words, i.e. the 'rubrics', that attributed various types of taumaturgic powers ('virtutes') to the act of devotion, ranging from instantaneous healing to success in affairs of the heart: 'All rubrics describing in most unseemly manner the alleged virtues of psalms and prayers are by order to be cut or deleted'.[7]

As to the second point, the *Instructio* – referring to the anonymous works condemned in the third class of the Pauline Index – made a significant distinction:[8] works published for the first time in the years subsequent to the dissemination of the Lutheran heresy (the 'last forty years') were to be considered in all cases prohibited, with certain specific exceptions.[9] This disposition was in fact nothing new. It is only natural, one might think, that the Pauline Index should concentrate on works presumed to have been contaminated by Protestant orthodoxy. The fact was, however, that this peremptory stressing of the *caesura* represented by the Protestant reform in the evolution of the Church of Rome takes on a particular connotation when considered in light of the indications contained in *Moderatio indicis librorum prohibitorum*, the decree signed by Pius IV two years later, in 1561, in order to diminish the impact of the bans that had targeted certain categories of books and to lighten the threatening atmosphere created by the Pauline Index.[10] This decree, referring to the same type of work, ordained that works printed before the spread of Lutheranism (i.e. the

---

[7] 'Rubricae quibus confictae, quaedam virtutes psalmorum sive orationum summa cum indignitate describuntur, in multis Psalteriis et communibus libellis precum iubentur vel rescindi vel deleri' (ibid.).

[8] Ibid., p. 101.

[9] 'Quae a quadraginta annis citra impressa sunt, ita ut compertum sit eadem ante XL annos nunquam fuisse alias impressa vel composita, censentur proibita.' The text of the *Instructio* continued as follows: 'Si tamen passim inter Catholicos recepta sint, et probata sine controversia et suspitione alicuius labis: et viri Catholici et eruditi id affirment cum licentia officii Sanctae Inquisitionis conceduntur' (*Index des livres interdits*, vol. VIII, p. 101). The licence of the Congregation of the Inquisition was therefore granted only for works that were above all suspicion.

[10] *Index des livres interdits*, vol. VIII, pp. 53–4. The text of *Moderatio* is on pp. 105–6; G. Fragnito, *La Bibbia al rogo*, p. 95; cf. also H. Jedin, *Storia del Concilio di Trento*, vol. IV, tome I, 1979, p. 153 et seqq.

same 'last forty years' of the *Instructio*) were to be tolerated except for cases of blatant heresy: 'Anonymous books printed more than forty years ago (provided they contain no errors of faith) are to be tolerated'.[11] In light of the norms contained in the *Moderatio*, the distinction that was barely hinted at in the *Instructio* now appeared in all its radicality: on the one hand, there was the inflexible anti-Lutheran battle and, on the other, an operation to recover Catholic traditions dating from before the diffusion of the reformed doctrines.

However, the censorial activity of the Pauline Index contained within it a striking contradiction. The radical offensive launched against the vernacular ran the risk of activating the church hierarchies in the opposite direction to that of the use and enjoyment of these same traditions, whether local or national. This contradiction was clear to, for example, Ludovico Beccadelli, Archbishop of Ragusa,[12] who reacted with incredulity and dismay at the ban on reading the Bible in the vernacular contained in the Pauline Index, despite this being a consolidated local tradition. Writing to Ghislieri just after the promulgation of the Index, he appealed in favor of the 'ancient practice' of using the vernacular languages, stating that it would be very difficult and also highly inappropriate to try to 'remove' them:

> And here in all the province of Slavonia, and not just in Ragusa, they have everything in their own language, they say, from St Geronimo onwards, all the holy books, and not only do they read them customarily in the women's convents and in private houses but they also celebrate Mass in the language of the Slavs throughout the country, in the cathedrals and the monasteries of the monks and elsewhere, and I have heard that the ceremonies for the ordaining of priests and doctors are also performed in that language. *And since this practice is very old, as I have said, it would be almost impossible to suppress it.*[13]

---

11 'Libri sine authoris nomine impressi ante quadraginta annos (dummodo nullum in fide errorem contineant) tolerentur'; *Index des livres interdits*, vol. VIII, p. 105.

12 On Beccadelli, cf. G. ALBERIGO, *sub voce*, *Dizionario Biografico degli Italiani* (DBI), vol. VII, pp. 407–13; G. FRAGNITO, 'Per lo studio dell'epistolografia volgare del Cinquecento: le lettere di Ludovico Beccadelli,' *Bibliothèque d'Humanisme et Renaissance*, 43, 1980, pp. 61–87; EAD., *In museo e in villa. Saggi sul Rinascimento perduto*, Venice, Arsenale, 1988, passim; EAD., 'Le contraddizioni di un censore: Ludovico Beccadelli di fronte al Panormita e al Boccaccio,' in *Studi in memoria di Paola Medioli Masotti*, F. Magnani (ed.), Naples, Loffredo editore, 1995, pp. 153–71.

13 'Et qui in tutta la provincia di Schiavonia, non pure a Ragusa, hanno nella lingua loro, com'essi dicono, da san Hieronimo in qua, tutti i libri sacri, et non solo gli leggono ordinariamente ne i monasterii delle donne e nelle case private, ma celebrano per tutto il paese, dalle cathedrali e monasterii de' frati in poi, la messa in lingua schiava et, per quel ch'intendo, in detta lingua si fanno preti et dottori anchora. *Et essendo questo uso molto vecchio, com'ho detto, sarebbe cosa quasi impossibile a levarla*' (Ragusa, 12 February 1559,

The Trent Commission, of which Beccadelli was an authoritative member, having been commissioned by Pius IV to mitigate the Index of Paul IV, corrected this evident contradiction and moderated the ban on reading the Bible in the vernacular. Rule IV of the Index of Trent, which that particular Commission prepared, allowed the Bishops and Inquisitors to authorize, after hearing the views of parish priests or confessors, the reading of versions of the Bible in vernacular languages, translated by Catholics, in all cases where it was their considered opinion that such reading would serve to increase the piety and devotion of the faithful.[14]

Thus, having resolved the contradiction, albeit only partially, the Trent Commission was able to resume the course taken by *Instructio* and *Moderatio*.[15]

On the one hand, another element was added to the above-mentioned process of 'recovery', clarifying that 'works written in the vulgar tongue on the reasons for good living or regarding contemplation, confession, and similar subjects are not to be prohibited if they contain sound doctrine; the same applies to popular sermons in the vulgar tongue' (Rule VI).[16] One glance at the catalogs of sixteenth-century reprints of medieval devotional texts[17] is sufficient to realize how all the topics identified by this last rule – from 'contemplation' to 'good living', and even including confession – were unmistakable features of this field of literature.

---

in BPP, Ms. Pal. 1010, f. 282r–v, quoted by G. Fragnito, *La Bibbia al rogo*, p. 101; my emphasis). The desire to observe local customs must have had considerable weight in the favorable attitude toward the translation of the Bible into the vernacular shown by the majority of the Italian Fathers in the Council (G. Fragnito, p. 79).

14 G. Fragnito, p. 98; the text of Rule IV is in *Index des livres interdits*, vol. VIII, pp. 816–7.

15 The first rule of the Trent Index faithfully presented the indication in *Moderatio* regarding pre-Reformation literature; by specifying that only books explicitly condemned in previous centuries were to be considered prohibited, it indirectly confirmed – as was already evident in *Moderatio* – that fourteenth- and fifteenth-century devotional and religious literature remained exempt from any ban: 'All books condemned by the Supreme Pontiffs or by Ecumenic Councils but not included in this Index are to be regarded as condemned, just as they were condemned in the past' ('Libri omnes, quos ante annum MDXV aut summi Pontifices, aut Concilia oecumenica damnarunt, et in hoc Indice non sunt, eodem modo damnati esse censeantur, sicut olim damnati fuerunt'; Rule I, *Index des livres interdits*, vol. VIII, p. 813).

16 'qui vero de ratione bene vivendi, contemplandi, confitendi, ac similibus argumentis vulgari sermone conscripti sunt, si sanam doctrinam contineant, non est cur prohibeantur, sicut nec sermones populares vulgari lingua habiti' (ibid., p. 816). The reference to 'sermones populares' introduced for the first time the approach of devotional literature towards 'unlettered' culture, a theme that was picked up again in the following years; cf. below, chapter 10.

17 For a first approach, see A.J. Schutte, *Printed Italian vernacular religious books*.

On the other hand, with regard to the second important issue addressed by the Pauline Index, i.e. superstition, the drafters of the Trent Index made a step forward. Listing the categories of works to be expurgated, the text of Rule VIII substantially equated heresy, on one side, and superstition, ungodliness, and divination, on the other, thus officially sanctioning – with the introduction of the instrument of expurgation – the beginning of the church offensive against all forms of 'superstitio': 'Books whose main topic is judged to be good, but in which there is occasional heretic, irreligious, divinatory, or superstitious matter, can be allowed, once they have been purged by Catholic theologians, on the authority of the general Inquisition'.[18]

It was, however, the whole field of 'morality' that, well beyond the confines of 'superstitio', became the object of a project whose purposes were essentially cultural rather than censorial and whose aim was to control every aspect of the life of the faithful: under the broad heading of 'lewd' and 'obscene' (Rule VII),[19] whole sections of vernacular literature, religious or not, fell into the hands of the Roman censors. A large part of sixteenth-century religious and devotional literature was considered by the Roman authorities in light of these new categories of censorship, often going well beyond the specific contents of the actual works.[20]

Closely in line with the design traced out by the Tridentine rules, the decrees issued on the occasion of the Council of Trent also emphasized

---

[18] 'Libri, quorum principale argumentum bonum est, in quibus tamen obiter aliqua inserta sunt, quae ad haeresiam, seu impietatem, divinationem, seu superstitionem spectant, a Catholicis Theologis, Inquisitionis generalis auctoritate, expurgati, concedi possunt'; *Index des livres interdits*, vol. VIII, p. 817. Rule IX also approached the subject, specifying the various forms of superstition lurking in the literature of the day, from spells to poisons and enchantments: '*Libri omnes, et scripta Geomantiae, Hydromantiae, Onomantiae, Chiromantiae, Necromantiae, sive in quibus continentur Sortilegia, Veneficia, Auguria, Auspicia, Incantationes artis magica, prorsus reiiciuntur*' (ibid., p. 818).

[19] In 'Regula septima' we read: 'Books that expressly describe, narrate, or teach subjects that are lewd or obscene, not only with regard to faith but also to customs that are liable to be corrupted by the reading of such books, are to be severely punished by the Bishops. Ancient books written by pagan authors may be permitted by virtue of their elegance and propriety of expression, but in no way should children be permitted to read them' ('Libri, qui res lascivas, seu obscoenas ex professo tractant, narrant, aut docent, cum non solum fidei, sed et morum, qui huiusmodi librorum lectione facile corrumpi solent, ratio habenda sit, omnino prohibentur, et qui eos habuerint, severe ab Episcopis puniantur. Antiqui vero, ab Ethnicis conscripti, propter sermonis elegantiam, et proprietatem permittuntur, nulla tamen ratione pueris praelegendi erunt'; ibid., p. 817).

[20] Despite the considerable reduction in the number of bans compared to the Pauline Index, and despite the introduction of an instrument of expurgation that in some way instilled new (albeit restricted) life into texts otherwise destined to oblivion – despite all this we have to take into consideration how the ten introductory rules of the Trent Index vastly increased church censorship's field of action.

the centrality of the problem of superstition. Having reiterated – always conforming to the rules of censorship – the principle of the authority of the holy texts and of patristic tradition[21] and having stressed the considerable value, in opposition to Lutheranism, of holy offices[22] and prayers,[23] which were deemed to be equal to all the other 'good works' of a devout Catholic, the Council Fathers declared that superstition and other similar deviant beliefs ('scurrilia, [...] fabulosa, vana, adulationes, detractiones, [...] impias et diabolicas incantationes, divinationes, sortes')[24] constituted one of the greatest dangers for the integrity and purity of the devotional system of Roman Catholicism. However, the Fathers did not merely point the matter out. Realizing the value of certain proposals already to be found in the *Libellus ad Leonem X*, the bishops of Trent resolved that the remedy to the problem lay in the peremptory affirmation of the central authority of the Church of Rome as the sole source of the legitimization of rites and prayers: 'to leave no room for superstition, they are to ensure by edict with accompanying penalties that priests do not celebrate at other than the proper times, nor use in the celebration of mass rites or ceremonies and prayers other than those approved by the church and considered traditional from long and praiseworthy usage.'[25] The very last

---

21 Session 4 (8 April 1546): 'First decree: acceptance of the sacred books and apostolic tradition' , *Decrees of the Ecumenical Councils*, Norman P. Tanner (ed.), vol. 2, *Trent to Vatican II*, Sheed and Ward, and Georgetown University Press, 1990, pp. 663–4.

22 'All are obliged to attend the divine office personally and not through substitutes, and to assist and serve the bishop when he is celebrating mass or other pontifical rites, and when in choir for sung worship to praise the name of God reverently, distinctly and devoutly in hymns and canticles' (Decree on reform, Session 24, canon 12, *Decrees*, p. 767).

23 'Decree on justification: [...] but also confession of them in the sacrament of penance, to be made at least in desire and in due season, absolution by a priest, and also satisfaction by fasting, almsgiving, prayers and other devout exercises of the spiritual life (Session 6, *Decrees*, p. 677).

24 'The Council wishes to check the lack of discretion by which the words and sentiments of sacred scripture are turned and twisted to scurrilous use, to wild and empty fancies, to flattery, detraction, superstitions, godless and devilish magical formulae, fortune telling, lotteries, and also slanderous pamphlets. So as to banish this kind of irreverence and contempt, and so that no one may in future dare in any way to make use of the words of sacred scriptures for these or similar purposes, the Council orders and prescribes that all persons in that category, violators and profaners of the word of God, should be checked by the bishops by legal and imposed penalties' (Session 4, 'Second Decree. Acceptance of the Latin Vulgate edition of the Bible; rule on the manner of interpreting sacred scripture', *Decrees*, pp. 664–5). Also with regard to superstition, cf. Session 25, 3–4 December 1563: 'On invocation, veneration, and relics of the saints, and on sacred images (*Decrees*, pp. 774–6): 'All superstition must be removed from invocation of the saints, veneration of relics, and use of sacred images; all aiming at base profit must be eliminated; all sensual appeal must be avoided, so that images are not painted or adorned with seductive charm'.

25 'Decree on things to be observed and avoided in celebrating mass', *Decrees*, p. 737.

words of the decree, referring to the 'ancient custom' of ceremonies and prayers as an alternative source of legitimization, provided evidence of the ultimate fusion of the two problems considered here, i.e. the battle against superstition and the exploitation of the traditional religious heritage.

The path that had to be covered was therefore uneven, but fairly straightforward. The reform of the Breviary, on which work had begun in those same years but was not completed until 1568, proved to be the first real test of this protracted period of normative gestation.[26]

During the preparatory work, which began under Paul IV and continued well after his death, many of the suggested changes put forward thirty years earlier by Quiñones were incorporated. In keeping with the informative spirit of the *Libellus to Leonem X*, in the mid-1530s the Franciscan Cardinal had planned a comprehensive reform of the Roman liturgic system. He proposed a radical reinterpretation of the functions and the ways of using the Roman Breviary – the liturgic text containing the divine office that the clergy were called upon to recite at various times of day. Quiñones' basic idea was to restore to the text its original function as a compendium of passages from the Scriptures, thus proposing a more internalized use of the texts than before. His suggested reforms answered a twofold requirement: on the one hand, to encourage direct, simplified reading of the Gospel text, using the passages in the Breviary, and, on the other, to return the Breviary to its *forma antiqua*, as consolidated in the patristic age: i.e. ease of use of the Holy Scriptures and affirmation of sacred church tradition. These two requirements were met in all the modifications in his reformed version, such as the simplification of weekday offices (and in particular a shortened and simplified rewriting of the Bible readings contained in them), the reduction in the number of feast-day offices (and of feast-days), hitherto dependent on an ever-growing number of saints to be honored, and the elimination of unnecessary responses and antiphons. Both of the subjects considered by Querini and Giustiniani – the problem of ignorance and that of the affirmation of church authority[27] – had thus received a concrete answer in the proposed reform. But the time was not yet ripe. The similarity of these reformist ideas to certain Protestant demands had the effect of causing Quiñones' project to arouse mistrust rather than support in the Roman Curia.[28] However, as the years passed, it became clear that the only real reason for the failure of the reform initiated in 1535

[26] On the reform of the Breviary, see H. Jedin, *Storia del Concilio di Trento*, vol. IV, tome II, 1981, pp. 344–8.

[27] See above, ch. 1.

[28] In 1558 (8 August) a decree desired by Paul IV prohibited the reprinting of Quiñones' breviary. This decree was never actually promulgated and in 1561 the Superior General of the Jesuits, Lainez, still allowed members of his Order to use the breviary. On these aspects,

was the fact that it was conceived thirty years too early. The same basic principles that in 1535 sounded like too early an admission of guilt, in the light of the still very recent Lutheran accusations of betraying the holy texts, now – after the process of doctrinal redefinition concluded at Trent and the 'closing of the ranks' achieved thanks to the two Roman Indexes – could be accepted as an essential component of the Roman liturgic reform.

The *Breviarium pianum* that was presented on completion of the work of the Commission responsible did in fact answer the requirement that it should restore the original form of thc Breviary (*ridur l'officio all'antico*; 'return the holy office to its ancient form'), eliminating whatever was 'new, absurd, and apocryphal' that had been added over the decades.[29] The first step was the reduction in the number of feast-days, thus returning the text to its main original purpose: to enable the readers (churchmen in the case of the Breviary and, as we will shortly see, ordinary worshipers in the case of the Missal) to say 150 psalms a week and at the same time give them the opportunity to read all the selected passages from the Holy Scriptures.[30] Church intervention was not however limited to altering the quantity of text – frequently the cardinals charged with the reform took it upon themselves to make qualitative changes too in particular passages, for example in texts of 'lessons' (*lezioni*) on the 'acts' (*azioni*) of the saints.[31] A report that Leonardo Marini, Bishop of Lanciano and a member of the cited Commission, addressed to Pius V, written with the intention of informing him about the development of the work of rewriting the hagiographic lessons, reveals some aspects of the kind of work involved: Marini concentrated on providing churchmen with a text written in 'concise and sober' style, an 'account' purified of any apocryphal elements and rid of any concepts not concerned with the life of the saint. The hagiographic narrative, again according to Marini, had to report only the most reliable information, plus any other deemed important for the edifying purpose it set itself. At all costs any words or expressions had to be avoided that might confuse the minds of the simplest or offend

cf. S. Ditchfield, *Liturgy, Sanctity and History in Tridentine Italy*, Cambridge, Cambridge University Press, 1995, pp. 24 and 29 and footnote 43.

29 Ibid., p. 35.

30 Ibid., p. 30. The number of feast-days, and of the offices corresponding to them, had increased, Ditchfield explains, not only to 'satisfy' the numerous requests coming from all corners of the Catholic world but also because of a 'human' reason. A feast-day dedicated to the worship of a saint dispensed the priest from the onerous task of reciting an elevated number of psalms and prayers to which had to be added the office of the day, the office of the dead, and the 'minor' office of the Blessed Virgin (ibid., pp. 31–2).

31 Ibid., p. 36.

Christian decorum.[32] Remarkable philological sensitivity was shown in the way every detail of the chronology of the lives of the saints was checked, with precise information being provided regarding the condition of the relics of each saint and their location. The sources on which the account was based were also given.[33]

The message that this reform of the Breviary was intended to offer was that the work was strictly one of 'restoration', i.e. there was no room for any imaginative or creative activity on the part of the revisers. There can be no other interpretation of the words carefully chosen by Sirleto[34] to synthesize the method of action: 'Nothing was added and nothing was put in the place of the new, absurd, and apocryphal.'[35] In this context one can appreciate the highly important role of local devotional traditions in the overall liturgical reform, particularly with regard to the indication that all breviaries used by dioceses and religious orders for more than 200 years were excluded from any such ecclesiastic action. In the years to come the principle of the 'antiquity' of liturgical texts thus became the most important factor that local dioceses would cling to when seeking from the Holy See what had become the mandatory approval of their offices and breviaries. We will return to this point later.

The radical revision of the Roman Breviary was followed, just two years later, by the reform of the Missal, the liturgic text used by the clergy during celebrations and by the faithful at times of individual prayer. The new version of the sanctorale made this procedure practically obligatory. The main intention of the reform – which, as said, was to restore the text to its original form, on the basis of precise philological methods – was explicitly formulated in the Papal Bull, *Quo Primum Tempore*, inserted at the beginning of the new Missal: 'to restore the mass to the original norms and rites of the Fathers.'[36]

---

32 Ibid., p. 37; P. BATIFFOL, *History of the Roman Breviary*, London, Longmans and Co., 1912 (first French edition: 1893), p. 228.

33 S. DITCHFIELD, *Liturgy, Sanctity*, p. 37.

34 On Sirleto, cf. P. PASCHINI, 'Note per una biografia del cardinale Guglielmo Sirleto', *Archivio Storico della Calabria*, V, 1917, pp. 44 et seqq; ID., 'Guglielmo Sirleto prima del cardinalato,' ID., *Tre ricerche sulla storia della Chiesa nel Cinquecento*, Rome, Edizioni liturgiche, 1945, pp. 155 et seqq; ID., 'Il cardinale Sirleto in Calabria', *Rivista di storia della Chiesa in Italia*, I, 1947, pp. 22–67; ID.,'Sirleto, Guglielmo,' *Enciclopedia Cattolica*, XI, Vatican City, 1953, coll. 757–8. On Sirleto's activity as a member of the Congregation of the Index, cf. G. FRAGNITO, *La Bibbia al rogo*, *ad indicem*.

35 'Niente è stato aggiunto o niente è stato messo al posto delle cose nuove assurde e apocrife' (S. DITCHFIELD, *Liturgy, Sanctity*, p. 35).

36 'Ad pristinam Missale ipsum sanctorum Patrum pristinam normam ac ritum restituerunt'; ibid., p. 43 and footnote 93. The reform of the Missal had become necessary following the revision of the calendar of saints, but the reform of the Martyrology had

It is in this context that the Papal Bull issued in 1571 by Pope Pius V 'on the recitation of the Blessed Virgin Mary, with the decrees and indulgences' is to be read.[37] It is a document that makes it possible to verify – with particular reference to the theme of prayer – the concrete methods of applying the censorial and 'reforming' criteria formulated with regard to liturgic and devotional material by the compilers of the Pauline and Tridentine Indexes. All the principles spelled out here – the prohibition on reading devotional text in the vernacular, the 'normative' value attributed to local ecclesiastic tradition prior to patristic tradition, the assertion of the central authority of Rome as the sole and indisputable source of legitimization in this respect, the battle against superstition – are principles that we find solidly and consistently applied in the Papal Bull of 1571. That the offensive against the vernacular was a basic aspect of Counter-Reformation strategy was clear – yet again – in the way the Bull insistently inveighed against offices and prayers in the vernacular:

> All offices in the vernacular, whatever the language, be it Italian, or Spanish, or French, or German, or any other vulgar tongue, are totally prohibited. [...] Prayers in the vernacular, whatever they are, even if they are included in the Latin offices, as likewise Litanies in the vernacular, are prohibited and laid under an interdict.[38]

The scope of the Bull was not, however, limited to the question of the vernacular – all sixteenth-century editorial production, in this case regarding the 'Offices of the Blessed Virgin Mother' (*Uffici della Beata*

---

become even more urgent, a task which Cesare Baronio, one of the greatest contemporary historians of the Church, accomplished with great industry in very few years (ibid., pp. 43 et seqq).

37 Bull dated 11 March 1571, in *Bullarium diplomatum et privilegiorum sanctorum romanorum pontificum, taurinensis editio* ..., tomus VII, Augustae Taurinorum, Seb. Franco et Henrico Dalmazzo editoribus, 1862, pp. 897–901. Here we follow the 'Sommario della Bolla del Santiss. padre Papa Pio V, sopra la recitatione dell'Ufficio della B. Vergine Maria, Colli decreti, et indulgentie, havuto da Tortona', quoted in *Scriniolum Sanctae Inquisitionis Astensis in quo quaecumque ad id muneris obeundum spedare visa sunt, vidilicet Librorum Prohibitorum Indices* ..., Astae, Apud Virgilium de Zangrandis, 1610, 55–7 et sqq. On this last important documentary source, see also M. FANTINI, 'Lo Scriniolum di Fra Giovanni Battista Porcelli (1612): da un archivio di lettere alla formazione di un manuale', *L'Inquisizione romana: metodologia delle fonti e storia istituzionale*, A. Del Col and G. Paolin (eds), Trieste, Edizioni Università di Trieste, 2000, pp. 199–256.

38 'Tutti gl'Ufficiali volgari, in qualonche lingua siano, o in Italiano, o in Spagnolo, o in Francese, o in Tedesca, o in qualonque altra volgare, sono totalmente proibiti. [...] Orationi volgari, qualonque siano, se ben fossero inserte ne gl'Uffici latini, e parimente Litanie volgari sono prohibite, e interdette' (*Scriniolum*, f. 56, under the title 'Modo, et regola di espurgare gl'ufficiali, et altri libri d'orationi').

Vergine Madre), was called into question for the sake of restoring the Pope's exclusive authority in liturgic matters:

> All Offices of the Blessed Virgin Mother composed in the vernacular or translated into it are annulled, whatever their manner or their language, as is also annulled the Office printed and published in Venice by Gionti last year, in 1570 with the following albeit false inscription: *Officium Beatae Mariae Virginis per Concilium Tridentinum Pius V Pontifex Maximus reformatum*, and indeed any other office of the said Blessed Virgin composed in Latin but with the inscription de *Hortulus animae*, or *Thesauri spiritualis compendium*, or presented under whatever other title or name.[39]

Addressing 'all persons, whether secular or regular of whatever order, and the laity of either sex, who in observance of whatever rule, militia, order, usage, custom, reason or cause are required to recite the Office of the Blessed Virgin', Pius V commanded

> that they shall not dare to speak, read or in any way hold any other Office of Our Lady, and that the correct commandment of Our Lord is that printed in Rome in the printing-house of the Roman People built for the purpose of printing holy books faithfully and continuously, and if they recite any other office they must know they are not performing their duty to recite this office, with the above exceptions.[40]

The delicate matter of local church tradition remained unresolved. Consequently, following the example of the compromise reached in the Tridentine decrees,[41] the compilers of the Bull sought out a formula capable of reconciling the assertion of Papal authority with the safeguarding of local

---

[39] 'Si annullano tutti li Uffici della Beata Vergine Madre, composti, o tradotti in lingua volgare in qual si voglia modo, e lingua, si come ancor si annulla l'Ufficio stampato, e pubblicato a Venetia appresso li Gionti l'anno passato 1570 con questa, se ben falsa inscrittione, *Officium Beatae mariae Virginis per Concilium Tridentinum Pio V Pontifex Maximus reformatum*, e in somma ciascun altro ufficio della detta Beata Vergine, composto ancor in lingua latina con inscrittione de *Hortulus animae*, o *Thesauri spiritualis compendium*, o sotto qual si voglia altro titolo, o nome divolgato' (*Scriniolum*, f. 55).

[40] 'che non ardiscano dire, leggere, o tener in alcun modo altro Ufficio della Madonna, che quello ch'è corretto di comandamento di Nostro Signore, è stato stampato in Roma nella stamparla del Popolo Romano eretta a fine d'imprimere fidelmente, e incorrottamente li libri sacri, e dicendo altro ufficio sappiano non satisfar al debito, che hanno da recitar tal ufficio, eccettuando come di sopra' (ibid). Pio V was addressing 'tutti quelli così secolari, come regolari di qual si voglia ordine, e laici dell'uno, e l'altro sesso, che per qual si voglia regola, militia, ordine, uso, consuetudine, ragione, o causa sono obligati a recitar l'Ufficio della Beata Vergine' (ibid.).

[41] Cf. above.

devotional practices. At first, the awkward embarrassment of the revisers seemed to have carried the day. The imperious tone of the prohibition was attenuated thanks to a somewhat ambiguous formula intended to combine the two factors of local tradition (implicit in the reference to the 'consent [...] of the Prelate') and of the reaffirmation of the Roman Curia's central authority masked behind the accommodating formula of the granting of a 'licence' (*licenza*): 'Licence is therefore granted whereby those who, for the above causes, could recite another office may indeed recite this, instead of that which they have hitherto recited, and therefore with the consent of the Prelate and all the Prelate's chapters.'[42] When they eventually had to return to the issue, however, they succeeded in resolving this underlying antagonism using much more straightforward terms that sanctioned the equal dignity of two principles:

> An exception [from the general prohibition] is however made in the case of Offices that from their first institution were approved by the Holy Apostolic See, and those that are found to have been instituted or practiced for over two hundred years, provided they are not in the vernacular.[43]

The apparent contradiction thus having been resolved, and the Bull's scope of action defined, the text then entered into the details of the censorship procedure. As they extended their in-depth analysis of the problems of the general type of prohibition, the revisors immediately came up against the problem of superstition: 'It is prohibited to say the office of the Blessed Virgin in the vernacular, as it is also prohibited to say any prayer in the vernacular, even if these may be included in Latin offices, for many of them are known to contain numerous superstitions.'[44] Using the tool of expurgation that was introduced by the Rules of Trent, Pius V's Bull acted directly on the texts, distinguishing between 'bad' parts (the 'rubrics' pointed out by the Pauline Index, plus others, as shall see) and parts 'to be saved'. The text of the Bull had ended with the invitation (or rather the command) to parish priests and believers in general to deposit the 'offices' in the hands of the 'inquisitors of heretic depravity' in order to 'abolish

---

42 'Si concede però licentia a quelli, che per le cause sopradette potessero recitar altro ufficio, che possano in loco di quello, che hanno recitato fino a hora dir questo, di consenso però del suo Prelato, e di tutto il capitulo d'esso Prelato' (*Scriniolum*, f. 55).

43 'Si eccettuano [dalla proibizione generale] però quelli Uffici, che dalla lor prima institutione furono approbati dalla santa sede apostolica, e quelli che consterà esser stati instituiti, o usati oltra duecento anni, purché non siano in lingua volgare' (ibid.).

44 'Si proibisce il dir l'ufficio d'essa Beata Vergine in volgare, si come ancor se li prohibisce il dir qualsivoglia oratione volgare, se ben fossero inserte nelli ufficii latini, poiché si è conosciuto esser in molte di esse orationi molte superstitioni' (ibid.)

completely all use of the vernacular and to *purge* the others'.[45] Thus we find in *Modo et regola di espurgare tutti gli uffici* a precise description of how this expurgation was to be carried out:

> All Rubrics, including those of prayers, are to be removed that do not come under the title of Prayer or the governing of the Office but instead speak of dubious Indulgences or vain or superstitious observations, or of the value of Prayer, saying things that are neither plausible nor reasonable. All such inserted parts, placed among the Prayers, that offend the holy writings or the teaching of the Holy Roman Catholic Church, or contain falsehoods, must be removed. Likewise, when any parts contain superstitious matter, or anything uncommon, or that is indecent, not known, or inappropriate, these parts should be removed.[46]

Before any indication of the 'places' to be expurgated, ecclesiastics and ordinary believers were thus provided with a list of 'prayers all of which are to be removed in their entirety' (*orationi le quali intiere, e tutte si levano*).[47] Among these are prayers whose title alone is sufficient to reveal their 'superstitious' nature, such as the *Oratione a ritrovar cose robbate* ('Prayer for finding things that have been stolen'), the *Oratione contra la tempesta* ('Prayer against storms'), the *Oratione contro il morbo* ('Prayer against disease'), the *Oratione contro gl'Inimici* ('Prayer against enemies'), one 'against fever', and one 'against gout', as well as prayers discarded as 'superfluous' in the course of the revision of the calendar of Saints linked to reform of the Breviary and the Missal, or texts that behind an apparently orthodox text concealed 'superstitious' messages and contents, as for example *II Confitemini della Beata Vergine*. A copy of *Confitemini della Madonna con le Litanie*, printed in Venice for Augustino Bindoni (1553) and kept in the Biblioteca Casanatense in Rome – a library where during the seventeenth century numerous texts once belonging to the Holy

45 Ibid., f. 55 (my emphasis).

46 'Tutte le Rubriche anco dell'orationi si levano via, le quali non appartengono al titolo dell'Oratione, overo al governar l'Ufficio; ma parlano d'Indulgenze incerte, o d'osservationi vane, o superstitiose, overo del valore dell'Orationi, con raccontare cose non verisimili, ne ragionevoli. Tutte le parte inserte, e poste nell'Orationi, le quali repugnano alle sacre lettere, overo alla dottrina della santa, e Cattolica Romana Chiesa, o importano falsità, devono esser levate via». E ancora, di seguito: «Parimente quando hanno del superstitioso, e dell'inusitato; o sono indecenti, incognite, o inette, o fuor di proposito inserte, debbano esser levate' (ibid., f. 56). The use of the term 'uncommon' is yet another reminder of the importance of 'ancient custom' as opposed to 'novelties', which were always given a negative connotation necessarily associated with the origin and the developments of the Lutheran Reformation.

47 For the prayers that follow, see ibid., ff. 56–7.

Office in Rome were deposited –[48] offers direct evidence of the quality and effectiveness of the act of censorship. The frontispiece of the document bears a handwritten comment that is unequivocally clear: 'Devotion showing foolish superstition', while on the first page there is another handwritten note confirming what had already been made clear in Pius V's Bull: 'The Confitemini ... [sic] the litanies of the Our Most Reverend Lady not approved, foolishly and therefore not without some room for superstition ... [sic], together with ridiculous promises.'[49] An analysis of the volume's contents thus provides an interesting testimony regarding the parts that were condemned, i.e. the 'rubrics', on the one hand, and superstitious passages, on the other. In the first of these categories we read comments such as the following:

> This devout psalm begins here. It must be recited with great reverence and contrition for certain matters, devoutly, when you have some tribulation with a special friend of yours or with some other person recommended to you who is in tribulation; you must say this psalm with the prayers written on it, kneeling before the image of the Virgin Mary and after each verse, as you will find it marked, you will recite the entire Hail Mary that appears on every verse, with an act of self-humiliation. And verily, when you have recited it devoutly, without fail, on seven mornings, before eating and not speaking to anyone, while you venerate her, your wish will certainly be granted and you will receive from God the gift and the grace that you seek.[50]

Or there are words like the following:

---

48 Clement XI's Bull dated 18 July 1703 made it possible for books prohibited by the Index to be kept also at the Casanatense Library: cf. V. De Gregorio, *La Biblioteca Casanatense di Roma*, Naples, ESI, 1993; see also the paper by A.A. Cavarra, 'La Biblioteca Casanatense a difesa dell'ortodossia: bibliotecari e teologi domenicani, segretari dell'Indice e Maestri del Sacro Palazzo', *Inquisizione e Indice nei secoli XVI–XVII. Controversie teologiche dalle raccolte casanatensi*, A.A. Cavarra (ed.), Vigevano, Diakronia, 1998, pp. 1–5.

49 'Il Confitemini ... [sic] le litanie della R.ma Vergine non approvate scioccamente, e perciò non senza qualche spazio di superstizione, ... [sic] unite delle promesse ridicole' (*Confitemini della Madonna con le litanie*, Venezia, Augustino Bindoni, 1553).

50 'Qui si comincia questo divoto psalmo che si vole dire con molta riverentia e contritione di cose divotamente quando tu hai alcuna tribulatione d'alcuno tuo amico speciale o d'altra persona divota che sia tua recomendata la quale fusse in tribulatione dirai questo psalmo con le orationi che sono scritte con esso ingenocchiati dinanci alla Imagine della Vergine Maria e doppo ogni verso come voi trovarete signato dirà tutta la Ave Maria con la invenia. Et veramente quando tu l'harai ditta divotamente senza fallo sette mattine a degiuno senza favellare a persona in tanto che tu la venerai a dire sarai essaudito senza fallo e receverai da Dio il dono e la gratia che tu dimanderai' (ibid., c. Alv).

> These are the Litanies of the glorious Virgin Mary which will save from the plague whoever says them or causes them to be said; and when the plague struck the Monastery of St Clare, the Virgin Mary miraculously saved it, thanks to these litanies.[51]

And yet again: 'To those who say this prayer I will give my body and with my precious blood I will sate them for all eternity.'[52] The superstitious passages contain irreverent and unreal portions, such as the following:

> It came about that this hermit was enrapt and it seemed to him that he was in a field where there was a delightsome river full of precious stones. And close by the river were all the nuns of the monastery. Of these, some were all wet from the water of the river, some were half wet, and some had merely bared their bellies. The hermit then prayed and the meaning of the vision was made clear to him: he understood that it signified the holy state of the nuns who had said this prayer.[53]

There are also passages containing incorrect doctrine that attributed to the Virgin Mary, more or less explicitly, salvific powers that orthodox Catholic doctrine did not recognize her as having: 'Now if you forsake me, where shall I go? What shall I do? Whom shall I call upon? Whom shall I ask for help, O *fountain of all grace*?'[54]

In the case of prayers like these, no corrective attempt would have been in the slightest way effective. In the case of other less compromised texts, the compilers of the Bull prepared a list of 'prayers, antiphons, litanies, and hymns that must be corrected'.[55] Without entering into the merit of each single prayer (and its corresponding expurgation), the precise identification of which is complicated by the difficulty of obtaining the actual texts, we are nevertheless able to offer some examples of 'vain

---

51 'Queste sono le Letanie della gloriosa virgine Maria le quali chi le dirà o farà dire serà scampato da pestilentia: la quale essendo intrata nel monasterio de santa Chiara per miracolo de la verzene Maria fu liberado per virtù de queste letanie' (ibid., c. B2r).

52 'Quello che dirà questa oratione io gli donerò el mio corpo e lo sangue mio precioso eternalmente li sacierò' (ibid., c. B7r).

53 'Advenne chel ditto solitario fu rapto e pareagli essere in uno campo nel quale era uno dilettevole fiume pieno de pitre preciose. Et appresso quel fiume era tutte le monache del ditto monasterio. De le quale parte erano tutte bagnate de la acqua del ditto fiume e parte erano meze bagnate e parte erano solamente spianzate. Allhora el solitario fece oratione che li fusse revelato che significava questa visione: fugli revelato che significava el stato santo de le sore che haveano ditta la ditta oratione' (ibid., c. B6v).

54 'Hora se tu m'abbandoni ove andarò? Che farò? Che chiamerò? A chi domandare aiuto o fontana d'ogni gratia' (ibid., cc. A8r–v; my emphasis).

55 *Scriniolium*, f. 56.

or superstitious observations' (*osservationi vane o superstitiose*) and of expressions that 'offend the holy writings [...] or contain falsehoods [...] [or] contain anything uncommon, or that is indecent'[56] that the censors in Rome thought should be 'removed'. The first category to be censored, as already said, was that of the 'rubrics'. Expressions such as 'by virtue of those words' and 'so that we shall always bear those words in our memory'[57] attributed almost miraculous powers to the simple words of the invocations that the faithful were required to address to God.

Besides this type of expurgation there were numerous other types of modification, e.g. the punctilious precision with which it was declared that the '*Hail Queen*, which in some minor Offices is entitled *Canticum Angelorum*, shall be entitled *Antiphona Beatae Mariae Virginis*'[58] or that the 'Oratio devotissima ad Beatam Virginem Mariam, *Stabat mater dolorosa*, is entitled *Planctus Beatae Virginis Mariae*';[59] there were also 'unseemly' (*sconvenienti*) expressions such as one in the *Litanie della Madonna* from which it was befitting 'to remove *Spiritus sancti solarium*'[60] as also the 'two words *ista manu*', to be 'struck out' of the *Oratio ad dexteram manum Christi*.[61] Finally, together with these comments, there were remarks pertaining to expressions that were linked too closely to Lutheran elements – sometimes in fact only linguistically, but in some cases this was decisive in prompting the action of censors whose knowledge of doctrine was frequently inadequate; or else there were other words that might mislead the reader. The compilers of the Bull therefore suggested removing the words 'Therefore, trusting in your pity' (*Ideo de tua pietate confisus*) contained in the prayer *Auxilientur mihi Domine Iesu*, or the even more ambiguous words 'all hope of remission of sins' taken from 'the confession sermon' contained in the *Instruttione alla Christiana religione*, words that might lead devote readers to make an erroneous interpretation of justification by works and by faith.[62]

---

[56] 'repugnano alle sacre lettere [...] o importano falsità [...] [o] hanno [...] dell'inusitato, o sono indecenti, incognite, o inette' (ibid.).

[57] 'per virtutem illorum verborum' and 'ut semper illa verba in memoria haberemus' (ibid., f. 57).

[58] 'La *Salve Regina*, dove in alcuni Ufficiali è intitolata, Canticum Angelorum, s'intitoli, Antiphona Beatae Mariae Virginis' (ibid.).

[59] Ibid.

[60] Ibid.

[61] Ibid.

[62] Ibid.

CHAPTER 6

Mental Prayer and Catholic Orthodoxy

There was thus a clearly recognizable strategy aimed at precise philological restoration, devotional purification, and recovery of the best pre-Lutheran ecclesiastic tradition, a strategy which – in both the thinking and the practice of the Tridentine reformers – proceeded parallel to the overcoming of the trauma of the Protestant schism and the rediscovery of an inward religious awareness that for decades had appeared to be the exclusive monopoly of the Reformation world. In other words, this orientation went along with the rediscovery of the theme of mental prayer, regarding which, starting with the Pauline Index, attempts had been made to return it to the regular course of Roman orthodoxy.

The figure who best reflected the religious and cultural aspects of what we might define the 'first Counter-Reformation' is Carlo Borromeo.[1] On the one hand, the third Milan Provincial Council (1573) immediately took precise cognizance of the rules and regulations that had been established up to that moment in the field of divine offices and superstitious prayers, in particular by the Bull promulgated by Pius V;[2] on the other hand – despite the

[1] A dialectical view of the relationship between two generations of cardinals in the second half of the sixteenth century – each with its own vision of the Church and the Counter-Reformation – lies at the base of Paolo Prodi's considerations in his 'Ricerche sulla teorica delle arti figurative nella riforma cattolica', *Archivio italiano per la storia della pietà*, IV, 1965, pp. 121-212. On Carlo Borromeo there is a vast bibliography; here it is sufficient to cite M. De Certeau, *sub voce*, DBI, vol. 20, pp. 260–69; G. Alberigo, 'Carlo Borromeo come modello di vescovo nella Chiesa post-tridentina', *Rivista Storica Italiana*, LXXIX, 1967, pp. 1031–52; *Il grande Borromeo tra storia e fede*, Cinisello Balsamo, 1984; G. Alberigo, 'Da Carlo Borromeo all'episcopato post-tridentino', H. Jedin and G. Alberigo, *Il tipo ideale di vescovo secondo la Riforma cattolica*, Brescia, Morcelliana, 1985, pp. 99–138; *San Carlo e il suo tempo*, Rome, Edizioni di Storia e Letteratura, 1986; *San Carlo Borromeo, Catholic Reform and Ecclesiastical politics in the second half of the Sixteenth Century*, J.M. Headley, J.B. Tomaro (eds), Washington, The Folger Shakespeare, 1988; *Carlo Borromeo e l'opera della grande Riforma: cultura, religione e arti del governo nella Milano del pieno Cinquecento*, F. Buzzi, D. Zardin (eds), introduction by G. Ravasi, Milan, Credito artigiano, 1997, and more recently D. Zardin, *Carlo Borromeo. Cultura, santità, governo*, Milano, VeP, 2010.

[2] *Acta Ecclesiae Mediolanensis ab eius initiis usque ad nostram aetatem opera et studio presb. Achillis Ratti*, Milan, ex typographia Pontificia Sancti Iosephi, 1890, tome II, col. 241; cf. C. Di Filippo Bareggi, 'Libri e letture nella Milano di San Carlo Borromeo,' N. Raponi and A. Turchini (eds), *Stampa, libri e letture a Milano nell'età di Carlo Borromeo*, Milan, Vita e Pensiero, 1992, pp. 39–96, in particular pp. 43–4; M.P. Fantini, 'Censura romana e orazioni:

conscious recognition of the importance of the process of 'collectivization of the sacred' for the purpose of a capillary social radication of orthodox values –[3] the individual quality of prayer was re-affirmed by the increased value attributed to prayer as a mental activity. It is no coincidence that in the early 1570s Carlo Borromeo, in the midst of all his pastoral activity, addressed confessors, asking them 'to get people who can read and can afford it to buy some spiritual and devout books'.[4] He suggested, among other texts, fourteenth- and fifteenth-century works such as 'the lives of the holy fathers [and] Gerson in the *Imitazione di Christo*', as well as 'the works of Brother Luigi di Granata ... [and] *Prattica dell'oratione mentale* by the Capuchin Father F. Mattia, and others of the same sort.'[5] Carlo Borromeo, the 'hero' of the Counter-Reformation, is of course first and foremost the author who in 1572 wrote and popularized the *Lettera pastorale ed instituto dell'orazione comune*. It was the collective dimension of prayer that particularly appealed to the Archbishop of Milan, for this was 'capable of imparting extraordinary power to prayer':[6]

> [and] because Christ said that if two of you agree upon this earth they will obtain from my celestial Father everything they may wish because where two or three persons meet together in my name, I am among them, therefore let us desire that all people agree together about this holy prayer so that the greater their common need, the more easily they may be satisfied.[7]

---

modi, tempi, formule (1571–1620)', *L'Inquisizione e gli storici: un cantiere aperto*, Atti dei convegni Lincei, Rome, Accademia Nazionale dei Lincei, 2000, pp. 221–44, in particular p. 228.

[3] Cf. J. Bossy's classic essay, 'The Counter-Reformation and the People of Catholic Europe', *Past and Present*, XCVII, 1970, pp. 51–70; A. Biondi, 'Aspetti della cultura cattolica post-tridentina. Religione e controllo sociale', *Storia d'Italia*, Annali 4: Intellettuali e potere, Turin, Einaudi, 1981, pp. 255–302; A. Prosperi, *Tribunali della coscienza. Inquisitori, confessori e missionari*, Turin, Einaudi, 1996, in particular the third part of the volume, pp. 551 et seqq.

[4] 'faccino comprare a quelli che sanno leggere, et hanno il modo alcuni libri spirituali, et devoti' (AEM, *Acta Ecclesiae Mediolanensis*, II, col. 1893; cf. C. Dì Filippo Bareggi, 'Libri e letture', p. 78).

[5] AEM, II, coll. 1893, cited by C. Di Filippo Bareggi, 'Libri e letture,' pp. 78–9. On the work of the Capuchin Mattia Bellintani da Salò, cf. D. Zardin, 'Mercato librario e letture devote nella svolta del Cinquecento tridentino. Note in margine ad un inventario milanese di libri di monache', N. Raponi and A. Turchini (eds), *Stampa, libri e letture a Milano*, footnote 16, pp. 157–8; and especially R. Cuvato, *Mattia Bellintani da Salò (1534–1611). Un cappuccino tra il pulpito e la strada*, Rome, Edizioni Collegio S. Lorenzo da Brindisi, Laurentianum, 1999; but cf. also below, ch. 7.

[6] C. Di Filippo Bareggi, 'Libri e letture,' p. 89.

[7] '[e] perché Christo dice, che se due di voi converranno sopra la terra, otterrranno dal mio Padre celeste tutto quello che loro dimanderanno, perché dove sono due o tre congregati nel nome mio, io sono in mezzo di loro, però desideriamo, che tutti convenghino insieme a questa santa orazione, per esser più facilmente esauditi, e tanto più che il bisogno è a

However, the institution of an authentically choral moment of prayer did not diminish the value of individual prayer, which was presented as a valid alternative to ordinary prayer (family prayer, in this specific case):[8] 'If someone in the course of time [...] happens to be away from home, or is prevented for some other reason from being with the other members of his family [...] he may pray alone [...] wherever he is.'[9] The indication – among the devout texts recommended to the faithful – of Granada's works[10] was in any case more than just a formal recognition of the individual dimension of prayer. The Archbishop of Milan had in fact established – thanks to his numerous Jesuit collaborators – a close relationship with the Dominican Luis de Granada in a series of valuable cultural and religious exchanges: it is therefore no coincidence that many of Granada's works were to be found in Borromeo's personal library.[11] This testifies to the acceptance by

tutti comune (AEM, III, col. 459, cited by C. Di Filippo Bareggi, p. 89). Besides the choral dimension, Borromeo, in his *Libretto dei ricordi*, praised the concept of prayer – a concept that to the same degree reflected typically Counter-Reformation thinking – as an 'instrument' that marks out the day of the faithful: 'If you can read you will say the Office of Our Lady, at least on feast days [...]. When the Ave Maria is rung in the morning, at midday, and in the evening, you will say the Ave Maria three times on your bended knees, and also the three verses that are to be found in the daily exercise printed in the small Office of Our Lady [...]. In the evening, after dinner, [...] read, if you can read, something from a book that is good for the spirit, or the lives of the saints, or something else [...]. If you are traveling, get in the habit of saying [...] those short prayers that are called the Itinerario, printed in the Office of Our Lady [...]. Make them read at table some book that is good for the spirit, if you have among them one who can do so, either children, or someone else, during meals, at least for a short while' ('Sapendo leggere dirai l'ufficio della Madonna, almeno le feste [...]. Quando si suona l'Ave Maria la mattina, a mezzogiorno, e la sera, dirai tre volte l'Ave Maria a ginocchione, ed insieme quei tre versetti, quali sono posti nell'esercitio quotidiano stampato nell'officiolo della Madonna [...]. La sera dopo cena, [...] leggi, se sai leggere un poco di un libro spirituale, o vite dei santi, o altro [...]. Se fai viaggio, usa di dire [...] quelle brevi orazioni e preci, che si chiamano *l'Itinerario*, stampato neU'ufficiolo della Madonna [...]. Facci leggere qualche libro spirituale alla mensa, se hai chi lo faccia, o figliuoli, o altri, mentre si mangia, almeno per un pezzo'; ibid., col. 653–5, cited by C. Di Filippo Bareggi, p. 79).

8 On the central role that Borromeo believed the family played, cf. C. Di Filippo Bareggi, pp. 90–94.

9 'Se alcuno si trovarà nel tempo [...] fuor di casa, o in altro modo impedito da poter trovarsi con gli altri della fameglia [...] potrà farla da solo [...] in ogni luogo dove si trova' (AEM, col. 462, cited by C. Di filippo Bareggi, p. 89).

10 On Luis de Granada (1505–1588), cf. the recent biography by A. Huerga, *Fray Luis de Granada. Una vida al servicio de la Iglesia, Madrid*, B.A.C., 1988; for a selection of his works, see M. Llaneza (ed.), *Bibliografia del V.P.M. Fr. Luis de Granada de la Orden de Predicatores*, Salamanca, Calatrava, 1926–28.

11 C. Di Filippo Bareggi, 'Libri e letture', p. 75. On the relationship between Granada and Borromeo, cf. A. Huerga, 'Fray Luis de Granada y san Carlos Borromeo. Una amistad al servicio de la restauracion catolica', *Hispania sacra*, 11, 1958, pp. 299–347, and R. Robres Lluch, 'S. Carlos Borromeo y sus relaciones con el episcopado Iberico post-tridentino,

Counter-Reformation spirituality of subjects like the annulment of human will and man's entrustment to the will of God, which in Spain, on the contrary, were the reason for these works' being condemned;[12] it also provides confirmation of the Archbishop's familiarity with the subject of mental prayer.[13]

Reading a book published in those same years (1574, to be precise) by the orthodox Capuchin monk Silvestro da Rossano[14] gives us a testimony of the way the subject of mental prayer had by then become an integral part of this particular form of Counter-Reformation treatises. The title of this one was *Modo come la persona spirituale che ora, si habbia a disporre nella Oratione verso Iddio e li suoi Santi* ('The manner in which a spiritual person at prayer must address his prayers to God and His Saints').[15] The orthodox tone of this work is clear from the start:

---

especialmente a través de fray Luis de Granata y s. Juan de Ribera', in *Anthologia Annua*, VIII, 1960, pp. 83–141.

12 Granada not only considered the ultimate aim of devotional practices to be the achievement of the union of the soul with God and the transformation of man into God (*Pie et devote orationi, raccolte da diversi e gravi autori, per il R.P.F. Luigi di Granata, dell'ordine de' Predicatori. E novamente tradotte di spagnolo in italiano da un devoto Religioso*, Vinegia, apud Gio. and Gio. Paolo Gioliti de' Ferrari, MDLXXX, c. A6v), but also insisted repeatedly on the nullity of human beings and the process of expropriation of the human will as an obligatory point of passage on the way toward the ultimate destiny of the faithful believer: 'I am dust and ashes; I am nothing' (ibid., c. A7r), and continued thus: 'For your sake I abandon all malignancy and vanity; all delight and personal will, personal passion, and personal ill inclination' (ibid., c. A8r); and also, further on, referring to the infinite distance between human 'vileness' and divine 'supremacy' (ibid.. cc. A9v–A10r, cf. also ibid. c. A9r.). Besides these themes in Granada's works there were also clear references to God's salvific mercy and to the 'merits' of 'Christ's precious blood' (ibid., c. A5v). It is presumably this kind of mixture of mystic elements and others of Lutheran inspiration that contributed to the prohibition by the Inquisition authorities in Spain of his *De la oración y Guía de pecadores* and his *Manual de diversas oraciones*, in the context of an ever greater identification between alumbrado and Protestant movements (on the censorship of Granada's works, cf. *Index des livres interdits*, vol. V, pp. 482–4 and vol. VI, pp. 611–14).

13 C. Di Filippo Bareggi, p. 80. To this regard, the texts 'advised' by Bishop Borromeo included a collection of sermons by Ludovico Pittorio, one of which was an anonymous work, *Espositione sopra l'oratione domenicale in forma di meditatione* (R. Bottoni, 'Libri e lettura nelle confraternite milanesi del secondo Cinquecento', N. Raponi and A. Turchini (eds), *Stampa, libri e letture*, p. 261).

14 See G. Carlini, 'Silvestro Di Franco da Rossano Calabro (1530–1596), Vicario Provinciale in Toscana', *Fra Noi*, XIII, 1996, pp. 5–33. The figure of Silvestro da Rossano was the subject of a conference held at Rossano Calabro, 16–19 May 1996, entitled 'Padre Silvestro da Rossano (1530–1596). A Capuchin amid cloisters, pulpits and the roads of Italy', the proceedings of which have not been published. Regarding Silvestro and his singular experiences with the Inquisition at the turn of the century, see below chapter 8.

15 *Modo come la persona spirituale che ora, si habbia a disporre nella Oratione verso Iddio e li suoi Santi: per tutti li giorni della Settimana tanto la mattina come la sera detta Consonantia Spirituale. Composta da Fra Silvestro da Rossano Cappuccino, mentre*

> We must go our way, and abound in the perfection of works [...]; we must exercise ourselves in the spiritual practices of Christian life, [...] although exercising ourselves every day in holy prayer has always been laudable among the spirituals and saints, and has been useful to the soul, it is also necessary for the salvation of all, and the Holy Roman Church has always upheld this exercise and taught it.[16]

In the course of the work the author analyzes at great length the 'reasons that induce us to pray [...] frequently, eagerly, and fervently'[17] as well as the 'effects of prayer',[18] always keeping strictly within the bounds of Catholic orthodoxy. However, it is Silvestro da Rossano's definition of 'correct prayer' (*orazione giusta*) that made him a paragon of Catholic orthodoxy, as it is the quintessence of the qualities of the perfect Catholic, a definition in which each element, on the basis of a typically Counter-Reformation concept of 'order' that was in the process of being consolidated, possesses its corresponding inevitable and immutable destiny:

> [correct prayer is that] which gives to everyone what is most fitting: in other words, to God, honor; to the saints, imitation; to the world, scorn; to demons, resistance; to the flesh, afflictions; to superiors, obedience; to equals, peace; to inferiors, good examples; to the poor, help; to friends, perseverance in friendship; and to enemies, forgiveness; and therefore when people pray in this manner, they pray correctly.[19]

---

predicava a San Salvatore di Venetia, nell'anno MDLXXII. Divisa in due parti, nella prima si tratta di quelle cose che sono necessarie da sapere, e nella seconda il modo che si ha da tenere. With privilege, in Vinegia apud Gabriel Giolito de' Ferrari, MDLXXIIII.

16 'Dobbiamo camminare, et abondare nella perfettione delle opere [...] dobbiamo essercitarsi nelli spirituali essercitii della vita Christiana, [...] nondimeno essercitarsi ogni dì alla santa oratione, sempre è stata cosa lodevole appresso gli spirituali, et santi, ha portato utile all'anime, oltre ch'egli è necessario per la salute di tutti, et la Santa Romana Chiesa sempre ha tenuto, et insegnato tale essercitio' (ibid., cc. A4r–v).

17 'ragioni che ci inducono all'oratione [...] frequente sollecita et fervente' (ibid., c. 13). The reasons include 'exemplariness', 'gratitude', and 'the need to remain in a state of grace', but it is also stated 'we are obliged by legal requirements to observe this, and also because God commands us to pray by every law' (ibid., c. 21).

18 Ibid., c. 59. Prayer has three effects, according to the author: that of 'meriting eternal life, an effect that is common to all good works done out of a sense of charity and active faith' (ibid., c. 59), that of 'impetrating that which we ask of our God in all His goodness' (ibid., c. 60), and that of 'a certain sweetness of the mind' (ibid., c. 60).

19 '[l'orazione giusta è quella] che dà a ciascheduno quello, che ti conviene; come a dire a Dio honore, ai santi imitatione, al mondo disprezzo, ai demonii resistenza, alla carne afflittioni, ai superiori obedienza; a gli eguali, pace, a gl'inferiori buoni essempii, ai poveri aiuto, a gli amici perseveranza nell'amicitia, et a gli inimici perdono, et però quando la persona ora in tal modo, ora giustamente' (ibid., c. 84).

It is therefore in this context that we find mental prayer being accepted by the author as one of the many possible forms of prayer; after sacramental prayer, laudatory prayer, and vocal prayer, here is Silvestro da Rossano's description of mental prayer: 'It consists of holy meditations and holy contemplations with acts of cognition by which we come to know God and our own soul.'[20] However, a distinction he had made shortly before had the effect of spoiling – to the great benefit of mental prayer – the egalitarianism that was implicit in this bureaucratic list of types of prayer. For when Silvestro da Rossano was examining the differences between outward and inward worship, he implicitly admitted that only prayer in which 'one seeks to elevate the mind' can be called 'true' prayer:

> Outward worship consists first of the ceremonies of the Church, and of religion; and second, of the reverences and the devout postures of the body that are performed before images and figures in the name of God, Jesus, the Holy Virgin Mary, and all the Saints according to what the places and times require, while inward worship means applying our intellect to know God, our will to love Him, and our memory to recall Him so that we may be grateful to him, and *'because that kind of outward worship can be performed without prayer, while inward prayer can never be performed without prayer because the intention is to elevate the mind, and we are all obliged to perform this worship.*[21]

However, the subject of mental prayer was not the only one to be brought back within the confines of correct Catholic faith. For example, Silvestro da Rossano adapted to the new Tridentine 'canons' certain concepts that belonged to the great bulk of mystic literature, using a demonstrably orthodox form of language; he did not therefore speak of union of the soul with God[22] but of concordance: 'The soul achieves concordance with the

---

20 '[Essa] consiste nelle sante meditationi, et sante contemplationi con li atti conoscitivi dove si conosce Iddio, et la propria anima nostra' (ibid., c. 45).

21 'L'esteriore culto consiste prima nelle cerimonie della Chiesa, et della religione: secondo nelle riverenze, et dispositioni del corpo divote, che si portano al nome d'Iddio, di Giesù, di Santa Maria Vergine, et di tutti i Santi all'immagini, et figure; secondo, che richiedono i luochi, et tempi, ma il culto interiore, consiste in applicare lo intelletto a conoscere Iddio, la voluntà in amarlo, la memoria in ricordarsi di lui per essergli grati, *et perché quel culto esteriore alquanto si può fare senza oratione, ma il culto interiore non si può fare mai senza oratione, perché si ricerca l'elevatione della mente, et a questo culto siamo tutti obligati*' (ibid., cc. 16–17; my emphasis).

22 On the occasions when he did in fact use this expression, it was always accompanied by typically orthodox concepts, as for example in the description of 'sacramental prayer', which 'consists in holy confessions and communions, for which reason it is called true prayer, in which the soul and the body are united with Christ his Lord' (ibid., c. 44).

Lord its Master by contemplation;'[23] he did not speak of the annulment of human will but of conformation: 'True righteousness [...] [consists] in conforming our will to that of God';[24] and when he spoke of 'peace of mind' he simply meant the tranquility and attention of someone engaged in prayer: 'Attention is no more than the firm and tenacious peace of mind and tranquility of a person engaged in prayer who directs all his attention to such prayer,'[25] and 'man can achieve peace of mind through association with holy matters'.[26]

Silvestro da Rossano reconsidered in his book all the harsh criticisms – pronounced by heterodox thinkers – of forms of devotion defined as 'sensitive',[27] 'curious',[28] 'superstitious',[29] and 'vainglorious',[30] and he warned the faithful that 'devotion is easily lost because of the desperation caused by the practices and offices and by the many different activities'.[31] However, as he did so, he declared that there was only one possible remedy i.e. the 'most Catholic' practice of 'holy confession, and communion': 'There is no better way than holy confession and communion, and holy silence, not speaking too readily of the things of this world, and above all of things that have no purpuse.'[32] As one reaches the final pages of the treatise, it is, therefore, hardly a surprise to discover in the text a citation of the same passage from the Bible which around the middle of the century

---

23 'Si concorda contemplando, l'anima con Iddio Signore suo' (ibid., c. A5r).

24 'La vera giustitia [...] [consiste] in conformare la volontà nostra con quella di Dio' (ibid.).

25 'L'attentione non è altro se non una ferma, et tenace quiete della mente, et tranquillità di quello che ora, il quale attende al fine di essa oratione' (ibid., c. 59).

26 'con le sante frequentationi potrà l'huomo acquistare la quiete della mente' (ibid., c. 62).

27 'Such devotion may be sensitive, as commonly happens with many people when they hear organs play, or hymns, psalms, or other spiritual music being sung; and although these things are necessary – and anyone denying it is a heretic – nevertheless, as St Augustine tells us, sensitive devotion alone is a very dangerous passion' (ibid., 55).

28 'Such devotion may be due to curiosity, as happens when a person seeks intrinsically to learn God's secrets in order to be able to speak of them, that is to say, without true need' (ibid., cc. 55–6).

29 'Devotion may also be superstitious, as for example when people pray more in one place than in another, at one time more than another, or most of all in one way more than in another' (ibid., c. 56).

30 'Devotion may also be vainglorious, as for example when for reasons of vanity a person possesses booklets, rosaries, and little crucifixes decorated with silk ribbons, and other such things, mostly among women; for verily adornment with objects must be done only for the honor and glory of God, and not otherwise' (ibid., c. 56).

31 'la divotione si perde facilmente per la disperatione de gli essercitii, et officii, et per li molti et varii negotii' (ibid., c. 56). The author's appeal continued with an exhortation to the reader to make sure 'that the exercises do not occupy him so much that he loses the great store of devotion in which the soul possesses God' (ibid.).

32 Ibid., c. 57

had become a symbol of Nicodemite practices,[33] but which here fits perfectly, and with added value, into an orthodox context. Regarding the question of what was the most suitable place for the faithful to say their prayers, Silvestro da Rossano without a moment's hesitation declared that 'the place of prayer, universally, is the Church'.[34] However, immediately after this, introducing a dichotomy between public and private practice that later on, at the end of the century, enjoyed considerable popularity in matters concerning the rules and precepts of Catholic morality,[35] he provided a most solemn legitimization for private and inward devotion:

> There are other special places *in houses*, where people find it convenient to perform their devotions; and so they adorn these rooms with the most devout of ornamentations [...]. But, speaking of the place most suited for spiritual prayer, I say that this place is *the heart, and our own will*, and also that holy places, decorated churches, and secret oratories are of little avail when the heart is full of vanity, and does not pray with diligence. Hence Our Savior Jesus Christ spoke rightly when He said that when you wish to pray, enter your secret chamber, lock the door, and there pray to your Father. The secret room is our heart, where God secretly dwells: the locked door is our appetite, which must be locked to all passion and the evils of the senses. This is the place to pray to God.[36]

---

33 Cf. above, ch. 2.

34 Ibid., c. 76. 'In particular', the author continued, 'it should be borne in mind that some churches possess holy relics, devout images, and in particular the most holy sacrament of the Eucharist, and in such places people pray with great devotional affection' (ibid.).

35 See below, ch. 9.

36 A]ltri luoghi sono particolari *nelle case,* dove le persone hanno commodità di farle; et così adornano quelle stanze con divotissimi adornamenti [...]. Ma parlando del luogo spirituale dell'oratione, dico, che è *il cuore, et la volontà nostra,* che poco ne gioveranno i luoghi santi, et le Chiese adornate, gli oratorii secreti, come il cuore è pieno di vanità, et non ora con diligenza. La onde bene disse il Salvatore nostro Christo Giesù, quando tu vuoi orare, entra nella tua camera secreta, et serrato l'uscio, ora là tuo padre. La camera secreta è il nostro cuore, nel quale secretamente habita Iddio: l'uscio serrato è il nostro appetito, il quale deve essere serrato ad ogni passione, et sensualità maligna. Questo è il luoco, dove si ora Iddio' (*Modo di orare*, cc. 76–7; my emphasis).

CHAPTER 7

Censorship and Self-Censorship in the 1580s

The process of re-incorporating mental prayer as an integral aspect of worship in the Counter-Reformation Church proved to be all the more delicate and difficult, the more necessary it became to continue to maintain an elevated level of vigilance in the censorship of the various doctrinal positions that the theme of prayer had adopted over this period of time. These consisted, on the one hand, of heterodox forms that had by then become familiar and which continued to proliferate and, on the other, of forms of heterodoxy other than Lutheran-Calvinistic forms that were time-honored in their theological and religious origins but quite new in the eyes of the Inquisitors and censors in Rome, whose attention had hitherto been 'distracted' by the danger of Protestantism. Although not representing an insurmountable obstacle along the path of the newly discovered devotional inwardness, this varyingly heterodox dress in which 'prayer' clothed itself in the course of the second half of the sixteenth century was, however, destined to have a negative affect on the pastoral and pedagogic activity of the church hierarchies and above all on the purifying action of prayer, in which large sectors of the Roman Curia had invested so much of their energy and hopes ever since the 1560s and 1570s.

The year 1560 saw the publication *apud* Giovan Battista Pinerolo of *La forma de le orationi ecclesiastiche e il modo d'amministrare i Sacramenti, e di celebrare il santo Matrimonio, secondo che s'usa ne le buone Chiese* ('The form of Church devotions and the manner of administering the Sacraments and celebrating Holy Matrimony, as practiced in good Churches'). Scarcely a year after the prohibition of *La Forma delle preghiere ecclesiastiche*[1] (an anonymous publication in which it is possible to discern, even at first reading, the hand of John Calvin), this work, almost as if to provoke the manifest severity of the Index desired by Paul IV, was, therefore, once again available on the book market thanks to a simple and almost imperceptible change of title. Far from being an orthodox instrument for teaching Catholic truths, as it was presented to the eyes of the more ingenuous and uninformed readers, this work contained some of the most lucid theoretical discussions of justification by faith alone:

1 *Index des livres interdits*, vol. VIII, pp. 472–3.

> Lord God, Everlasting and Almighty Father, – the first pages of the text immediately proclaimed – we confess and sincerely recognize [...] that we are miserable sinners conceived and born in iniquity and corruption, prone to commit evil acts, and incapable of good deeds and we confess that because of our vices we never cease to transgress your holy commandments. And by so doing, so we merit ruin and perdition by your right and proper judgment. Nonetheless, O Lord, we rue having offended you, and we condemn ourselves and our sins with true repentance, desiring that your grace may assist us in our misery and misfortune.[2]

The church hierarchies thus soon learned how to recognize some of the most fearful and insidious vehicles of doctrinal heterodoxy lurking behind the reassuring façade of apparently orthodox titles.

This stratagem of using a pseudo-orthodox frontispiece was tried out again by some imaginative crypto-Lutheran editors, causing considerable anxiety among the sentinels of Catholic orthodoxy. Mockingly exploiting the great editorial success of the Tridentine *Catechismo*, which had been continuously reprinted since the early 1560s,[3] a faithful transposition of all book 15 (1–43) of Calvin's *Institutio* was published in 1580, bearing the 'most Catholic' title *Il piovano, cioè sedici sermoni composti da Messer Vittor de Popoli di san Germano sopra 'l Catechismo Romano* ('The Parish, that is, sixteen sermons composed by Messer Vittor de Popoli of San Germano on the Roman Catechism').[4] In an edition of impeccable form – one need only take a rapid glance at the 'order of sermons contained in this book', which faithfully reproduced the index of the contents of the

---

[2] 'Signore Iddio, Padre eterno e onnipotente, noi confessiamo e riconosciamo sinceramente [...] che noi siamo miseri peccatori, conceputi e nati in iniquità e corruttione, inclinati a mal fare, e inutili ad ogni bene, e che per nostro vitio non cessiamo già mai di trasgredire i tuoi santi comandamenti. Il che facendo, ci acquistiamo per tuo giusto giuditio mina e perditione. Nondimeno Signore, noi habbiam dispiacere in noi stessi d'haverti offeso, e condanniamo noi e i nostri peccati con vero pentimento, desiderando che la tua gratia sovvenga a la nostra miseria e calamità' (*La Forma de le orationi ecclesiastiche e il modo d'amministrare i Sacramenti, e di celebrare il santo Matrimonio, secondo che s' usa ne le buone Chiese*. Stampato da Giovanni Battista Pinerolo, 1560, c. A2r–v).

[3] The last part of the Tridentine catechism was entirely devoted to the subject of prayer: *Catechismus, ex decreto Concilii Tridentini, ad parochos, Pii Quinti Pont. Max. iussu editus*, Romae, In aedibus Populi Romani, apud Paulum Manutium, 1566, pp. 292–359; on the Roman catechism, cf. the recent research of M. Catto, *Un panopticon catechistico: l'arciconfraternita della dottrina cristiana a Roma in età moderna*, Rome, Edizioni di Storia e Letteratura, 2003.

[4] T. Bozza, 'Italia calvinista. Il Piovano di messer Vittor de' Popoli', *L'uomo e la storia. Studi storici in onore di Massimo Petrocchi*, vol. I, Rome, Edizioni di Storia e Letteratura, 1983, pp. 267–98; in particular, the transposition of Calvin's Book 15 corresponded to the five 'Sermoni sopra l'Invocatione' (cc. 452–408) in *Piovano*.

Tridentine catechism ('5 Sermons on the Symbol of the Apostles, 5 on the Ten Commandments of the Law, 6 on the Lord's Prayer') – the Genevan printers had put together a product capable of aspiring to circulate on the Italian editorial market, avoiding the tight web of church censorship. The frequent and alarmed exchange of letters between the members of the Congregation of the Index and the local inquisitors regarding the work's dangerous nature is an indication both of the partial success achieved by this refined editorial venture and of the church hierarchics' newly acquired awareness that an act of censorship could no longer stop at mere appearances: in the face of material presenting an ever-higher level of perfection, it was necessary to react with scrupulous attention, carefully checking the contents of every work in circulation and therefore not limiting the examination to a mere perusal of the frontispiece.[5] The work was soon condemned and duly included in successive Indexes of prohibited books;[6] however, the ghost of a treatise on the Lord's Prayer – with which prayer the heterodox salvific message that '[God] *ab eterno* had predestined them to be Sons of Jesus Christ, as He so willed', had erroneously been associated[7] – was in the years to come destined to influence the attitude of the Roman Inquisitors and censors.

As already said, in addition to the more recent manifestations of Lutheran and Calvinist heresy, other forms of doctrinal heterodoxy appeared to be menacing the subject of prayer.

A renewed sensitivity now made it possible to appreciate shades of doctrinal meaning that previously were difficult to detect. In the course of the 1580s the church hierarchy resumed its gentle Inquisitorial action, interrupted in the 1530s, against degenerative forms of a tradition – a mystic and unitive tradition – whose roots in Italy were far off and long gone. This consisted of a series of acts of censorship which, though far

---

5 On 25 July 1603, in a letter to the Modena Inquisitor, Cardinal Tagliavia referred to Piovano's 'feigned, false frontispieces' and undertook to 'issue instructions that those involved in admitting new and foreign books should not consider only the frontispiece, although the title, the author, the place of printing, and the licence suggest it is a Catholic book, but instead they should diligently examine and consider the doctrine contained in the book before permission is given for it to circulate' ('dar ordine che li deputati in admetter libri novi e forestieri non riguardino al solo frontispitio, con tutto che per il titolo autor luogo stampator e licenza apparisca il libro catholico, ma con diligenza sia revista et essaminata la dottrina che contiene il libro prima che sia permesso e divulgato;' cf. A. Rotondò, 'Nuovi documenti per la storia dell'Indice dei libri proibiti (1572–1638)', *Rinascimento*, 2nd s., 3, 1963, pp. 145–211, in particular p. 177; the same recommendation is also directed to the Bologna Inquisitor in a letter sent the same day, cf. ibid., p. 178).

6 The work appeared for the first time in the Sixtine Index and subsequently in the Sixto-Clementine Index of 1593. cf. *Index des livres interdits*, vol. IX, p. 362.

7 '[Dio] ab eterno gli ha predestinati ad essergli figliuoli per Giesù Christo secondo il beneplacito della sua volontà' (*Il Piovano, cioè sedici sermoni*, c. 295).

from manifesting any organic or methodically planned unity, were clear enough to define the features of an offensive that repeatedly touched on the theme of prayer and helped to define its orthodox character (i.e. orthodox from the Catholic point of view).

Let us start by considering a singular case of self-censorship, singular because it concerns a religious personality of the day, a Capuchin friar called Mattia Bellintani da Salò,[8] and a devotional work of his, *Prattica dell'orazione mentale*[9] ('Practice of mental prayer') which has often been described as a model of Counter-Reformation devotional literature. In 1573 Carlo Borromeo asked Bellintani to write an ascetic treatise on the subject of prayer, with the intention of codifying once and for all the exercise he had practiced during his apostolate, an exercise that was now widespread and much liked;[10] it had also been Borromeo who determined its great editorial success in the years immediately following, possibly even more successfully than the orthodox treatise of that other member of his confraternity, Silvano da Rossano.

Bellintani's ascetic masterpiece combined a contemplative dimension (inward teaching) and the aspect of evangelic preaching, 'practices', method, and written rules (outward teaching).[11] His intention was to provide a guide for the concrete exercise of mental prayer: after an introduction dealing with the theoretical utility of meditation, and after some indications of a general nature regarding the concrete aspects of the practice of meditation, he presented 52 meditations or 'practices' (a number destined to increase in subsequent editions)[12] organized around the mysteries of the life of Christ – from the Incarnation to the Passion

---

8 See the recent biography by R. Cuvato, *Mattia Bellintani da Salò (1534–1611)*.

9 Mattia Bellintani da Salò, *Prattica dell'orazione mentale di fra Mathia Bellintani da Salò dell'Ordine dei Frati di S. Francesco Capuccini. Parte prima: Di nuovo dallo stesso autore riveduta, corretta, ed in alcune parti ridotta a miglior forma. Parte seconda: Nuovamente posta in luce*, Venice, apud Pietro Dusinello, 1584, critical edition by Father Umile da Genova, O.M.C. (Order of Capuchin Minors), Assisi, Collegio S. Lorenzo da Brindisi dei Minori Cap., 1931 (henceforward edition of 1584). However, see also the first edition of 1573, edited for the first time only recently (cf. below, footnote 14).

10 Introduction by Father Umile to the 1584 edition, p. XII.

11 'The teaching imparted by the Holy Spirit is of two sorts, for it teaches us inwardly in secret manner and outwardly in manifest style. Inward teaching is the concealed descent of the Holy Spirit into the soul, prompting it to pray. This is the demand that the spirit asks of us with ineffable weeping, of which St Paul spoke. Outward teaching concerns the precepts and orders that we receive from sacred writings and from holy men who, enlightened by God and experienced in such matters owing to their long practice they have had in prayer, have been able to give us this singular doctrine [...] because the Holy Spirit, despite being the first operator in all our good works, nonetheless seeks man's cooperation' (*Prattica*, edn 1584, p. 35; R. Cuvato, *Mattia Bellintani da Salò*, p. 112).

12 R. Cuvato, *Mattia Bellintani da Salò*, p. 109.

– each of which was composed of three elements destined to guide the faithful along their spiritual path: '*Preambolo*, *Meditazione*, e *Azione*' ('Preamble, Meditation, and Action'). The author explained, illustrating the importance of the three moments:

> As man has to pray, he must first prepare his soul and make himself ready for the acts that has to perform, and for the receiving of grace, which God desires to give him, in order to help him to perform his deeds. Having completed his preparation for the preamble, he must begin to meditate mentally on some holy mystery [of the faith] which serves as fuel to light the fire of our will. Thus, when through meditation the will has caught fire, it breaks out into its own acts, and this is where the power of prayer lies; and these are placed in the third part called action.[13]

The contemplative dimension was therefore tempered by being solidly anchored to the daily needs of prayer of the faithful, steering clear of any uncontrolled mystic outbursts. Yet when in 1584 he prepared to reprint his *Prattica* with the addition of a third and fourth part, Bellintani must have perceived that the contemporary atmosphere was different from that of only ten years before, at the time of the work's first edition. In the absence of any further relative documentation, it is hard to say whether the 'rewriting' of the eight introductory chapters of his work was dictated by a voluntary act of self-censorship or whether, as a Capuchin friar, he was possibly subjected to pressure from within his Order. What is certain is that if we compare the text of the first edition of 1573[14] with that of the

[13] 'Dovendo l'uomo pregare ha prima da preparare l'animo suo, e disporsi agli atti che deve compiere, e al ricevimento della grazia, che Iddio gli vuole dare, per aiutarlo a far tali atti. Fatta la preparazione per il preambolo, si entra a meditare qualche mistero santo con l'intelletto, il quale ci serva per esca onde accendere il fuoco nella volontà. Pertanto, quando per la meditazione la volontà si è infiammata, prorompe negli atti suoi, nei quali sta la forza dell'orazione; e questi si pongono nella terza parte chiamata azione' (*Prattica*, edn 1584, pp. 44–5; R. Cuvato, *Mattia Bellintani*, p. 109). Bellintani displayed particular sensitivity in his firm intention to relate the effort required to the believer's actual capacities and spiritual 'potential', when he made the following distinction according to the conventional subdivision: 'For beginners the movements of fear are better suited [...] than the desire to improve the ways of their lives. For the proficient the best suited are the movements of hope and of the desire to do as much good as possible [...]: For the perfect the most suitable is the movement of love and of the desire to love more'. (*Prattica*, edn 1584, pp. 51–2; R. Cuvato, *Mattia Bellintani*, p. 110).

[14] *Prattica dell'oratione mentale, di f. Mathia Bellintani da Salò, dell'Ordine de' frati di S. Francesco Capuccini. Opera molto utile per quelle divote persone, che desiderano occuparsi nell'oratione con frutto e gusto* ('Practice of mental prayer, by Brother Mathia Bellintani da Salò, of the Order of the Capuchin Friars. A very useful activity for the devout who wish to practice prayer with benefit and zest'). Con privilegio dell'Illustrissimo Senato di Milano per anni dieci. In Brescia, appresso Vincenzo Sabbio, 1573, in *I Frati Cappuccini.*

successive edition of 1584,[15] we can no longer interpret Bellintani's allusive words at the beginning of his work of 'rewriting' as a simple rhetorical introductory formula:

> I let the first edition slip hastily out of my hands, – he wrote in 1584 – without keeping it long enough to reconsider it with greater care when the first fervor of creative invention had died down, and consequently it was with considerable sorrow that when I glanced at it again for the first time since I wrote it, I realized that in this addition I would have to cut something out of the introductory part; therefore let no one who finds this book again be surprised to see that it is in some way different from before.[16]

All this was very likely an embarrassed attempt to mask the way the text had been adjusted to suit the religious and cultural climate of those later years,[17] in an adaptation that necessarily presented intentional omissions and small but significant textual additions. The first fundamental observation that arises from a comparative reading of the two editions is that all the alterations tend toward a reinforcement of the element of the affirmation of man's will. By eliminating words that were inappropriate or might be misunderstood or, on the contrary, by adding expressions that clarified the meaning of his statements, the author's intention throughout was to re-establish the central role of man's free will. Bellintani's alterations ranged from substantial modifications to minor adjustments. As he self-critically reread the introductory pages of his *Prattica*, this Capuchin friar must have realized that his overwhelming love and his uncontrolled passion for the act of prayer had drawn him away from what might be termed the spirit of the age. He had written in 1573:

> And these should know, from the teaching of St Bernard and the experience of holy men, that the excessive neglect of prayer, in order to perform acts of charity, is a desire that goes beyond God's command to love one's neighbor more that oneself; *and whoever gives himself up too much to outward actions, however good they may be, suffers so many impurities of the spirit that a thousand disorderly passions enter therein, and though he may think that he*

Documenti e testimonianze del primo secolo, C. Cagnoni (ed.), III/l, Letteratura spirituale ascetico-mistica (1535–1628), Perugia, EFI Edizioni Frate Indovino, 1991, pp. 665–736 (henceforward edn 1573).

15 For the full title, cf. above.

16 Proemio, edn 1584.

17 For other considerations regarding the widespread anti-mystic sensitivity of the early 1580s, cf. below.

acts out of charity, he acts for the eyes of others, forfeits the fruit of his deeds, and in some cases commits a sin.[18]

To state that whoever charitably devotes himself to 'good outward actions' may be committing a sin and be liable to impurity of spirit was evidently a rash thing to do, even though it concerned a faithful believer culpably neglecting the activity of prayer. Thus, ten years later, Bellintani took the opportunity to adjust his sights, reversing the meaning of his previous statement; still referring to the position of those who claim that 'they have no time for prayer', he wrote:

> This sometimes happens because people are driven to it by the Devil, who when unable to do aught else distracts us from prayer by setting good deeds before us, so that, having put away the spirit of prayer, we also put away good works and perform evil ones instead.[19]

This possibly involuntary devaluation of good works required corrective action, and Bellintani must have thought that the devaluation of man's free will which appeared elsewhere in his book was equally in need of correction. When dealing with the subject entitled *L'orazione è la via più breve per acquistar le virtù* ('Prayer is the quickest way to gain virtues') and commenting on the line in the Lord's Prayer 'Thy Kingdom come', in an impetuous outburst of exultation of divine power and glory, he had written:

> There are two ways of achieving common virtues: one is our own practice of virtuous acts [...] the other is to beseech them from God in the same moment as the prayer and this precisely is his Kingdom, which we pray may come to us when we say, 'Thy Kingdom come', because God then reigns in us in singular manner, *when our soul is humbly subject to His rule, and it does not move unless it is moved by the Holy Spirit;*[20]

---

18 'E questi dovrebbero sapere, secondo la dottrina di san Bernardo e la isperienza di santi uomini, che il lasciare così notabilmente la orazione, per fare opere di carità, è un volere oltra il precetto divino amare più il prossimo che se stesso; e *chi si dà tanto in preda alle opere esteriori, quantunque buone, contrae tanta impurità di animo che vi entrano mille passioni disordinate, e pensandosi di operare per carità, opera per umani sguardi e perde il frutto e qualche volta pecca*' (edn 1573, p. 687).

19 'Cosa che talvolta si fa per istigazione del demonio; il quale quando non possa con altro, ci svia dall'orazione ponendoci innanzi l'opere pie, acciò, lasciato lo spirito dell'orazione, lasciamo anche l'opere buone e prendiamo l'empie' (*Prattica*, edn 1584, p. 33).

20 'Due sono i mezzi d'acquistar le virtù in commune: uno è il nostro proprio essercizio che facciamo negli atti virtuosi [...] l'altro è l'addimandarle a Dio istantissimamente nella orazione e questo apunto è il regno suo, il quale preghiamo che venga in noi, dicendo: "Venga il regno tuo", perché allora con modo singolare Iddio regna in noi, *quando l'anima nostra sta*

and a little further on, confirming this interpretation, he uses the following words to comment on the successive verse in the Lord's Prayer, 'Thy will be done':

> For this reason Christ taught us to say when we pray to our Heavenly Father: 'Thy will be done in Heaven as on Earth'; because if here on earth we do as God wills, it means that we are observing His holy precepts and His counsel, and this observance consists of virtuous acts, *because there is no act of virtue that is not ordered or counseled by God.*[21]

The rewriting was bound to include a redefinition of these ambiguous statements, eliminating anything that might mislead an ingenuous reader into forming a Lutheran vision of man's way to salvation. Restoring the right doctrinal weight and the correct theological value to the 'consent and participation of our will', he provides us in the new version with his comment on these two verses of the Lord's Prayer:

> Therefore it is necessary not only to beg God to give the garb of virtue, which makes the soul willing to be moved by the Holy Spirit [referring to the invocation 'Thy Kingdom come'] but also the act itself of virtue, which is the movement of God *with the consent and participation of our will* [referring to the invocation: 'Thy will be done'].[22]

Likewise, in the same paragraph, certain ambiguous expressions are omitted, such as one proclaiming that 'we perform acts of virtue badly if in prayer we do not beforehand obtain this grace from God',[23] and incautious declarations such as 'if virtues are God's gifts and *if our strength is feeble*'.[24] He had to repeat the operation a few pages further on, where he had used terms which, though not infringing strict orthodoxy,

---

umilmente soletta al suo imperio, e non si muove se non tanto quanto è mossa dallo Spirito Santo' (edn 1573, p. 676; my emphasis).

21 'Per questo ne insegnò Cristo a dire, pregando il Padre nostro celeste: "Sia fatta la volontà tua qui in terra come si fa in Cielo;" perché il farsi da noi qui in terra la volontà d'Iddio altro non è che osservare i suoi santi precetti e consigli, e questa osservanza consiste negli atti virtuosi, *perché non è atto di virtù alcuno che non ci sia da Dio o commandato o consigliato*' (edn 1573, p. 677; my emphasis).

22 'Però non solo s'ha da chieder a Dio l'abito della virtù, che renda l'anima facile a lasciarsi muovere dallo Spirito santo [il riferimento è all'invocazione "Venga il regno tuo"], ma ancora l'atto stesso della virtù, che è il movimento di Dio *col consentimento e concorso della volontà nostra* [il riferimento è all'invocazione "Sia fatta la tua volontà"]' (ibid.).

23 'malamente ci essercitiamo negli atti virtuosi, se nella orazione non otteniamo prima tal grazia da Dio' (ed. 1573, pp. 676–7).

24 'se le virtù sono doni d'Iddio e *se le nostre forze sono deboli*' (edn 1573, p. 680).

he thought wise to eliminate: although the Council of Trent had recently solemnly reaffirmed the theological validity of the dogma of cooperating grace (the cooperation of human works and divine grace for the purpose of eternal salvation), the memory of not so remote anti-Lutheran battles evidently engendered the doubt that statements such as 'so that man might know that his labors were in vain without the hand of God',[25] or 'as for us, we fall into every evil if God does not sustain us',[26] might persuade a pious reader to trust exclusively in the help of God for his salvation.

The same type of action was applied in some small adjustments that Bellintani made when he inserted into the text certain short expressions in order to clarify the meaning of a sentence, eliminating every last possibility of doubt regarding the orthodoxy of his work. The following example may suffice: 'And you could little by little reach the point where you would be ready to suffer hell itself, *with regard to the punishment alone*, if that were possible and God so willed',[27] where the addition of 'with regard to the punishment alone' (*quanto alla pena solo*) was intended to set a precise and insurmountable barrier that the unitive impulse and the desire to annul the human will could never overcome. In other cases, the purpose of an almost imperceptible addition was to stress more vigorously what had been said eleven years before; for example, one may note that in 1573, when introducing the subject of 'the affective part we have called *action*' (*parte affettiva che abbiamo chiamato azione*), Mattia da Salò had illustrated the relationship of dependence that links the 'act' to meditation using the following words:

> Meditation produces many results: the first result [i.e., affections] is to light up the spirit either to love or to desire, or to hope or to cause it to fear, and so on. The second result [i.e., acts] is to produce the operations generated by the affections of love, hope, desire, and fear.[28]

There was nothing deceptive about these statements; the ascetic and mystic pathway traced out by Bellintani proceeded along lines drawn by the most orthodox contemplative tradition: it was meditation, as the

---

[25] 'accioché conoscesse l'uomo che le sue fatiche sarebbero vane senza la mano d'Iddio' (edn 1573, pp. 682–3).

[26] 'quanto sia per noi, caschiamo in ogni male, se Iddio non ci sostiene' (edn 1573, p. 684).

[27] 'e potresti a poco a poco venire a tanto che ti troveresti pronto anche a patire l'inferno, *quanto alla pena solo,* se ciò fosse possibile e a Dio piacesse' (ibid.)

[28] 'Dal meditare si cavano più sorti de' frutti: il primo [gli affetti] è di accendere l'animo o all'amore, o al desiderio, o a speranza, o farlo temere, e simili. Il secondo [gli atti] è di farlo uscire alle operazioni nascenti da quelli affetti di amore, di speranza, di desiderio, di timore' (edn 1573, p. 702).

Capuchin friar pointed out, that warmed man's heart and guided him in the 'action' that was born of this warmth and love.

Nonetheless, in the adjusted edition of 1584, two significant additions altered the original import of the text. These were two expressions which – once again – were intended to highlight the role performed in this course by the human will: for it is the human will, Bellintani now specified, that was the prime motor of love from which all our 'acts' draw their origin; meditation is an 'irrigating source' (*fonte irrigatrice*) that cannot be renounced but, without the act of will on which love is based, man's action would lose all meaning:

> 'When *our will* has been irrigated by holy meditation, it produces in itself, with the strength of the Holy Spirit, two very useful and sweet effects. These are affections and acts. The affections are: love [...]. The word love implies first of all a burning desire to be joined to what we love [...]. It also implies *an act of will* with which we freely love someone, just as the soul, which loves God, cherishes him, in other words desires and is pleased that he should have that divine good which is the infinite ocean of all perfection'; or, to put it differently, 'All acts are born of love, for the first action that our will performs is love.'[29]

'Mattia's thinking', as his most recent biographer tells us, providing an efficacious interpretation of certain doctrinal contradictions present in his work, 'though inherited from the theology of St Augustine, to which he was indebted, was formed from the point of view of his vocation by the thinking of St Francis and by that of Bonaventura [...] and appears sometimes to waver between a form of anthropology in which the human being seems in all cases inadequate and therefore incompatible with the diversity of God, and an anthropology that lucidly proclaims the dignity of a human being made in the image and likeness of God and therefore

---

[29] 'Irrigata *la nostra volontà* dalla sacra meditazione, produce in se medesima, col vigore dello Spirito Santo, due effetti molto utili e dolci. Questi sono gli affetti e gli atti. Gli affetti sono: l'amore [...] Il nome di amore importa prima un desiderio ardente di unirci con la cosa che amiamo [...] Importa poi *un atto di volontà*, col quale liberamente vogliamo bene a qualcuno, come l'anima, che ama Iddio, gli vuol bene, cioè vuole e si compiace ch'egli abbia quel suo bene divino, ch'è l'infinito pelago di ogni perfezione [...]. *Nascono [...] tutti gli atti da l'amore, perché la prima operazione che faccia la volontà nostra è di amare*' (edn 1584, p. 51; my emphasis). Before Costanzo Cargnoni's publication of the 1573 edition in 1991, the edition of *Prattica* to which everyone referred was Father Umile da Padova's critical edition, itself based on the 1584 edition. On the various editions of *Prattica*, cf. F. Umile, Introduzione to edn 1584, pp. xxviii–xxxiii; see also R. Cuvato, *Mattia Bellintani*, pp. 107–8. A few years later Bellintani's Commento all'Apocalissi was ready for publication when this was prevented – for reasons that do not however concern the topic of prayer – by firm action on the part of the Inquisition authorities (ibid., pp. 162–6).

capax Dei.'[30] This subtle interpretation may accurately represent the inner conflict in the Capuchin friar's theological and doctrinal thinking but it does not altogether clarify the reason for these repeated acts of self-censorship, which become fully comprehensible only if *Pratica*'s vicissitudes are considered in a wider cultural and religious context, bearing in mind the developments in church censorship in those years and the troubled events that occurred within his Order.[31] The year that saw Bellintani take up his *Prattica dell'orazione mentale* with the intention of 'expanding' it and also, as we have seen, of toning down the harshest expressions also procured the official condemnation of the *Dialogo dell'unione dell'anima con Dio*, written by a Franciscan monk, Bartolomeo Cordoni da Castello.[32] This was certainly not the first time this book had drawn the attention of the censors in Rome. Eight years earlier, in 1576, Cordoni's *Dialogo* had appeared on an unpublished list (or possibly an Index) of prohibited books (this is now kept in the Archive of the Congregation for the Doctrine of the Faith).[33] This list was compiled by Giovanni di Dio, who according to De Bujanda was Censor of books in Rome by order of the Congregation of

[30] Ibid., pp. 223–4.

[31] Another noteworthy case of sixteenth-century self-censorship is that concerning Antonio Pagani, author of the well-known work, *Rime spirituali*, first published in Venice in 1554 and placed on the Roman Index in 1559. In 1570, in an attempt to cover up his tumultuous past in the ranks of the Barnabites, this former follower of Paola Antonia Negri, now known as Brother Antonio, an Observant Friar Minor, sent to be printed a new version of his collected spiritual works, specially adapted for the occasions. 'The entire text', as Elena Bonora puts it, 'was reworked. It was transformed from a pure and simple apology of disobedience to the Church in the name of inner illumination and Christian freedom into a Counter-Reformation exaltation of the supremacy of "the shepherd who represents the divine throne on earth".' (E. BONORA, 'Nei labirinti della censura libraria cinquecentesca: Antonio Pagani (1526–1589) e le "Rime spirituali"', *Per Marino Berengo. Studi degli allievi*, L. Antonielli, C. Capra, M. Infelice (eds), Milan, Franco Angeli, 2001, pp. 114–36, citation p. 128; to be integrated with the considerations presented in EAD., *I conflitti della Controriforma*, pp. 583 et seqq).

[32] On Cordoni, see the entry in the DBI by P. ZAMBELLI (vol. VI, Rome, 1964, pp. 707–8) and that by E. D'ASCOLI, *Dictionnaire de Spiritualité, Ascétique et Mystique. Doctrine et Histoire*, file IV, Paris, 1935, pp. 1266–7; see also STANISLAO DA CAMPAGNOLA, 'Bartolomeo Cordoni da Città di Castello e le due prime edizioni del suo "Dialogo"', *Bollettino di storia patria per l'Umbria*, LXXX, 1983, pp. 89–152.

[33] *Index Authorum, qui vel aperti haeretici sunt, aut certi de haeresi valde suspecti esse videntur aut contro bonos mores, vitaeque pudicitiam aliqua continent. Postremo etiam addita sunt opera Sanctorum Doctorum sive etiam prophanorum, quae ratione impressionis, aut Interpretis, sive quod scholia, atque Annotationes haeretici alicuius Authoris contineant minus probanda videntur.* Authore D. Jo. DEI FLORENTINO, Romae MDLXXVI [ACDF, Index, series XIV, one vol.]. In the tenth and last volume he edited, De Bujanda, who in the meantime had been authorized to view the Index but not to publish it, devoted a few lines to the document, merely pointing out its importance in the context of sixteenth-century censorship (*Index des livres interdits*, vol. X, *Thesaurus de la littérature interdite au XVI siècle. Auteurs,*

the Inquisition and Master of the Sacred Palace –[34] and it was prepared on the suggestion of Cardinal Guglielmo Sirleto that a catalog be created of prohibited books not on either the Pauline or the Tridentine Index:[35] this was, therefore, the first Roman source of the 'long lists' and of the Indexes of prohibited books appearing in the late 1570s and early 1580s.[36] At the

---

ouvrages, éditions, Centre d'Etude de la Renaissance, Editions de l'Université de Sherbrooke Librairie Droz, 1996, pp. 825–6).

34 *Index des livres interdits*, vol. X, p. 825.

35 Giovanni di Dio announced his intention in a prefatory letter but in substance never fulfilled it, for his list includes books that had previously been condemned, including the *Beneficio di Cristo*. Too little is known of him for us to speculate on his decisions on what was to be censored. There can be no doubt he was a man of outstanding culture, and his refined sensitivity is clearly shown by, among other things, the presence among the prohibited titles of the *Oratione di m. Benedetto Varchi fatta in Fiorenza il Venerdì santo nella Compagnia di San Domenico, la quale oratione è nell'Orationi raccolte dal Sansovino nel 2 libro a carte 58* ('Oration by Monsignor Benedetto Varchi pronounced in Florence on Good Friday at the Company of St Dominic, which oration is among those collected by Sansovino in Book 2 on page 58'), a work which, as pointed out by E.-M. Jung-Inglessis – 'Il Pianto della Marchesa di Pescara sopra la passione di Christo' [1957], *Archivio italiano per la storia della pietà*, 1997, vol. X, pp. 115–204 (see also P. Simoncelli, *Evangelismo italiano*, chap. VI, pp. 330 et sqq; and M. Firpo, *Gli affreschi di Pontormo*, pp. 218 et sqq) – contains whole passages literally transcribed from the *Beneficio di Cristo*. Not only did Varchi's delicate but heretic transposition go unnoticed but none of the successive sixteenth-century Indexes ever mentioned Varchi's *Oration*. We are far from understanding this figure and the reasons for his decisions in matters of censorship, but it is useful to note that, in light of the scanty information to be gathered from the introductory note to the Index, he must have acted in total concord with Cardinal Sirleto and the entire Congregation of the Inquisition and that the letter of dedication he composed for the Giolito edition of Luigi di Granada's *Pie et devote orationi* provides sufficient evidence of di Dio's particular sensitivity to mystic tradition, for on 18 November 1567, writing to 'the Very Reverend Father, Giacomo Pasqualigo, of the Order of Preachers, my Most Honorable Father in Christ' (*Pie et devote orationi, raccolte da diversi e gravi autori, per il R.P.F. Luigi di Granata, dell'ordine de' Predicatori*, c. A2r), Giovanni di Dio warmly recommended that people should read the work (ibid., c. A2r). In light of this impassioned exaltation of Granada by the censor Giovanni di Dio, the editorial positioning of the *Pie et devote orationi* assumes particular importance, for in the Giolito edition of the 'Terzo fiore della ghirlanda', kept in the Biblioteca Angelica in Rome and mentioned by Paolo Simoncelli (*Evangelismo italiano*, p. 222, footnote 6), this work is placed among texts by Vittoria Colonna, one of which being the *Pianto della Marchesa di Pescara sopra la Passione di Christo* (texts reproduced in their entirety by Jung-Inglessis, pp. 124–30; see also Simoncelli in the appendix of his volume, pp. 423 et seqq). Evidently the choice made by the Venetian editor Giolito de' Ferrari, who detected an element of affinity and assonance between the writings of Vittoria Colonna and those of Granada, traced a boundary line of Catholic orthodoxy in the field of religious mysticism (on Vittoria Colonna's mysticism, cf. A. Aubert, 'Misticismo, valdesianesimo e riforma della chiesa in Vittoria Colonna', *Rivista di Storia della Chiesa in Italia*, XLVI, 1992, pp. 143–66; on Granada cf. also above, ch. 6).

36 J.M. De Bujanda, *Index des livres interdits*, vol. X, p. 826. On the long lists and the Indexes of these years, cf. U. Rozzo, 'Index de Parme', *Index des livres interdits*, vol. LX, pp. 17–185.

end of the list of prohibited books in Latin, in the appendices to the lists of 'suspected books in the vernacular' and arranged alphabetically, we find for the first time in this Index some mystic works that hitherto had been ignored by the Roman censors, one of which was this particular work, the *Dialogo dell'unione dell'anima con Dio*.[37] Added a few years later to the Parma Index of 1580, this text was closely scrutinized by certain censors and theologians and was eventually officially banned by the Holy Office in March 1584.[38]

The text of the condemnation that was prepared at the time focused on the censors' ultimate objective and contained the following significant expression regarding *novum et insolitum orandi modum* ('the new and unusual manner of praying'). The Cardinals forming the Congregation of the Inquisition, after examining the censures *theologorum* ('of the theologians'),[39] pronounced the following judgment:

> The propositions containing errors of faith as well as the many others that were false, scandalous, rash, and offensive to the ears of the pious were to be suppressed and prohibited as they induced the reader to fall into the heresies that abound in these ill-fated times, or into other heresies condemned long ago.[40]

At this point, if we consider that this allusion to doctrines 'long condemned' (*iamdiu damnata*) probably contained an implicit reference

---

37 *Index Authorum*, cc. unnumbered. The *Dialogo* was put on the Parma Index of 1580 (which itself owed much to Giovanni di Dio's Index) and on the unpromulgated Indexes of 1590 and 1593, but was 'excluded' from the Clementine Index of 1596.

38 ACDF, Inquisizione, Decreta, 1584, cc. nn. In the course of a meeting held on 8 March 1584 the Congregation of the Index recorded the Holy Office's condemnation: 'Before the Most Holy Lord Gregory XIII in the Congregation of the Holy Office, the book Dialogo dell'Unione spirituale de Dio con l'anima by the Observant Friar Minor Bartolomeo da Castello was condemned' ('*Registrum Actorum et decretorum Sacrae Congregationis Indicis ab anno 1571 usque 1606*, in ACDF, Indice, Diaria vol. I, c. 14v). The text of the condemnnation was also published independently by the heirs of Antonio Biado, chamber printers, in the same year of 1584; this last version was reproduced by Paolo Simoncelli in the appendix to his paper 'Il "Dialogo dell'unione spirituale di Dio con l'anima" tra alumbradismo spagnolo e prequietismo italiano', *Annuario dell'Istituto storico italiano per l'età moderna e contemporanea*, vols XXIX–XXX, 1977–78, Rome, Istituto storico italiano per l'età moderna e contemporanea, 1979, pp. 565–601, text on 600–601; cf. also Stanislao da Campagnola, who notes the presence of the same text also in 'Études sur l'Index romain', *Analecta iuris pontificii*, II, 1857, Rome, cc. 2632–3 (S. da Campagnola, 'Bartolomeo Cordoni', p. 123, footnote 116).

39 On these censures, see below.

40 'iudicaverunt [...] esse supprimendos et prohibendos, tamquam continentes errores in fide, et plures propositiones erroneas, scandalosas, temerarias ac piarum aurium offensivas, quaeque per apertas consequentias ad haereses hoc infelici tempore grassantes, et ad alias iamdiu damnatas dedecunt' (P. Simoncelli, 'Il "Dialogo"' p. 601).

to the now remote beghard heresy of the Free Spirit,[41] the mention of this 'new and unusual manner of praying' – besides being a warning light indicating a growing aversion to 'novelties' (*novitates*) that might upset the current order – represented an important testimony of the attention that the Roman censors continued to pay to the subject of prayer. What is, however, more significant is the fact that the censor's allusion (to the 'new and unusual manner of praying') did not refer to the famous text by the Franciscan Cordoni but to a short work attached to it, *Circolo del divino amore,* now attributed with a fair degree of certainty to Francesco Ripanti da Iesi – the former General of the recently founded and restless Capuchin Order, to whom the heads of the Roman Curia had allotted the tricky task of closing the ranks in the wake of Bernardino Ochino's sensational flight. Briefly reconstructing the parallel editorial vicissitudes of these two works, Cordoni's *Dialogo* and Ripanti's *Circolo*, it is not only easy to verify that it was the latter text that must have attracted the Roman Inquisitors' greatest attention; it is also possible to observe how the Inquisition's action ended up by calling into question – through Ripanti's implicit condemnation – the Capuchins' entire and as yet still young spiritual tradition.

The first edition of the *Dialogo* had been published posthumously in 1538 by a Franciscan, Ilarione Pichi da Borgo San Sepolcro.[42] Cordoni's decision to forgo publication can be seen as an indication of his awareness of the risks implicit in a 'dialogue' that dwelt entirely on the 'perfect freedom of the soul' (*perfetta libertà dell'anima*) and 'enlightenment' (*illuminazione*) – risks that certainly did not escape the attention of the editor of the work if we consider the great care and energy he devoted to the work of 'cleansing' the text (*pulitura*), during which process he probably expunged the most esoteric statements, i.e. those that ran the greatest risk of action on the part of the censor.[43]A few months later, in January 1539, heedless of the dangers involved in this first delicate editorial adventure, or possibly unaware of them, Girolamo da Molfetta, a fine orator and a follower of Ochino, published in Milan a new edition of the text.[44] This

[41] Ibid., p. 600, but *passim*.

[42] *De unione animae cum supereminenti lumine. Opera nuova et utile ad ogni fidel Christiano. Composta per il Reverendo padre frate Bartolomeo da Castello de l'ordine de l'observantia*, Perugia, per gli Cartolari, October 1538.

[43] P. Simoncelli, 'Il "Dialogo"', pp. 573–4. Simoncelli corroborates this hypothesis, indicating, on the basis of a Franciscan chronicle of 1572, the existence of two other works by Cordoni which presumably circulated in manuscript form (ibid., p. 573).

[44] *Dyalogo dell'unione spirituale de Dio con l'anima*, Milan, per Francesco Cantalupo et Innocentio da Cicognara, 1539. Stanislao da Campagnola believes that the 1539 edition edited by Girolamo da Molfetta was based on a manuscript that was not the same as that used by Ilarione, i.e. that the two editions of 1538 and 1539 relate to two different manuscript forms (S. da Campagnola, 'Bartolomeo Cordoni,' pp. 130 et sqq.). Simoncelli put

time, together with Cordoni's work, Molfetta also published an 'Epilogue' entitled *Circulus charitatis divinae*, or *Circolo del divino amore* ('Circle of Divine Love') (a 53rd chapter added to the original 52), plus a short work of his own called *Alcune regule de la Oratione mentale con la contemplatione de la Corona del nome di Iesu* ('Some rules of mental prayer with the contemplation of the Rosary of the name of Jesus').[45] Barely two years after this editorial initiative, Molfetta, emulating the deeds of his master, Brother Bernardino Ochino, then the General of the Capuchin Order, fled across the Alps: a rash, instinctive decision taken perhaps more to conform to his model of human and religious life, i.e. Ochino himself, than out of any effective inward maturing of thought, a hasty decision that it is not unreasonable to suppose was one of the reasons that drove Molfetta to his dramatic decision to commit suicide.[46] Over and above the sad end to his short life, Molfetta's unexpected decision to flee and his abrupt break with Catholic orthodoxy, which was implicit in such behaviour, had the effect of irredeemably compromising the fortunes of his work. It is not hard to understand why the next edition of Cordoni's *Dialogo*, published in Venice in 1548, lacked Molfetta's *regule per l'oratione mentale*: it was not so much the presence of dubious doctrinal content that provoked the omission of his text from the mid-sixteenth century edition as an automatic censorial mechanism set into action by his flight. Molfetta's short work, *Alcune regole de la Oratione mentale con la contemplatione de la Corona del nome di Iesu*, did not present any elements that could be taken as being heterodox from the doctrinal point of view.[47] A short introduction preceded a *Rosary* that led the reader by the hand through an account of all Christ's life, from the Incarnation to Pentecost, condensed into thirty-three mysteries regularly arranged in a manner corresponding to the succession of the thirty-three years that Jesus Christ spent on this earth. From the meticulous list of introductory rules to observe during prayer[48] to the 'five degrees' of 'those acts of grace that God Himself wishes should be asked

this hypothesis forward with some doubt, opting however for an interpretation according to which Girolamo da Molfetta used the second edition to oppose the order's desire to cover up the first edition (P. Simoncelli, 'Il "Dialogo"', pp. 575–6).

45 *Alcune regule de la oratione mentale con la contemplatione de la Corona del nome di Iesu, predicate da Fra Hieronymo da Molfetta*, in *I Frati Cappuccini. Documenti e testimonianze del primo secolo*, C. Cargnoni (ed.), III/1, *Letteratura spirituale ascetico-mistica (1535–1628)*, pp. 429 et sqq.

46 On Molfetta's flight and suicide, cf. P. Simoncelli, 'Il "Dialogo"', pp. 577 and 579.

47 On the close dependence of this short piece of writing on one of the opening chapters of the Dyalogo, cf. C. Cargnoni, 'Fonti, tendenze e sviluppi della letteratura spirituale cappuccina primitiva,' *Collectanea Francescana*, 48/3–4, 1978, pp. 311–98; pp. 361–2.

48 *Alcune regule de la oratione mentale*, pp. 435–6.

of Him',[49] to the virtues to be practiced during contemplation[50] and the list of mysteries of the life of Christ before which one must pause,[51] the entire contents of the work remain strictly within the bounds of utter orthodoxy. If the unexpected outcry against the moral and religious corruption of the clergy may possibly have aroused some suspicion in the more sensitive readers[52] – for it is legitimate to suppose that certain insinuations made by the author around the time when the work was written, in 1539, were little tolerated ten years later in a radically changed context – the faithful and heartfelt appeal to return to the 'Roman Church'[53] would certainly set their minds at rest. Not even the possible suspicion of a similarity of content to that of the coeval work *Trattato dell'oratione* by his master Ochino[54] could have led to the exclusion of Molfetta's short work. Recognition of the fact that Ochino's *Trattato dell'oratione* was printed in 1544, i.e. after Molfetta had written his work, would not by itself exclude a dependence of thought and ideas between the two, especially in light of the intensity and closeness of their contacts before they fled. But the difference of approach and content between the two works is evident from the very first reading. The only aspect really worth mentioning is that in Ochino's *Trattato* the mystic-unitive element appeared to be marginal[55] to its clearly Calvinistic approach. While, on the one hand, the work collected together the nascent

---

[49] 'cinque gradi di quelle grazie, le quale vole esso Dio li siano domandate' (ibid., pp. 437–8).

[50] Ibid., p. 439.

[51] Ibid., pp. 440–45.

[52] 'Then I remembered that I had not sought Him [Christ the Divine Spouse] in the state of men of religion; and great hope sprang within me. I saw that these men of religion were of two sorts, whence I addressed those who were nearest to me, and asked of them: "Have you seen my beloved?" And the voice answered before them: "Here you seek Him in vain, for all those who are here seek their own things, not those of Jesus Christ"' ('Dapoi io mi ricordai che non l'avea cercato [il divino Sposo Cristo] nel stato de' religiosi; ce venne a me alquanto di speranza. Questi religiosi viddi essere di dua sorte, onde domandai a quelli prima che mi stavano più appresso, e dixi a quelli: "Avete visto il mio diletto". E la voce rispose prima che loro: "Qui invano il cerchi, perché questi tutti sonno che cercano le cose sue, e non quelle de Iesu Christo"', ibid., p. 434).

[53] Besides the act of Grace to ask of God in favour of the 'Christian Militant Church', see also the passage that follows: 'And when saying this rosary, you should contemplate one by one the following mysteries, praying to God at the end for the states of the Roman Church' (ibid., p. 440).

[54] *Sermones Bernardini Ochini Senensis*, [Geneva] 1544, 15 March (Sermons I–XIII). Cargnoni mentions a different edition of the treatise in *La seconda parte delle prediche di M. Bernardino Ochino Senese…*, in which the *Trattato dell'oratione copiosissimo* is included between Sermons 52 and 64 /C. Cargnoni, 'Fonti, tendenze e sviluppi', pp. 333–4.

[55] The only sermon containing mystic elements is Sermon VIII *(Delli vani modi che doveremo tenere per bavere delle grafie da Dio;* cf. *Sermones Bernardini Ochini*, cc. E3r–v; on which cf. also Cargnoni, 'Fonti, tendenze, sviluppi', p. 333).

germs of Ochino's ultimate doctrinal positions, protagonist as he was – with his *Dialogi Triginta* – of the great debate in Europe on tolerance,[56] on the other hand, Ochino's work was the mature product of his new religious credo, and thus clearly distinguished itself from Molfetta's orthodox *Regule*. The central nature given in the economy of the work to the doctrine of the 'benefit of Christ'[57] enabled the author to present side by side – even at the risk of a certain degree of conceptual and doctrinal stretching[58] – a rigid Calvinistic predestination-oriented conception[59] and a universalist vision which, by exerting pressure on elements such as the law,

[56] Cf. M. Firpo, '"Boni christiani merito vocantur haeretici". Bernardino Ochino e la tolleranza', *La formazione storica della alterità. Studi di storia della tolleranza nell'età moderna offerti ad Antonio Rotondò*, promossi da H. Méchoulan, R.H. Popkin, G. Ricuperati, L. Simonutti, Firenze, Olschki (Studi e testi per la storia della tolleranza in Europa nei secoli XVI–XVIII, vol. 5), 1.1, pp. 161–244. See also Id., *Il problema della tolleranza religiosa nell'età moderna*, Turin, Loescher editore, 1978, pp. 95–6.

[57] Cf., for example, Sermon IV – *Per qual mezo si debbano domandare le gratie a Dio (Sermones Bernardini Ochini*, c. B5r; c. B6r; and also cc. B6v–B7r.

[58] See, for example, the following passage where Ochino attempts, not very straightforwardly, to soften the rigidity of Calvinist predestination by introducing elements contradicting the immutability of the word of God: 'Since it will never be our intention to pray to God that He change His word, but that He should act in accordance with His divine will; we must therefore pray for all, in the manner that has been prescribed [...]. Therefore, we are obliged to pray more for believers than for non-believers, although it may be that God, divining that non-believers, by their conversion, will be more fruitful and may inspire us to pray with greater fervor for them than for believers' ('Impero che non sarà mai nostra intentione di pregar Dio che muti la sententia, ma che ne disponga secondo el suo divino beneplacito; debba adunque pregarsi per tutti, nel modo che è dicto [...]. Però siamo più obligati a pregar per li fedeli che per li infideli, ben che 'l potrebbe anco essere, che Dio prevedendo che uno infidele convertendosi, farà molto fructo, ci inspirasse a pregar con maggior fervor per epso *[sic]*, che per li fideli'; ibid. cc. C7v–C8r).

[59] 'Knowing that Christ in Heaven our defender assists us before the eternal Father, and prays for us as our only mediator, we are sure by our faith that we shall be saved' ('Noi sapendo che Christo in celo nostro advocato, assiste inanti al Padre, et prega per noi, chome unico nostro mediatore, siamo per fede certi, che ci salvaremo'; Sermon II, A che fine si debba fare oratione, ibid., c. A7r; but cf. also Sermon V, *Per chi debba farsi oratione*, ibid., c. C5r) and also expressions such as: 'God is [...] immutable' ('Dio è immutabile;' ibid., C6v), or: 'You shall not pray to God that He save the sinful and change His word, but rather you shall pray that He may use it in His honor and glory and in the way that in all eternity has been foreseen and determined' ('Non debbi adunque pregar Dio che salvi li reprobati, et muti la sententia, ma si ben pregarlo che se ne serva in suo honore, et gloria et in quel modo che ha ab etterno previsto, et determinato;' ibid., c. C7r); 'The chosen ones [...], although they do not pray continuously and do not read the divine law, nonetheless this failure to observe the law is not held to their account as a sin, and the same is true of the followers of Christ, and they have nothing within them that deserves damnation.' ('Li electi, [...] se ben non orano di continuo, et non observan la divina legge, niente dimeno tale inobservantia, non li è imputata a peccato, imo per esser membri di Christo, non hanno in se cosa alchuna la quale sia degna di damnatione'; Sermon VII, *Quando debba farsi oratione a Dio*, Ivi, cc. D7v–D8r).

natural reason, and the religion of the heart, was destined to lead him to the doctrine of divine mercy that is granted to all believers.[60]

If therefore Molfetta's sudden flight – and not some reason related to this short work – was the only real cause of the disappearance of his *Regule* from the Venetian edition of the *Dialogo* (1548), it would appear that the orthodoxy of the Capuchin spiritual tradition with regard to prayer came out of the 'Ochino affair' unscathed, at least for the time being.

The Venetian edition of 1548 did, however, still contain the anonymous *Circolo del divino amore*. Difficult though it may be to explain why the eye of the Roman censors did not fall upon this work until the early 1580s – but not that of Giovanni di Dio, who drew attention to the work as early as 1576 – thus allowing more than three decades to pass after the previous edition, it is interesting here to underline that it was precisely this text, even before the *Dialogo*, that aroused the Inquisitors' attention and led to the condemnation of the entire work. This is what emerges, in particular, from the censures prepared by the Capuchin Evangelista Canobio, now kept among the Protocols of the Congregation of the Index.[61] For, as

60 'God is all benign, sweet, pious, clement, and full of charity, His mercy is infinite and does not need to be moved by our prayers' ('Dio è tutto benigno dolce, pio, clemente, et pien di carità, la sua misericordia è infinita, et non ha bisogno di esser commossa, con le nostre orationi;' Sermon II, ibid., cc. A5r–v); 'Because God is an infinite ocean of all goodness, from which all graces emanate, all gifts, and all our good' ('Perché Dio è uno infinito pelago di ogni bontà, dal quale emanano tutte le gratie, tutti li doni, et tutto '1 nostro bene;' Sermon III, *A chi debbano demandarsi le gratie*, ibid., c. A7v); the same expression is used by Ochino a few pages further on, on c. D1r: 'immense and infinite ocean of goodness, all graces emanate' ('immenso et infinito pelago di bontà, emanano tutte le gratie'). The amplitude of divine mercy hypothesized by Ochino in this passages seemed at certain moments to open up the way towards an actual theorization of religious tolerance, as we saw in the treatises on Pico and Stancaro's prayer (cf. above, ch. 1): 'Rarely will you find that they have ever said a prayer for the Turks, the infidels, the Jews, the heretics, the schismatics and the excommunicated, so they hold them in hatred and they think it is an act of zeal to persecute them, and an act of evil to pray for them; so they never pray sincerely in their hearts for their enemies' ('Rarissimi trovarai che habbin facto mai oratione per li turchi, per li infideli, per li hebrei, per li heretici, scismatici, et scomunicati, imo li hanno in odio, et pensano che '1 sia zelo persequitarli, et male il pregar per loro; imo non pregano mai di core per li loro inimici'; Sermon V, ibid c. C4r); '[God] desired that in prayer we should seek that God is universally honored by all, and also, we should ask grace for all' ('[Dio] volse che nella oratione, cercassemo, che Dio fusse universalmente honorato da tutti, et così anco, che per tutti domandassemo le gratie'; ibid, c. C4v).

61 ACDF, Index, Protocolli G, cc. 201r–202v and cc. 215v–216v (these were respectively censures 'in libello Circulus charitatis divinae' and censures regarding the 'Dialogo dell'unione spirituale di Dio con l'anima'). These were clearly the censures pronounced by the 'theologians' on the basis of which the Congregation of the Inquisition resolved to condemn the text. This text, published by Paolo Simoncelli in the appendix to his above-cited paper, ran as follows: 'They gave instructions to the Most Reverend Theological Fathers that the aforementioned Booklet of the Union of the Soul and the treatise entitled Circle of Charity should be diligently examined so that – when the propositions pointed out by the above theologians

already suggested, the expression 'novus modum orandi' contained in the Inquisition decree alluded to the *Circulus*, not to Cordoni's *Dialogo*,[62] i.e. to the orthodox General of the Capuchins, Francesco Ripanti, called upon to repair the damage done by Bernardino Ochino, and not therefore to the Franciscan heretic Cordoni.[63] It was above all to this 'new and unusual way of praying' that Canobio chose to dedicate most of his attention. It was a contemplative method 'of extremely difficult interpretation', as has recently been rightly pointed out,[64] which through a complex 'circular operation' (*operatione circolare*) was intended to guide the believer first to a vision of Jesus Christ and then to a perfect union with God. Without going into all the insidious intricacies of the text,[65] we will simply point out the objective difficulty encountered by the Capuchin censor, occupied as he was trying to see his way through the theological and doctrinal subtleties of a work which stood at a point where heretical traditions of various origin and background all flowed together. The simultaneous presence of theological elements going back to the beghard tradition of the Free Spirit and of doctrinal traces of clearly Lutheran descent prevented the censor from providing a unitary and organic interpretation of the text, compelling him to proceed passage by passage and sentence by sentence without any attempt at a global understanding of the work, and in some cases had the effect of misleading this Capuchin friar, for all his care and attention. That is what, for example, can be deduced from one of Canobio's final remarks in which, in a significant forced interpretation, he detected a contradiction in the text. At a certain point in the last chapter, as the censor pointed out in amazement, the author maintains that once man reaches the end

in the above Congregation had been taken into consideration, as also the censures expressed by the theologians regarding the propositions that they themselves had reported – they might judge whether the above-said Booklet of the Union of the Soul and the said Epilogue were to be suppressed and prohibited' ('mandaverunt Reverendiss. Patribus Theologis ut praedictos libellum de unione anime et tractatum Circuii charitatis divinae diligenter examinarent, ac demum intellectis in Congregatione praedicta propositionibus per praedictos Theologos notatis, consideratisque censuris eorundem theologorum mature desuper factis, ac per eosdem relatis, indicaverunt praedictos libellum de unione animae, et dictum Epilogum [...] fore et esse supprimendos et prohibendos'; P. Simoncelli, 'Il "Dialogo"'p. 601).

62 The Inquisition's entire decree appears to concentrate more on the Circulus than on Cordoni's work, apart obviously from including this work in the decree of condemnation; cf. P. Simoncelli, 'Il "Dialogo"', pp. 600–601 and S. da Campagnola, 'Bartolomeo Cordoni,' p. 124; see also C. Cargnoni, 'Fonti, tendenze,' p. 345; and above, pp. 96–7.

63 It is difficult to establish whether Brother Canobio had any precise idea about the true identity of the author of the Circolo; however, considering what is said in the decree of condemnation, the Inquisitors had realized it was not Cordoni.

64 C. Cargnoni, Fonti, tendenze, p. 344.

65 For an in-depth analysis of Ripanti's text, cf. C. Cargnoni, Fonti, tendenze, pp. 340–42; and especially Id., *Introduzione* in *I Frati cappuccini*, III/1, pp. 46 et seqq.

of his circular course – when he has been permitted to contemplate the long-desired 'circulus divinus' – *tendit in nihilum* ('tends toward nullity'). Shortly afterwards, however, Canobio continued, the author plainly denies this statement, asserting that once divine grace has been obtained (*informatus gratia, et cum ea operante*), man is made powerful and capable of everything, and 'therefore' 'non tendit in nihilum':

> In the last chapter we read that a man who contemplates this Circle as he may be able and as he may wish, morally and gratuitously, tends toward nullity; and in the same chapter we read that a man who is informed by grace and acts with grace is enriched, and having the capacity to do all things he therefore does not tend toward nullity.[66]

It was therefore clear to the eyes of the censor that 'this doctrine is the opposite of itself'.[67] His misleading objection was probably originated by his imperfect knowledge of the subtleties of beghardism inherited from sixteenth-century mysticism and by a theological and doctrinal reasoning that was still subject to an over-rigid alternation between Catholic orthodoxy and Lutheran orthodoxy. For Canobio was unable to appreciate how, in the mystic circular course that it was thought would conduct man to his union with God, the author distinguished two quite separate moments. The first of these coincided with the phase that is commonly defined as that of annihilation, when through contemplation of the object of his desire (God), man – maintaining his free will – succeeds in ridding himself of all the affections and ties that bind him to the terrestrial world, reaching the point where he desires for himself only nothingness. The second of the two moments (the unitive phase) leads man to unite his will to that of God and, through this unitive act, makes him potentially able to do all that is within the power of God: in this final stage, and only then, man in fact loses his free will, but only indirectly, as a consequence of his identification with God, and not – as sustained by Lutheran orthodoxy – because free will is 'corrected' by the intervention of divine grace. The contradiction, in other words, was only apparent: the result of a mechanical, but culpable, juxtaposition of two expressions taken out of their original context; or else, more simply, it was the result of a certain amount of comprehensible confusion on the part of the censor himself. It was a difficulty of interpretation that it is not surprising one may also find in the shortest and most schematic censures of

---

66 'In ultimo cap. habetur quod homo habens contemplationem huius circuii potens et volens moraliter et gratuite tendit in nihilum, et in eodem capite habetur quod homo informatus gratia, et cum ea operans factus est dives et potens omnia non igitur tendit in nihilum' (ACDF, Index, Protocols G, c. 202r).

67 'haec doctrina est contraria sibi ipsi' (ibid.).

Cordoni's *Dialogo*.[68] Far from attempting to reconstruct the doctrinal origin of statements that at times were conflicting, the censor limited himself to listing the incorrect statements, specifying the corresponding page number, but this time without making any attempt at a comment or marginal note and putting together concepts that theologically were mutually remote. Thus, in the brief list of *loca notata* ('points noted') it was possible to read, one after the other as if in some sort of bureaucratic list, statements that vilified free will and the role of good works for the purposes of salvation, such as *Bona opera sunt nihil* ('Good works are nothing'), or *Videtur negare ieiunia, vigilia et labores, et opera humilitatis* ('It appears to deny the value of fasts, wakes, and the works of charity'), side by side with concepts that dangerously exalted the mystic effects of the 'deifying' union: *Uniti operatio non est humana* ('The operation of the union of the soul is not a natural quality of man'), or which promised man the chance to take upon himself all the merits recognized in Christ: *Unitus usurpat sibi virtutes, et merita Christi* ('He who attains the state of union with God usurps to himself the virtues of Christ'); or guaranteed an even more fearsome sensation of omnipotence: *Unitus possidet omnipotentiam Dei* ('He who is united to God possesses God's almightiness'), or *Unitus concurrit omnibus operationibus creaturarum, et Creatoris, etiam divinis conceptibus* ('He who is united takes part in all the works of human beings and of the Creator, including divine operations'), or a dangerous conviction that freed man of the obligation to perform any virtuous deeds: *Licentiat se unitus a virtutibus charitatis* ('He who is united to God is rid of the virtues of charity'), *Non utitur actualiter virtutibus* ('He does not make use of virtues').

Over and above these introductory considerations, however, the 'censor's difficulty'[69] detracted nothing from the effectiveness and incisiveness of Canobio's fault-finding. His Lutheranocentric vision was possibly less sophisticated in its manner of interpretation but it had the virtue of putting clearly into focus the danger lurking in these pages. The doctrinal enemy was already well identified and defined: the devaluation of human free will and the consequent devaluation of good works for the purposes of eternal salvation; the certainty of salvation and the state of impeccability guaranteed by the union with God. Once having overcome

---

68 Ibid., cc. 215v–216v.

69 An expression is borrowed here that was used by A. Rotondò, 'Cultura umanistica e difficoltà di censori. Censura ecclesiastica e discussioni cinquecentesche sul platonismo', *Le pouvoir et la plume. Incitation, contrôle et répression dans l'Italie du XVI siècle*. Actes du Colloque international organisé par le Centre Interuniversitaire de Recherche sur la Renaissance italienne et l'Institut Culturel Italien de Marseille (Aix-en-Provence, Marseilles, 14–16 May 1981), Paris, 1982, pp. 15–50.

this first difficult impact with the text, the Capuchin Canobio was in fact immediately able to locate the work's key points.

Rigidly following the sequence of the chapters, the censor began his work, listing and commenting on some of the *proprietates quas Auctor tribuit huic Circulo* ('properties that the Author attributes to this Circle').[70] The first fault that Canobio found concerned the need to make a clear distinction between the level of contemplation and that of action. Far from wishing to contest the definition of the *Circolo* as a contemplative *tractatus* ('treatise'), he took pains to emphasize that it was not right to attribute to this *esercitio* ('exercise') and to this contemplative dimension also the value and the characteristics peculiar to an 'active' and charitable life, thus raising the Circulus to the status of being a perfect synthesis of the 'Vita apostolica':

> That the Circle means Apostolic Life. [...] This proposition is false because the Circle also makes men contemplative, whereas the apostolic life required not only a state of contemplation but also a state of action, as is clear in the Acts of the Apostles 4.[71]

By reducing active life to contemplative life, the censor seemed to be insinuating, one ran the risk of discouraging the faithful from the concrete performance of good deeds. The purpose of his next observation had the same objective. Further clarifying the meaning of his previous remark, he pointed out the author's mistake in attributing an unspecified 'magnitude of charity' to an 'exercise' that was merely contemplative, as was that which he was about to present to his readers: if anything, it might have been possible to speak of a 'magnitude of contemplation' (*magnitudo contemplationis*). As charity is an act that cannot be performed without the element of man's voluntary participation, it was decidedly misleading to speak of *magnitudo charitatis* with reference to a contemplative 'treatise' in which there was not the slightest trace of human will:

> The characteristic feature of this Circle is the magnitude of charity. This proposition is also false because charity is subject to human will, and therefore, since contemplation is an act that concerns the intellect, this Circle should be called the magnitude of contemplation rather than the magnitude of charity.[72]

---

70 ACDF, Index, Protocols G, c. 201r.

71 'Quod [Circulus] sit Vita apostolica [...] Haec propositio est falsa de rigore sermonis, quia hic Circulus facit homines etiam contemplativos, vita autem Apostolica consistebat ne dum in contemplatione sed etiam in actione ut patet actu ap. c. 4' (ibid.).

72 'Proprietas huius Circulis est quod sit magnitudo charitatis. Ista propositio etiam est falsa quia charitas subiectatur in voluntate, Circulus iste cum sit contemplatio quedam

However, proceeding further with his reading of the text, Canobio must have soon realized that in order to emend it, it was not sufficient to propose a clear distinction between the level of contemplation and that of action, nor was it enough to insist on the separation between the sphere of the intellect and affection from that of the will and charity. As he himself seemed to have understood from his very first observation, the author's confusion of levels concealed a hidden danger – and one that was indeed much more to fear – of the devaluation of human acts. *Cultus divinus* ('Divine worship') could not exhaust itself in the inner union that man establishes with God, directing on high his mental prayer; man, according to Canobio, must find his necessary and indispensable completion in 'outward worship' made up of sacrifices, outward acts of devotion, and offers of money, in other words in the complex armamentarium of good deeds 'advised' by the Catholic Church:

> At the beginning of this *Circle* it is said that the *Circle* consists in the supreme worship of God; this proposition also appears to be false, because the worship of God does not consist only in the inward conjunction with God through the intellect and through love, that is to say through devotion of the mind, but also in acts of outward worship, in sacrifices, and in oblations.[73]

Before beginning to occupy himself with the author's doctrinal speculations in the final phases of his unitive pathway, Canobio set himself the primary task of re-establishing the central value of man's free will and of denying all trace of *certitudo gratiae* ('the certainty of grace').[74] In the face of rash statements such as that according to which 'this circle is of immense value intensively and extensively' (*hic Circulus est infinitus intensive, et estensive, immensi valoris*), Canobio – reproposing the centrality of Christ's merits, something that could in no way be taken for granted – rapidly intervened, repeating that 'no work of the wayfarer, whether inward or outward, can possess infinite value and merit. This is because every work of man is effective, as regards its satisfaction and its merit, only insofar as it

---

spectat ad intellectum et ideo potius dici debet magnitudo contemplationis quam charitatis' (ibid., c. 201r).

73 'In principio declarationis huius Circuii, dicetur quod circulus iste est supremus cultus divinus quae praepositio falsa etiam videtur, quia cultus divinus nedum consistit in interiori coniunctione ad Deum per intellectum et affectum, hoc est in devotione mentis, sed etiam in exteriori reverenda, et in sacrificiis et oblationibus' (ibid.).

74 'Dicetur quod exercens hunc circulum habet actum perfectissimum amoris circumstantio natum [...] Quae prepositio videtur presuntuosa, quia ponit certitudinem gratiae' ('It is said that if one frequents this Circle one experiences a most perfect act of love generated by the circumstance. This proposition appears to be presumptuous because it presupposes the certainty of grace; ibid., c. 201v).

derives its effectiveness and satisfaction from Christ'.[75] And where he read that 'contemplating this Circle [man] offered free will to God, regarding it only as an instrument that was dependent on God's will',[76] he took it upon himself to remind the author of the clear and unequivocal decrees of the Tridentine Church: 'This proposition is heretic because it makes free will inactive, against the Tridentine Council session 6 canon 4'.[77]

Finally, we see the Capuchin censor at grips with the last mystic outbursts of the author of this 'new and unusual manner of prayer". The assumption that the 'exercise' (*essercitio*) of this 'circle' (*circolo*) would guarantee a full and clear understanding of all God's attributes was a falsehood that had to be to be resisted: 'In the same [last] chapter we read that he who devotes himself to the practice of this Circle has in his mind a distinct and orderly vision of God and a circular similarity to him. This statement is presumptuous and false because during the path of our life we cannot have a distinct vision of all God's attributes and God's ideas, as this Circle declares and affirms'.[78] It was a falsehood to be resisted at least as much as the erroneous belief that one was in the presence of a 'perfect and final' (*perfetta e finale*) union with God: as St Thomas Aquinas had in his day made clear, the characteristic feature of man's spiritual pathway must be a continuous tending towards divine perfection, although he will never be able to reach his final goal since the achievement of this result would lead to the exhaustion of this indispensable spiritual tension: 'In the same place we read that if one frequents this Circle one achieves a perfect union with God, one that is effective, formal, and final. This statement is false because during the course of human life such a perfect union is not possible but can always be further perfected, [...] as St Thomas says 22 questio 23'.[79]

It was, therefore, clear to anyone reading Canobio's censures that Ripanti's *Circolo* was the real danger that had to be eliminated, even

---

75 'nullum opus viatoris sive internum sive externum, potest esse infiniti valoris et meriti, cum omne opus hominis satisfactorium et meritorium efficaciam habeat ex satisfactione et merito Christi' (ibid.).

76 'contemplans hunc Circulum obtulit Deo liberum arbitrium tenens ipsum solumodo ut instrumentum sub voluntate Dei'.

77 '[Haec] propositio [est] heretica quia tollit activitatem a libero arbitrio contra concilium Tridentinum sess. 6 can. 4'.

78 'In eodem cap. [ultimo] habetur quod qui exercit se exercitio huius circuli habet in mente sua distinctam et ordinatam speciem et similitudinem circularem presentis exercitii Dei quae assertio est presuntuosa et falsa quia in via non possumus habere distinctam speciem omnium actributarum Dei et etiam idearum, ut declarat et ponit hic Circulus' (ibid., c. 202r).

79 'Idem habetur quod exercens se in hoc circulo consequitur perfectam unionem cum Deo effectivam, formalem, et finalem. Falsa assertio quia in vita non datur unio, ita perfecta, quin perfectior fieri possit [...] ut ait S. Thom. 22 q. 23' (ibid., cc. 202r–v).

more urgently than Cordoni's *Dialogo*. This message must have reached its intended target if we consider that the promoters of the new editorial enterprise that, immediately after the Inquisition's ban, presented Cordoni's *Dialogo* once again on the Italian book market chose this time to publish it without the 'Epilogue' (*Epilogo*) by the former General of the Capuchin order, perhaps hoping that if they omitted a work that had most attracted Rome's censorial atention, the text might have a better chance of circulating undisturbed.[80] However, over and above the hopes of those who endeavored to get round the Church's prohibitions, the omission of the 'new manner of praying' (the *Circolo*) marked the beginning of a full-scale process of repression of its author, i.e., this Francesco Ripanti da Iesi, who until a few decades before had been hailed as the savior of Capuchin orthodoxy – a process of repression to which Capuchin historiography itself appears to have added its own considerable contribution, the effects of which are still perceptible.[81] Ripanti was thus destined to oblivion, just like Giovanni Pili da Fano, another important figure in sixteenth-century Capuchin spiritual thinking. This much-appreciated, pugnacious author of controversial works such as *Opera vtilissima uulgare contra le pernitiosissime heresie luterane per li simplici* ('A work in the vulgar tongue most useful for simple folk against pernicious Lutheran heresies'),[82] was himself the author of a work entitled *Arte di unirsi a Dio* ('The Art of Uniting with God', 1586), which followed Cordoni's censured *Dialogo* almost to the letter.[83] Subsequently, in 1622, after a refined and subtle

---

[80] Not only the well-known edition of 1593 but also that of 1589, hitherto unknown, presented once again – only a very few years after the Inquisition's censures – the very first edition (1538) of Cordoni's text, without Ripanti's *Circolo*. See Bartolomeo Cordoni da Castello, *De vnione anime cum Deo*, Perugia, per Girolamo Cartolaro, 1538. Ristampata in Bologna per Fausto Bonardo, 1589.

[81] It cannot be a coincidence that the Capuchins' bibliography on Ripanti is extremely limited not only with regard to the decades following his death but throughout the subsequent centuries, as pointed out by C. CARGNONI, 'Fonti, tendenze, sviluppi', pp. 346–7.

[82] In Bologna, Giouan Battista Phaello, 1532. On this work, cf. G.L. BETTI, 'Alcune considerazioni riguardo all' 'Incendio de zizanie lutherane' di Giovanni da Fano pubblicato a Bologna nel 1532,' *L'Archiginnasio*, LXXXII (1987), pp. 235–3; see also S. CAVAZZA, '"Luthero fidelissimo inimico de messer Iesu Christo". La polemica contro Lutero nella letteratura religiosa in volgare della prima metà del Cinquecento', L. Perrone (ed.), *Lutero in Italia*, Casale Monferrato, Marietti, 1983, pp. 65–94, in particular pp. 69 et sqq. On Giovanni Pili da Fano, see OPTATUS a VEGHEL, 'Jean de Fano', *Dictionnaire de spiritualité*, VIII, Paris, 1974, pp. 506–9 with relative bibliography.

[83] C. CARGNONI, 'Fonti, tendenze sviluppi', pp. 349 et sqq. It would therefore be useful to conduct a separate study of the doctrinal reasonings and compromises by which Pili's impassioned anti-Lutheranism could come to terms with certain affirmations of clearly Protestant intent that were faithfully taken from Cordoni's *Dyalogo* and then contained in his *Operetta devotissima chiamata Arte de la Unione*, Bressa, per Damiano and Iacomo Philippo Bros., 1536.

process of mystification, Dionisio da Montefalco reworked the text and gave it an air that was more in tune with the standards of the day, purifying a work that was 'incomplete and defective [...] foul, rough and formless' (*manchevole e difettosa [...] rancia, rozza e sformata*) and thus returning it to devoted readers in a decidedly 'improved' condition.[84] While the copies of the 1536 and 1548 editions of *Arte* were probably taken off the editorial market,[85] Pili was therefore fated to be remembered only and exclusively as a much-praised champion of Catholic controversial writings and an impassioned supporter of evangelical poverty.[86]

This brief reconstruction serves to show the origin of Bellintani's self-censuring scruples, when, in 1584, he set about rewriting his *Prattica dell'oratione mentale*.[87] There is no need to carry out a comparative reading of the respective passages that were censured to realize how much Canobio's action must have influenced the choices made by the author of *Prattica*.

This was not, however, just a matter limited internally to the recently founded yet important Capuchin Order. It was the more general religious and cultural climate of the early 1580s that influenced the development of sixteenth-century mystic spirituality. Two examples should suffice to spotlight the main lines of the political censorship exerted by the church authorities of the day. It cannot be a coincidence that the latter part of the 1580s saw the presentation and discussion by the Congregation of the Index of the censures directed at two of Battista da Crema's condemned

---

84 *Arte d'unirsi con Dio, del RP.F. Giovanni da Fano Predicator Capuccino. Ridotta in miglior forma, accresciuta, e in quattro parti divisa, cioè nella vita purgativa, nell'illuminativa, nell'unitiva e negli esercizi...*, in Rome, per Andrea Fei, 1622, cc. 8–9. A short comparison between the old edition and the altered one was made by U. D'Alençon, 'Le Père Jean de Fano', *Etudes franciscaines*, 47 (1935), pp. 636–47, in particular p. 643; cf. also C. Cargnoni, 'Fonti, tendenze, sviluppi,' pp. 326–7.

85 Extremely few copies are extant: a first count finds only two copies of the first edition and two of the second printed by Damiano Turlino, in Bressa, 1548 (cf. C. Cargnoni, 'Fonti, tendenze,' footnote 79, p. 326).

86 *Regula et testamentum seraphici patris nostri s. Francisci. Compendioso discorso dil fra Giouanne da Fano, sopra il stato dell'altissima pouertà euangelica de frati minori.* Milan, for Bros. Francesco & Simone Moscheni, 1554; on this point, cf. F. Elizondo, 'El 'Breve Discorso' de Juan de Fano sobre la pobreza franciscana', *Collectanea Francescana*, 48 (1978), pp. 31–65.

87 Cf. above,

works:[88] *Specchio interiore*[89] and *Della cognitione et vittoria di se stessi.*[90] These works had been scheduled for expurgation since the promulgation of the 1564 Index:[91] to be precise, ever since – on the request of Cardinal Ludovico Simonetta, one of the legates who were members of the Tridentine commission charged with preparing the new Index – the works had been condemned *donec corrigentur* (moderating the previous prohibition pronounced by the Pauline Index) and entrusted to the General of the Company of Jesus, Giacomo Laìnez, *ut, ab eo expurgatae, excudi rursus possent et legi* ('so that, once purged by him, they might be immediately published and read').[92] As Laìnez fell ill shortly after being given this task, and in fact soon died,[93] this task had been set aside. It was only during the 1580s that times were again ripe for the work to be resumed. One remark, however, should first be made. The choice of the two texts to be expurgated out of the many written by the Dominican monk, or at least of his four most important works, was by no means fortuitous. Accepting the traditional subdivision of the path towards perfection into four 'stages',corresponding to the categories of the devout, defined respectively as beginners, the proficient, the perfect, and the most perfect, Battista da Crema had dedicated particular attention to each of these levels, writing

88 ACDF, Index, Protocolli G, cc. 203r–207v; and 193r–198r. The text of these censures appears in the appendix to S. Pagano, 'La condanna delle opere di fra' Battista da Crema. Tre inedite Censure del Sant'Offizio e della Congregazione dell'Indice,' *Barnabiti Studi*, 14 (1997), pp. 259–80.

89 Battista da Crema, *Specchio interiore opera divina per la cui lettione ciascuno devoto potrà facilmente ascendere al colmo della perfettione*, Milan, apud Calvo, 1540.

90 Battista da Crema, *Opera utilissima de la cognitione et vittoria di se stesso ... Composta per il reverendissimo Battista da Crema maestro di scientia spirituale pratica et perfettione, christiano rarissimo* (I edn, Milan, 1531), Venice, Nicolò Bascarini, 1545.

91 The memorial written by Paleotti in 1583 and debated that same year by the Congregation of the Index [full text published by A. Rotondò, 'Nuovi documenti per la storia dell'Indice dei libri proibiti (1572–1638),' pp. 163–71; cf. also P. Prodi, *Il cardinale Gabriele Paleotti (1522–1597)*, vol. II, Rome, Edizioni di storia e letteratura, 1967, pp. 241–2; and G. Fragnito, 'La Bibbia al rogo', pp. 125–7] enables us to deduce (albeit indirectly) that until that year Battista da Crema's works had not yet been expurgated, for in the response to 'Doubt 5' we read as follows: 'The works of Brother Battista da Crema are in the second class of the Trent Index, quandiu expurgata non prodierint, but it is better to keep them' ('L'opere di fra Battista da Crema sono nella 2a classe dell'Indice di Trento, *quandiu expurgata non prodierint*, però è bene ritenerle'; A. Rotondò, 'Nuovi documenti', p. 165). The date attributed by Sergio Pagano to the censures confirms this deduction as it is subsequent to that date; using biographical data regarding the only censor we can positively identify, the Augustine Brother Evangelista Bosio da Padova, Pagano opts for the period 1587–1593 (S. Pagano, 'La condanna delle opere di fra' Battista da Crema', pp. 251–4).

92 *Index des livres interdits*, vol. VIII, p. 106; cf. also ibid., p. 81.

93 M. Scaduto, *L'epoca di Giacomo Laínez 1556–1565. L'azione*, Rome, Edizioni La Civiltà Cattolica, 1974, p. 248.

four separate works: *Aperta verità* and *Philosophia divina*, intended for those taking their first steps up Battista da Crema's mystic stairway, and *Della cognitione et vittoria di se stessi* and *Specchio interiore*, meant for those who had already completed part of the way. While the object of the first two works was to persuade beginners to abandon all ties and earthly passions, the other two treatises selected by the church hierarchies for 'cleansing' were addressed to the proficient and the perfect, i.e. to those who had already come to terms with passions and earthly vices and only had to complete the process of nullification of their personal will, overcoming their last 'suspicions' (*suspitioni*) and 'fantasies' (*fantasie*), the last remaining obstacles along a path that was to lead them 'to become very similar to God' (*farsi ben simili a Dio*).[94]

These then were the two treatises that the author had dedicated to the devout who, having achieved 'a perfect victory over themselves', now 'do not fear the smoke of human praise, nor the insults of devilish confusion' and, 'like lamps on a candelabra […], firm and steady columns', 'are strengthened, so that not only do they not fall but being so pure […] it is always their pleasure to grow'.[95] *Specchio* and *Vittoria et cognitione* were without a doubt the writings which – in the framework of Carioni's typical theological gradualism – went furthest along the path of man's 'deification', revealing to readers hidden truths which no one else was permitted to know: in other words they were the writings that more than any other made Battista da Crema's productions comparable to the heretic doctrines of Cordoni's *Dyalogo* and Ripanti's *Circulus divinis amoris*.[96] The choice, as already said, was no chance matter. Precisely because of this particular function and destination, the space allowed in these two works to the element of will was practically non-existent. In *Philosophia divina* and *Aperta verità* the author clearly stressed the need to exercise human will as a privileged means to find within oneself the strength to abandon earthly ties and passions in order to turn freely to God. In contrast, in the works where Battista da Crema addressed the proficient and the perfect, the value of human free will and of human works was destined to lose a large part of the role they had been recognized as possessing: as the faithful believer gradually came nearer to God, ridding himself of the burdens that kept him tied to the earthly globe, he was called upon to forsake his own

94 E. Bonora, *I conflitti della Controriforma*, p. 152.

95 'giunti alla perfetta vittoria di se stessi, non temono fumo di laude bimana né vituperio di confusione diabolica e, come lucerne sopra de candeliere [...], colonne ferme et stabilite, sono fortificati, di sorte che non solo non cascano, ma stando in tal purità [...] sempre si dilettano di crescere' (ibid.).

96 For a comparison between Battista's writings and Cordoni's *Dyalogo*, cf. ibid., pp. 175 et seqq.

will to the point of total annulment in the will of God. The Dominican's other two works (*Aperta verità* and *Philosophia divina*) could wait. Even at a first reading of the censures made of the two texts, it is clear – as it is in Cordoni and Ripanti – that the censor's main objective was to reassert the centrality of human will in Catholic theology and to oppose any attempt to minimize the value of man's good works. Here, for example, is how, after transcribing one of the sentences that had most struck his imagination ('folio 175 side 2, line 12 it says, you shall glory in your good works as much as a donkey may glory when carrying a load of manure, etc.'),[97] he proceeded to deny it most categorically: 'The example is worthless, for when a man performs a good deed can he glory in God, as the Apostle says, *qui gloriat in Domino gloriet*?' ('Whoever glorifies God will be glorified').[98] He noticed another apparently rash statement by the author which suggested a vilification of human nature: 'It seems that it is not right to say that our Lord God made us as we are and that He subjugated us to these [evil] inclinations, for as our nature became corrupt and disorderly, not so much in ourselves as in Adam, we subjugated ourselves to God, placing upon us this yoke. And furthermore, if Adam had not sinned, man would not have borne this yoke.'[99]

The re-establishment of theological and doctrinal centrality to the element of human will thus remained, as a result of a persistent anti-Lutheran current of thought, the pivot around which the censors' action was destined to revolve and the main filter through which mystic literature – or rather its more extreme derivations – was also subjected to the control of the Church, following a censorial logic and sensitivity whose effects were felt without any great difficulty even within the Jesuit order. One who paid the cost of all this was Achille Gagliardi, the author of a *Breve compendio della perfezione cristiana*, which was written as an epilogue to his short but intense mystic experience, during which, in 1584, he was the spiritual counselor of Isabella Berinzaga. The *Compendio* was heavily attacked by his own brethren and after being subjected to strict censorial control was destined to be the victim of a series of tormented editorial vicissitudes.[100]

[97] 'fol. 175 fa. 2 lin 12 dice, tanto e non più ti devi tu gloriar delle tue buone opere quanto si può gloriar un asino a portar letame etc.'

[98] 'Par che l'esempio non vagli, perché quando l'huomo fa una buona opera si puole gloriar in Dio, come di' l'Apostolo qui gloriat in Domino gloriet?' (ACDF, Index, Protocolli G, 'Censura in libro Della cognitione e vittoria di se stesso', cc. 193r–198r, in particular c. 196r).

[99] Ibid., c. 194r.

[100] The text was written in about 1585 and published in Paris, in French, in 1596 with the title *Abrégé de la perfection*, without the author's obtaining authorization from his Order and probably without its knowledge. The first editions in Italian (Brescia, 1611, and Vicenza, 1612) were published anonymously (to be precise, the second of the two

While it is to be hoped that the whole episode may be reconstructed in full detail, it is striking that most of the censor's actions – intended to minimize the echo of the experiences of Isabella Berinzaga and in particular the most extreme points in her *via perfectionis* – rotated around the topic of human will. The deceptive claim of theological 'clarification' was in fact a cover for the censor's substantial alteration of the text: where, for example, Gagliardi had written that the soul leaves 'complete and immediate mastery of the entire body to God's pleasure [...] as if it no longer had any will of its own', he adjusted the spiritual master's words, adding: 'As if it no longer had possession of its will' (*come se non havesse più proprietà ne la sua volontà*). Or again, when the author developed his line of reasoning and compared this 'subtraction and renunciation' (*sottrazione e rinuncia*) to that of Christ in the Garden of Gethsemane, when He allowed himself to 'suffer the cross' (*patir croce*) not because that was His will but because it was His Father's, commenting: 'And thus [His will] became non-will' (*e così [la sua volontà] diventò non volontà*), and the censor punctually advised an opportune correction: 'It became not his own will' (*diventò non propria volontà*).[101]

gave as the author the generic definition of a 'Servant of God'). The first Italian edition to attribute its authorship to Gagliardi was *Breve compendio intorno alla perfettione cristiana. Dove si vede una pratica mirabile per unire l'anima con Dio. Del M.R.P. Achille Gagliardi. Teologo della Compagnia di Giesù*. In Napoli, per Giovan Giacomo Carlino, 1614. For this information, cf. *Breve compendio di perfezione cristiana. Un testo di Achille Gagliardi S.I. Introductory essay and critical edition* (M. Gioia (ed.), Rome-Brescia, Gregorian University Press – Morcelliana, 1996 ('Aloisiana', 28), in particular pp. 18–23). Regarding the text's reception by the censor, see ibid., pp. 39–43, and especially S. Stroppa, 'L'annichilazione e la censura: Isabella Berinzaga e Achille Gagliardi', *Rivista di storia e letteratura religiosa*, n. 3, 1996, pp. 617–25, in which the author makes use of the different manuscript readings of the text and corresponding variations pointed out in Mario Gioia's recent edition. A little-studied source, the series of 'Censurae librorum' internal to the Jesuit order and a source that might well add much to an in-depth study of this topic, was first drawn to the attention of scholars by U. Baldini, 'Una fonte poco utilizzata per la storia intellettuale: le 'censurae librorum' et 'opinionum' nell'antica Compagnia di Gesù', *Annali dell'Istituto storico italo-germanico in Trento*, XI, 1985, pp. 19–50. On the relationship between Achille Gagliardi and Isabella Berinzaga, cf. also P. Pirri, 'Il P. Achille Gagliardi, la dama milanese, la riforma dello spirito e il movimento degli zelatori', *Archivum Historicum Societatis Iesu*, XIV (1945), pp. 1–72; on his mystic masterpiece, see Id., 'Il breve compendio di Achille Gagliardi al vaglio dei teologi gesuiti', ibid., XX, 1951, pp. 231–53 and Id., 'Gagliardiana 1. Un nuovo importante codice del Breve compendio di perfezione cristiana', ibid., XXLX, 1960, pp. 99–129.

101 S. Stroppa, 'L'annichilazione e la censura', p. 624. The vicissitudes of Gagliardi's *Compendio* have to be seen also in relation to the evolution during those years within the Company of Jesus, with particular reference to the important change in matters concerning spirituality which had started during the Generalship of Mercuriano and continued under General Acquaviva. The Jesuit Order in fact viewed with favor a change from 'a contemplative and almost mystic spirituality to one that was much more active and practical', with the intention of 'replacing meditation that rotates around the focusing of the soul in its inward

The presence, among the Siena trial documents kept in the Roman archive of the Holy Office, of an Inquisition trial in 1585 against a Jesuit Father found guilty of 'writing and pronouncing' rash statements about the salvific and glorifying power of prayer does not seem to be a mere chronological coincidence. Antonio Francesco Ghelfucci, a Jesuit lector of grammar, was invited to 'correct' some sentences which appeared to suggest, according to the Inquisition authorities in Siena, that 'a Christian who prays may very soon [...] gain perpetual glory both for himself and for others' and that prayer was the 'most useful, most honest exercise in this life without any limitation', and an 'exercise' of even 'greater perfection' than the 'theological virtues'. To the precise question asked of him by the Inquisitor of Siena whether 'he who prays can be sure he is in a state of grace and that whomsoever he prays for is in a state of grace', the Jesuit's answer was evidently deemed to be too evasive. Ghelfucci replied, 'I say that whoever prays cannot know, without God's revelation, whether he or any other is in a state of grace because it cannot be known whether his prayer has been granted. If I say it is sure I mean this in the ordinary way in which people speak' [shortly before he had used the expression 'the common manner of speech']. To overcome any remaining doubts about terminology and contents, the Inquisitor made the 'accused' sign his name to three 'propositions' by which he corrected the meaning of what he had stated, thus permitting the Siena authorities to shelve the case: '1. Nothing more delightful etc. than prayer, I mean this to be taken as an exaggeration [...] rejecting any error that may derive therefrom; 2. Whoever prays for himself and others perpetuates glory in this life [...] I mean for those who are in a state of grace etc. [...]; 3. Whoever prays in this life [...] will surely receive help'. Besides providing evidence of the sensitivity of the Inquisition censorship authorities, who were particularly on the watch for the dangers arising from any minimization of the value of the intervention of divine Grace to the advantage of the excessive confidence of those among the faithful who placed excessive trust in an earthly 'means' such as prayer, this short trial provides documentary evidence of the specific attention paid by the Inquisition to Members of the Company of Jesus in those

process, taking into account above all the attributes of God, with another that contemplated more the function of Jesus Christ in the spiritual life of each person, whose figure became the center of meditation' (see J. Martinez Millán, 'Transformacióon y crisis de la Compañía de Jesús (1578–1594)', *I religiosi a corte. Teologia, politica e diplomazia in antico regime*', F. Rurale (ed.), Rome, Bulzoni, 1998, pp. 101–29, in particular pp. 106–7 (my translation from the Spanish); but cf. also I. Iparraguirre, 'Para la historia de la oraciòn en el Colegio Romano durante la segunda mitad del Siglo XVI', *Archivum Historicum Societatis Iesu*, XV (1946), pp. 77–126; and A. Guerra, *Un generale fra le milizie del Papa. La vita di Claudio Acquaviva scritta da Francesco Sacchini della Compagnia di Gesù*, Milan, Franco Angeli, 2001, pp. 115–20).

years as soon as they approached the subject, so dear to them, of prayer, allowing themselves to be transported by its supposed immense spiritual and earthly powers.[102]

The anti-Lutheran slant that we have seen as being characteristic of the approach of the Inquisition authorities in Rome to the subject of 'mystic-unitive' prayer seemed to be destined to interfere with the censors' capacity of interpretation even in those few cases when, considering matters of prayer, they perceived dangers other than that of the Lutheran certainty of faith.

A first sign in this sense can be seen if we read a censorial note – a further testimony of the attention paid by the Roman authorities under the leadership of Sirleto to the theme of prayer and the act of praying in the late 1570s and early 1580s – concerning a work by the Bishop and Cardinal John Fisher, a future saint of the Church of Rome,[103] entitled *Tractatus de orando Deum, et de fructibus precum, modoque orandi* ('Treatise on praying to God, the fruits of prayer, and the way to pray'), published posthumously in Rome in 1578.[104] The censorial authorities' oversensitivity to this subject may explain an interest which otherwise is

[102] ACDF, Inquisition of Siena, Processi, vol. 10, trial against Antonio Francesco of the Company of Jesus, Grammar Lector, 1585, cc. 712r–715r. With regard to this matter, must one do not neglect the general situation of the relationship between the Roman Inquisition and the Jesuit Order, with the Holy Office in those same years siding with the Pope against some influential members of the 'Castellanista' party which for some time had taken control of the running of the Order to the disadvantage of the opposing 'Papist' party. (cf. J. Martinez Millán, 'Transformación y crisis', p. 114).

[103] John Fisher was born at Beverley in about 1469 and died in London in 1535. He was a Cardinal, humanist, theologian, Bishop of Rochester [Roffense], confessor and spiritual father of Henry VIII's entire family, and an extremely bitter anti-Lutheran polemicist. On Fisher, cf. A. Stewart, *The life of John Fisher cardinal Bishop of Rochester; with an appendix containing the bishop's funeral sermons, letters*, London, Burns & Oates, 1879; C. Eubel – W. van Gulik, I, vol. III, Monasterii, sumptibus et typis Librariae Regensbergianae, 1923, p. 286; Enciclopedia Cattolica, Vatican City, Ente per l'Enciclopedia cattolica e il libro antico, 1948–1954, vol. VI, 1951, pp. 626–7; on his friendship with Erasmus, cf. Erasmus and Fisher: their correspondence, 1511–1524, by Jean Rodschausse, Paris, Vrin, 1968. Fisher is rightly remembered as a keen anti-Lutheran polemicist: his best-known writing is his *Assertionis Lutheranae confutatio iuxta verum ac originalem archetypum, nunc ad vnguem diligentissime recognita. Per reuerendum patrem Ioannem Roffensem episcopum, academie Canthabrigien cancellarium.* Aeditio vltima, variis annotationibus in margine locupletata, Venice, in aedibus Gregorii de Gregoriis, August 1526.

[104] *Ioannis Roffensis episcopi et S.R.E. Cardinalis, Tractatus de orando Deum, et de fructibus precum, modoque orandi*, Rome, apud Franciscum Zanettum, 1578. The document of censure (which bears no indication either as to the date or to the author) is to be found in ACDF, Index, Protocolli G, c. 151r. The observation that the only known printed edition, dated as said 1578, lacks the two expressions deemed by the censor to be dangerous (cf. below) might suggest a pre-emptive intervention by the censor himself, in other words an intervention prior to publication. However, we cannot exclude the possibility that two

inexplicable.[105] Scrupulously careful as he was, showing great zeal but also a basic lack of any overall theological or doctrinal vision, Fisher's censor noted down in two short pages, and without any comment, passages by the author that contained a minimization of the importance of human works, as in Lutheran thinking, plus others in which he discerned (not without some stretching of his interpretation) a Pelagian-style exaltation of the human will. Thus, on the one hand, he noted a point in the text where men's prayers were defined as 'profane and unclean,implicitly rebuking the author for minimizing the value of human works:

> Sheet 20 page 2, where he says: God lends His most sacred ears to our profane and impure prayers etc.; up to this point there is no error in meaning (as the author himself says below); however these two words, profane and impure, are placed at this point most improperly, for profane and impure prayers can surely be defined as prayers in which one asks God for something wrong, such as revenge for a murder, etc., these are the prayers that God in no way answers.'[106]

---

editions were printed in the course of the year 1578 and that, of the two editions, only the second (the corrected one) is extant today.

[105] There is nothing in the life of Fisher that seems to me to contain any elements capable of damaging post mortem his completely orthodox image and therefore of indirectly justifying any posthumous interest by the censorial authorities. The consequences of this fleeting action by the censors were in any case extremely limited, as the year 1592 saw the publication of the work's Italian translation (*Breue trattato di Giovanni Vescouo Roffense ... del modo di pregare Iddio, e de' frutti che si cauano dall'oratione*. Napoli, ex officina Horatii Saluiani, appresso Giovanni Giacomo Carlino & Antonio Pace, 1592). The Clementine Index of 1596 would appear to have contained the name of the Cardinal – not however with reference to this publication but rather as the presumed author of a volume entitled *De fiducia et misericordia Dei*, which was, as expressly stated, a work falsely attributed to him (*Index des livres interdits*, vol. IX, p. 704).

[106] 'Fol. 20 pag. 2 ibi: Deum aures suas sacerrimas ad prophanas et immundas nostras preces inclinare etc. quamque in sensu nullum omnino vitium est (ut autor ipse inferius exponit) adhuc tamen haec duae voces: prophanae et immundae; impropríssime ponuntur hoc loco, prophanae enim et immundae preces proculdubio eae dicuntur in quibus, res iniuste postulante a deo, scilicet vindicta homicidium etc. has autem preces nullo modo Deus exaudit' (ACDF, Index, Protocolli G, c. 151r). As foreshadowed in the previous footnote, this reference to the 'prophanas et immundas nostras preces' was changed in a later edition (or possibly in the first – cf. the considerations made above in footnote 103) into a more innocuous 'nostras preces': 'Quamquam divina maiestas' (this is the 'purified' passage) 'supereminentissimae fuerit celsitudinis, est nihilominus adeo pia, clemens et dulcis, ut non dedignetur aures suas sacerrimas ad nostras preces inclinare, modo non desit nobis animus resistendi peccatis' (I. FISCHER, *Ioannis Roffensis episcopi et S.R.E. Cardinalis, Tractatus de orando Deum, et de fructibus precum, modoque orandi*, Rome, *apud* Franciscum Zanettum, 1578, pp. 29–30). This version of the passage in question was faithfully preserved in the vernacular Italian translation published in 1592: 'Although our Lord God is immense in His majesty, he is nonetheless so clement and so bountiful that He does not disdain to bow down and lend His most holy ears to our prayers, if we promise to flee our vices and abandon our

On the other hand – without in the least troubling himself about the contradiction into which he was falling – he proffered a passage from the piece that enabled him to dwell on the dangers of an interpretation of the relationship between faith and good works in the Pelagian sense:

> Sheet 41 page 1, ibid., but whatever we do (up to the point where our sins were caused by us alone), it does not seem possible to sustain that these words – 'by us alone' – exclude the general help of God, who moves man to action, and I shall certainly say that we are nearly unable to think of anything by ourselves, or to perform any effective work, nor is it possible in this case to doubt the cause. If the above words exclude grace, which is a customary gift, in the manner in which it seems necessary to understand it, then it contradicts canon 7 on justification pronounced by the Council of Trent.[107]

The emergence of Pelagian demands in relation to the subject of prayer was recorded by the Roman authorities in the early 1580s, also in connection with the 'Mocenigo case'. Filippo Mocenigo, Archbishop

---

sins' (*Breue trattato di Giouanni Vescouo Roffense ... del modo di pregare Iddio, e de' frutti che si cauano dall'oratione*, p. 27).

[107] 'Fol. 41 pag. 1 ibid., sed quaecumque nos agimus quatenus a solis nobis processerint peccata magis etc. non videtur sustinendum nam si per illa verba / solis nobis / excluditur, generale Dei hominem moventis, auxilium, fatebor equidem, nos ne sufficientes quidem esse aliquid cogitare quasi ex nobis, ne dum opus aliquod vel minimum efficere, neque in hoc casu potuit esse dubitandi causa. Si vero per praefata verba excluditur gratia qua est donum habituale quemadmodum videtur necessario intelligendum. Tunc contradicit Concil. Tridentinum Cano. 7 de iustificatione' (ACDF, Index, Protocolli G, c. 151r). In this case it seems that the elimination of the expression marked by the censor required a reworking of the entire section, which in the 'new' version runs as follows: 'It is certainly true that no one, however heavily he may be burdened by the most serious of sins, will be entirely without merit, thanks to his prayer: for either he will be rewarded in the present age with temporal prizes or he will at some future time be treated less severely, at least as regards the punishments that he will suffer' ('Certum equidem est, neminem quantumvis gravissimis onustus peccatis fuerit, orationis suae merito prorsus omni cariturum: remunerabitur enim aut in praesenti saeculo praemiis quibusdam temporariis, aut saltem quantum ad poenas mitius in futuro tractabitur'; I. Fischer, *Tractatus de orando Deum*, p. 56). And here is the vernacular translation: 'It is quite true that when each man prays, although he is laden with sin, he does not pray without some merit because either he will be rewarded in this world with temporal prizes or in the next world his torments will be lightened, but his prayer will never gain him the glory of Paradise' (*Breve trattato*, p. 53). Another testimony of the Inquisition authorities' anti-Pelagian sensitiveness was provided by Paolo Simoncelli with reference to certain writings by Chiari (P. Simoncelli, 'Documenti interni alla Congregazione dell'Indice', p. 200 and footnote 35). This sensitiveness was not yet however perfect if it is true, as Adriano Prosperi pointed out, that none of the censors recognized in the clearly Pelagian tenor of these writings the unmistakable influence of Giorgio Siculo's Epistola (A. Prosperi, '*L'eresia del Libro grande. Storia di Giorgio Siculo e della sua setta*, Milan, Feltrinelli, 2000, footnote 2 at p. 470, and p. 376).

of Cyprus and brother of Marcantonio, was a member of a distinguished Venetian patrician family, another branch of which was that of Alvise di Marin, who had once been condemned by the Holy Office in Venice for Lutheran heresy.[108] In 1583 he was tried by the Inquisition after oral testimonies of various origin had been officially pronounced against him over the course of the previous two decades.[109] The trial was so unusual that a record of it is preserved in the series of *Censurae librorum* kept in the Inquisition archive in Rome:[110] most of the proceedings concerned an analysis of a manuscript book written by Mocenigo (entitled *Circa la via et progressi spirituali*) in which the Inquisitors strove to find confirmation of the charges laid against him.[111] In the course of the detailed analysis

108 Regarding Alvise Mocenigo and his experiences with the Inquisition, cf. F. Ambrosini, *Storie di patrizi e di eresia nella Venezia del '500*, Milan, Franco Angeli, 1999, pp. 110–12 and 122–35; on Marcantonio and Filippo Mocenigo, cf. ibid., p. 114, footnote 49 and P. Grendler, The 'Tre Savi sopra eresia', 1547–1605: a prosopographical study, in 'Studi veneziani', new series, 3 (1979), pp. 283–340, in particular p. 314.

109 ACDF, Inquisition, series Censurae librorum, vol. I, file 5 (1583), against Filippo Mocenigo, cc. 47r–191v. Immediately after Brother Antonio da Venezia was accused in 1561, the Inquisition opened a file on this Venetian ecclesiastic. His influential friends in the Curia and his noble ancestry won him immunity for some years, until 1572, when the accusations against him were reiterated in evidence given by Teofilo Martino da Siena. Like his previous accuser, this monk from Monte Cassino sowed the doubt that Mocenigo might be suspected of Pelagianism. But once again no action was taken. It was only in the early 1580s, to be precise in 1583, that the Holy Office in Rome decided to get to the bottom of the matter and attempted to ascertain the truth of the allegations that had been made against him. This time the Roman Inquisition was able to use not only oral testimony but also documents written by the accused himself which the Inquisitional authorities could verify directly (cf. also P. Godman, The saint as censor. Robert Bellarmin between Inquisition and Index, Leiden, Brill, 2000, pp. 21 et sqq).

110 There is still much to investigate regarding this archive series of 'Censurae librorum' of the Congregation of the Holy Office (for a first approach, cf. P. Godman, The saint as censor, p. 20). However, we know that after the creation of the Congregation of the Index, the Holy Office did not renounce its special rights in the field of book censorship, faithful as it was to a broad interpretation of its powers. On the conflicts between the two Congregations, ample documentation has been provided by Gigliola Fragnito (*La Bibbia al rogo*, *passim*; and Ead., 'La censura libraria tra Congregazione dell'Indice, Congregazione dell'Inquisizione e Maestro del Sacro Palazzo (1571–1596)', *La censura libraria nell'Europa del Cinquecento*, U. Rozzo (ed.), Convegno Internazionale di Studi, Cividale del Friuli, 9–10 November, 1995, Udine, Forum, 1997, pp. 163–75).

111 In 1581 Mocenigo published a work on 'human perfection' entitled *Philippi Mocenici archiepiscopi Nicosiensis regni Cypri, etc. Universales institutiones ad hominum perfectionem; quatenus industria parari potest* (Venetiis, *apud* Aldum). However, this work, dedicated to Gregory XIII and solemnly approved by the Pope himself, as also by the Emperor and the kings of France and Spain, must not be confused with the Latin version of the vernacular work which attracted the Inquisition's attention. Regarding *Universales institutiones* and the inquisitorial process against Mocenigo, see now E. Bonora, *Giudicare i vescovi. La definizione dei poteri nella Chiesa postridentina*, Roma-Bari, Laterza, 2007,

of Mocenigo's manuscript, it became evident that the censor's attention was directed at the bombastic over-estimation of man's capacity to undertake and successfully conclude the mystical *via perfectionis*: 'If the soul can rise to the understanding of God's immense goodness and unfathomable wisdom', he observed in his notes, after reading one of the most emblematic sentences,[112] 'then the soul can become God, which is impossible, as that which comprehends cannot be less than that which is comprehended, and for that reason the learned doctors say that no created being, whatever its absolute perfection, can comprehend divine wisdom and goodness but only itself'.[113] To the mind of the Holy Office Consultor, this Pelagian danger appeared to become increasingly more dangerous as the author gradually approached the theme of prayer. The reading of the text of a prayer, *Oratione, la quale frequentata potria giovar non poco al progresso spirituale, et seria bene dirla innanzi l'Imagine del Crucifisso, et più presto in modo di meditatione, che leggondola* ('Prayer, the use of which may no little benefit spiritual progress; it would be good to say it before the Image of the Crucifix, meditating upon it rather than reading it'),[114] kept among the papers in the Mocenigo file, in the appendix to the manuscript work by the Venetian ecclesiastic, had given him forewarning. Here the echoes of a still-active Christocentricism took on a Pelagian-type slant, in an unusual doctrinal combination. The emphasis which from the beginning of the *Oratione* was laid on the 'Most Holy Body [of Jesus Christ] who died with such suffering' (*santissimo corpo [di Iesu Christo] morto con tanta afflitione*) and the impassioned invocation of the 'fruit of Your Divine Mercy' (*frutto della Divina vostra Misericordia*) accompanied

pp. 263–86. Nothing remains of the printed matter examined by the Inquisitors (*Circa le vie et progressi spirituale*) except for a manuscript version kept in the Roman archive of the Holy Office in the 'Raccolta dei Libri della Censura Librorum'. The text of the condemnation explicitly refers to 'exemplaria edita' of this vernacular work, but as far as I can ascertain no trace remains of any printed edition.

112 The censor himself cited the sentence in question before pronouncing his comments: 'At c. 61 f. 2 we read: 'and they can raise their soul to the understanding of the immense goodness of Our Lord in His desire to give new strength to His creatures and to reduce the universe not only to its own harmony but to one more noble yet, as [to the understanding] of His unfathomable wisdom and providence which are beyond our understanding, etc.' (ACDF, Inquisition, series Censurae librorum, vol. I, file 5 (1583), Contra Filippo Mocenigo, c. 73r).

113 'Se l'anima si può elevare alla comprensione dell'immensa bontà, et incomprensibil sapientia divina, già l'anima può diventar Dio, il che è impossibile, poiché il comprensore non è minor della cosa compresa, et per questo dicono li dottori, che qualsivoglia creatura, benché perfettissima non può comprendere l'incomprensibil sapientia et bontà divina, ma solo essa stessa' (ibid., c. 73r).

114 The text is in Mocenigo's manuscript volume (*Circa le Vie e Progressi Spirituali*) at cc. 129v–130v.

each other in a design that was substantially consistent with the reflected image of the faithful believer who, with the 'most excellent gift of the Intellect' (*dono eccellentissimo dell'Intelletto*), having won his personal struggle against vices and earthly passions (pride, wrath, avarice, gluttony, lust, sloth), begged the Son of God to permit him 'to perform Thy will in full' (*penetrare al pieno adempimento della volontà vostra*). Here below are a few passages of the forbidden prayer:

> O Lord, my Redeemer Jesus Christ, I pray Thee, by virtue of Thy Most Holy Body that died with such suffering and rose again with such glory, to mortify all my earthly, worldly, and fleshly affections and revive me in my spirit with Thy divine spirit. Wherefore, all pride having been extinguished, may there live within me true humility, and with the gift of Thy Most Holy Awe may it be protected from all evils, and become part of Thy Most High Celestial Kingdom. [...]
>
> All gluttony having been extinguished, and love of bodily comforts, may there live in me the capacity for true mercy, and with the most noble gift of Thy Counsel may I be permitted to accomplish Thy will in its entirety and, following it with all my strength, may I always receive the fruit of Thy divine Mercy.[115]

The Pelagian stress on man's merit, confirmed by the phrase 'trusting to enjoy it fully' (*con fiducia di doverla fruir pienamente*) used by Mocenigo, must have persuaded the censor that his suspicions were fully justified. But he became even more sure of his convictions when he began to read the remarks dedicated by the author to the Lord's Prayer. Thus wrote the censor, repeating Mocenigo's comment on the sixth invocation in the Lord's Prayer ('Deliver us from evil'):

> It says on the same page [c. 50], side 2, that in the sixth invocation in the Lord's Prayer we ask to be delivered from temptation, and the following words are said: "Always considering not temptations from which we can free ourselves

115 'Signor, et Redentor mio Iesu Christo vi prego, ch'in virtù del S.mo Corpo vostro morto con tanta afflinone, et risuscitato con tanta gloria vogliate mortificare ogni affetto mio terreno, mondano, et carnale, et vivificarmi nello spirito con il divino spirito vostro. Siche estinta ogni superbia viva in me una vera humiltà, et con il dono del S.mo timor vostro meriti essere assicurata da tutti i mali, et constituita in parte dell'altiss.mo vostro Regno celeste. [...] Estinta ogni Gola, et affetto di commodità corporali, viva in me la efficacia della vera misericordia, et con il dono altissimo del Consiglio vostro meriti di penetrare al pieno adempimento della volontà vostra, et seguendola con tutti li spiriti miei, riceva sempre il frutto della Divina vostra Misericordia.'

by avoiding the opportunity but those to which we are violently drawn by evil spirits and by the men who follow them".[116]

To maintain that man was able to flee certain temptations without the help of God meant for the censor choosing to follow Pelagius beyond the bounds of Catholic orthodoxy:

> This sentence confirms that there are certain temptations from which we can free ourselves by dint of our own industry, without any need to ask the Lord for help, a concept that clashes with another sentence among His pronouncements, *sine me nihil potestis facere* ('without me you can do nothing') and also with another of the Apostles, *non summus sufficientes cogitare aliquid ex nobis, sed sufficientia nostra ex deo est* ('we are not capable of thinking anything by ourselves – all but our capacity comes from God')[117]

'It is not wrong,' he went on, referring explicitly to the doctrinal clash which in antiquity set St Augustine at odds with Pelagius,

> to be mindful, when we pray, to beg God to help us not only to avoid falling into the violent temptations of demons and evil men but also to save us from those temptations which, once the opportunities are removed, are easy to decline, because without God's grace we shall in fact not shun the opportunities; and as this avoidance of opportunities is the reason and cause of our incapacity to resist when violent temptations come, it follows that everything depends on our own determination when we defeat the demon and gain Paradise, as St Augustine said when persuading the Pelagians, who held that, although to act more easily we needed God's grace, consenting to grace was nonetheless a matter of our own; which, being heretic, was condemned, for if by his natural strength or industry a man can recover from an evil, provided it is small and then only with difficulty, it follows that, by strengthening himself with similar exercises, he will be able to recover from all evils, above all if we suppose that he gains for himself the help of God by shunning the opportunities and consenting to inspirations of goodness.[118]

116 'Alla carta medesima [c. 50] faccia 2, si dice che nella sesta petitione dell'oratione del signore domandiamo essere assecurati dalla tentatione, et pongonsi queste parole: "Havendo sempre risguardo non a quelle tentationi dalle quali potemo liberarci fuggendo l'occasioni, ma da quelle nelle quali possono condurci violentemente li maligni spiriti, et gl'huomini seguaci loro" ' (ibid., c. 72r).

117 'Questa sententia conferma che ci sono alcune tentationi dalle quali possiamo liberarci per industria nostra, senza bisogno di domandare aiuto al signore, il che è contra quella sua sententia, *sine me nihil potestis facere* et quell'altra dell'apostolo, *non sumus sufficientes cogitare aliquid ex nobis, sed sufficientia nostra ex deo est*' (ibid.).

118 'Non è mal fatto haver l'ochio quando oriamo a domandar aiuto a Dio per non cascar non solo nelle tentationi violenti delli demoni et huomini maligni, ma ancora da quelle che con levar le occasioni si possono declinare, perche senza aiuto della gratia di

'True Catholic faith', he vigorously asserted, 'maintains that although free will plays its part, nonetheless it is not sufficient without God's help either to justify oneself or to keep oneself in a state of righteousness, as was declared in the Tridentine Council *de Iust. Can. 22* ('about justification canon 22')'.[119]

However, it would appear that the Consultor's learned argument did not prove very convincing, as the Members of the Congregation of the Holy Office fully acquitted the accused. In fact, following a practice that was quite frequent, though not for that reason any the less equivocal, the Roman Inquisitors in one and the same breath decreed the Venetian cleric's complete innocence (*non esse haereticum, neque suspectum de haeresi*: 'he is not heretical, nor suspected of heresy') and hastened to order the suppression of all copies in circulation of the incriminated work. The ambiguity of the verdict, which certainly can be seen as being related to Mocenigo's influential connections in the Curia and the upper levels of the aristocracy, reflected the existence of a hierarchic scale in the evaluation of heretical doctrines, on which scale Pelagianism clearly did not occupy a very high level. Thus runs the text of the Inquisition's controversial decision:

> This booklet on spiritual progress is written in the vernacular and composed by the same author, and although it has been revised by these men and approved by them as also by the former Inquisitor of Venice in a report prepared both by the former censors and by himself, it must be further examined and revised so that, should it contain any ambiguous, obscure, or dangerous affirmations, it may be suppressed and the copies that have already been, or are about to be, published may be prevented from circulating, and they should be taken to the Holy Office so that they too may be suppressed.[120]

Dio ne manco fuggiremo le occasioni, et essendo questo guardarsi dalle occasioni principio et causa che ancora quando vengono le violenti tentationi non resistiamo, seguitaria che il tutto dependaria dalle forze nostre quando vinciamo il demonio, et acquistiamo il paradiso, come convince S. Agostino i Pelagiani, quali dicevano che se bene era bisogno della gratia di Dio per più facilmente operare, nondimeno il consentire alla gratia era tutto nostro; il che come heretico è stato damnato, percioché se per sua naturai forza o industria può l'huomo resipiscer da un male benché piccolo et con dif-ficultà, seguitata che rinforzandosi per simili esercitii potrà restaurarsi da tutti, massime se poniamo che per se stesso si guadagni l'aiuto di dio fuggendo le occasioni, et consentendo alle buone inspirationi' (ibid.).

[119] 'La verità catholica è che se bene concorre il libero arbitrio, nondimeno esso non è sufficiente senza l'aiuto divino né a giustificarsi, né a conservarsi in giustitia, come si dice nel Concilio Tridentino *de Iust. Can. 22*' (ibid.).

[120] 'Libellum autem de spiritualibus progressibus vulgari lingua ab ipso composito licet a piis quibusdam viris revisum, et ab eis et ab Inquisitore olim Venetiarum ad relationem tamen alterius sibi factam probatum cum denuo recognitus, et examinatus, non nullas propositiones ambiguas, et obscuras, et periculosas, [...] continere dignoscatur, fore et esse supprimendum, et exemplaria edita, vel aliis communicata ab eo fore, et esse colligenda, et

As has recently been written, 'the atmosphere created by the triumph of the Counter-Reformation, with the violent polemic against the Augustinism of the Reformation, was favorably inclined toward accentuated mystic and devout expressions of the goodness and importance of man's work. [...] The lack of attention, or indeed the favor, shown toward mystic accentuations and the impulse to achieve sanctity through human works were therefore popular trends'; in other words, 'the polemic against the ideas propounded by Luther led to a shifting of mainline Catholic doctrine towards Pelagian leanings'.[121] When dealing with Fisher's *Tractatus de orando Deum*, the censor had shown little knowledge of the topics treated and the emergence of Pelagian elements had been only fleetingly noticed and pointed out; while on the contrary, in the case of Mocenigo, the dual formula of acquittal/condemnation evidently marked a limit that the Roman authorities were not yet ready to cross.[122]

These reflections should make it clear that mystic prayer attracted the action of the censor only, or almost only, when it was equated to the message of Lutheranism, as we have seen with reference to the topic of free will. It is also clear that, parallel to the weakening of the drive to repress Protestant doctrines, even the most passionate manifestations of the rich spiritual tradition of mysticism were destined to regain the ground they had lost.

The late 1580s saw what seemed to be the conclusion of an intense and important phase of censorship by Rome – a phase in which the character and personal viewpoint of Pope Gregory XIII must have occupied a not insignificant position, still to be fully studied.[123]

---

in sancto officio exhibenda, ut similiter supprimantur, prout illum, et illa supprimi'. The decision was taken in the course of the meeting held on 6 October 1583 (ibid., cc. 191r–v).

[121] A. Prosperi, *L'eresia del Libro grande*, p. 376.

[122] It is clear that in the absence of any complete study of sixteenth-century anti-Pelagianism we have to limit ourselves here to mentioning isolated cases and to outlining trends that need to be inserted into a more organic framework.

[123] A fine letter written by Agostino Valier a few years later, in 1600, provides a good illustration of Gregory XIII's particular sensitivity towards mystic and ecstatic degenerations. Responding to questions put to him by the Inquisitor of Turin, who wished to know how he should react in the presence of 'many accidental falls that appear to occur in what appears to be a state of ecstasy or loss of consciousness and even of rapture occurring during the admirable devotion of Our Lady of Vico at Mondovì', the Cardinal of Verona recalled to our attention the legacy of the teachings of Gregory XIII: 'as can be seen from the example of Pope Gregory XIII, who once, when a devout believer fell into a state of ecstasy before him, had the person taken away and never asked what became of the person' ('Come si vede dall'essempio di Papa Gregorio decimo terzo inanti a cui andando in estasi una divota persona se la fece levar d'avanti, né mai più dimandò che ne fosse'; 'Consideratione sopra le cadute d'alcuni di quelli che vanno alla divotione della santissima Vergine di Mondovì;'

It is no coincidence that in 1588 – after a delay of some fifty years – the last of a long series of works devoted to the Lord's Prayer was published. This was the treatise *Della unione dell'anima con Dio sopra il Pater noster* by the Venerated Mother Battista Vernazza,[124] daughter of Ettore Vernazza, the celebrated founder of the Oratory of Divine Love. The original version of the work dates from 1538, the same year incidentally as the first edition of Cordoni's *Dyalogo*. The similarity of the title, as also of the content, had perhaps discouraged a 'hasty' (*frettolosa*) publication of the text. The work remained unpublished for five decades until it finally appeared after the death of its author (9 May 1587). Some questions inevitably arise, for Battista Vernazza's obstinate reluctance throughout the course of her long life to have the work published is worthy of inquiry. The generous attempt made by the promoter of the editorial venture in 1588, Don Dionisio da Piacenza, to explain this long chronological gap from 1538 to 1588 as being caused exclusively by the shy nature of this mystic Genoese lady and by her proven avoidance of all public life ('the truly humble person [...] is one who shuns all honor') is not sufficient to explain the episodes of a life that was far more complex than it was intended it should appear. Indeed the 'apology' – placed by don Dionisio in the form of a dedication at the head of the complete edition of Vernazza's works ('To the most Illustrious and most Reverend Monsignor Nicolò Sfondrato, Cardinal and Bishop of Cremona', Piacenza, 5 January 1587) revealed a certain measure of anxiety. 'The Works of the Venerable Mother Dame Battista Vernazza', thus the Lateran Canon begins, 'which have now been printed are in themselves so spiritual and full of divine feelings and sentiments that they would appear to need no human protection to defend them from any

Letter from the Cardinal of Verona to the Inquisitor of Turin, Rome, 4 October 1600, in *Scriniolum*, f. 617 et sqq).

[124] Battista Vernazza, *Della unione dell'anima con Dio sopra il Pater noster. Tratt. della Reverenda, et Devotissima Vergine di Christo, Donna Battista da Genoa, Can. Regolare Lateranense*, in *Opere spirituali della Reverenda et Devotissima Vergine di Christo, Donna Battista da Genova, Canonica Regolare Lateranense*. In tre tomi distinte, nelle quali tutta l'altezza della Christiana perfettione, et intima amorosa union con Dio (quanto sia possibile) chiaramente s'insegna. Hor prima date in luce, con tre tavole utilissime et copiosissime. With privileges. Venice, apud the heirs of Francesco Ziletti, 1588. For some biographic information about Battista Vernazza, cf. L. Ferrari, *Onomasticon. Repertorio biobibliografico degli scrittori italiani dal 1501 al 1850*, Milan, Hoepli, 1947, p. 686; P.L. Ferri, *Biblioteca femminile italiana*, Padua, Crescini, 1842, pp. 380–1; *Elogi di Liguri illustri*, second edition re-edited, corrected, and expanded by D.L. Grillo, Genoa-Turin, 1846–77, 4 vols, vol. I, pp. 17–25, R. Soprani, *Li scrittori della Liguria e particolarmente della marittima*, Genoa, P.G. Calenzani, 1667, p. 55, and especially D. Solfaroli Camillocci, 'La monaca esemplare. Lettere spirituali di madre Battistina Vernazza (1497–1587)', *Per lettera. La scrittura epistolare femminile tra archivio e tipografia, secoli XV–XVII*, G. Zarri (ed.), Rome, Viella, 1999, pp. 235–61.

calumny that may be devised by the envy or maliciousness of others.'[125] The immediate sensation that this is a case of *excusatio non petita* is confirmed in the continuation of the Dedication:

> But rather let these works succeed in persuading and in clearly convincing all who read them with a sincere mind that they were written more with supernatural inspiration and with continual use of prayer than with human industry or other manner of study; whence it seems to me quite superfluous to spend on them many long words as a formal Apology.[126]

Despite Don Dionisio's attempted cover-up, reading between the lines one can clearly discern the shadows of the polemics, of the diffidence, and possibly also of the suspicions that had gathered around Vernazza's works. Almost as if to provide some legitimate support for his editorial enterprise, as if he wished to share with others the responsibility for his choice, he invoked in his aid the authority of 'my spiritual Father' and of 'some Fathers of Theology':

> I therefore recall not only the great diligence and scrupulous attention which the Very Reverend Father Don Gasparo, Joint Canon and my spiritual Father, God rest his soul, desired to devote to these Works, spending many years on them, but also recalling the attention that was given to them by the Most Illustrious Carlo Borromeo of St Praxedes, when he showed them to some Fathers of Theology, most distinguished for their wit and erudition, by whom the works were carefully revised, undersigned, and approved.[127]

Thus the work was solemnly and officially undersigned, as was usual, especially for works by members of religious orders, and preceded by a

---

125 'Le Opere della Veneranda Madre Donna Battista Vernacia, le quali hora si mandano in luce, sono per se stesse tanto spirituali, et ripiene di affetti, et sentimenti divini, che pare, che non habbiano bisogno di altro presidio humano, per diffendersi da qualsivoglia calonnia, che loro potesse esser machinata da altrui invidia, o malignità' (Dedicatory Epistle prefaced to the edition of the *Opere spirituali della Reverenda et Devotissima Vergine di Christo, Donna Battista da Genova, Canonica Regolare Lateranense*, c. A2r).

126 'Ma anzi che siano atte a persuadere, et convincere chiaramente chiunque con sincerità di mente le leggerà, che esse più con lume sopranaturale, et con uso continuo d'oratione, che con industria humana, o con altro studio siano state composte; la onde mi è parso del tutto soverchio a fare sopra di ciò longo discorso per modo di Apologia' (ibid.).

127 'Dico per tanto, che oltre la diligenza grande, et scrutinio che il molto Reverendo Padre Don Gasparo concanonico, et Padre mio spirituale di buona memoria volse fare intorno a dette Opere, spendendovi de gli anni; et oltre a quella che vi aggiunse l'Illustrissimo di Santa Prassede da poi, dandole da vedere ad alcuni Padri Theologi di spirito et di eruditione molto segnalati, da quali furono accuratamente vedute, et con la loro sottoscrittione approvate' (ibid., A2r–v).

protracted revision of the text ('spending many years'), which probably involved also the Congregation of the Index, and which makes it possible to advance the hypothesis that some 'corrective' action was taken.[128] The hypothesis of an involvement of the Congregation of the Index is corroborated by the content of a letter written in September 1582 in which the General of the Lateran Regular Canons asked Cardinal Sirleto to have the Congregation produce an official 'revision' of the three volumes of Vernazza's works, which thus followed that of 'our theologians'. He also asked be advised as to the name of a possible censor for Vernazza's works:

> 'It is now some forty years,' ran the text of the missive, which considering the abundance of information it provides is well worth quoting in full, 'since Our Lord God began to put very great and important ideas into the mind of one of our Lady Canons, Dame Battista da Genoa in the Monastery of Graces, then 46 years of age, a most pure and humble woman untaught by man except how to read and write. When the Virgin enjoined her to refuse to believe these ideas, lest she should be deceived by him who transfigures himself as an angel of light, and being much in doubt, she was reassured by one of her confessors, a man of holy life and great learning – having recited her prayers to God and having had others recite many prayers – that this matter really was the work of God and she was comforted and revived in spirit, and indeed she was instructed that out of obedience she must take account of it all and set it down in writing. And so she did, but always in the greatest of secrecy. She has now written three entire volumes. Now it has pleased God that the matter should come to our knowledge. I have seen a large part of these writings, and everything from beginning to end has been submitted to our theologians, all learned and enlightened men, so that they may examine them with great care to see if there are any impediments, and I have approved them as you will see, and wishing for the honor of God and the advantage of many (as we hope) to set them before the light of day, I have resolved, in order to prevent the works from being approved in one city and then being prohibited in another, and not wishing them to appear without the approval of this most Illustrious Congregation, to send them to you, and humbly present them at your feet, and I accept the correction and the judgment of Your Most Illustrious Lordships, and as it would perhaps be difficult to find any other person who has the time and the ability and the desire to attend for so long to such an important undertaking, and having learned that the Reverend Father Emanuelle di Sa' of the Company of Jesus, who knows the Reverend Mother very well, is in Rome, I beg Your Most Illustrious Lordships to entrust it to him so that he may examine it all with due diligence and provide a report thereon. For this, I myself and all our Congregation, besides our other obligations, shall remain

---

[128] On this long process of 'internal' revision, which involved Cardinal Carlo Borromeo, Cardinal Niccolò Sfondrati, and her spiritual director Gasparo Scotto da Piacenza, among others, and on the genuine reluctance and sincere devotion of the Vernazza, see D. Solfaroli Camillocci, 'La monaca esemplare'.

most obliged and devoted. May Our Lord preserve you and I humbly kiss your hand. Piacenza, 9th September 1582. Don Theodosio General of the Lateran Regular Canons'.[129]

However, hypotheses apart, the fact that we have to stress here is that it was only at the end of the 1580s that conditions became ripe for the publication of such a work. Certainly, as already said, this was also a consequence of Vernazza's death, which ruled out any last possibility of overcoming the author's reluctance to publish, but it was also a clear sign of a new cultural and religious climate. In actual fact, Vernazza's text, whether purified or not, continued to possess theological and doctrinal features that were worthy of attention. Starting from a profound reflection on the 'unitive' nature of the Lord's Prayer – a 'prayer intended to join man with God' (*orazione [che] tende ad unire l'huomo con Dio*)[130] – Vernazza provided a careful analysis of the seven invocations composing

---

[129] 'Sono anni circa 40, – recitava il testo della missiva che, data la ricchezza di informazioni, vale la pena riportare per intero – che ad una nostra Canonica D. Battista da Genoa nel Monasterio delle Gratie, d'anni all'hora 46, purissima, et humilissima et alla quale non è mai stato insegnato da huomo se non leggere et scrivere, cominciò il Signore mettere in mente concetti grandissimi et importantissimi. Alli quali ricusando la Vergine di dar fede per non essere ingannata da colui che si traffigura in Angelo di luce, et stando molto sospesa, fu assicurata da un suo confessore huomo di santa vita et molta dottrina, fatta prima et fatto far molte orationi a Dio, che la cosa era dal S.re et fu confortata et inanimata, anzi gli fu imposto per obedienza, che dovesse tenerne conto, et mettergli in scritto. Così fece et sempre la cosa è stata secretissima. Di modo che a questa hora ha scritto tre tomi intieri. Hor è piacciuto a Dio che la cosa è venuta a nostra cognitione. Per il che havendogH visto io in gran parte, et poi per gli impedimenti il tutto dal principio insino al fine fatto vedere et essaminare con somma diligenza da nostri theologi huomini dotti et illuminati, gli ho approvati come vedrà et volendogli ad honor di Dio, et utilità di molti (come si spera) mandare in luce, mi son risoluto, acciò non sia in facultà d'alcuni in una città approvargli, et altri in un'altra riprovarli over sospendergli, non volere che venghino fuori senza l'approbatione dell'Illustrissima Congregatione così glieli mando, et a piedi loro humilmente gli presento, al tutto rimettendomi alla correttione et giudicio di S. S.rie Ill.me et perché sarebbe forsi difficile trovar persona che habbia tempo, et sappia et voglia attendere a così lunga et importante impresa, però intendendo che in Roma si trova il R.P. Emanuelle di Sa' theologo della Compagnia di Gesù, qual molto bene conosce essa Madre, supplico V.S. Ill.ma degnarsi commettergliela, che lui vegga il tutto diligentemente, et riferisca quanto gli pare. Dil che gli ne restarò io et tutta la Congregatione nostra, oltre gli altri oblighi inclinatissimo et deditissimo N.S. la conservi, et gli bascio humilmente la mano. Di Piacenza, alli 9 di settembre 1582. Don Theodosio Generale de Canonici regolari lateranensi;' BAV, Vat. Lat. 6194, Letters to Cardinal Sirleto, part II, c. 475r. At this point in time, we have no record of any documentation that might enable us to ascertain whether the revision by the Congregation of the Index was ever actually carried out and whether the author of this intended censorial revision was in fact the Jesuit Sa' indicated by the General of the Lateran Regular Canons in his letter to Sirleto, but there is also no reason to believe that the revision did not take place.

[130] Battista Vernazza, *Della unione dell'anima con Dio sopra il Pater noster*, cap. XLV, f. 94.

the Lord's Prayer, each of which she interpreted as a step in the direction of the achievement of the final goal: union with God.[131] The various stages of the *via perfectionis* were carefully analyzed in Vernazza's concentrated reading: from the annihilation of one's earthly passions and will to the contemplation of the figure first of Christ and then of God, and to the unitive transformation and the achievement of peace and perfection.

It was along this thin borderline between heresy and orthodoxy traced by the repeated action of the censors in the 1580s that the *Unione dell'anima con Dio sopra il Pater noster* by the Genoese mystic attempted to create a theological and doctrinal space for itself.

In the initial phases of her ideal spiritual journey, for example, Vernazza spoke with great mystic intensity and unitive outpouring about the 'inward crucifixion' (*crocifissione interiore*)[132] and the 'nothingness' (*nichilità*) of man, explaining to devout readers that 'the soul, which desires to be a sister of Christ, must with all its might plunge to the very depths of the abyss, as deep as it possibly can, for various reasons [...] mainly in order to obey His Majesty; [...] because that is what our nothingness deserves'.[133] She also stressed the necessity that

> whoever truly wishes to humble himself should make a true light of his nothingness, which is acquired when the mind is in the presence of God. [...] Those who ardently love Christ alone feel the greatest delight when they abase themselves below every rational creature, in order to stay together with Christ in the abyss: and they cannot do otherwise if they have understood His divine meaning.[134]

Yet, immediately after this, to prevent any unwanted misunderstanding, Vernazza specified that 'this annihilation, considered in itself is certainly

131 *Pater* (chapters I–IV), *qui es in coelis* (V–IX), *santificetur nomen tuus* (X–XVII), *adveniat regnum tuum* (XVIII–XXII), *fiat voluntas tua* (XXIII–XXX), 'recapitulation of the first part of the Lord's Prayer' (XXXI–XXXV), *panem nostrum quotidianum da nobis hodie* (XXXVI–XLV), *dimitte nobis debita nostra* (XLVI–LV), *sicut et nos dimittimus debitoribus nostris* (LVI–LXIII), *et ne nos inducas in tentationem* (LXVIII–LXXIX), *sed libera nos a malo* (LXXX–LXXXIX), *Amen* (XC–CXX).

132 The title of chapter XXVI f. 58 is: 'Outward crucifixion is not sufficient; it is necessary to crucify oneself inwardly with Christ and sacrifice oneself'.

133 'quell'anima, che desidera essere sorella di Christo, debbe con tutto '1 suo sforzo profondarsi, et abbissarsi in tutto, più ch'ella può, per diverse ragioni [...] principalmente per obedire a sua Maestà; [...] perché così merita la nostra nichilità' (ibid. f. 58).

134 'chi vuole in verità humiliarsi, bisogna che della propria nichilità habbia un vero lume, il quale, stando la mente nella divina presentia, s'acquista. [...] Chi ardentemente, et unicamente ama Christo, grandissimo diletto sente in profondarsi sott'ogni rational creatura, per star insieme con l'istesso abissato Christo: et non può far di manco, se ha ricevuto il suo divino senso' (ibid.).

nothing but a *voluntary* and loving way of dying in which one sacrifices one's spirit and puts it in the hand of the Father'.[135] As she approached the last stages of the unitive journey in a growing literary and spiritual crescendo, the author's threshold of attention became increasingly higher. This was where the danger of heresy lurked, more feared than ever; this was where many others before her, speaking of 'deified or deiform lovers' (*deificati, over deiformi amatori*),[136] had crossed the uncertain doctrinal boundaries of Catholic orthodoxy. The union of human will with that of God, the dissolving of the one into the other, and the achievement by 'deified' (*deificato*) man of divine perfection and the state of impeccability were dangerous topics which since the days of the medieval heresy of the Free Spirit had been condemned by Rome. Also in this case the Genoese mystic (or her 'reviser') must have realized in time the limit beyond which she could go no further. Man, Vernazza very shrewdly stressed, cannot help striving toward divine perfection – he may be able to come very close to God but he will never succeed in having a perfect vision of God's appearance: 'We cannot comprehend the Almighty /…/ So that until I return my body to the earth, / may my mind be in Heaven with you, / Where you are in yourself, but it is beyond my understanding'.[137] Even in that very moment when man succeeds, thanks to the divine Grace granted to him, in reaching the highest level of prayer – even if by love and participation he becomes a *quid unum* with God – he will always remain distinct in his singularity and his human nature:

> And although it is not possible to equate being deified by Grace to being God by nature, there is however so much similarity that we can say with confidence: *on earth as it is in heaven*. It is the same when His Majesty invites us at another point to imitate his fatherly perfection, when He says: *Estote perfecti, sicut et pater vester caelestis perfectus est* (Be perfect as your Heavenly Father is perfect). This surely does not mean equality but imitation and similarity.[138]

---

[135] 'questo annichilarsi in sé considerato, certo non è altro, che un *volontario*, et amoroso morire, nel quale si sacrifica il proprio spirito, mandandolo in mano del padre' (ibid., my emphasis).

[136] Ibid., f. 151.

[137] 'Noi non possiam capir l'onnipotente /… / Si che fin tanto che alla terra rendo / il corpo, in cielo sia mia mente teco, / Dove in te stesso sei, ma non l'intendo' (ibid., ff. 201–3).

[138] 'Et avenga che equiparar non si possa l'essere deificato per gratia all'esser Dio per natura, pur vi è tanta similitudine, che possiamo fiducialmente dire: *Come in deh, così sia in terra*. In quel modo, che sua Maestà c'invita in un altro luoco ad imitare la paterna perfettione, quando dice: *Estote perfecti, sicut et pater vester caelestis perfectus est*. Siate perfetti, come è perfetto il vostro padre celeste. Dove per certo non s'intende a equalità, ma a imitatione, et simiglianza' (ibid., ff. 63–4).

Even at the highest point of the unitive journey – the author thus made clear – man and God will always constitute two entities that are quite distinct from each other: however hard the cord was pulled, even almost to breaking point, the fine borderline between orthodoxy and heresy still remained inviolate.

Even considering the importance of these acts of censorship or self-censorsship, the publication of this work would thus appear to testify to a considerable reduction in the attention which in previous years had characterized the Roman censors' repressive action against a wide variety of productions of mystic content. As we have endeavored to demonstrate in the foregoing pages, the watchful defenders of Catholic orthodoxy, only a few years before, would not have tolerated dramatic minimizations of human 'strength,' such as that contained in the following passage: 'It is not by one's own strength but by Grace that this perfection is achieved. Just as Divine Goodness has always recompensed evil with good'.[139] Nor would they have tolerated categoric amputations of human free will, such as that we can read, slightly attenuated by the initial reference to the 'readiness' of human will, in another passage dedicated to 'outward crucifixion' and to the 'purging of the affections':

> Wherefore my will is ready, but *my strength indeed is nothing*. Thus, my beloved, *You who have given me the will*, add the power, or rather, with Your power, make me able to say in truth: 'Pater autem in me manens ipse facit opera.' The Father, who by Grace is within me; *it is He who does all things*.[140]

Statements like these, as I was saying, would not have been tolerated. Now, on the contrary, they successfully overcame a dual process of revision. There had been a clear change of approach.

Although it is difficult to assess the extent and quantity of the work of 'cleansing' performed by the 'Theological Fathers', and by the Congregation of the Index, it is legitimate to hypothesize that the addition of certain adjectives and adverbs was due to them: 'If the Lord had not helped me', as we can read in the pages of the 'commentary on the Lord's Prayer', 'I would *almost* have been in Hell. Where he shows not only that he was unable to obtain something perfect, but rather, had it not been

---

139 'Non per proprie forze, ma per gratia, questa perfettione s'acquista. Et come la divina bontà ha sempre bene per male retribuito'.

140 'Sì che la volontà è prontissima, ma *le mie forze in verità sono nulla*. Però amor mio, *tu che hai dato il volere*, aggiungi il potere, anzi con tua virtù fa in me l'effetto, sì ch'io possa veramente dire: "Pater autem in me manens ipse facit opera". Il Padre, che in me sta per gratia; *egli fa le opere tutte*' (ibid., f. 16).

for Your divine help, he would *nearly* have plunged down into Hell'.[141] Another example: 'In such a way that the bodily and animal senses become *almost* spiritual, not wishing, nor seeking to receive consolation, or nurture from outward proportioned objects. And so, even our outward man becomes *very* similar to Christ on the Cross'.[142] The adverbial expressions 'almost' (*quasi*), 'very' (*grandemente*), and again 'almost' were probably deliberately added by some scrupulous censor in order to blunt the temper of the harder statements and to tone down what was being said when this appeared to become too compromising.

This last hypothesis is confirmed in another censorship 'case' dating to those years. These minor interventions of theological correction are very similar in nature to the slight alterations which Dionisio da Piacenza himself – this time as a censor and no longer as a promoter or guarantor of the publication of the text as he had been in the case of Vernazza's works – suggested in his *Annotationi fatte intorno all'operette del R. P. D. Serafino da Fermo da Don Dionisio da Piacenza, Abbate della Badia di Fiesole, secondo le stampate in Piacenza da Francesco Conti 1570* ('Notes regarding the works of the Reverend Father Serafino da Fermo made by Don Dionisio da Piacenza, Abbot of Fiesole Abbey at Fiesole, as printed in Piacenza by Francesco Conti 1570').[143] The manner and the nature of the suggested alterations were in fact completely alike, as we can see in some of the more significant cases: 'Chap. 6 [from the treatise *Dell'oratione interiore*] at the end: I praise the work of Giovanni Cassiano. In the margin I would put:

141 'Se il Signore non m'aiutava, io era già *quasi* nell'inferno. Dove dimostra non solo da sé stesso non poter ottener cosa perfetta, ma anzi che se stato non fusse il tuo divino aiuto, seria *quasi* profondato nell'inferno' (ibid., f. 112; my emphasis).

142 'In modo tale, che i sensi corporali, et animali diventano *quasi* spirituali, non volendo, né curandosi di ricevere consolatione, né pascimento dalli esteriori proportionati oggetti. E così etiandio l'huomo nostro esteriore si fa a Christo crocifisso *grandemente* conforme' (ibid., f. 195).

143 ACDF, Index, Protocolli N, cc. 337r–339v. The only work by Serafino da Fermo to appear in the Roman Indexes was *Apologia di Battista da Crema*, condemned in 1559 and in 1564. We know that Serafino's works had a different fate in Spain, where in 1559 they were totally banned (cf. *Index des livres interdits*, vol. X, p. 181; see also above, ch. 3). The same volume of protocols that contains these censorship notes presents (Prot. N, c. 391r) a letter datemarked Piacenza, 19 May, 1605, in which Brother Francesco Strada reported finding in the 1570 edition of Serafino da Fermo's works two dedicatory epistles taken from the already condemned *Apologia di Battista da Crema*, in which Serafino poured out his praises of Master Battista and invited his interlocutor (presumably a Cardinal belonging to the Congregation of the Index) to advise him whether the text in question was to be considered forbidden or not. The available documentation does not permit us to establish accurately the relationship between this letter and Don Dionisio da Piacenza's censures, which are preserved a few pages before in the same volume of Protocols. The possibility however cannot be ruled out that it was this letter that triggered the mechanism to examine Serafino's works, a mechanism that did not in fact lead to any condemnation or official comment.

Take this to mean therefore in those places where it is not disapproved';[144] and again: 'Chap. 8 of the same Treatise of Conversion; at the end where it says that no one if compelled etc. has ever desired Hell, I would put in the margin: *Again take this to mean, if it is possible, and God willing; and with regard to the penalty*';[145] and a little further on, 'In the little Epistle preceding the Trattato della Cognitione et Vittoria di se stesso [Treatise of Cognition and Victory over oneself], line 19, weed out passions (I would say: 'weed out passions, *as far as possible*';[146] and again: 'Chap. 1 [of the treatise *Specchio interiore*], When man has suppressed every passion, and temptation, and is so strengthened that he not only does not fall etc., I would put in the margin: *Take this to mean, in matters of importance*'.[147] The expressions and additions which the censor suggested inserting into Serafino da Fermo's writings ('in those places where it is not disapproved', 'as to the penalty', 'in matters of importance'), in other words, recalled very closely the adjectival and adverbial expressions to be found in the pages of Vernazza's *Commento al Pater* (i.e. the words 'almost' and 'very', to which we have referred), thus strengthening the hypothesis that some action was taken on the text of the mystic lady of Genoa (action that was certainly pre-emptive in this case and not subsequent to publication, as in the case of Serafino's works). Vernazza's text therefore increasingly appears to be the final result of a delicate process of revision in which the censor, Dionisio da Piacenza, must have been involved. Thanks to the attentive 'care' of the Abbot of Fiesole, the work of Serafino and that of Vernazza were destined to become more similar than they were before his intervention. When correcting some of the more delicate passages in the Canon of Fermo's work concerning the unitive moment of man with God, Dionisio proposed, for example, the same doctrinal expressions that had permitted the publication of the *Commento al Padre*: while in the work

[144] 'Cap. 6 [del trattato *Dell'oratane interiore]* in fine: Laudo l'opera di Gio. Cassiano. In margine porrei: *Intendi però in quelle cose, dove non è riprovato*' (ibid., c. 337r).

[145] 'Cap. 8 dell'istesso Trattato della Conversione; al fine ove dice, che alcuno mosso etc. ha desiderato l'inferno. Porrei in margine: *Intendi sempre, se possibile fosse, et a Dio piacesse; et quanto alla pena*' (ibid., c. 337v). It must be pointed out that this last correction, 'with regard to the penalty', is exactly the same as that made (spontaneously by the author or on the recommendation of a third party) by Mattia Bellintani in a passage of the 1584 revised edition of his *Pratica dell'oratione mentale* (cf. above).

[146] 'Nella Pistoletta precedente al Trattato della Cognitione, et Vittoria di se stesso, lin. 19 sterpare le passioni (direi: sterpare, *quanto si può*, le passioni)'; (ibid., c. 337v). This other correction is very similar both in content and manner: 'Chap. before the end of this treatise, "we shall gain perfect victory over ourselves and all sin", I would put in the margin: Understand as far as is possible in this life' (ibid.).

[147] 'Cap. primo [del trattato *Specchio interiore]* Quando l'huomo ha suppeditato ogni passione, et tentatione, et talmente è fortificato, che non solo non casca etc. Metterei in margine: *Intendi, in cosa rilevante*' (ibid., c. 338r).

of the venerated lady of Genoa one read 'which surely does not mean equality but imitation and similarity',[148] the same expressions were to be used in Serafino's *Specchio interiore*: '[chap. X of the Treatise] Aspiring *to equality* with God; I would say *to similarity*. And thus [...] if man does not make himself similar and equal, I would add *in his way* to God'.[149]

The renewed emendatory function attributed in this case to the censor's intervention was an important confirmation of the evolution of the attitude of the Roman authorities toward mystic literature at the turn of the century. It was no longer just an act of destruction intended to suppress whole passages but – returning to the original Tridentine-humanistic spirit of expurgation – it was a genuine attempt to save the text from oblivion and from its otherwise inevitable disappearance as a publication. Dionisio da Piacenza's professional fortune was in this sense emblematic. On the one hand he was a promoter of the shrewd posthumous publication of the works of the mystic Vernazza, while on the other – just a few years later – he was a benevolent censor of the mystic Serafino da Fermo.

Very likely motivated by his intention to prevent the worrying possibility of much more severe action by some 'theologian', the desire to establish a clear dividing line between orthodoxy and heterodoxy that is apparent in his action as a censor emblematically reflected the unexpected authorization granted in the last years of the century by the Church hierarchies to mystic-unitive prayer. There was a slackening in the severity of censorship that opened the doors to the editorial recovery of a mystic and spiritual genre which otherwise was destined to oblivion. Now instead it was destined to become the bedrock of the subterranean proliferation of a literary form that was about to re-emerge, with all its potential danger for standard doctrine, with the *orazione di quiete* (the 'silent prayer') of the mid-seventeenth century, from the inner reaches of the Church itself.[150]

---

148 'dove per certo non s'intende a equalità, ma a imitatione, et simiglianza'.

149 '[cap. X del trattato] Aspirare alla *equalità* di Dio; direi *(alla simiglianza)*. Et così [...] se l'huomo non si fa simile et equale, aggiongerei *(nel modo suo)* a Dio' (ibid., c. 338v; the italics are all taken from Dionisio da Piacenza). For the reference to Vernazza's 'Commento al Pater', cf. also above, pp. 125–6.

150 P. Simoncelli, Il 'Dialogo', pp. 600–1; G. Signorotto, *L'eresia di Santa Pelagia*; A. Turchini, 'Il libro delle 'Rivelazioni' di Francesco Negri detto il Fabianino. Orazione mentale e dispositivi di controllo inquisitoriale nel Seicento veneto', *Annali dell'Istituto storico italo-germanico in Trento*, XVII, 1991, pp. 379–559; A. Malena, 'Inquisizione, "finte sante", "nuovi mistici". Ricerche sul Seicento', *L'Inquisizione e gli storici*, pp. 289–306, in particular pp. 301 et sqq.; Ead., *L'eresia dei perfetti*; S. Stroppa, *Sic arescit. Letteratura mistica nel Seicento italiano*, Florence, Olschki, 1998.

CHAPTER 8

From Heresy to Liturgy

Although the Church hierarchies were beginning to glimpse final success, and therefore the end of the Inquisition's harsh censorial action in the last decades against a wide variety of forms of religious heterodoxy, the effect of these battles was long to exert an influence on Catholicism's process of renewal.

The first to realize this was Angelo Rocca, a learned member of the Congregation of the Index and a future founder of the extremely well-endowed Angelica Library in Rome,[1] when – intending to offer to an unlettered public a Catholic compendium of the Lord's Prayer – he found he had to reckon with a series of acts of unconscious psychological resistance. At the beginning of the 1570s, encouraged by the success of the considerable number of acts of censorship intended to rid Catholic devotional rites of any pagan and superstitious accretions,[2] Carlo Borromeo had succeeded, in his proposals regarding matters of religious education, in combining the mystic works of Granada with his own pastoral invitations to indulge in the practice of 'common' prayer, thus taking an important step in the direction of a renewed integration of the topic of mental prayer within the cultural and religious heritage of the Catholic religion.[3] Twenty years later, in 1594, Rocca's Spositione intorno all'orazione domenicale was printed, eight years after it was first conceived.[4] The long time-lag between the author's original intention and the work's final appearance is an indication that his creative impulse lost some of its initial impetus. What was intended to be, in Rocco's own words, a 'commentary' (spositione) 'for the use of the less learned' (per utilità de' meno intendenti) turned out at the end of his labors to be an erudite dissertation that even his most expert readers must have found hard to disentangle. Moreover, it was not merely a presumptuous display

[1] On Angelo Rocca, see A. Anselmi, *Cenni biografici di mons. Angelo Rocca d'Arcevia: fondatore della biblioteca Angelica in Roma*, Fabriano, apud Gentile, 1881; *Sacerdote Angelo M. Rocca*, Turin, Ufficio delle Letture Cattoliche, 1908; and L. Ferrari, *Onomasticon*, p. 581.

[2] Cf. above, ch. 5.

[3] Cf. ibid.

[4] *Spositione intorno all'oratione domenicale raccolta da' più famosi Scrittori antichi et moderni che in ciò hanno scritto fin'hora, da F. Angelo Rocca da Camerino, dottore in Theologia dell'Ordine Eremitano di S. Agostino*. Rome, apud Guglielmo Facciotto, 1594. For the reference to the long time-gap between the author's original intention and the work's actual publication, see Rocca's own comments at cc. A2r–v.

of erudition and an exemplary testimony of his rigorous philological and humanistic approach to sacred subjects, for the work's overdependence on the Scriptures was at one and the same time an unmistakable sign of the continuing psychological insecurity of the Church hierarchies regarding this kind of devotional theme and an untoward literary weighing-down of the Spositione. What with the 'Alphabetical catalog of the authors who the author of this Exposition found, had considered the Lord's Prayer, except for those authors who illustrated the Lord's Prayer with Commentaries, as an opportunity for presenting the sacrosanct Gospels',[5] and the list of the 'Authors whose words are cited in this Exposition',[6] the 'less learned' reader was obliged to tackle long passages in which even the most erudite scholar would have been hard put to pick out the meaning of the author's devotional message from the mass of learned quotations surrounding and at times completely obscuring it:

> In this Proemium directed to Our Lord God – as one reads for example in a certain passage – it was not necessary to make him [the reader] willing to learn for He gives this docility to all men, as Solomon did, and to others: and he is only an examiner of hearts; as he himself says to Samuel; and as the Prophet, David, and Jeremiah say; and Wisdom knows the secrets of our hearts and our thoughts: and calls things that are not in being in the same way as those that are in his being, as St Paul wrote to the Romans. Nor was it necessary to maintain his attention for not only is he an examiner of hearts but also, in the words of Jeremiah, the Prophet, he exhorts us to turn to him, invoking him.[7]

It was, therefore, clear, reading the text further, that Rocca's *Spositione* was certainly not the best instrument that the market for devotional literature could offer in order to 'cultivate the devotion of the less learned' (*coltivar la devotione de' meno intendenti*): this was all the more true

[5] 'Catalogus auctorum, quos in Orationem Dominicam conscripsisse invenit Expositionis huiusce Auctor (iis exceptis, qui eandem Commentariis illustrarunt ex occasione exponendi sacrosancta Evangelia) ordine Alphabetico digestus' (ibid., c. A6v et sqq.).

[6] 'Auctores, quorum sententiae hac in expositione citantur' (ibid., c. A6v et seqq.).

[7] 'In questo Proemio drizzato al nostro Signore Iddio, non occorreva renderlo docile [il lettore], poiché egli da la docilità a gli huomini, come fece a Salomone, et a gli altri: et solamente è scrutatore de' cuori; come esso stesso dice a Samuele; et come dice il Profeta, David, Geremia; et la Sapienza, conosce i secreti de' cuori nostri, et i nostri pensieri: et chiama le cose, che non sono in essere, come quelle, che sono nel suo proprio essere, et nella sua propria natura, sì come scrive S. Paolo a Romani. Né faceva bisogno di renderlo attento, poiché non solamente è scrutatore de' cuori, ma anco per bocca di Geremia profeta ci essorta a ricorrere a lui invocandolo' (ibid., p. 4). One single page contains no fewer than nine indications of the original sources: 3. Kingdoms 3; 1. Kingdoms 16; Psalms 7 and 43; Jeremiah 17; Wisdom 7 and 7; Romans 4; Jeremiah 33; Psalms 106; Wisdom 3.

if we compare its style with the directness and spontaneity of certain Lutheran and Calvinist *sposizioni* (commentaries) on Our Lord that were still circulating.

Rocca's *Spositione del Pater Nostro* was destined, as far as I know, to remain (at least in the decades to come) the last isolated voice of this literary genre among Catholic works: it therefore testified to a relationship – i.e. the relationship maintained by the Church hierarchies with the forms and manners of a renewed (and refound) devotional inwardness – that was still far from a final positive solution.

Rocca's intention – clear in every page he wrote – that the subjects dealt with should be stoutly anchored to a rich and erudite store of precise ecclesiastic sources reflected the gradual development in the rules that in those same years were being worked out by the Inquisitors and censors with regard to devotional literature: in the course of this process of legislative codification, marked out by the Rules prefacing the three Indexes of forbidden books in the 1590s, the desire (already apparent in the Indexes of 1559 and 1564) to revive Catholic literary traditions dating back to before 1515, i.e. before Luther and the Reformation (the advent of which, as a precautionary measure, was brought forward a few years), found a new place for itself.[8] This important operation was not limited to recognizing the reconciliation of the authorities in Rome – now at last freed from the ghost of Luther – with a precious and unrenounceable spiritual patrimony that was a constituent part of the Christian religion. While on the one hand there was an attempt to recover and revalorize pre-Lutheran ecclesiastic traditions, on the other there also began to develop – as a consequence of the introductory rules of the Sistine and Sisto-Clementine Indexes and of the Clementine Index of 1596 – an attitude of total rejection of any form of devotional novelty. This was a prelude to an ambitious but also utopian project to achieve liturgical uniformity, which in the phase of its application became the main and possibly the only motivation inspiring the Church's repressive action.

Rule III of the Sistine Index condemned only 'books and other writings, whatever their title and whatever their subject, that prior to the year 1515 were condemned by the Sovereign Pontiff, by decretal epistles, by Councils recognized by the Church, or in whatsoever other manner',[9] i.e. only those explicitly forbidden by the Church before 1515. Among such works the Sistine rules provided for another exception, according to which 'the Holy Church has recognized as a testimony of the rites of old,

8 For the references to the 1559 and 1564 Indexes, cf. above, ch. 5.

9 'libri, et scripta cuiuscunque sint titulli, aut argumenti, quae ante annum MDXV a summis Pontificibus, epistolis decretalibus, conciliis ab ecclesia receptis, vel alio quocunque modo damnata sunt' (*Index des livres interdits*, vol. IX, p. 795).

of ecclesiastic traditions, or of the condemnation of heretics':[10] once the errors they contained had been noted, the work could circulate freely.[11] These few lines thus enable us to perceive a profound sense of ecclesiastic tradition, according to which the customs and ancient practices of liturgical ceremonies were to be defended from all 'novitates': 'All those that introduce novelties regarding the rites and sacramental ceremonies compared with the customs and practices accepted by the Church' were to be 'weeded out', added Rule XXI of the same Index.[12] Anything not falling within the limits of the now redefined Catholic dogmas and rituals thus came to be profoundly distrusted. Any 'editorial novelty' in this sector had to obtain the specific approval of the authorities in charge of inspecting texts: 'So that in future there shall be no publication, without such approval [of the Congregation of the Index, of the Inquisition, or of other relevant authorities], of any books dealing with holy matters or regarding dogmas of the faith and church rites, even if written in Latin by laymen, however expert, or by women, which are not allowed to be taught publicly in church' (Rule XVII).[13]

The Sisto-Clementine Index fully confirmed this line. While on the one hand the *Instructio* – the document that 'replaced' the Sistine rules[14] – repeated that books by Catholic authors published before 1515 did not need to be altered except in cases of gross error: 'In books by Catholic writers of the past nothing may be changed, except where there is evidence

---

[10] 'ecclesia sancta in antiquorum rituum, ecclesiasticarum traditionum, haereticorumque damnationis testimonium recepit' (ibid.).

[11] Ibid.

[12] 'Omnes illae, quae circa ritus, et cerimonias sacramentorum aliquam novitatem inducunt contra receptum usum, et consuetudinem' (Rule XXI, in *Index des livres interdits*, vol. IX, p. 799).

[13] 'Nec in posterum [...] libri [...] de rebus sacris, aut fidei dogmatibus, ecclesiasticisve ritibus, etiam latino sermone a laicis etiam peritis, aut a foeminis, quas in ecclesia *publice* docere prohibitum est, sine tali approbatione [of the Congregation of the Index, of the Inquisition, or other relevant authorities] in lucem emittantur' (ibid., p. 798, my italics, cf. also G. FRAGNITO, *La Bibbia al rogo*, p. 151). On the meaning to be attributed in the framework of Church practice to the adverb *publice*, cf. the remarks made above, ch. 9.

[14] 'Instructio eorum, qui libris tum expurgandis et corrigendis, tum imprimendis diligentem oc fidelem (ut par est) operam sunt daturi' (*Index des livres interdits*, vol. IX, p. 859). The document, edited by Bellarmino and Miranda, synthesized the rules regarding expurgation and preventive censorship, see FRAGNITO, *La Bibbia al rogo*, p. 158. For more general information about the Sisto-Clementine Index, cf. ibid., pp. 156 et sqq.; see also V. FRAJESE, 'La revoca dell'Index sistino e la curia romana (1588–1596)', *Nouvelles de la République des Lettres*, I, 1986, pp. 15–49; and ID., 'La politica dell'indice dal tridentino al clementino (1571–1596)', *Archivio italiano per la storia della pietà*, XI, 1998, pp. 269–356, and now ID., *Nascita dell'Indice. La censura ecclesiastica dal Rinascimento alla Controriforma*, Brescia, Morcelliana, 2006.

of falsification by heretics or a misprint due to evident carelessness;'[15] on the other hand, the document further refined the instruments of scholarship that the censors could use in defense of tradition. Besides taking up once again the Sistine indications condemning *novitates* that tended to set the faithful 'against the rites and sacramental ceremonies, and against the consolidated use and custom of the Holy Roman Church'[16] and those that imposed the expurgation of parts of the Holy Scripture taken from heretical versions,[17] the philological precision of the *Instructio* was taken to such an extreme that all words 'sacrae scripturae non fideliter et integre prolata' ('from the Holy Scriptures that were not faithfully and integrally reproduced') were forbidden.[18] Despite the failure to promulgate either

---

15 'In libris autem catholicorum veterum nihil mutare fas sit; nisi ubi fraude haereticorum, aut Typographi incuria manifesta error irrepserit' (*Index des livres interdits*, vol. IX, pp. 860–61). Bellarmino's action was probably also responsible for the 'softening' of the rules concerning the works of Catholic authors published after 1515. As co-author of 'Instructio' he must have been preoccupied to prevent his *Controversie* from ending up once again in the Index (albeit *quamdiu non corrigantur*), as in the case of the Sistine Index. Even as soon as the preparatory work of the Congregation of the Index, Bellarmino did not lose the opportunity to impose his point of view; very likely it was he who inspired the decree approved on 19 September 1592 which established 'quod Catholicis scriptoribus obiter errantibus inter scribendum nulla fiat iniuria annotando eosdem in Indice sed in margine notentur errores et apponantur censura et nullatenus mutilentur delendo sententias sed solum notando errores' ('With regard to Catholic writers who accidentally make mistakes in their books, they should not be made to suffer the insult of having their names placed on the Index, but rather a note should be made in the margin of the page and a censure should be inserted, but in no case should such books be cut by eliminating entire sentences: only the mistake should be noted'; ACDF, Index, I/1, f. 52r). While editing the 'Instructio', Bellarmino not only presented this decree but also chose to 'abrogate' the censorial prescriptions contained in the Sistine Index which authorized the circulation of 'libri catholici de controversiis fidei, vulgariter editi' only in its 'tantum locis, ubi catholici cum haeretici permixti habitant, vel ob propinquitatem aliquod commercium habent' ('controversial Catholic books in the vernacular' only 'in those places where Catholics live together with heretics or have dealings with them for reasons of trade'; Rule VIII, *Index des livres interdits*, vol. IX, p. 796). In its stead, the 'Instructio' recalled that easily correctable works by Catholic authors were to be immediately rectified and authorized to circulate freely throughout the territory: 'in the books of recent Catholic authors written after 1515, if it seems necessary to correct the text with a few alterations or by making some additions to it, the correctors should make the necessary changes, while on the contrary, if it is not sufficient to make just a few small corrections, the book should be entirely eliminated' ('In libris autem Catholicorum recentiorum, qui post annum Christianae salutis millesimum quingentesimum decimum quintum conscripti sunt, si id quod corrigendum occurrit paucis demptis, aut additis emendare posse videatur, id correctores faciendum curent, sin minus omnino deleatur'; *Instructio*, p. 860).

16 'contra Sacramentorum ritus, et caerimonias, contraque receptum usum et consuetudinem Sanctae Romanae Ecclesiae' (ibid., p. 860).

17 Ibid.

18 Also extending the prohibition to all words 'of the Holy Scriptures that have been used for profane purposes, as also those that have been so distorted that their meaning is totally

of the Indexes under consideration here[19] and despite the fact that the reintroduction of the Tridentine rules authorized by the Clementine Index in theory cancelled many of the rules approved in those years, the 1596 Index did not modify, as far as these sectors were concerned, the regulatory system thus far defined. Whenever there happened to be – as precisely in the case of the sectors described above – a substantial similarity between the position of the two Indexes as also – a not insignificant element – between the two Congregations of the Inquisition and the Index (frequently instead they were at loggerheads),[20] the standard established rules were destined, in the medium term, to guide the controlling action of the authorities in charge of censorship and the Inquisition in Rome.

Around the time of the promulgation of the Clementine Index, this elaborate theoretical reasoning immediately found its first practical application. Reproposing the list of prohibitions contained in the Tridentine Index, with some necessary modifications,[21] the 1596 Index brought to the censors' attention an action of expurgation left for the most part incomplete. Among the many texts indicated in the 1564 Index as requiring emendation there were nearly all the writings of the mystic Battista da Crema, while the only two of his works subjected to emendation in the course of the second half of the 1580s were, as we have seen, *Della vittoria e cognitione di se stesso* and *Specchio interiore*.[22] As has already been pointed out, this choice was not fortuitous, and the decision to submit to censorship *Philosophia divina* and the treatise *Della devotione* (contained in the volume *Via de aperta verità*) likewise corresponded in these last years of the century to a precise Inquisition logic.[23] In the overall

---

contrary to that of the unanimous interpretation of Catholic Fathers and Doctors' ('Scripturae sacrae quaecunque ad profanum usum impie accomodantur, tum quae ad sensum detorquentur abhorrentem a Catholicorum Patrum, atque Doctorum unanimi sententia'; ibid.).

19 The failure to promulgate the Sistine Index was mainly due to the death of Pope Sistus V. The bitter, protracted conflicts that divided the Congregation of the Index and the Pope during the compiling of the Index (on which see G. FRAGNITO, *La Bibbia al rogo*, pp. 147 et seqq.) seem to have had no direct bearing on the Index's non-appearance, notwithstanding it had in fact reached its definitive version.

20 G. FRAGNITO, *La Bibbia al rogo*, p. 195. On the conflicts between the two Congregations, EAD., 'La censura libraria'.

21 P.F. GRENDLER, Index de Rome 1590, 1593, 1596. Introduction historique, in *Index des livres interdits*, vol. IX, p. 287.

22 Cf. above, ch. 7.

23 It is necessary to mention only briefly that in those same years, i.e. between March 1596 and December 1599, Cordoni's *Dyalogo* – which was reprinted in 1593 – was once again subjected to censorship within the Order by the Capuchin Girolamo Mautini da Narni. In the course of the session held on 29 January 1600 the Congregation of the Index received Mautini's work and decided to instruct the Venice Inquisitor to investigate the editorial and other responsibilities involved in this edition, which ignored an official

structure of the gradualistic devotional project of Battista da Crema, these two texts corresponded to the lowest levels of an ideal mystic journey: in these writings the author mainly addressed those who were defined as *incipienti* (beginners), i.e. those who were moving their first steps along a religious pathway they still had to complete. The greatest risks that the ecclesiastic censors could see in the writings of the Dominican friar derived from the belittling of Roman liturgical and ceremonial practice contained in the stirring admonishments that Brother Battista addressed to these 'neophytes', in which he invited them to refuse not only vices and human passions but also certain ornamentations of outward religious behavior that were often both useless and harmful. If one reads the list of *Correttioni generali* ('General corrections') compiled by the censor at the end of the work – the list is therefore a summary of his acts of censorship regarding Battista da Crema's two texts – one receives an immediate and clear example of the changed attitude and especially of the new objectives of the ecclesiastic authorities at the end of the sixteenth century, and one is set before a totally new hierarchy of values or, to put it better, an uncommon scale of priorities. According to the censor's final very efficient formula, there were four categories of dangerous propositions that needed to be expunged from the text, because:

decree of condemnation pronounced by the Holy Office: 'Censura in libellum inscriptum Dialogo dell'Unione dell'anima con Dio Fratris Bartholomaei de Castello, ordinis minorum de observantia, olim Decreto Congregationis Sancti Officii damnatum et nuper cum eisdem erroribus Venetiis impressimi sub fido nomine fratris Bartholomaei de Castello, cappuccini, recepta fuit a frate Hieronimo de Narnia cappuccino et Inquisitori veneto scribendum ut diligenter ad impressore inquirat quomodo impressa sit hic liber ut officio Sanctae Inquisitionis significari possit a quo olim liber damnatus fuit' ('The censure was made by Brother Geronimo da Narnia regarding the book entitled Dialogo dell'Unione dell'anima con Dio by Bartolomeo da Castello of the Order of Observant Friars Minor. This book had already been condemned by a decree of the Congregation of the Holy Office but nevertheless printed a second time in Venice, repeating the same mistake and under the false name of Bartolomeo da Castello, Capuchin; it is necessary to write to the Venetian Inquisitor, instructing him to investigate with all due diligence, through the printer, how the book came to be published, thus making it possible to inform the printer who it was that condemned the book in the first place') (ACDF, Index, 1/I, cc. 119v–120r). The text of the censure is kept in the Casanatense Library, manuscript 345: *Censura del libro intitolato Dialogo dell'unione spirituale di Dio con l'anima*; Cargnoni published the text of the 14 'paradoxes' singled out by the censor in the text, without, however, including the lengthy doctrinal and theological arguments that were developed (C. Cargnoni, 'Fonti, tendenze e sviluppi,' pp. 394–8); on these acts of censorship, cf. also Stanislao da Campagnola, 'Bartolomeo Cordoni da Città di Castello,' pp. 122 et sqq.; and V. Criscuolo, *Girolamo Mautini da Narni (1563–1632): predicatore apostolico e vicario generale dei Cappuccini*, Rome, Istituto Storico dei Cappuccini, 1998, pp. 131–6. On Girolamo Mautini da Narni, an interesting figure in the context of Counter-Reformation's spirituality, see also *Girolamo Mautini da Narni e l'ordine dei Cappuccini fra '500 e '600*, V. Criscuolo (ed.), Rome, Istituto Storico dei Cappuccini, 1998.

> 1) it teaches that a spiritual man must so much hate himself that he must not act for any good, not even spiritual good, and indeed must beg God sincerely and without objection to be perpetually condemned to Hell;
>
> 2) it reasons excessively against vocal prayers and indulgences;
>
> 3) it seems to promise such a sure state in this life that man cannot sin or lose grace;
>
> 4) it teaches such purity that it seems to want man to be able to unite in this life with God so that he may see Him face to face and it seems that he is almost like a *comprehensore* and that he can no longer grow in perfection and that there is within him no further source of sin.[24]

'Lutheran' certainty of faith[25] and the 'unitive' impeccability of man, which as we have seen constituted until then the main and possibly the only objective of the powers in Rome, were therefore relegated to the last places in this 'table' of doctrinal perils that had to be resisted. With a radical inversion of intentions, the censor's absolute priority became the defense of the Church's liturgical and devotional system. If, on the one hand, the invitation 'not [...] to act for any good' (*non [...] operare per bene alcuno*) formulated by Battista da Crema as an inescapable corollary

---

24 '1) insegna che l'huomo spirituale deve tanto odiare se stesso che non deve operare per bene alcuno neancho spirituale, anzi che deve domandare a Dio con verità et senza resistentia di essere condannato all'inferno perpetuamente. 2) eccede in raggionare centra l'orationi vocali et indulgentie. 3) par che promete un tal stato sicuro in questa vita che l'huomo non possa peccare né perdere la gratia. 4) Insegna tal purità che par che voglia che l'huomo possa in questa.' These censures date from the late sixteenth century or the very first years of the seventeenth: 'Correttione del libro de Fra Battista da Crema intitolato Philosophia divina di quel solo vero maestro Iesu Christo Crocifisso' ('Correction of the book by Brother Battista da Crema entitled Divine Philosophy of the sole true Master Jesus Christ crucified') in ACDF, Indice, Protocolli N, cc. 530r–534r, in particular 'Correttioni generali' ('General corrections').

25 Regarding the doctrine of the certainty of salvation, the following were the most significant points singled out for this purpose by the censor: 'In the proemium he says whether these three Maries wish to stay by the Cross where I, who so many times ardently with material heart have tied myself to the Cross, must not and cannot go. Sooner will fire be cool and water be naturally hot [...] than I can leave the Cross for I am certain that neither death nor life nor other being shall ever be able to part me from the Cross and His love, etc. *From which words it appears that he considers himself certain of Grace and of continuing in such state*' (ibid., c. 530r; my emphasis). Or again: 'In chapter 14 he makes a comparison between the inward and outward signs of the Christian and says you will be more content not to have this outward sign but to have some other inward sign by which you would know that you had the Holy Spirit and that the Spirit remained with you; if you have wit to understand you shall say that you would have little care for the outward sign so long as you have within you clear signs that you have the Holy Spirit. *De certitudine spiritus sancti et perseverantia*' (ibid., c. 530r; my emphasis).

of the annihilation of human will[26] contained within it – to the mind of the scrupulous consultor of the Congregation of the Index – an intolerable belittlement of the value of the good works of 'charity' that had to be fought with might and main, on the other hand, the attacks by the author 'on oral prayers and indulgences' seemed to be part of an intolerable offensive intended to undermine the very foundations of the ecclesiastic institutions in Rome.

Thus, among his papers, the anonymous censor diligently noted the many 'points' where Battista da Crema had gone beyond the tones of a calm and orthodox discussion of the theme of prayer, starting from the passage where the author dared to use the terms 'senseless and mad' to describe all those who, like good Catholics, 'put their trust in vocal prayers and indulgences':

> In chapter 30 he reprimands [...] those who put their trust in vocal prayers and indulgences and Papal bulls, believing them to be absolute, and it seems to me that he oversteps the limit when he calls them senseless and mad, and then he says, do as Christ did for then you shall have His indulgence, and true and constant absolution, and this will be a good and true jubilee, not to say prayers [...] therefore, for such persons it will be [...] right to do good works and to let them perform their office of vocal prayers and attend to necessary matters,[27]

passing then to the rash statement that 'God is displeased by those who wish to say any prayers and psalms':

> In chap. 18: I know not how much God will like, or rather I know how much God dislikes, those who wish to say many prayers and psalms and spend all day in similar words as if God were deaf and needed people to chatter continuously in His ears so that good souls are left without good advice. God rejects these prayers of yours and is not grateful for your manner of contemplation but rather wishes you would abandon it in order to attend to the needs of others,[28]

---

[26] With reference to this point, the censor had, for example, noticed among his papers: 'In chapter II, praying he says, Lord God if anything else were dearer to me than my soul, and if there were a greater glory than that of Paradise, then all would I abandon, and everything would I despise, I would that everything were sunk in Hell, and worse, if this can be said to win over my neighbor. *It seems to me that the order of charity wishes me to love first my own soul before my neighbor's*' (ibid., c. 530r; my emphasis).

[27] 'Nel cap. 30 reprehende [...] quelli che si confidano nelle orationi vocali et indulgentie et bolle di essere absoluti et par a me che passi chiamando costoro insensati et matti et puoi dice fa come ha fatto Christo che puoi haverai una sua indulgentia et absolutione vera et ferma et questo sarà un buono giubileo et vero, non di far orationi: [...] per tanto a tali sarà [...] bene far di buone et farli lassare tanto affido et attendere alle cose necessarie' (ibid. c. 531r).

[28] 'Nel cap. 18: Non so quanto piacerà anzi so quanto dispiacciono a Dio quelli che vogliono pur dire molte orationi et salmi et tutto il giorno spenderlo in simili parole come

and finally, going on to another passage in which the scorn manifested by the Dominican possibly reached its peak:

> In chap. 58 [he writes]: I do not praise you for taking upon yourself many vocal prayers and offices because God does not need your words, nor is He deaf and can be made to hear only by the great din of many words [...] it would be better to sweep the house than chew words because one of these acts has some purpose while the other is just empty words.[29]

The desired elimination of vernacular passages derived from the Holy Scriptures ('which I would believe if he were to remove all the vernacular texts and replace them with Latin')[30] and the meticulous checking of the apocryphal nature and falsity of certain other passages related to the Scriptures that had been inserted ('First he adds numerous gospels in the vernacular, including the entire passion of Christ. And although he calls it a historical text, despite that – with all he puts into it – many things are not in the text')[31] appeared to be clear signs of the cultural climate of those years.[32] Yet, the censor's distinctive stroke was of a different nature: his anxious desire to defend the Catholic devotional system was simply one aspect of the now irreversible movement of the Church toward the creation of liturgical uniformity. 'It appears to me that this idea is new, for the words we find in this prayer are very different':[33] that is how the

---

che Iddio sia sordo et bisognasse continuamente cianciarli nelle orechie et lassar le anime senza qualche conseglio Dio non accetta queste vostre orationi né ha grata questa tal vostra contemplatone ma più presto vuole che la lassate per attendere il bisogno d'altri' (ibid., c. 531v).

29 'Nel cap. 58 [scrive:] Non ti laudo che tu ti charichi molte di orationi vocali et di tanti officii perché Dio non ha bisogno di parole ne anci è sordo che per strepito di parole si faccia odire [...] saria meglio di netare con la scopa la casa che masticare parole imperoché questo contiene qualche utilità et quelle sono parole senza altro utile' (ibid., c. 532v). Except when moderating his scorn after reading the continuation of Battista's statements: 'It is true that what he says mainly refers to things said by the mouth alone and not by the heart'.

30 'onde crederei se dovesse levar tutti questi testi volgari et mettervi il latino' (ibid., c. 530r).

31 'Prima ve mette molti evangeli! volgari et tra gl'altri tutta la passione di Cristo. Et se bene l'intitola testo della historia con tutto ciò vi mette dentro molte cose quali non sonno del testo' (ibid.).

32 The severe remarks on some 'lewd' passages in the Dominican's work were other indisputable signs of the times, as for example in the following passage that was marked by the censor: 'In chap. 17, o Jews, drunk on wine, with your mouth full of poisonous phlegm, besmear this face well, befoul it so that we may be ashamed and confused by having so much care of our face, so that we may cast away all these little boxes and all these colors. Displicent verba' (Displeasing words) (ibid., c. 530v; my emphasis).

33 'Parmi questo pensier novo havendo noi le parole di detta oratione molto differenti' (ibid.).

censor emblematically stigmatized the author for arbitrarily introducing unauthorized 'liturgical innovations,' recording among his notes the actual words of the incriminated passage:

> In the same chapter, discussing the prayer Christ recited in the Garden of Gethsemane, he says that one may in all pity say that He was praying for those who were in limbo [...] and in purgatory and that he freed many both in the one and in the other place although they had been confined there for their sins and did not deserve to be liberated.[34]

The Capuchin friar Silvestro da Rossano – known already as the author of *Modo come la persona spirituale che ora, si habbia a disporre nella Oratione verso Iddio e li suoi santi*, an exemplary literary model of Counter-Reformation spirituality published in the 1570s[35] – was one of the first to suffer the effects of the Church's new offensive. The year before *Modo di orare* was published, in 1573, he had printed another short spiritual work entitled *Modo di contemplare, et dire la devotione del preciosissimo sangue del nostro Signor Gesù Christo, sparso pietosamente per noi*, reprinted two years later, in 1575, by the Venetian publisher Giolito.[36] The title, and therefore the delicate subject considered, inevitably

---

34 'Nel istesso cap. ragionando dell'oratione che fece Christo nel horto dice che pietosamente si può dire che orasse per quelli che erano nel limbo [...] et nel purgatorio et che ne liberò molti dall'uno et l'altro loco se bene erano impregionati per sue negligentie et non meritassero la liberatione' (ibid., c. 530r).

35 Cf. above, ch. 6.

36 SILVESTRO DA ROSSANO, *Modo di contemplare, et dire la devotione del preciosissimo sangue del nostro Signor Giesù Christo, sparso pietosamente per noi*. Composto dal R.P. Fra Silvestro Rossano Cappuccino, Predicatore evangelico, et insegnato alla Compagnia dell'Oratorio di Santa Maria dell'Humiltà di Venetia. Opera molto utile all'anime che l'useranno ('Manner of contemplating and reciting the devotion of the most precious Blood of Our Lord Jesus Christ, shed for us in all pity. Composed by the Reverend Father Brother Silvestro Rossano, Capuchin, Evangelical preacher and taught at the Company of the Oratorio of Santa Maria of Humility in Venice. A most beneficial work for all those souls that use it, newly reprinted, With privilege in Venice, apud Giorgio Marescotti'). The entire text of this short spiritual work by Rossano was recently published by C. CARGNONI, 'La devozione al sangue di Cristo in un opuscolo censurato e finora ignorato di Silvestro da Rossano', *Collectanea Francescana*, 69 (1999), 3–4, pp. 573–628 (text on pp. 593–628), now also in *Clavis scientiae. Miscellanea di studi offerti a Isidoro Agudo da Villapadiema in occasione del suo 80° compleanno*, V. Criscuolo (ed.), Rome, Istituto Storico Cappuccino, 1999, pp. 315–74. The reconstruction of the experiences Rossano's work went through at the hands of the censors – carried out by Cargnoni on the basis of a document kept in the Archibishopric Archive in Florence and brought to our attention by Giacomo Carlini, and thus not having had the benefit of the documentation that we have consulted – contains new elements that, with regard to the reasons for the work's condemnation, contribute to the greater importance now given to the liturgical aspect than had previously been known;

jarred on the nerves of the still keenly anti-Protestant sensitivity of the Inquisition authorities in Rome. The work was immediately added to the local list then being circulated.[37] And yet, after these first attempts to block its circulation, the episode seemed to come to a close there and then: apart from a brief reference to the matter made during a meeting of the Congregation of the Index held in October 1594,[38] no one showed any special interest in the work: evidently everyone was relaxed about the orthodoxy of the contents and confident of the author's reliability. None of the official Roman Indexes mentioned the text. It was only with the excessive desire for 'uniformity' that began to spread at the end of the century, developing in the austere courtyards of Rome, that the censor's attention was redrawn to Rossano's innocuous work – the reason was certainly not related to doctrinal matters regarding the controversial spiritual heredity of the Capuchins.

As we learn from the reports prepared by the Secretary of the Congregation of the Index, in the summer of 1599 the *Procuratore generale* of the Capuchin Order presented to the members of the Congregation a detailed censure of Silvestro da Rossano's *Preciosissimo sangue*: 'Procurator Cappuccinorum censuram in libellum de Sanguine Christi f. Silvestri de Rossano Cappuccini tradidit' ('The Attorney of the Capuchin Order presented the censure of the book *De Sanguine Christi* by Brother Silvestro da Rossano, Capuchin').[39] As soon as he was warned of the dishonorable shame looming over his reputation, Silvestro da Rossano approached the censuring Cardinals and demanded immediate justice: 'I

Carlini's essay on this aspect is entitled 'Silvestro Franco da Rossano Calabro (1530–1596). Un'ignorata vicenda devozionale', *Fra Noi*, XIV, 1997, pp. 13–15.

[37] The date of the work's first condemnation was June 1576; after the emanation of this decree by the Inquisition (on which cf. C. CARGNONI, 'La devozione al sangue', p. 583), Rossano's work was added to Giovanni di Dio's Index (ACDF, Index, series XIV, one volume, cc. nn.), and to the 1580 Parma Index (*Index des livres interdits*, vol. IX, p. 63).

[38] 'Lecta censura in tractatum de sanguine Christi R. di Fratris Sylvestri de Rossano Capp.ni et commissum Ill.mo Card.li Asculano ut Rev.mum Fratrem Thomam de Senis ordinis Praedicatorum Theologum Ill.mi Card.lis Florentini eiusdem libri censorem advocet, et examinatur Censura et libro Congregationi referat si merito condemnandus est liber, interim vero Ill.mus Card.lis Florentinus iuxta facultatem in indice ordinarijs traditam si videbit poterit in sua diocesi librum prohibere' ('The censure of the treatise De Sanguine Christi by Brother Silvestro da Rossano, Capuchin, was read, and Cardinal Ascolano was instructed to appoint as its official censor Tommaso di Siena of the Order of Preachers, Theologian of the Cardinal of Florence. He was also instructed to inform the Congregation, once having examined the censure and the book, whether it deserved to be condemned; in the meantime, by virtue of the powers granted by the Index to the Ordinaries, the Cardinal of Florence may, if he deems fit, prohibit the book throughout his diocese') (ACDF, Index, I/1, meeting of 8 October, 1594, c. 81v). The matter was considered without any final outcome, at least so far as we know on the basis of the available documentation.

[39] ACDF, index, I/1, c. 120v (meeting of 31 July, 1599).

wish to know where error may lie', the Capuchin friar wrote indignantly, 'and where there is suspicion; error, there is none, because the teaching is that of St Bernard, of St Bonaventure [...] at most the doctrine of St Thomas; suspicion, there is none, as can be seen in the way devotion proceeds to the greatest advantage'.[40] However, despite his sincere indignation, Rossano seemed to have understood the reasons for this interest:

> One thing is true – the impassioned text of the missive went on – namely that heretics glory in the blood of Christ and therefore this devotion must be removed. It is a serious matter indeed that heretics impiously, irreverently, erroneously, faithlessly [...] name Christ's precious blood. Therefore must we Catholics not name and contemplate Him and speak of this faithfully, Catholically, piously, devoutly, fruitfully?[41]

Although reluctantly admitting that the tribute paid to Christ's blood had been raised by the Lutheran enemies as a kind of symbol and spiritual flag, this in no way diminished the validity of a text that attempted to promote the reappropriation of the cult from an orthodox point of view. However, when he received the text of the censure for his personal perusal, Rossano must have realized to his great surprise that most of the criticisms made by the anonymous censor had nothing to do with the subject of the blood of Christ. The conciliatory 'answer to the censures' (*risposta alle censure*), written by the Capuchin friar in his own hand,[42] i.e. the document he sent to the Congregation of the Index after becoming aware of the 'censures' made of his text, indicate that the question of devotion

40 'Vorrei sapere dove è l'errore, dove è la suspitione; errore non ce ne è, perché è la dottrina de San Bernardo, de San Bonaventura [...] al più la dottrina de San Thomaso; suspitione non vi è poiché si vede la devotione quanto va inanti con summa utilità.'

41 'Una sola cosa di vero che gli heretici si gloriano del sangue de Christo però si deve levare questa devotione. Gran cosa certo gli heretici impiamente inreverentemente erroneamente infidelmente [...] nominano il sangue precioso de Christo. Donque noi catholici non lo dobbiamo nominare contemplare e di questo parlare fidelmente catholicamente piamente devotamente fruttuosamente?' (letter from Silvestro da Rossano to the Secretary of the Congregation of the Index, Paolo Pico, undated, in ACDF, Index, Protocolli M, cc. 47r–v).

42 The content of the text was certainly conciliatory, but one cannot fail to notice the irritated tone of Rossano's opening words: 'Although by demonstrating my sound and complete conformity with Catholic truth and theological doctrine I have fully answered the above Censures, nonetheless, to avoid dispute and to comply with the sound judgment of your Illustrious Lordships, I deemed it proper that I should accept with all due propriety the above censures and without any difficulty whatsoever correct the matters that are noted' (the text of the 'Censure sopra il libretto de sanguine Christi' is in ACDF, Index, Protocolli T, cc. 501r–504r; that of the 'Resposte... lette inanti all'Ill.mo Santa Severina et alla Congregatione' is ibid., cc. 505r–510r, citation at c. 508v; and the other censures of Rossano's text, written in Latin, are at cc. 511r–515v.).

was now inseparably linked to the Counter-Reformation project of a rigid uniformity of the whole liturgical system. Interspersed here and there with remarks on the question of Christ's blood,[43] the observations of a liturgical nature made on the text by the anonymous censor were greater by far than those concerning any other topic. Moreover, they did not so much concern the specific content of prayers and litanies as the 'order' (*ordine*) and the 'choice' (*eleccione*) followed by the author in their arrangement; i.e. objections of a procedural nature, as we might say, rather than of merit, to which Brother Silvestro necessarily showed himself to be compliant:

> Where it is said that one must not observe such and such an order and sequence of a prayer but that one must follow the order of the Holy Mother Church, I say we must put it more expressly so that Catholic virtue according to the order of the Holy Church may be all the better known;[44]

and

> where he speaks of the choice of the Litanies, I say that however ancient they may be and though they may be said by particular brotherhoods, I am content nevertheless, in order to avert the danger that is highlighted in the censure, that new litanies should not be made public while those used in the breviaries of the Holy Church should be left, [...] and that they should be removed and instead the simple litanies used by the Holy Mother Church should be printed as prayers.[45]

---

43 According to what Silvestro da Rossano himself tells us in his 'reply': 'Where [the censor] says that the Holy Mother Church attributes Christ's merits to itself because of Christ's death and not because of His blood, I am content to put because of Christ's death and blood' (ibid., c. 508v; text of the censure at c. 502r]. The statement immediately following struck the same tone: 'As for the third one, where it states that it should not say twelve effusions of blood (text of the censure, ibid., c. 502r), I say that it would be better to put twelve considerations or contemplations of Christ's blood' (ibid, c. 508v).

44 'Ove se dice che non se deve servare tale ordine et disposicene di oracione ma che si deve tenere lo ordine della santa Madre Ecclesia dico che lo metteremo più espresso acciò più si conosca la virtù Catholica secondo l'ordine de santa Chiesa' (ibid., c. 509r; text of the censure, ibid., c. 502v).

45 'ove parla del eleccione delle Litanie dico che quantunque siano antiche et si dicono da particolari fraternite non di meno mi contento per deviare il periculo che si ripone nella censura acciò non vadano queste nove in publico et si lassino quelle che usa Santa Chiesa nelli breviarii, [...] che siano tolte queste et poste per modo di oracione stampino le semplici litanie ch'usa la santa Madre Chiesa' (ibid., c. 509v; text of the censure, ibid., c. 503r). The following 'observations' quoted by Brother Silvestro were very similar in nature to these last two 'censures': 'Where he says that one must not put the form using 'most', this prayer is most necessary and most devout and most useful, I say that although I mean, with regard to the Lord's Prayer, that it should be said with this meditation of the precious blood of Christ,

Once the modifications imposed by the censors had been made, the case was shelved: a few simple modifications made by the well-meaning Capuchin thus sufficed to put an end to a matter that had kept the entire Congregation of the Index busy for months on end.[46]

The ease and above all the manner in which the whole matter was brought to a conclusion provide a very good example of the quality of the goals that Church censorship set itself in this part of the century: in other words they illustrate very well the important and central role of a commitment, on the liturgical front, that before long was to lead to massive disciplining action in the multifaceted editorial world of missals, indulgences, and prayers. As we can see, this project was destined to be successful only as long as it was accompanied, in the proper terms, by the action of ridding Catholic devotional material of pagan superstitions and accretions and by the careful philological restoration of ecclesiastic tradition that had been set in motion by the Church hierarchies in the 1560s.

we will nevertheless omit the term 'most' and put the simple form devout, necessary, and useful' (ibid.; text of the censure, ibid.; c. 503v.).

[46] A few years before, on the occasion of the preparation of the Sistine Index, the *Commentarius de oratione horis canonicis* by Dr Navarro, Martín de Azpilcueta, had been the object of censorship of a similar tenor. On his own admission the anonymous censor had inserted the notes 'magis quia mihi nova visa fuerunt quam falsa aut censura digna'. This consisted mainly of notes of a liturgical nature that urged greater adherence 'to the letter' officially approved by Rome. Cf. Vatican Apostolic Library, Vat. lat. 6207, cc. 75r–77r, cit. at c. 75r, my emphasis. Regarding Navarro, cf. Vincenzo Lavenia, 'Martín Azpilcueta: un profilo', *Archivio italiano per la storia della pietà*, 16, 2003, pp. 15–144.

PART III
Toward the Failure of the Struggle against Superstition: The Clementine Index in its First Years of Application

CHAPTER 9

The Making of Liturgic Uniformity: Mere Wishful Thinking?

The early years of the seventeenth century saw the development of an editorial and economic quarrel concerning the circulation of certain editions of Venetian missals that were so full of mistakes that the Holy See forbade their sale. The disagreement between the ecclesiastic hierarchies and the Venetian booksellers and printers went back very far in time.[1] When the Roman authorities, in the 1570s, began to impose throughout Italy the principle of the uniformity of liturgic texts, they encountered the systematic opposition of the Venetian printers, who were not slow to rise up to defend their economic interests: every new edition approved by Rome meant – at least in theory – a loss of income due to the impossibility of marketing the works already printed.[2] The Church hierarchies in the past had been compelled to reach some kind of more-or-less dignified compromise with the powerful Venetian printers' corporation, but in the early 1600s they attempted to accelerate the action by which they controlled texts. It was no chance matter that the Congregation of the Index took a direct interest in handling the problem.[3] Clement VIII had noticed the existence of an imperfect edition (i.e. not corresponding to the version approved by Pius V) of the Roman missal published and printed in Venice at the Giunti printing-shop,[4] and accordingly, during a meeting of the Congregation of the Index held on 20 January 1601, he instructed the Congregation to take serious measures 'lest it should spring up again' (*ne in futurum repullulet*); beginning with a reassertion of the complete validity of Pius V's Bull, the Pope took pains to guarantee that no one should modify the liturgic order established by Rome:

---

[1] For a detailed reconstruction of the various episodes that, from the 1570s on, set the Venetian printers and the Church hierarchies against each other over various problems – mainly economic – related to the printings of missals and breviaries, cf. P.F. Grendler, *The Roman Inquisition and the Venetian Press, 1540–1605*, Princeton, Princeton University Press, 1977, pp. 169 et seqq.

[2] Cf. ibid.

[3] The direct interest of the Congregation of the Index was in fact a rational application of the regulations contained in the Sistine and Clementine-Sistine Rules, on which cf. above, ch. 8.

[4] ACDF, Index, 1/1, f. 140r. On Pius V's missal, cf. above, ch. 5.

> So that no one shall dare to add, reduce, or eliminate anything in ecclesiastic worship and rites without special license from the Holy See and so that in the meantime any reckless transgressors may be punished and any inventions of the sort prohibited, particularly missals, because the missals printed in Venice at the Giunti printing house contain the same mistakes as made by the proof-readers who emended them on the basis of Sixtus V's Vulgate edition.[5]

During the same meeting the Master of the Holy Palace was instructed to ban all missals printed in Venice – not only those published by the Giunti printing house – after 1596, the year the incriminated edition was printed: 'The Master of the Holy Palace has been instructed to interdict booksellers who do not sell missals printed in Venice after 1596.'[6] Once these first emergency measures had been adopted the Master of the Holy Palace – as we can read in the minutes of the meeting – was to discuss with His Holiness whether this 'negotiation' was a matter that concerned the Congregation of the Index rather than the Congregation of the Holy Office. It is legitimate to deduce that the Pope must have favored the first of these two solutions considering that within a matter of weeks, on 17 February, the Cardinal Members of the Index – organizing and completing the indications coming out of that same meeting – pronounced an edict 'regarding the prohibition of missals' (*super Missalium prohibitione*).[7] Mindful from the very first lines of the Pope's explicit request,[8] the Cardinals of the Index – having

[5] 'Ne quis audeat absque speciali Sedis Apostolicae licentia in ecclesiastico culto et rito aliquid addere, minuere, vel detrahere et interim puniantur temerarii transgressores et interdicantur huiusmodi adinventiones et praesertim missalia et quoniam ne dum missalia apud Iunctas Venetiis impressa verum etiam apud alios ibidem continent eosdem errores correctorum culpa qui iuxta editionem Vulgatae Sixti V iussu editam missalia emendare ausi sunt, ne dum in Epistolis et Evangeliis, verum etiam in reliquis, quod minime esse faciendum' (ibid., c. 140r).

[6] 'Commissum Magistro Sacri Palatii ut ab anno 1596 quaecumque missalia Venetiis impressa interdicat librariis ne vendant' (ibid.) The Secretary of the Congregation, on the other hand, along with Giovanni Battista Bandini, was instructed to examine the various editions of the missals published in Venice that had to be corrected, so that it should be clear which were the authorized editions and which the banned. The subject, it was said, would be rediscussed at the next meeting of the Congregation.

[7] *Edictum Illustriss. D.D. Card. a Sanctiss. D.N. Clem. Papa VIII Congregationi Indicis Deputatorum super quorundam Missalium contra formam Bullae Pii Papae V Impressorum prohibitione,* in ACDF, Index, Protocolli S, cc. nn.; the same text is also to be found in ACDF, Index, Protocolli X, c. 566r; and in *Scriniolum*, ff. 188–9 (owing to a typographical error, sheet 188 is numbered 178).

[8] So that this matter should not remain unpunished and not give rise to more serious evils and problems, our Most Holy Lord has ordered vivae vocis oraculo that measures should be taken to find an appropriate solution to this problem as soon as possible' ('Sanctiss. D. N. ne ea impunita remaneret, et ut gravioribus malis, et detrimentis aditus praecluderetur, vocis oraculo mandavit, ut quantotius super his de opportuno remedio provideremus'; *Edictum*).

taken cognizance of the ineffectiveness of Pius V's Bull concerning missals[9] – ordered the prohibition of all copies printed 'at the Giunti, Sessa, and Misserini printing-houses, and at the sign of the Siren and of Europe, and any other missal printed after 1596' (*apud Iunctas, Sessas, Misserinum, et ad signum Syrenae, et Europae, et quoscunque alios ab anno 1596*): all the Church authorities were to occupy themselves with the supervision of the correction of the copies circulating in the area of their jurisdiction, taking as their model the Missal of Pius V.[10] However, the situation proved to be more difficult to manage than the Roman authorities could have possibly expected. Far from providing a solution, or at least putting an end to the matter, the action taken by the Index authorities opened up a whole series of problems of a practical nature, thus contributing indirectly to the impression that the Roman project was merely wishful thinking.

It may be useful at this point to recall the exemplary case of the Inquisitor of Asti, Giovan Battista Porcelli, certainly one of the most active of the Inquisitors to have dealings with the Congregation of the Index.[11] The obstructive behavior and the opposition rising out of the economic interests of the Venetian publishers and printers once again played a key role in bringing round the Pope in Rome from his rigid and intransigent initial position toward a softer conciliatory attitude.[12] However, a not insignificant role in this process must also have been played by Porcelli's two well-informed and extremely precise letters which laid bare the aporias of the Roman project and contributed to the reshaping of the Church hierarchies' lines of action. Writing from his home town on 27 June 1601, a few days after viewing the text of the edict, he expressed the regret that there was no 'note of the errors to be corrected nor was there even one single Missal that we can be assured is truly accurate.'[13] However, the

---

9 *Edictum.*

10 Ibid.

11 The collections of letters relative to these years sent by and to the Congregation of the Index and now kept at the ACDF (Index III/5 and Index V/1) contain frequent references to the missal problem. It is not intended to offer in this ontext a detailed and complete reconstruction of this correspondence, but the Porcelli case that is under consideration here seems to provide – for the purpose of our analysis – sufficient examples of the content of the reports. For general background information we refer readers to the work of Paul F. Grendler cited above.

12 The definition is by P. GRENDLER, *The Roman Inquisition*, pp. 246 et sqq., who deals amply with the conclusion of the entire episode, highlighting the Venetian booksellers' complete success (ibid.).

13 'Nota delli errori da doversi corregere, né tampoco un Missale, che possiamo assicurarsi, che sia veramente corretto;' Letter from the Inquisitor of Asti to Cardinal Valier, in *Scriniolum*, ff. 176–7. He also warned that it was important to examine the frontispieces with great care as they were often falsified by the printers in order to deceive the church authorities. As he wrote later in the same letter, he found 'the year of printing falsified: for there isa Missal printed by Gionta in Venice in the year 1580 and although the first page of

problems deriving from the Congregation of the Index's project were not limited to the lack of a sure base on which to make the corrections.

For when Porcelli received the requested 'note',[14] he was far from satisfied and returned to the charge, listing a whole series of punctilious 'observations'. First of all, he wrote, 'I found there to be scarcely a single Missal not requiring some correction, not so much only from '96 onward as in the other old ones';[15] secondly, not even Pius V's official edition could be considered correct if compared with the text to be found in the censures in question: 'I found that there were some mistakes even in the 1571 edition, of which a printed copy is also sent'.[16] In other words there was no escape from this tortuous maze of versions and corrections; there were even

> two Missals from Venice that were taken to be correct, one printed by Gionta in 1598 and the other for Giorgio Varisco in 1602, on which I thought I could count in order to be establish the accuracy of all the Missals. But when

---

the reprinted edition bears the date 1598 the last page says 1580. With the addition of the Masses from Gregory XIII up to Clement VIII, which are placed in their normal positions, even if it is known that most of them were added by Sistus V, who was made Pope only in 1585. And this same mistake may have been repeated elsewhere by others and for this reason I deemed it my duty to advise Your Most Illustrious Lordship thereof so that he may instruct us how we should act in order to perform that which the Holy Congregation desires, and not bootlessly cast away the fruit of our labor' ('trovando che è falsificato l'anno dell'impressione: che vi è un Missale stampato dal Gionta in Venetia dell'anno 1580. Se bene nel primo foglio ristampato di nuovo dice del 1598. Nell'ultimo però dice del 1580. Con l'aggionta delle Messe da Gregorio XIII fino a Clemente VIII e sono poste a suoi luochi ordinarii, e pure si sa che la maggior parte furono aggionte da Sisto V che fu fatto Papa solo del 1585. E questo istesso errore può anco esser commesso in altri, per questo mi è parso doverne dar aviso a S.S. Illustrissima acciò ci ordini come havemo a governarsi per effettuare quanto desidera quella Sacra Congregatane, e non gettare via la fatica senza frutto alcuno';ibid., f. 177).

[14] The text of these censures is given in *Scriniolum*, ff. 200 et sqq.

[15] 'trovai non esservi quasi Missale alcuno, che non havesse bisogno di correttione, non tanto dal '96 in qua, quanto anco delli altri più antichi;' Letter from Asti dated 24 December 1602, ACDF, Index III/5, ff. 41r; also in ACDF, Index, Protocolli, X, ff. 26r–v and in *Scriniolum,* ff. 191–2. The cited passage continued as follows: 'In the pages containing the words that have to be put in the Missals instead of the mistakes contained therein, it is found that they took as their model the Missal printed in Venice for the heirs of Bartholomeo Faletti 1575, as can be seen from the printed copy found in a similar Missal corresponding to this – I noticed the mistakes contained in the Missals printed for Giovanni Varisco and Heirs of Bartholomeo Faletti, and his companions in 1570, 1572, 1573, 1574, 1580, and 1589, of each of which I send a printed copy' ('Et perché in quelli fogli nelli quali sono stampate le parole che si hanno a rimetter ne' Missali in luoco de gl'errori, vi si contiene, che havessero preso per essemplare il Missale stampato in Venetia per li heredi di Bartholomeo Faletti 1575 come si potrà vedere per la copia stampata, ritrovata in simil Missale, conforme a quello notai li errori, che si contenvano ne i Missali stampati per Giovanni Varisco, e Heredi di Bartholomeo Faletti, e suoi compagni del 1570,1572,1573, 1574, 1580, 1589, de quali tutti ne mando copia stampata').

[16] 'Anco in quello del 1571, ritrovai esservi qualche error, mandandone pur copia stampata' (ibid., f. 41r).

I compared them I found them to be very different one from the other, with many discrepancies.[17]

In short, since 'all the corrections made by the Printers are wrong, and only need some marks of correction to enable them to get off their hands various issues of incorrect Missals which they find they have',[18] Porcelli personally undertook to send the text of the correction although, having no illusions, he realized it would serve little purpose. The situation was therefore bleak.

The cardinals in Rome – exposed to the pressure exerted by the Venetian printers who wanted the abolition of the privilege of the Vatican Apostolic Typography and to the difficulties caused by the abolition of the ban on selling old versions of the Missal, and hard struck by these two incisive letters – must have begun to realize how difficult it would be to realize their plans. An indication of the embarrassing deadlock can be seen in the action of Cardinal Terranova who, when thanking the Inquisitor of Asti for the censures sent to him, limited himself to saying that 'Venice has been instructed by letter to take greater care in the printing of Ecclesiastic books, otherwise appropriate measures will be taken that will not please the booksellers of Venice'.[19] This last threat, one may suppose, must have seemed to those at whom it was directed the manifestation of a wearily repeated rite rather than a sign of true conviction, for on 7 July, 1604, with the promulgation of the new missal, the booksellers of Venice found all their requests granted.[20]

A similar attempt to set up rules and regulations and a degree of uniformity was initiated in those same years also in the delicate sector of indulgences. The matter had got beyond the control of the authorities in Rome long before the violent attacks by the Lutherans began to question their theological basis, constructing around them a mass of radical criticism

---

17 'duoi Missali da Venetia che si spendevano per corretti, uno stampato dal Gionta del 1598, e l'altro per Giorgio Varisco del 1602, sopra de i quali credevo potermi assicurare per stabilire la correttione di tutti i Missali. Così confrontandoli insieme trovai esser tra loro molto differenti, e discrepanti' (ibid.).

18 'tutte le correttioni, che vengono per via di Stampatori sono false, e attendono solo a far qualche segno di correttione, per scaricarsi di qualche numero de Missali scorretti, che si trovano havere' (ibid.).

19 'a Venetia si è scritto che si usi maggior diligenza nelle stampe de libri Ecclesiastici, altrimenti si piglierà rimedio opportuno che non piacerà a librari di Venetia' (letter from Rome, 19 March 1603, in *Scriniolum*, f. 196).

20 The Venetians' only concession to the requests from Rome was the launching of a reform of the press, desired by the Senate, by virtue of which the Venetian printers were admonished to exhibit greater rigor and more care in the exercise of their trade (P.F. Grendler, *The Roman Inquisition*, pp. 246 et seqq).

against external devotion and superstition. There was an excessive number of religious confraternities and companies that abused their true or claimed Papal privileges in order to entice the faithful into their churches and, above all, to get their money; likewise, the selling of false indulgences by unscrupulous ecclesiastics was a practice that had gotten quite out of control. While as late as 1571, in Pius V's Bull, indulgences were still regarded as a means to 'urge the faithful more vigorously' to observe Catholic precepts,[21] at the beginning of the seventeenth century the attitude of the Church began to change. On 22 July 1603 the Inquisitor of Milan showed the first signs of stiffening, when he issued an edict prohibiting

> certain Indulgences, which are vainly claimed to have been liberally granted to certain Rosaries, or to the Rosary of the Grand Duke of Tuscany of ten Hail Maries, and a Lord's Prayer, by Pius IV, or Pius V, God rest their souls, and confirmed by Pope Clement VIII, of which some copies have fallen into our hands.[22]

---

[21] 'And to urge the faithful to show greater vigor in saying this office, which is newly corrected and printed, all persons who recite it, although under no obligation to do so, will have fifty days taken off the number of days of Penitence imposed upon them. Whoever says the Office of the dead included in the said Office, likewise fifty days. Whoever says the Seven Psalms or Graduals included in this Office, another forty days. Whoever says any of the prayers likewise included in this Office, also fifteen days' ('et per incitar più vivamente ogni fedele a dir questo ufficio nuovamente corretto e stampato, a tutti quelli, che non essendo obligati, lo diranno, per ogni volta si relassano cinquanta giorni delle Penitenze a loro imposte. A chi dirà l'Ufficio de morti inserto in detto Ufficio altri cinquanta simili. A chi dirà li Sette Salmi, o Graduali in esso ufficio inserti altri quaranta. A chi dirà alcuna delle orationi parimente in esso ufficio inserte quindeci giorni simili'; *Scriniolum*, f. 55).

[22] 'Alcune Indulgenze, le quali vanamente si pretendono essere state concesse grandissime a certe Corone, o Corona del Gran Duca di Toscana di X Ave Marie, et un Pater noster, da Pio Quarto, o Pio Quinto di Santa Memoria et confirmate da Papa Clemente Ottavo, delle quali anco alcune copie sono capitate alle nostre mani' (*Editto della S. Inquisitione per le prohibitioni infrascritte. Noi frat'Agostino Galamini dell'Ordine de Predicatori, Maestro nella Sacra Theologia, Inquisitore Generale nella Città di Milano, suo stato, e dominio. 22 Luglio 1603*, in *Scriniolum*, f. 314). It is interesting to quote the text of the incriminated Indulgence that followed the edict: 'Indulgence granted in happy memory of Pius V to the Rosary of the Grand Duke of Tuscany, confirmed by His Holiness Clement VIII 1601. This Rosary is called the Rosary of the Merits of the Passion of Our Lord Jesus Christ, which is ten Hail Maries and a Lord's Prayer, whence all persons saying this Rosary will obtain remission for all their sins and plenary indulgence. And every time they hold this Rosary in their hand, or look upon it in all good faith, saying Lord Jesus Christ, I pray Thee, for the merits of Thy Most Holy Passion, to have mercy on my soul and on my most grievous sins, they will receive remission for them. Likewise, looking at it, or kissing it for the souls of the dead, each time they say it they will set free a soul from Purgatory, and if they say it a thousand times a day they will set free as many souls [...]. The said Grand Duke is empowered to bestow these Rosaries upon seven devout persons, who then may give it to seven others, and so on, but with the warning that any person who wishes this Rosary must ask for it for God's sake, and for the merits of His Most Holy Passion. And this Rosary must be given without recompense,

In the wake of this edict Clement VIII decided in 1604 to publish a 'Constitution' (*Costituzione*) with which he attempted to set some order in the whole matter.[23] The Pope instructed the local Inquisition and episcopal authorities to gather as soon as possible all information regarding indulgences, whether true or false, in the possession of 'persons in Cloisters and Monasteries and Mendicants' (*persone Claustrali, Monastice, e Mendicanti*), of 'religious Confraternities and Companies' (*Confraternite e Compagnie religiose*), and of 'secular and regular Churches' (*Chiese secolari e regolari*), charging them to send them to Rome to be verified and newly granted, should such be the case. It was therefore an enormous undertaking for which Clement VIII 'deemed it almost necessary to create a Congregation' (*giudicò quasi necessario erigere una Congregatione*), specially formed, as revealed by Cardinal Baronio in a letter to the Archbishop of Milan, Cardinal Federico Borromeo, a few months after the approval of the 'Constitution'.[24]

It is difficult to assess how far and in what way this ambitious project bore fruit,[25] but we can get some useful information from the parallel

---

and if the Rosary is by chance lost, that person can choose another one but can no longer dispense it to others. Received in Milan, 1 January 1603' ('Indulgenza concessa dalla felice memoria di Pio quinto alla Corona del Gran Duca di Toscana, confirmata dalla Santità di Clemente Ottavo 1601. Questa Corona si dimanda Corona delli meriti della Passione di N.S. Giesù Christo, qual'è di dieci Ave Marie, et un Pater noster, onde qualonche persona haverà detta Corona otterrà la rimissione di tutti li suoi peccati, e indulgenza plenaria. Et ogni volta che terrà in mano detta Corona, overo con buona fede la guarderà dicendo, Sig. Giesù Christo io ti prego che per li meriti della tua passione santissima habbi misericordia all'anima mia, e de miei gravissimi peccati, otterrà la remissione di quelli. Similmente guardandola, o bacciandola per le anime de morti, per ogni volta che la dirà, caverà un'anima di Purgatorio, et se mille volte il giorno la dicesse tante anime caveria [...]. Si da facoltà a detto Gran Duca, che possa dispensare dette Corone a sette persone divote, quali ancor essi possino darla ad altri sette, et così di mano in mano. Avvertendo però che qualonche persona vorrà detta Corona la deve dimandar per amor di Dio, e per li meriti della Passione sua santissima. Et questa Corona si deve dar senza premio alcuno, et se detta Coruna per sorte si perdesse se ne può quel tale eleggere un'altra da sé, ma non può poi esso più dispensarla ad altri. Ricevuta in Milano del 1603 al primo di Genaro'; *Scriniolum*, ff. 314–15).

23 The text of the 'Constitution' concerned in general various aspects of the life of the confraternities; cf. the Papal Bull 'Quaecumque a Sede Apostolica', 7 December 1604, in *Bullarium diplomatum et privilegiorum sanctorum romanorum pontificum, Taurinensis editio*, tome XI, 1867, pp. 138–40.

24 Letter dated 10 December 1605, in *Scriniolum*, ff. 630–31; this long and informative letter from Baronio conveyed Paul V's intention to continue the work of his predecessor, and indeed Paul V took official action with regard to the matter just three months later (cf. *Scriniolum*, ff. 631–2. A Congregation of Indulgences and of Relics was created only some decades later, in 1669, in a *motu proprio* by Clement IX entitled *In ipsis pontificatus nostri primordiis* (cf. N. Del Re, *La Curia romana. Lineamenti storico-giuridici*, Rome, Libreria Editrice Vaticana, 1998 (IV ed.), pp. 382–4).

25 Further research will throw more light on this aspect. Here we will limit ourselves to mentioning a document that shows the Inquisition in action. The Congregation of the

experience of 'prayer', which has to be read and interpreted in the framework of the same project.

Soon after the promulgation of Pius V's Bull on offices and prayers[26] it was immediately clear that the objective of the overall process of regulation of the sector pursued by the Church hierarchies would be much more difficult to achieve than the compilers of the Bull had expected. All the difficulties that a ban of the sort – mainly aimed at positively identifying prayers to be censured or condemned – would entail in its practical application[27] immediately became apparent in a letter in which the Inquisitor of Pisa, a few months after the publication of the Papal Bull, answered the request of the Cardinals who were members of the Congregation of the Holy Office. Overwhelmed by the mass of devotional material, which went far beyond the detailed list of prayers contained in the Bull, the Inquisitor of Pisa could do no more than send back a copy of each *operetta* that was suspect:

> I send you a selection of these legends and prayers (as you asked me), of which for the most part I have copies, and I should appreciate it if you would confirm that there is not one of them that does not contain either a false title or indulgence [...] or vain or superstitious observations, or prayers of dubious value, or reasonable but to be considered false [...], incompetent or improper in their expression or ridiculous lies, or things that cannot be permitted, or words [...] that are out of place, as you in your more mature and wise judgment may

---

Index decreed in 1605 the prohibition of a very popular book entitled *Tesoro pretiosissimo d'indulgenze*: this can be deduced from the text of the letter sent in reply by the Inquisitor of Bologna Brother Pietro Martire to Cardinal Girolamo Bernieri, a Member of the Congregation of the Index, in which the former wrote that once having received his letter of 8 October, the Archbishop and he would arrange 'for the publication by Preachers and Curates of the prohibition of the book entitled *Thesoro pretiosissimo d'indulgenze* gathered together for Giulio Cesare Nanni and printed in Bologna for Vittorio Benaccio in 1590, which will be an excellent remedy to open people's eyes to other similar books, and I have never permitted the publication of books containing indulgences or new miracles until I have sent them to the Archbishopric for them to be approved, in accordance with the instructions imposed by the sacred Council of Trent' ('in modo che sarà publicata da Predicatori et Curati la prohibitione del libro intitolato *Thesoro pretiosissimo d'indulgenze* raccolto per Giulio Cesare Nanni, stampato in Bologna per Vittorio Benaccio 1590, il che sarà buonissimo remedio per aprire gl'occhi ad altri libri simili, et io non ho mai lasciato dare alla stampa libri continenti indulgenze, o miracoli novi, che prima non gl'habbi mandati all'Arcivescovato aciò fossero approvati conforme a quanto gl'impone il sacro Concilio di Trento'; letter from Bologna, 29 October 1605, in ACDF, Index III/5, c. 172r).

[26] On which cf. above, ch. 5.

[27] The criteria of censorship indicated by the Bull were in any case too vague and too recently adopted to be applied with any certainty by individual local Inquisitors or Bishops to the numerous examples they came across, each of which was different from the next.

perceive, and that you will prohibit because, as most people in the world are idiots, [...] [these said] prayers exist to deceive Idiots.[28]

In no way satisfied by the instructions received from Rome, he invited the Roman authorities to proceed even further: 'Just as books were dealt with in the indexes of the Sacrosanct Council of Trent and of the Holy Office, let measures be taken to prohibit those papers so that [...] women and simpletons do not trust them and printers no longer circulate them.'[29] In order to justify his feelings of malaise, he decided to provide a sample of the tangle of such prayers and writings from which the defenders of Catholic orthodoxy were expected to learn how to extricate themselves:

> I also send you three booklets, the first entitled *Scelta d'orationi* (A Selection of Prayers), the second, *Giardino Spirituale* (Spiritual Garden), and the third, *Selva d'orationi* (Forest of Prayers), and so when you have seen them either you send them back to me [...] or you keep them and let me know whether they must be purged (and in what way) or whether they must be prohibited. [...] In the first and second, besides many prayers composed *ad placitum*, and in the vernacular there are [...] some prayers that deserve to be purged: in addition to the fact that they promise uncertain indulgences, [...] I find that the Lord's Angelical salutation, the Symbol, the Hymns, and the Psalms set out in verse, and others which seem to me become worthless when taken from Latin. The third, apart from containing what we find in the first and second, presents the seven penitential psalms set out in verse unlike other cases (as you will see); however, as I did not know [...] *whether these are to be permitted or not, I thought it my duty to write about it and ask you for a solution.*[30]

---

28 'gli mando un mazzo di queste leggende et orationi (come ella mi domanda) havendone io le copie della maggior parte, dove harò caro che ella si chiarisca che non ve n'è alcuna che non contenga o falso titillo, o indulgenza [...] o osservatane vane, super-stitiose, o valore dell'oratione non verisimile, o ragionevole, ma da reputarsi finto [...] incompetente, o parlar inpto, o bugie ridiculose, o cose da non permettersi, o parole [...] malposte come ella dal suo più maturo e savio giuditio saprà scorgere, et che eUa ne farà prohibitione, perché essendo la maggior parte del mondo Idiota, [...] [dette] orationi siano per inganar gli Idioti' (Letter from the Inquisitor of Pisa, Brother Girolamo, Pisa, 29 December 1571, ACDF, St. St. HH 2-d, cc. 206r–v). The frequent use of dots is due to the fact that some words have worn away over time and are therefore illegible. The overall meaning of the sentences however remains comprehensible and it has been necessary to make only a few additions, all duly marked, in order to facilitate the reading of the text.

29 'Come con gl'indici del Sacrosanto Concilio Tridentino, e del santo Offitio s'è previsto ai libri, così con prohibitioni si proveda a queste carte, acciò non [...] confidarsi *[leggi:* non confidino] tanto in queste le donne et i semplici, né gli stampatori in mandarne *[leggi:* ne mandino] più fuora.'

30 'Gli mando anche tre libretti di titulo uno Scelta d'orationi, il 2° Giardino spirituale, il 3° Selva d'orationi a fin che doppo gli harà visti, o me gli rimandi [...] o ritenendogli mi facci saper se purgar (et in che modo) o abolir si debbono. [...] [N]el primo et secondo, oltre

Also – as if that were not enough – to make the situation even more complicated there were those *historiette* ('tales') freely taken from the Holy Scriptures, which were more or less directly affected by the prohibition contained in Rule IV of the Tridentine Index:

> In the selection, I send you copies of acts of many representations of the Old and New Testaments and many representations of Saints, both men and women for the simple reason that if we do not allow each of them Bibles in the vernacular, how will it be that the mysteries reach the hands of everyone [...] expressed in poetic verse, with poetic license and very often incorrectly, or with inappropriate or misplaced words?[31]

Far from offering a definite solution to the uncontrolled proliferation of devotional material, Pius V's Bull thus stirred up more problems than it solved. The restatement of the Bull's formal validity at a meeting of the Congregation of the Index on 10 April 1587[32] must thus have appeared to be at one and the same time a testimony of the ineffectiveness of the prohibitions and a sign of the deadlock reached by the Church hierarchies.

It was necessary to wait for the end of the century for the authorities in Rome to tackle the question with renewed strength and to try to stem the flood of uncontrolled editorial production.

For it was in the Clementine Index that the sensitivity of the censors toward *historiette et orationi* ('tales and prayers'), typical expressions of 'unlettered' (*senza lettere*) religious expression, found its indispensable normative legitimization.[33] It was therefore no coincidence that in the years immediately following the promulgation of the Index there was a sort of long-range competition among the local authorities, which busied themselves drawing to the Roman Cardinals' attention every suspicious

---

molte orationi composte ad placitum, et in lingua vulgare, sono [...] dell'orationi degne di purgatione: oltre che promettono indulgentie incerte, [...] trovo la domenicale salutatione Angelica, il Simbolo, Inni, et Salmi esposti in verso, et altre che pare a me doventino vili cavandosi dal latino. Nel terzo oltre che vi si trova quanto si trova nel primo e nel secondo, vi si vedono i sette salmi penitentiali diversamente da diversi in verso esposti (come ella vedrà); però non sapendo io [...] se si debbino permettere o no, m'è parso scriverne e domandarne a lei risolutione.'

31 'Nel mazo gli mando copie di molte representationi d'atti del vechio et nuovo [testamento] et molte representationi di Santi et Sante mosso di qua, che se non si concedono bibbie vulgari a ogn'uno, come in mano d'ogn'uno perverranno i misterii [...] esposti in verso poetico, con licentia poetica, et bene spesso iniustamente, o con parole incompetenti o mal poste?' (Letter from the Inquisitor of Pisa, 29 December 1571).

32 'Decretum quod observetur constitutio Pii quinti dehoris Beata Virgine aliisque precibus vulgaribus' (ACDF, Index, 1/1, cc. 18r–v).

33 Cf. also below, ch. 10.

example of this literary genre.[34] If at first these testimonies must have been isolated cases, driven more by a desire to show the Roman authorities their eagerness than by any real awareness of what censorship consisted of or what cultural project lay behind such an action, before long they began to have a certain organic relationship between them.

An edict issued on 26 July 1599 by the Inquisitor of Asti[35] was the first real sign of the Inquisition's new attitude toward this sector of publishing: from this moment on, the censor's interest in *historiette et orationi* ('tales and prayers') would be constant and long lasting. It is no coincidence that this sign came from the city of Asti. Brother Giovanni Battista Porcelli d'Albenga, the Inquisitor of Asti, as already mentioned, soon attracted the attention of the authorities in Rome as one of the most scrupulous appliers of the Clementine Index. From the moment the edict was drawn up, he showed all his skill in his grasp of the censors' intentions and in his manner of translating these into concrete action. Rereading Pius V's Bull in the light of the subsequent prescriptions elaborated in the two published but unpromulgated Indexes (the Sistine and Sisto-Clementine Indexes) and incorporated in the Clementine Index, we can perceive that the Inquisitor of Asti foresaw – and therefore in some way even suggested – many of the rules and regulations which the Church of Rome would eventually officially adopt. He warned 'all faithful Christians' (*tutti li fedeli christiani*) against using 'any sort of prayer that is not approved by the Holy, Catholic, Apostolic, and Roman Church, and that is not consistent with the way it

34 Among these testimonies we will cite two letters: one from the Vicar of Naples Ludovico Boido to Cardinal Terranova, which read: 'Here people have been tearing up sheet upon sheet of 'tales' and other similar trifles that sometimes circulate and they say are printed in Naples even though without authorization [...] and it is suspected [...] that they come from other cities in merchants' bales of cloth or with other goods' ('Qui si sono stracciate e si stracciano spesso molti fogli de historiette, et altre simili cosette che vanno a volta e dicono d'essere stampate in Napoli se ben falsamente [...] e si dubita [...] che vengano da altre città in balle del mercanti de panni, o d'altre merci'; letter from Naples, 12 September 1597, in ACDF, Index, III/3, cc. 202r–v); and the other from Brother Cipriano, the Inquisitor of Rimini, to Cardinal Agostino Valier, which recounted that he had come across a booklet in the style of a short office in the possession of an Italian soldier who had just returned home from Germany, 'in which I saw some extravagant kinds of litanies and therefore resolved to send it'('dentro al quale havendo visto una sorte di lettanie stravaganti, mi sono risoluto di mandarlo'; letter from Rimini, 8 March 1598, in ACDF, Index, III/2, c. 75r): it cannot be ruled out that this letter triggered the Inquisition's interest in the Jesuit Sailly (see below).

35 *Noi frate Gio. Battista Porcelli d'Albenga, dell'Ordine de Predicatori, Professore di Sacra Theologia, e Inquisitore Generale della Città, e Diocese d'Asti, dalla Santa Sede Apostolica specialmente delegato* ... Asti 26 luglio 1599 (*We Brother Giovanni Battista Porcelli d'Albenga, of the Order of Preachers, Professor of Holy Theology, and Inquisitor General of the City and Diocese of Asti, specially delegated by the Apostolic Holy Seat* ... Asti, 26 July 1599), in *Scriniolum*, f. 171.

is properly used'.[36] But above all he introduced the principle of referring to official liturgic offices as the only yardstick for establishing whether prayers and litanies were legitimate or not: all prayers 'that are not printed in the approved and reformed Missals, Breviaries, and Offices'[37] were in no way to be allowed to circulate ('unless they are first seen by the Holy Office and judged to be good or bad').[38]

The problem of limiting and regulating the number of texts in circulation was not the only one to face the Church hierarchies, and such a set of rules and regulations could scarcely by itself be the best of solutions. As had anyway already become clear following the considerations on the reform of Breviaries and Missals during the 1570s, one of the trickiest questions in the devotional field was the control of consolidated local traditions, which were extremely hard to root out without serious jeopardizing the religious faithfulness of entire outlying areas. When on 11 June 1600 the members of the Congregation of the Index received in their hands a supplication from the provincial Father in Apulia of the Order of the Eremetics of St Augustine (*eremitani di Sant'Agostino*), the matter cannot have surprised the Roman Cardinals. This letter requested permission 'to sing the undermentioned litanies, which since time immemorial it has been the custom to sing before the most devout image of the Most Holy Savior situated in the Church of the Most Holy Savior of Barletta, in the diocese of Trani, of the Fathers of the aforesaid Order of the Eremitics of St Augustine' (this was followed by a detailed list of the litanies that were sung).[39] But the Congregation's official answer, pronounced forthwith, was a peremptory '*nihil*'. On the contrary, a few months before, on 12 February 1597, responding to a similar request (albeit referring to lauds in vernacular verse, not litanies)[40] from the Vicar Capitular of Cortona, Evangelista Ridolfini,[41] the Congregation of the Index had answered – with all due caution – in quite a different tone:

36 'sorte alcuna d'orationi, che non sia approbata dalla Santa, Catholica, Apostolica, e Romana Chiesa, e conforme all'uso d'essa' (*Scriniolum*, f. 171).

37 'che non siano stampate nelli Missali, Breviarii, e Officioli approbati, e reformati' (ibid.).

38 'se prima non saranno vedute dal S. Officio, et giudicate buone o cattive' (ibid.).

39 'potersi cantare l'infrascritte litanie, quali antichissimamente che non vi è memoria soleno cantarsi avanti la devotissima immagine del Santissimo Salvatore sita e posta dentro la Chiesa del Santissimo Salvatore di Barletta, nella diocesi di Trani, deli padri dello detto ordine eremitano di Sant'Agostino' (ACDF, Index, series XIX (one volume), cc. 162r–163v).

40 This might indeed have been a cause of greater preoccupation, considering the lack of belief in any sacred matter presented in poetic form.

41 "Letter written from da Cortona on 25 January 1597, in ACDF, Index III/3, c. 72r. In this letter the Vicar Capitular related that 'the Brotherhood known as the Brotherhood of the lauds [...] has for more than two centuries had the obligation to have lauds sung during all

> With regard to the 200-year-old custom of singing these lauds in vernacular verse regarding the current epistles and Gospels of the year, as testified by Monsignor the Bishop, and as it is more than fifty years since the book was printed, and as it does not contain the bare text of the Holy Scriptures but is also accompanied by some added moralities [...], my Most Illustrious Colleagues have judged that for the above reasons and in view of the devotion of the People it should be permitted that the said lauds be sung according to the ancient use in the customary churches but that nothing new should be introduced and that this grace and permission should not be extended to other churches.[42]

The Inquisitorial decree issued the following year thus came up against matters of this sort which, as we have seen, remained unsettled.[43]

If we briefly reconstruct the stages leading to the compilation of the decree, it is useful to point out that on 20 January 1601 the Pope himself considered the matter, thus providing the highest possible legitimization for the battle that was about to break out. Clement VIII was clearly sensitive to the reports which by now were reaching him from all directions and he took pains to make it clear that he was aware of the multiplication of the number of printed litanies and of 'the many rubrics added to the prayers and some others translated into the vernacular' (*multas rubricas orationibus additas et quasdam etiam in vulgari lingua translatas*), officially instructing the Congregation of the Index to resolve the matter immediately 'lest it should spring up again'(*ne in futurum repullulet*). With regard to the reasons which in a mere six months were to see the Congregation of

---

Lent in the Cathedral and in four other churches of the said town [...], where with the great concourse of many people with all their devotion it is not possible to put an end to these lauds without causing a great upset in the City; I therefore resolved to give your Illustrious Lordship an account of the matter together with which I send the booklets intended for this purpose'.

[42] 'Havendo riguardo alla consuetudine antica di 200 anni in cantarsi quelle laudi volgari in versi sopra l'epistole et evangelij correnti dell'anno, come attesta Mons.r Vescovo eletto et essendo più di 50 anni che il libro è stampato e non contenendo il semplice testo della S. Scrittura, ma d'alcune moralità interposte ... [sic] accompagnato, perciò han giudicato questi Ill.mi Sig.ri miei colleghi, che per le ragioni predette et attesa la devotion del Populo si permetta che si cantino dette laudi conforme all'uso antico nelle Chiese solite ma non si introduchino altre di nuovo né in altre chiese si stenda questa gratia e permissione' (Letter in ACDF, Index, V (one volume), c. 49r).

[43] On the decree in July 1601 concerning litanies, cf. below. Even if we grant that the Congregation's changing attitude possibly concealed reasons of some political importance (we cannot exclude – even if it is not apparent in the documentation we have examined – reasons related to the changed attitude of the Church toward this or that Company or Confraternity) or rules and regulations that differed one from the other, we cannot forget the role that local devotional tradition had been recognized as having (nor the sensitiveness that this tradition had encountered among the Church hierarchies) in the course of the compilation of the reformed Missals and Breviaries and in the text of the Sistine and Sisto-Clementine Rules of the early 1590s.

the Holy Office claim the matter for itself, taking it literally out of the hands of the Cardinals who were Members of the Index, to whom the Pope himself had solemnly turned, it is difficult – in the absence of any further documentation – to make a firm pronouncement: one can only consider this episode in the context of the steady and irresistible process of expansion of the Inquisition's field of action, which had now being going on for many years.[44]

Meanwhile, alarming reports from local defenders of Catholic orthodoxy continued to reach Rome one after the other. One particular letter, written on 26 May that same year by the Inquisitor of Venice and particularly rich in information, must have persuaded even the most reluctant to take concrete action to remedy the situation. A considerable number of unauthorized *libretti di litanie* ('litany books'), some well known and others less, came to the attention of the cardinals in Rome:

> *Forty hours of prayers* by Don Ferdinando Bongiorno with various litanies, and judged there to be impertinent, and compositions full of new rites and therefore prohibited, as your Lordship writes to me, have been printed again here in Venice. [...] I wish however to tell your Lordship that these sundry litanies have been authorized to be printed because before them various others were printed: in particular, in Venice in 1599, a book in 12mo containing 34 sorts of litanies besides the Ordinaries after the seven psalms; and, of these, many were taken by Bongiorno [...] and the title of the book is *Thesaurus sacrarum precum sive litaniarum* [...]; and there is another large book composed by Father Thomaso Saillyo of the company of Jesus printed in Paris in 1599 and in Cologne in 1601, [...] the title of the book is *Thesaurus litaniarum, ac orationum sacer*;

and also:

> in a booklet printed in Venice in 1598 at the workshop of Cornelio Arrivabene composed by Father Gaspare Loarte, Doctor of Theology, of the Company of Jesus, and at the end there are some litanies regarding the Most Holy Sacrament of the Eucharist, and regarding the name of Jesus composed by Father Ignatius [...]; in another booklet printed in Venice at the Sign of the Lion [...] by Brother Alberto Cecho, Carmelite, and composed by Claudio Cuardino da Macerata there are all sorts of litanies that are different from the Ordinaries. In another printed in 1596 entitled *Litanies*.[45]

---

44 See G. Fragnito, *La Bibbia al rogo, passim*; and A. Prosperi, *Tribunali della coscienza, passim*.

45 '*L'orationi delle 40 hore* composte da Don Ferdinando Bongiorno con diverse lettanie, et giudicate costì impertinenti et compositioni piene di novità di riti, et perciò prohibite, come V.S. mi scrive, sono state stampate et novamente qui in Vinetia. [...] Voglio però dire a V.S. che tanta diversità di letanie sono state concesse alla stampa, perché avanti di esse ne sono state stampate diverse altre: di singolare in Venetia del 1599 un libro in 12 con

The report of this letter very likely resolved the Pope's last doubts: on 14 June, during a meeting of the Congregation of the Holy Office, the first official measure with regard to litanies was taken. The specific reference was, for the occasion, directed at the most voluminous and the best known of the books indicated from Venice, i.e. the text by the Jesuit father Sailly,[46] but the intention to act generically throughout the entire field of publishing was by now becoming clear:

> Regarding the Thesaurus Letaniarum of Father Tommaso Saiglio, S.J. which contains 365 forms of litany and other types of litany by various authors, the Pope, having read the letters dated the second of this month from the Inquisitor of Venice, has decreed the suspension of all the aforesaid forms of litany, except the ordinary litanies contained in the missal and in the breviary and those that are customarily recited in honor of the Blessed Mary of Loreto; he also ordered that a letter should be written to the Inquisitor requesting him to send some examples of these types of litany. Furthermore this suspension was to be communicated to the other Inquisitors, and the Master of the Holy Palace was to carry out inspections in the city of Rome.[47]

dentro 34 sorte di letannie, oltre l'ordinarie, doppo i sette salmi; et da queste sono state prese molte dal Bongiorno [...], et il titolo del libro è *Thesaurus sacrarum precum sive litaniarum* [...]; vi è un altro libro più grande composto dal padre Thomaso Saillyo della Compagnia di Giesù stampato in Parisi del 1599, et in Colonia del 1601, [...] il titolo del libro è *Thesaurus litaniarum, ac orationum sacer*;'and also: 'in un libretto stampato in Venetia del 1598 appresso Cornelio Arrivabene composto dal padre Gaspare Loarte dottor theologo della Compagnia di Giesù nel fine vi sono alcune litanie sopra il Santissimo Sacramento dell'eucarestia, et del nome di Giesù composte dal Padre Ignatio [...]; in un altro libretto stampato in Venetia ad Signum Leonis [...] da frate Alberto Cecho Carmelitano et composto da Claudio Giardino da Macerata vi sono sorte di lettarne tutte diverse, et distinte dall'ordinarie. In un altro stampato del 1596 intitulato *Litanie*' (Letter from Brother Giovanni di Ravenna, Venice, 26 May 1601, in ACDF, Index III/6, cc. 296r et seqq.). Here are the full titles of the cited works that we have been able to verify: *Il bongiorno overo orationi delle quaranta hore*, 1601; *Thesaurus sacrarum precum sive Litaniae variae ad Deum Patrem, ad Deum Filium, ad Deum Spiritum Sanctum, ad B. Virginem, ad Sanctos Angelos et ad plures Sanctos et Sanctas Dei. Una cum septem Psalmis penitentialibus ... [et aliis] devotis orationibus ...*, Venice, apud Beretium, 1599; Tommaso Saiglio, *Thesaurus litaniarum, ac orationum sacer cum suis adversus sectarios apologiis ... Novo ordine dispositus et Litaniis de Martyrologio in singulos anni dies sumptis autus*, Paris, apud Claudium Chappellet, 1599.

46 Some time later the Congregation of the Index decided it was advisable to have Cardinal Bellarmino write to him in order to clarify that only the public use of his volume of litanies had been prohibited in obedience to Clement VIII's decree *circa Litanias*, thus reassuring him that the prohibition did not concern the contents of the text and that his integrity as a man of the cloth was in no way damaged by this condemnation (ACDF, Index, Diarii, vol. I, Meeting of 3 December 1605, c. 180v). Regarding Sailly (1558–1623), cf. C. Sommervoegel, *Bibliothèque de la Compagnie de Jesus*, Brussels-Paris, Schepens-Ricard, tome VII, coll. 403–8.

47 'De Thesauro Letaniarum Patris Thomae Sayllii gesuitae continente trecentas sexaginta quinque formas Letaniarum ac aliis modiis Letaniarum diversorum authorum,

Side by side with the litanies contained in Missals and Breviaries, the litanies of the Blessed Virgin of Loreto also found their place among the invocations that were expressly permitted: the final formula of the Inquisition's decree was gradually taking shape. Cardinal Giulio Antonio Santoro meanwhile hastened to carry out the desire of the Pope and the Holy Congregation of the Inquisition and informed the local Inquisitors and Bishops of the content of the new measure, announcing to them at the same time Clement VIII's intention to proceed before long to issue a decree, which by now had become indispensable.[48]

The last question that remained to be solved was the position to be taken with regard to local liturgical and devotional traditions. The suspension of Sailly's volume of litanies, communicated by Cardinal Santoro, had not helped to resolve the doubts which, as said, were already widespread and which indeed continued to arrive ceaselessly in communications from

lectis literis Inquisitoris Venetiarum datis 2 huius, Sanctissimus decrevit suspendi omnes praedictas formas letaniarum, exceptis letaniis ordinariis in Missali ac Breviario contentis, ac etiam Letaniis recitari solitum in honore Beatae Mariae de Laureto: item mandavit rescribi Inquisitori ut mittat exemplaria huiusmodi Letaniarum, et hanc suspensionem significari caeteris Inquisitoribus et magister Sacri Palatii faciat diligentiam in Urbe' (ACDF, Inquisition, Decreta, 1600–1601, copia, c. 573: feria quinta die 14 June 1601, coram Sanctissimo).

48 'It having come to the notice of the Holiness of Our Lord that a book by Father Tomaso Saiglio, Jesuit, entitled *Thesaurus litaniarum*, contains 365 sorts of litanies, and that another book entitled *Thesaurus sacrarum precum sive litaniae variae*, like other booklets, contains sundry varieties of litanies, His Holiness has temporarily suspended the said books, as well as the use of the above litanies, excepting only the ordinaries that are in the Missal, and in the Breviary, and also the litanies in honor of Our Most Holy Lady of Loreto; *if your Beatitude wishes at some later time to pronounce the deliberation and the resolution that are appropriate regarding the diversity and the number of these litanies.* I therefore beg Your Lordship not to fail to notify this suspension and its details to all booksellers and Episcopal Vicars in the places under his jurisdiction and to all others as necessary; and let it be done in such a way that the intention and the desire of His Beatitude are obeyed' (letter from Cardinal Giulio Antonio Santoro to the Inquisitor of Florence, in J. Tedeschi, *Documenti fiorentini per la storia dell'* Indicedei libri proibiti, in Id., *Il giudice e l'eretico. Studi sull'Inquisizione romana,* Milan, Vita e Pensiero, 1997, first English edition 1991, pp. 174–5; my emphasis). A letter in the same tone and with almost the same text was sent to the Archiepiscopal Vicar of Naples (Asdn, Archivio Storico Diocesano di Napoli, *Arcivescovi, Alfonso Gesualdo*, file 1,cc. nn.; the letter is kept together with the edict issued by the Vicar on 10 July as ordered by the Pope, as also the list of Neapolitan booksellers to whom it was notified; I have to thank Gigliola Fragnito for drawing this document to my attention). The Pisa Inquisitor – and probably many other local Inquisitors and Bishops – also received a similar letter: on 4 July 1601 his reply to Santoro announced 'I have also notified to all the booksellers and also to Monsignor the Archiepiscopal Vicar the suspension which our Master has pronounced regarding those books containing different sorts of litanies, and in obedience to the orders of His Holiness I have declared that the above books and the use of the above litanies are suspended, and the only ones to be observed are the ordinaries, which are in the Missals and the Breviary' (Pisa, 4 July 1601, in ACDF, St St HH 2-d, cc. 191r–v).

outlying areas: in a letter dated 18 July, for example, the Inquisitor of Pisa pronounced the following warning:

> The Fathers of St Dominic's Church have begun to doubt whether they can say their customary litanies in the name of Jesus, which by ancient practice they have always been accustomed to say on the occasion of every third Sunday of the month, and now the same doubt has come to our Fathers of St Francis' Church regarding whether they can use the litanies which hitherto they have sung in honor of our St Francis every fourth Sunday of the month.[49]

The congregation of the Holy Office bided its time. The extreme embarrassment, or paralyzed deadlock, in which the Roman Cardinals must have found themselves was thus emblematically attested by the *supersedeat* with which they replied to yet another request for clarification received from Venice:

> With regard to the ancient litanies that are sung in many churches in Venice, and in particular in St Mark's Church, following the reading of the Venetian Inquisitor's letters dated 30 June, it was decreed that he should ascertain their ancient origin and send us a copy of them, and then put the matter off to a later date.[50]

It was necessary to wait more than a month for the *Palazzo Apostolico nel Monte Quirinale* ('Apostolic Palace on Monte Quirinale') to announce, on 6 September, that the *Decreto di N. S. Papa Clemente Ottavo da osservarsi circa le Litanie* ('Our Lord Pope Clement VIII's Decree on Litanies') had finally been perfected.[51] The first part of the decree simply took cognizance of the problem and summarized the decisions that had already been taken:

> Considering that today many persons, including ordinary citizens, under the pretext of their increasing devotion, every day popularize new Litanies,

---

49 'è nato dubio ai Padri di S. Domenico, se puosso dire le consuete loro littanie del nome di Giesù, quali per uso anticho, son sempre stati soliti di dire ogni ritornata, che fanno ogni terza domenica del mese, l'istesso dubio hanno i Nostri Padri di S. Francesco se possano servirsi delle Iettarne, che fin adesso hanno usato in honore del nostro S. Francesco ogni quarta Domenica del Mese' (Letter from Pisa dated 18 July 1601, in ACDF, St St HH 2-d, cc. 192r–v).

50 'De Litaniis antiquiis quas plurimae Ecclesiae habent Venetiis, praesertim Ecclesia Sancti Marci, lectis literis Inquisitoris Veneti datis 30 Junii, decretum ut certioret antiquitatem, mittat illarum exemplum, et *supersedeat*' (ACDF, Inquisition, Decreta 1600–1601, copia, cc. 664–5, feria quarta die 25 luglio 1601).

51 Ibid. The vernacular text, together with that in Latin, is also to be found in *Scriniolum*, f. 173.

so much so that innumerable forms are circulating, and in some there are inappropriate expressions and in others (which is more serious) expressions that are dangerous and false; His Holiness Our Lord Pope Clement VIII in his pastoral care, wishing to ensure that people's devotion and invocation of God and of the Saints be without any danger of causing any spiritual harm, orders and commands that considering that the most ancient and common litanies, such as are to be found in Breviaries, Missals, Pontificals and Rituals and also the Litanies of the Blessed Virgin that are customarily sung in the Holy House of Loreto.[52]

All others, presumably, were normally prohibited. It was the second part of the decree that contained something really new:

Whoever wishes to make known other litanies, or wishes to use some of those already sent to the Churches, Oratories, or Processions, is obliged to send them to the Congregation of Holy Rites to be recognized and, if necessary, corrected; furthermore, without the permission of the above-said Congregation, these litanies shall not be circulated or *publicly* recited, on pain of punishment (in addition to the sin committed), as may be ruled by the Ordinary and the Inquisitor with all due severity.[53]

Thus, the Holy Office recalled – at least on the formal level – that the problem of the legitimacy of the ancient litanies (as also of those that might be composed in the future) concerned the Congregation of Rites. But this was not the most significant feature of the decree. This decree took cognizance of the impossibility of acting in capillary fashion in such a wide and indeterminate field as that of prayers, but also assumed – in line with theoretic considerations and the regulations until then followed by the Roman authorities – a position that showed the greatest respect for a certain medieval devotional tradition that had laid value on individual and private prayer. It also officially introduced a dual level of

[52] 'Perché molti in questo tempo, anche huomini privati, sotto pretesto d'accrescimento di devotione, ogni giorno divulgano nuove Litanie, a tal che se ne va portando attorno quasi innumerabili forme, et in alcune si trovano sentenze inette, et in altre (quel ch'è più grave) ve ne sono delle pericolose, et erronee; la Santità di N.S. Papa Clemente Ottavo per la sua pastoral sollecitudine, volendo provedere, che la devotione delle anime, et invocatione di Dio, et de Santi sia senza pericolo d'alcun danno spirituale mantenuta, Manda, e comanda che, ritenute le antichissime, et comuni Litanie, quali ne Breviarii, Missali, Pontificali, et Rituali si contengono, et anche quelle Litanie della Beata Vergine, che si sogliono cantare nella Sacra Casa di Loreto' (*Decreto di N. S. Papa Clemente Ottavo da osservarsi circa le Litanie*; ibid.).

[53] 'Chiunque vorrà mandar fuori altre Litanie, overo delle già mandate nelle Chiese, Oratorii, o Processioni vorrà usare, quelle siano tenuti mandare alla Congregazione de Sacri Riti a riconoscere, et correggere, se sarà bisogno, né meno presumano senza licenza della sudetta Congregazione mandarle fuori, *né publicamente* recitare, sotto pene (oltre il peccato) all'arbitrio dell'Ordinario, et dell'Inquisitore, severamente da imponersi' (*Decreto*, ibid.).

action and assessment. The emphasis placed on the adverb *publicamente* ('publicly') was not fortuitous. All Counter-Reformation cultural and religious prospective thinking in the years to come was to revolve around the distinction between public and private. The ambition to succeed in controlling every single aspect of the religious practice of the faithful – an ambition that the Counter-Reformation Church had cultivated since the early years of its long history – soon clashed with a reality in which the means available were few and far between, and resistance strong. In a certain sense the ecclesiastic hierarchies had admitted defeat but at the same time this was the result of a precise strategic decision that enabled the Pope to legitimize this dual level of prayer: here 'private' prayer did not mean only that practiced in the home by the faithful but also the private use that individual confraternities or religious companies, especially local ones, might make of it.[54] Thus, as if to sublimate (or to officialize) this distinction, we find at the foot of the text of the decree, transcribed among the (private) internal papers, i.e. the minutes, of the Congregation of the Inquisition, a significant addition that was not subsequently included in the (public) printed text of the decree: 'As for litany books already published, His Most Holiness decreed that they were permitted for private use, provided they were first examined by the Ordinaries and the Inquisitors'.[55] It is not hard to see behind the tortuous twistings and turnings that accompanied the preparation of this decree the influence of Cardinals Bellarmino and Baronio, who in those same years were the leading figures in a heated debate about the discipline of the worship of saints that took place in the newly founded *Congregazione dei Beati* (Congregation of the Blessed), from which base they also supported a compromise solution authorizing the use in private of acts of devotion that in public were prohibited.[56]

[54] In this regard, see, for example, the letter sent, some years after publication of the decree, by the Apostolic Nuncio at Graz, the Bishop of Troia, to Cardinal Millino about a *libretto delle litanie* ('litany book'), in which the writer gives the following assurance: 'I have already written to all the Bishops in this State that they shall not permit public use of this, private use thereof having been granted only to the local Oratory of the Holy Spirit' ('Ho già scritto a tutti i Vescovi di questo Stato, che non permettano l'uso pubblico di quello havendolo concesso in privato solamente all'Oratorio dello Spirito Santo di qui'; letter dated 13 December 1610, in ACDF, St St TT-1 a, ff. nn.; regarding which, also see below, ch. 12).

[55] 'Quo vero ad libellos Letaniarum iam editos, Ssmus decrevit *pro usu privato permiti,* prius tamen revisos ab ordinariis et Inquisitoribus' (ACDF, Decreta, 1600–1601, copia, c. 664). For the printed text, see ACDF, Index Protocolli O, cc. nn. (not numbered papers); and *Scriniolum*, f. 173.

[56] The specific aim of this compromise solution was to reach a diplomatic agreement between those who, on the one hand, in the name of ecclesiastic custom tended to admit all manifestations of devotion shown to those who died in the odor of sanctity (i.e. the topic under discussion) and, on the other, intransigent hard-liners; cf. M. Gotor, 'La fabbrica dei santi: la riforma urbaniana e il modello tridentino', *Storia d'Italia, Annali 16: Roma, la città*

But what was even clearer was the Pope's desire to apply to the Roman devotional and liturgical system the principles and guidelines that had up to then inspired his own personal policy with regard to censorship. New documentary evidence now makes it possible to see through the veil of apparent unanimity that was always a characteristic feature of censorship choices and decisions, and make it possible to distinguish shades of opinion and varying standpoints that previously it was impossible to define. In particular, the text of some handwritten considerations made by the Pope in 1594 in reply to certain *dubia* ('doubts') expressed by the cardinals engaged in revising the Sisto-Clementine Index, today known as the Clementine *Animadversio*, makes it possible – also through an assessment of the distance separating it from the official decision taken in the last instance by the Congregation of Index – to observe the specific nature of Clement VIII's proposal. Regarding the tricky question of the difficulties of applying an overstrict and excessively rigorous index, the Pope immediately offered the first sample of a methodological approach that was firmly rooted in reality and in his own problems, ready as he was to confront a complex network of resistance and practical obstacles. Acting on an inspiration that was not lacking in intellectual daring, the Pope proposed to the Congregation of Index that the titles added to the much more moderate Tridentine list should be printed separately in an appendix attached to the main text of the Index:

> It appears much simpler and more convenient that the Indexes should not be mixed together, and that an Appendix to the Index of Pius IV should be published under the name of that Most Holy Pope, in particular because, if otherwise, they would be mixed up together without any indications, and the Indexes – with great difficulty for the readers – would have to be compared on every occasion in order for it to be possible to understand which books were added. With the passing of time Pius IV's Index may fall into total disuse, as happened with that of Paul IV, which is now hard to find because of the publication of the other Index by Pius IV. In conclusion, Pius IV's Index has been recognized and accepted by all the Catholic countries so that, if the Appendix were also not recognized and accepted because of this intermixing, both Indexes would be jeopardized.[57]

del papa. Vita civile e religiosa dal giubileo di Bonifacio VIII al giubileo di papa Wojtyla, L. Fiorani and A. Prosperi (eds), Turin, Einaudi, 2000, pp. 679–727, in particular pp. 696–701; and Id., *I beati del papa. Santità, Inquisizione e obbedienza in età moderna,* Florence, Olschki, 2002, pp. 127 et seqq.

[57] 'Videretur longe facilius et commodius ut Indices non miscerentur sed Appendix ederetur a S.mo ad Indicem Pii quarti praesertim quia ita sine ullo signo commisti sunt, ut cum magna difficultate lectori in singulas vices conferendi Indices sint, ut dignosci possint libri additi. Potest etiam procedente tempore interire penitus ob hanc commistionem Index Pii, sicut accidit Indici romano Pauli IV, qui vix invenitur ob editionem alterius Indicis sub

Faced by the risk of a recurrence of the deadlock that was created when the Pauline Index was issued in 1559, when several Catholic countries had refused to adopt the severe repressive measures decreed by the first Roman universal Index, the Pope envisaged, as has been acutely remarked, 'two levels on which the Index could be used, one for those who accepted everything and one for those who used only the Tridentine list':[58] for whenever the added titles were mixed with the previous titles, any refusal of the first would automatically also mean the refusal of the books already contained in the Tridentine Index, whereas, on the basis of the hypothesis he had floated, any country that refused to accept the condemnations contained in the appendix would be able in any case to make use of the Tridentine list (already accepted without any protest), which was specially reprinted for the occasion. By about 1595, full awareness of the insurmountable difficulties that any further tightening of book censorship would entail had become a characteristic feature of the attention paid by the Pope to censorship. This awareness was consequently enriched and complemented by the demand of the faithful for greater responsibility in matters of devotion. Tackling the thorny problem of possible punishment and, on a more general plane, of what was to be done with those who possessed books in need of expurgation, thus raising a question that before long was to become one of immediate urgency for the authorities in Rome,[59] Clement VIII showed his political long-sightedness. Once he had realized the vast gap between the severity of the current legislation and the evident difficulties of applying it,[60] the Pope found two different solutions, each of which was characteristic of his concrete way of reasoning and acting.[61] Only the second of the two that he proposed was accepted and

Pio. Postremo Index Pii iam apud omnes nationes catholicas receptus est, si additamentum forsan non reciperetur ex hac admistione uterque Index periclitaret' (*Oppositiones a S.D.N. per Illustrissimum dominum Silvium Antonianum transmissae contra Indicem*, published in the appendix by V. Frajese, 'La politica dell'indice dal tridentino al clementino (1571–1596)', *Archivio italiano di storia della pietà*, XI, 1998, pp. 269–356; document on pp. 346–9; p. 346).

58 V. Frajese, 'La politica dell'indice', p. 325.

59 With regard to the way in which censorship in Rome became overwhelmed to the point of paralysis by the endless number of books to be expurgated, as also to the difficulty of achieving any coordination between the central Congregation and local advisers, cf. G. Fragnito, 'In questo vasto mare de libri prohibiti et sospesi tra tanti scogli di varietà et controversie: la censura ecclesiastica tra la fine del Cinquecento e i primi del Seicento', *Censura ecclesiastica e cultura politica in Italia tra Cinquecento e Seicento*. Atti della VI Giornata Luigi Firpo, C. Stango (ed.), Turin, Luigi Firpo Foundation, 5 March 1999, Florence, Olschki, 2001, pp. 1–35.

60 V. Frajese, 'La politica dell'indice', p. 348.

61 'Unde, ut pareat facilior, videtur *ad oboediendum* excogitanda via, quae duplex esse poterit' ('whence, to make things easier, it seems that a form of obedience has to be found, and this can be of two types'; ibid., my emphasis).

adopted by the Congregation of the Index, which was too jealous of its prerogatives to accept any limitation of its field of action: the readers and sellers of book to be expurgated were obliged to hand in a complete list of the titles of the books in their possession, leaving to the Congregation the power to grant any reading license after a careful examination of the personal and social qualities of the person in question.[62] But it is the first of the two proposals – the solution that the Congregation was careful not to accept – that better indicates the Pope's attitude to censorship, and also illuminated *a posteriori* the reasons and motivations of the 1601 decree on prayers and litanies, which otherwise is difficult to contextualize: 'So that, without any sin being committed, the books may be kept – but not read – until they have been expurgated in accordance with the instructions in the expurgation Index. The penalties established by the Constitution of Pius IV are thus reduced'.[63] Readers, the Pope decided, would be allowed to keep prohibited books in their possession, but without reading them, pending publication of the index of expurgation.[64] Between the moment a reader came into possession of a book and the moment of actually reading it, the Pope created a shadowy area where good Christians and their conscience were to become the sole arbiters of their fate. Behind these three simple words (*non tamen legi*: 'they must not however be read') a concept of censorship began to take shape that was based on a dual level of control (outward/inward or public/private), thus transforming the reading of books to be expurgated into a matter of personal conscience that all could judge for themselves, with respect to which the Inquisition authorities were expected to take a step back. What then happened was that this principle of the faithful reader's cultural responsibility, over and above his religious responsibility, apparently involving only a small minority of humanists and intellectuals (*dotti*),[65] was soon extended to the field of devotion and even to the world of the *senza lettere* ('unlettered') devout. The decree issued by the Holy Office in 1601 to discipline the vast editorial sector of litanies and prayers seems therefore to take its place in a wider

[62] V. Frajese, 'La politica dell'indice', p. 328.

[63] 'Ut retineri possint sine peccato libri, non tamen legi, donec expurgati ad praescriptum expurgatorii Indicis fuerint, et sic temperanda pena constitutionis Pii IV' (ibid., pp. 348–9).

[64] The index of expurgation, on the basis of which the appropriate authorities or individual authors would be enabled to emend texts (*Indicis librorum expurgandorum in studiosorum gratiam confecti Tomus primus. In quo quinqinginta auctorum libri prae coeteris desiderati emendatur per Fr. Jo. Mariam Brasichellen. Sacri Palatii Apostolici Magistrum in unum corpus redactus et publicae commoditati aeditus*, Rome, ex Typographia R. Cam. Apost., 1607), was published many years later, only to be withdrawn from circulation, amid great clamor, within a matter of months (cf. G. Fragnito, 'In questo vasto mare de libri prohibiti et sospesi', p. 31).

[65] V. Frajese, 'La politica dell'indice', p. 328.

cultural and religious project that had been conceived and realized by the Pope and his most authoritative collaborators. It was at one and the same time a high-minded theoretic compromise aimed at achieving a Utopian totalizing project, i.e. the establishment of complete liturgical uniformity among the faithful in their daily religious practice, and an attempt to create new emotional spaces to enable the faithful to rediscover a lost religious inwardness based on the principle of individual responsibility.

The results did not, however, come up to expectations, partly because of the objective intrinsic impracticability of this Utopian project of creating any such uniformity and partly because of the lack of interest shown in successive decades by the ecclesiastic hierarchies with regard to the question of giving more responsibility to devotional pedagogy.

For despite the significant theoretical compromise achieved by the higher echelons of the Roman Church, Clement VIII's decree did not produce the results that had been hoped for. While disconsolate messages reporting devotional anarchy[66] continued to arrive from the rest of Europe, on the Italian scene it was inevitably the habitually painstaking Inquisitor of Asti who drew attention to the first signs of weakness in the Inquisition's action in Rome.[67] In a highly informative letter dated 12 March 1602,

66 Again it was the Bishop of Troia, the Apostolic Nuncio at Graz, Pietro Antonio da Ponte, to write, this time to say that 'nearly all the Saints have their own personal litanies and on their feast days these are customarily recited even if they have not been approved, for one day I heard them myself when I was [...] here at St Paul's, and it happened to be the Saint's festivity. However, as this is an ancient and widespread custom, I think it would be almost impossible to abolish it and I fear it would cause great disturbance. Nevertheless I shall await your Illustrious Lordship's orders and I bow most humbly before you' ('quasi ogni Santo ha le sue litanie particolari, et nelle lor feste si soglion recitare, ancorché non siano approvate, havendole sentite io stesso un giorno, che mi trovai con S.A. qui in S. Paolo, la cui festa all'hora correva. Però essendo questo costume antico, et generale, credo che sarebbe quasi impossibile il torlo, et dubito che ne seguirebbe gran disturbo. Attenderò nondimeno gli ordini di V.S. Ill.ma alla quale fo humilissima riverenza'; Letter from Graz, 14 March 1611, ACDF, St St TT – 1 a, cc. nn.). It was around this time (1614) that Bellarmino wrote his famous letter, commented on by Antonio Rotondò ('La censura ecclesiastica e la cultura', pp. 1399–1401), in which the Jesuit cardinal expressed his opinion that it was impossible to extend the Counter-Reformation cultural and religious project beyond the Italian border.

67 Regarding Porcelli's absolute scrupulousness – a quality that has frequently been remarked upon – a significant comment he made reveals the annoyance (but also the poorly concealed self-satisfaction) caused to him by the carping voices of other Inquisitors and ecclesiastics who pointed their finger at him as a classic example of the 'top of the class', interested only in drawing to himself the attention of the authorities in Rome: 'which would deny people the opportunity to murmur that one Inquisitor wishes to be wiser than the other' ('Che leveria l'occasione al mondo di mormorar, che un inquisitore vogli esser più savio dell'altro'; Letter to Cardinal Valier, Asti, 12 March 1602,in ACDF, Index III/5, cc. 37r–v, and 47r; also in *Scriniolum*, ff. 186–7; owing to a misprint, page 187 is numbered 177).

addressed to Cardinal Valier,[68] Porcelli, with his customary sharpness of mind, remarked that 'if no sure form is given [to the 'Litanies, that are customarily sung in the House of the Most Holy Virgin of Loreto'], in a few days we shall see an infinite number of them, all with that title'.[69] But while this problem could be solved quite easily – as testified by the detailed list of 'Loreto litanies' sent a few months later (not however without a second sharp reminder)[70] by Cardinal Borghese –[71] it was harder to tackle other objections of a practical nature presented by the Inquisitor of Asti:

> It appears to me there is a state of great confusion with so many sorts of Latin and vernacular prayers that circulate in printed form with innumerable other stupidities written by charlatans on which it is necessary to waste much time, tiring one's brains examining and examining them again, for if they are not scrutinized carefully some very obscene things will get through, things that go against good morality and apocryphal and in a thousand other ways indecent, and it seems to me that in this way ordinary people are free to make up prayers

68 Regarding Valier, cf. L. TACCHELLA, *S. Carlo Borromeo ed il card. Agostino Valier (carteggio),* Verona, Istituto per gli studi storici veronesi, 1972; L. and M.M. TACCHELLA, *Il cardinale Agostino Valier e la riforma tridentina nella diocesi di Trieste,* Udine, Arti grafiche friulane, 1974; A. CISTELLINI's introduction to A. VALIER, *Il Dialogo della Gioia cristiana,* Brescia, Editrice La Scuola, 1975, pp. XIII–LXXXI; and now A. CIPRIANI, *La mente di un inquisitore. Agostino Valier e l'Opusculum De cautione adhibenda in edendis libris, 1589–1604*, Firenze, Nocomp, 2008.

69 'se non s'haverà una forma sicura [delle 'Litanie, che si sogliono cantare nella Casa della Santissima Vergine di Loreto'] fra pochi giorni se ne vedranno infinite, tutte sotto quel titolo' (Letter from the Inquisitor of Asti to Cardinal Valier, Asti 12 March 1602).

70 'I wrote as long ago as March that as the Litanies customarily sung in the Holy House of the Most Glorious Virgin in Loreto continued to be permitted, many examples of them appeared under this title, and I sent two different ones so that they might decide which were proper ones that could be allowed, but I have never had a reply; so I continue to be undecided, and, whatever the case, confusion is caused, and I would not like to be accused of negligence, because I know how I should behave and I shall use all possible diligence' ('Già sin questo marzo scrissi, che poiché restavano admesse le letanie, che si sogliono usar nella S. Casa della Gloriosissima Vergine in Loreto, ne uscirono diverse sorti sotto quel titolo, e ne mandai due differenti, acciò ansassero quali sono le vere, che si possono admettere, non ho mai havuto risposta; così resto ancora irresoluto, e a tutta via si causa confusione, non vorrei che a me fusse imputato negligenza, poiché come saprò in che maniera habbi a governarmi, usarò ogni diligenza possibile'; Letter from the Inquisitor of Asti to Cardinal Valier, Asti, 24 December1602, *Scriniolum,* ff. 191–2).

71 Letter from Cardinal Borghese to the Inquisitor of Asti, Rome, 30 January 1603, *Scriniolum*, f. 193: 'Herewith you receive an example of the Litanies that are sung in the Holy House of Loreto, which may serve to guide you in the places that come under your jurisdiction' ('Se le manda l'essemplare delle Litanie, che si cantano nella S. Casa di Loreto, secondo il quale potrà regularsi ne' luochi della sua giurisdittione'; this is followed by a complete list of the litanies).

in their own head, to present them using saints' names as titles, and to say whatever they like to say.[72]

What was therefore emerging was the need – perceived by Porcelli as a moral imperative but at the same time impossible for a single Inquisitor – to check on every single one of the flysheets which in their hundreds were sweeping through Italy, in town and country alike. But his letter was not limited merely to blaming a lack of staff for the failure of the Roman censors to carry out their plans. He also inveighed against the disarming lack of co-ordination, which here is indicated as one of the main causes of the uncontrolled proliferation of 'Latin and vernacular prayers [...] which are held in higher esteem by the masses [...] than those in common use by the Holy Church':[73] 'And although I have many times been against admitting any of them, even if I have seen they were printed elsewhere and that they are permitted for all purposes, I have decided to let things be, lest I might appear wiser than the others'.[74]Thus, in order to show his counterparts in Rome that besides being a shrewd critic he was also capable of making concrete proposals, he suggested to Valier that

> the Inquisitors of Savoy and Monferrato (only one of whom is from Casale) should be ordered to meet at least twice a year, so that they may discuss all the cases of abuses committed every day in printing, and on other occasions, and then jointly refer to the Holy Congregation, which after hearing their opinion should order whatever it felt to be most expedient: it might not be such a bad thing if we were all to agree on everything, for that would deny people the opportunity to murmur that one Inquisitor wishes to be wiser than the other.[75]

---

72 'Una cosa parmi d'avisare d'una gran confusione di tante sorti d'orationi latine, e volgari, che si portano attorno stampate, con infinite altre bagattelle da ciarlatani, che ci bisogna perdere gran tempo, con rompimento di capo a starli a rivedere, e non le rivedendo passeriano cose assai obscene, e contra bonos mores, apocrife, e in mille altri modi indecenti, e parmi che sia in libertà d'ogni privato far orationi di suo capo, darle fuori sotto titolo de santi, e dire tutto ciò che piace loro' (ibid.).

73 'orationi latine, e volgari [...] che sono da populazzi stimate più [...] che quelle che sono in commune uso di Santa Chiesa' (ibid.).

74 'E se bene sono stato più volte per non admetterne alcune, pure vedendo che sono stampate altrove, e che per tutto sono permesse, per non parer più savio d'altri, l'ho lasciate così' (ibid.).

75 'ordinar alli Inquisitori di questi stati di Savoia e Monferrato (che è uno solo di Casale) che si ritrovassero insieme almeno per due volte l'anno, e tra loro si trattasse di tutti gli abusi, che nascono alla giornata intorno allo stampar, e altre occorrenze, e tutti unitamente riferirne a quella Sacra Congregatione, che co '1 parer loro, ordinasse lei quanto li paresse più espediente: forsi non saria male, e si troveressimo tutti conformi in ogni cosa, che leveria l'occasione al mondo di mormorar, che un Inquisitore vogli esser più savio dell'altro' (ibid.). Regarding the final words of the quoted text, cf. the remarks contained above in footnote 67.

There can be no doubt that the Inquisitor of Asti was an exceptional man, but not the only one to realize the existence of loopholes in the decree issued in September 1601.[76]

[76] See, for example, the remarks of the Inquisitor of Pisa which laid bare the inadequacy of a prohibition that limited itself to an appeal for the formal conformity of prayer and litany texts to liturgical texts: 'In these parts of the world they sell psalteries, booklets for schoolchildren containing the ordinary litanies of the breviary but with *saints removed, added and transposed*, I know not whether, according to the Constitution regarding litanies, these may be permitted, and I hereby send you two examples'. Letter from the Inquisitor of Pisa, 2 October 1606, in ACDF, St St HH 2-d, c. 879r.

CHAPTER 10

A Fight against Superstition or a Struggle against the Illiterates?

The first to accept the Inquisitor of Asti's invitation to set some order in this somewhat vague and confused mass of rules and regulations was the Inquisitor of Modena, Arcangelo Calbetti. Singling out, title by title, all the *historiette et orationi* ('tales and prayers') circulating in his home town, he drew up a special list of books to be censured. This list, inserted in the appendix to *Sommaria instruttione a' suoi Vicari* ('Summary instructions to his Vicars') published in Modena in 1604,[1] was mainly intended to establish a clear point of reference in a context that allowed wide scope with undefined margins of personal powers of decision. It consisted of a list of twenty-eight titles of popular works, both devotional and non-devotional, written in verse (mostly octaves), and variously comprising *orationi* ('prayers'), *vite di santi* ('lives of saints'), *historie* ('stories'), *contrasti* ('disputations'), and *legende* ('legends'). The words Calbetti used in his official motivation of the reasons for banning the twenty-eight titles rang loud and clear: 'There shall be no sale', he wrote at the end of the *Instruttione* in his *Avvertimenti in materia di libri prohibiti e sospesi* ('Warning regarding prohibited and suspended books'), 'of any of the following Stories because they contain

[1] The text of *Sommaria instruttione a' suoi Vicari* is contained in *Scriniolum*, ff. 335–43; the list of censured works was to become the basic model for all successive lists of *orationi prohibite* ('prohibited prayers') which, first on a local level and later more centrally, were printed during the course of the century – each list bearing more banned titles than the one before (cf. below). Calbetti's *Instruttione*, in which the list was contained and published, was – together with the analogous *Breve informatione* by the Inquisitor of Bologna, Pietro Martire Festa – the first of a long series of 'instructions for vicars'. These 'instructions' provided vicars from outlying areas with a clear and simple compendium of the rules governing Inquisition procedure, with particular reference to occasions when vicars were called upon to play some important role, such as conducting preliminary inquiries and gathering evidence. However, these texts were not directed specifically at the Inquisitors and it is wrong to speak of them as Inquisition manuals or concise instructions for Inquisitors. Cf. A. Errera, *Processus in causa fidei. L'evoluzione dei manuali inquisitoriali nei secoli XVI–XVIII e il manuale inedito di un inquisitore perugino*, Bologna, Monduzzi Editore, 2000, pp. 259–62. For a broader view of these topics in a more general context, see also J. Tedeschi, 'The Question of Magic and Witchcraft in Two Inquisitorial Manuals of the Seventeenth Century', Id., *The Prosecution of Heresy. Collected Studies on the Inquisition in Early Modern Italy*, Binghamton, New York, Medieval and Renaissance Texts and Studies, 1991, pp. 229–58, and A. Borromeo, 'A proposito del Directorium Inquisitorum di Nicolas Eymerich e delle sue edizioni cinquecentesche',*Critica storica*, 20 (1983), pp. 499–547.

either false or superstitious or apocryphal or lewd matter.'[2] It is therefore clear that the action taken by the censor of Modena, like that of the few other Inquisitors who followed his example in the years immediately after, constituted the last act in order of time of a process which, according to the initial intentions and projects of Roman authorities, was expected to combine the impelling need to achieve uniformity in the complex matter of devotional literature by purifying the sources that the humbler classes incessantly devoured. The reading of some of these texts – their identification is facilitated by the information provided in the *incipit*s, especially in the later (and more exhaustive) editions of this list of banned works in Modena – gives this first impressionistic observation the required documentary confirmation. The action of the Inquisitors as far back as the 1560s and '70s had already enabled the Roman authorities to identify what were known as *rubriche* ('rubrics') as one of the main sources of popular superstition. The 'rubrics', phrases that were usually placed at the end of the actual text, in the end attributed to the devotional verses a merely mechanical and material value.[3] Thus, to give an example, in *La historia et oratione di Santo Giorgio Cavallero* ('The Story and Prayer of St George the Knight') we read that any soldier carrying this text about his person would be safe from all danger:

> Protect whoever in perfect faith carries my prayer / about his person, / be he man-at-arms or foot soldier, / at sea, on land, and in every battle, / let him not die nor even be wounded / and let not one link of his armor be damaged, / and as I fought for your sake / go and help whoever calls my name.[4]

The *Oratione devotissima alla Matre di Dio, trovata nel Santo Sepolcro di Christo* ('The Most Devout Prayer to the Mother of God, found in Christ's Holy Sepulcher')[5] was believed to have even more portentous miraculous powers:

> This Holy Prayer was found in Christ's Holy Sepulcher in Jerusalem, and any Christian who carries it with devotion and says a Hail Mary every day shall not fear the sentence of Judges against him [...], nor shall he die in water or by fire,

---

[2] 'Non lascino vendere alcuna delle Historie seguenti, per contenere esse respettivamente cose false, superstitiose, apocrife, e lascive' ('Avvertimenti in materia di libri prohibiti e sospesi', *Sommaria instruttione*).

[3] Cf. above, ch. 5.

[4] 'Chi con perfetta fe' la oration mia / porterà adosso fa ch'ella gli vaglia / in gente d'arme, e per la fanteria / in mare, in terra, e per ogni battaglia, / non sia morto né ancor offeso sia / né danneggiato pur sol una maglia, / si come per tuo amor ho combattuto / chi chiama il nome mio dagli aiuto' (*Historia et oratione di Santo Giorgio Cavallero*, In Venetia, in Frezzaria al segno della Regina, 1586).

[5] In Barzelona, e ristampata in Venezia, con licenza de'superiori, senza data.

nor shall false witness be brought against him, nor shall he die of the plague or rabies, and he shall be victorious in all battles, and if a woman cannot give birth, this prayer, placed upon her, will immediately set off her labor, it works its power against those possessed by the devil, and the Most Holy Virgin will appear to all who always carry this prayer about their person, and all has been tried and proven by his Lordships the Inquisitors of Barcelona.[6]

The desired objective would be equally well achieved if faithful believers, rather than *portare addosso* ('carrying about their person') the text of the prayer or the story, recited the recommended words: for among the censured works we find *La confessione di Santa Maria Maddalena* ('St Mary Magdalene's Confession'), in which the Inquisitor spotted yet another superstitious pronouncement:

> Whoever recites, or gets others to recite, this confession / for thirty days, for himself or for his family, / will receive contrition for every sin, / Mary Magdalene will be his defender / before our good Lord Jesus with devotion / such that this soul shall always be exalted / high in the Kingdom of Heaven where the blessed are, / whence all great sins are in the end forgiven;[7]

[6] 'Questa santa oratione fu trovata nel santo sepolcro di Christo in Gerusalem, qualsivoglia Christiano che la porta con devotione dicendo un'Ave Maria ogni giorno non havrà paura di sententia di Giudici contro di sé [...], né morirà in acqua, né foco, né falso testimonio potrà contro di sé, né morirà di pesta, né rabia, e in ciascuna battaglia sarà sempre vincitore, se alcuna donna non potrà partorire, mettendol *[sic]* sopra questa oratione subito partorirà, vale contro l'indemoniati, e portando sempre questa oratione addosso gli apparirà la Madonna Santissima, et è cosa esperimentata dalli Signori Inquisitori di Barcellona' (ibid.). The Roman Inquisitors, together with the local ones, continued to check on material of this kind in the years to come; it is therefore no chance matter that among the prayers added in the Bologna edict of 1614 (about which see above), there were other texts accompanied by superstitious rubrics such as the *Oratione di Santa Maria de Loretto*, in Siena, undated, which says: 'Again I pray to you in all your power, / sweet Mary, I pray as much as I can / that you may save from disease and pestilence / *whoever wears this prayer upon his person,* / defend him, Mother, from unjust sentences, / let him not be the victim of spells and magic, / and let him be free of all displeasures / I pray to you for all your joys' (ibid.,cc. nn.; my emphasis); there is also *La devotissima contemplatione del peccatore al Crocifisso,* in Venetia, in Frezzaria, al segno della Regina, 1586, where we find the following words: 'Whoever recites with humble heart / this lament and whoever causes it to be recited / for the five wounds that our Savior received, / on thirty mornings without fail, I say, / or wears it only for His sake / he may rove where'er he pleases / and he shall not die without repenting / and from sentence to Hell he shall be saved'.

[7] 'Chi dirà, o farà dir questa confessione / trenta giorni per sé o per sua brigata, / d'ogni peccato haverà contritione, / la Maddalena sarà soa advocata / dinanzi al buon Giesù con devotione / accioché quest'anima sia sempre essaltata / su nel regno del ciel dove stanno i beati / onde i gran falli al fin son perdonati' (*La confessione di santa Maria Maddalena*, In Venetia, dalla bottega del Guadagnino, al segno dell'Hippogrifo, 1585).

likewise, he could not help noticing *La Benedizione di Nostra Donna* (Our Lady's Blessing'), in which there was the triumphant invocation:

> Ever praised and blessed / be our protectress, Mother of Jesus, / save us from pestilence, and illness, / and save us at the end of our days / from anger, hatred, and evil company, / protect us and let the soul / of every good and faithful Christian be recommended to you, / so that in the end, we may go to Paradise.[8]

The censors and Inquisitors engaged in the delicate battle against popular superstition had already learned that their work could not be deemed to be over simply when they had identified the 'rubrics' attached to the texts. Much of the *cose false, superstitiose, apocrife o lascive* ('false or superstitious or apocryphal or lewd matter') that they were seeking was hidden between the lines of the actual text of the *orationi et historiette* ('prayers and stories'). It is true that except for the first three prayers cited in the Modena list, namely *Oratione di San Daniele*, *Oratione di Santa Helena in ottava rima* and *Oratione, e scongiuri di Santa Marta* ('St Daniel's Prayer, St Helen's Prayer in ottava rima, and St Martha's Incantations to ward off evil') – '*orationes ad amorem*' ('love prayers'), i.e. texts of love spells used by witches and necromancers on payment of small sums of money[9] – the texts of the banned prayers presented themselves deceptively as orthodox narratives of the lives of the saints or as episodes in the life of the Blessed Virgin, and other biblical characters, always with an introduction that was above all suspicion, such as 'In the name of Jesus with devotion / and of sweet Mary our protectress', or 'To you, kneeling with clasped

---

8 'Sempre laudata, e benedetta sia / la madre di Giesù nostra avvocata, / de pestilenza ci guardi, e malattia, / anchor ci guardi l'ultima giornata / da ira, da odio e trista compagnia, / ci guardi e sia a te raccomandata / l'anima d'ogni buon fidel Christiano, / acciò che al fine, al Paradiso andiamo' (*La Benedittione di Nostra Donna*, In Siena, 1578).

9 Concerning these magic spells – which were often transcribed by the notaries during Inquisition trials of women who used them and are therefore more easily accessed in the archives of the Inquisition than in the catalogs of 'popular' libraries – the term 'archive literature' has been used: cf. M.P. Fantini, 'Saggio per un catalogo bibliografico dai processi dell'Inquisizione: orazioni, scongiuri, libri di segreti (Modena 1571–1608)', in *Annali dell'Istituto storico italo-germanico in Trento*, XXV (1999), p. 587; Ead., 'La circolazione clandestina dell'orazione di Santa Marta: un episodio modenese,' *Donna, disciplina, creanza cristiana dal XV al XVII secolo. Studi e testi a stampa,* G. Zarri ed., Rome, Edizioni di Storia e Letteratura, 1996, pp. 45–65. see also M. O'Neil, 'Sacerdote ovvero strione: ecclesiastical and superstitious remedies in 16th century Italy',*Understanding Popular Culture. Europe from the Middle Ages to the Nineteenth Century*, S.L. Kaplan (ed.), Berlin-New York-Amsterdam, Mouton, 1984, pp. 53–83; Ead., 'Magical Healing, Love Magic and the Inquisition in Late Sixteenth Century Modena', *Inquisition and Society in Early Modern Europe*, S. Haliczer (ed.), London, 1987, pp. 88–114; and, more generally, the fine work by M. Duni, *Tra religione e magia. Storia del prete modenese Guglielmo Campana (1460?–1541)*, Florence, Olschki ('Studi e testi per la storia religiosa del Cinquecento', 9), 1999.

hands / I turn, o sweet Virgin Mary', or again 'Hail gracious Virgin Mary / more than any other woman you are blessed', and so on.[10] But this deceptive exterior concealed the dangers of 'lewdness', of 'apocrypha', and of 'falsehood'. In *Oratione devotissima della gloriosa Santa Catherina Vergine, e Martire. Con un nuovo Sonetto in laude di quella nuovamente aggiorno* ('Most Devout Prayer of the Glorious St Catherine the Virgin and Martyr. With the addition of a new Sonnet in Her praise'), for example, the anonymous author, singing the legend of the Saint of Alexandria, told of the violence that the emperor Maxentius inflicted upon her to make her marry him: 'he stripped Saint Catherine bare / and threw her on the wheel' and 'he had her breasts severed, / and her head cut off clean';[11] in *Oratione devotissima di Santa Margarita, con i sette Gaudii di Santa Maria Maddalena* ('St Margaret's Most Devout Prayer with St Mary Magdalene's Seven Joys') describing – in the manner of martyrological *formulae* that by then were well established – 'how painfully she lost her life / because of that cruel and cursed tyrant' (*con quanti stratii lei perse la vita / per quel Tiranno crudele e maladetto*), and the story was told of his 'intention to lie with her'(*intention di giacersi con ella*) and of the cruelty with which he ordered her to be 'taken and bound, / when she was naked without a moment's respite, / and had her whipped with supple canes':[12] a lascivious allusion to female nudity that was unlikely to leave the Inquisition authorities indifferent.[13] In like manner the Inquisitors must have been vexed by the magic virtues unduly attributed in the same 'prayer' to a mysterious *segno della Croce* ('sign of the Cross'), which on this particular occasion possessed unprecedented material qualities: 'And then he had her thrown back into prison, / and sorely beaten and all whipped, / when to one side appeared a dragon / and all the prison was bright / with the fire

[10] 'nel nome di Giesù con devotione / e della dolce Maria nostra advocata'; or 'A te con le mani giunte inginocchiato / ricorro, o dolce Vergine Maria'; and 'Ave Maria Vergine gratiosa / più che altra donna voi sete beata'.

[11] 'Santa Catherina nuda ei la spogliava / e sopra quelle rode la gettava [e]troncar gli fé le mammelle del petto, / tagliar gli fé la testa senz'alcun difetto' (in Venetia, Frezzaria, al segno della Regina, 1584).

[12] 'prendere e legare, / essendo nuda senza prender sosta, / con sottil verghe la fece frustare' (stampata in Siena nell'anno 1581).

[13] The Counter-Reformation discomfort caused by female nudity is well exemplified – on a culturally more elevated level – in the matter of the tomb of Paul III. This tomb, completed by Guglielmo Della Porta in 1574, presented statues of Justice and Prudence, which Clement VIII ordered to be covered up. This episode was reconstructed by R. Zapperi, *La leggenda del papa Paolo terzo: arte e censura nella Roma pontificia*, Turin, Bollati Boringhieri, 1998.

that the monster breathed out, / and it gobbled Margherita up, / but she with the holy sign of the Cross / made the beast explode'.[14]

In addition to 'superstitious' and 'lewd' matter,[15] there was also that defined as 'false' and 'apocryphal' to attract the attention of the scrupulous Inquisitor of Modena. Expressions that were contrary to official doctrine and stories that were philologically unreliable had to be removed as far as possible from the pious ears of the faithful. This was so in the case of certain clear doctrinal deviations in the worship of Mary and the saints that ultimately attributed to the Virgin Mary exceptional salvific powers[16]

---

14 'Dipoi la fé rimetter in prigione, / così battuta, e tutta flagellata, / dove da canto v'apparse un dragone / che tutta la prigion ha illuminata / col fuoco che sbuffava quel fellone, / e hebbe Margherita lui ingollata / e lei col santo segno della Croce, / fece scoppiar quella bestia feroce' (*Oratione devotissima di Santa Margarita*).

15 The category defined by the censors as *lascivia* ('lewd') had expanded to such an extent in the mentality of the Inquisition that it is no exaggeration to suppose that it might have included *Il contrasto dell'Angelo et del Demonio. E come l'Angelo mostra la via de salvatione al peccatore di questa vita presente, per andare alla gloria di vita eterna*. The main purport of the text – that of the effectiveness of the sacraments independently of the virtues of the person actually administering them – was a perfectly orthodox answer to a doubt that was widespread among people at the time; however, the Church hierarchies must have found it intolerable to entertain even the thought of the possibility of the existence of a 'murderous' confessor. Here are the salient points of this work: '[Angel] You must know that God has not abandoned him, and therefore do not tell me these words, / I include him among the others who are saved, / Because he did what reason dictates, / And if he sinned it is because he lived, / And when his end came he repented, and he suffers, / With pure faith, and contrition, / He took Holy Communion and he confessed [...] / [Demon] ... . Why do you say that he confessed, / that priest can never give absolution / because *that priest was a murderer*, /and such a confession is worthless. [Angel] I will reply to what you have said, / O false Demon full of iniquity, / Even if a Priest commits freely / all the sins in this world / our gracious God and Lord and Father / does not deprive him of his power / to be always able to confess / those whom in all purity Christ wishes to forgive' ('[Angelo] Tu dei saper pur che Dio non l'ha privo, / si che a me non dir queste parole, / fra gli altri che son salvi io già il scrivo, / Perché ha fatto ciò che ragion vole, / Se fallato ha nel mondo è stato vivo, / E nel suo fine s'ha pentito, e duole, / con pura fede, e con contritione, / Comunicossi, e prese confessione [...] / [Demonio] ... . Perché tu dici che gli è così confesso, / assolver non lo può giamai quel Prette / perché *quel Prette fu humicidiale,*/e tal confession giamai non vale. [Angelo] A quello che tu hai detto io ti respondo, / O Demonio falso pien d'iniquitade, / Se tutti peccati che fanno al mondo / Havesso un Prette in sua libertade, / il nostro Padre Dio Signor giocondo / non leva però a quel l'autoritade / che lui non possa sempre confessare, / Chi puramente Christo vuol perdonare;' ibid., cc. nn.; cf. also C. Ginzburg, 'Folklore, magia, religione',*Storia d'Italia,* 1: *I caratteri originali,* Turin, Einaudi, 1974, pp. 601–76, in particular p. 653).

16 See, for example, the *Oratione delli confitemini della Madonna, dal R.P.F. Nicolò Aurifico Carmelitano*, Palermo, for Rosselli, 1630. In this text the anonymous author attributes to the Virgin Mary the power of conceding salvific grace: 'I know very well, and I certainly know for my own merits, I am not worthy to have prayers granted or to receive grace, but your vast pity and goodness are such that they are always ready to grant grace to all those who with pure heart recommend themselves to you' ('Io conosco bene, e so certamente che per gli meriti miei, io non son degna d'esser esaudita né di ricever gratia, ma la tua grandissima

or to St Catherine of Siena the undeserved recognition that 'thanks to the merits of this Holy Virgin, God rid many other people, in infinite number, of this pestilential sickness'.[17] But they were clearly also texts in which the borderline between 'false' and 'apocryphal' was extremely faint and treacherous. While the story told in *La devota oratione di San Francesco con una laude bellissima*[18] might call to mind the witty and ironic pages written by Vergerio around the middle of the century,[19] and while the adventures of the tempting Demon disguised as a *donzella* ('maiden') illustrated in *La devota orazione di Santo Antonio* ('St Anthony's devout prayer')[20] might be considered 'falsehoods' that could not be tolerated in the light of the strict distinction between holy and profane theorized by the Tridentine canons, a clear case of 'apocrypha' can be seen in *Transito di Nostra Donna* ('Our Lady Transit'), a little work that some years later did not escape the meticulous attention of the Inquisitor of Bologna, whose knowledge of philology was clearly more solid than that of his colleague from Modena. It is not our intention to track down and point out all the cases of apocrypha spotted in the first decade of the seventeenth century by learned and zealous local Inquisitors of the time, but it may nevertheless be useful to present here, just as an example, some passages from *Transito*, accompanying the

pietà e benignità è tanta che sempre sta sollecita a fare gratia a tutti quelli che con puro core si raccomandano a te'). He then addresses to her the same words that are dedicated in the Lord's Prayer to the figure of the Son of God: 'I pray to you devoutly and with great faith and fervor that you may bountifully grant me your holy mercy, and deliver me from all evil, and let me do your will and this you do out of your great charity [...] you alone can help me, and this I believe in all certitude, without any doubt, that you receive from God all grace and all gifts, and complete power to beseech grace for anyone who asks you' ('Pregoti divotamente con gran fede, e fervore, che tu mi dia largamente la tua santa misericordia, e liberami d'ogni male, e fammi fare la tua voluntà, e questo fai per tua grandissima carità [...] tu sola me poi aiutare, e questo credo certamente, senza dubitare, che tu hai da Dio ogni gratia, e dono, e piena potestà d'impetrare gratia a qualunque te adimanderà;' ibid., cc. A2v–A3r), and finally puts his life entirely into her hands: 'If you forsake me, where shall I go, what shall I do, whom shall I call, to whom shall I turn for help [...] and I recommend to you, our Most Sweet Lady, the souls of my mother and father, so that you for your merits may save them from the pains of Purgatory, and lead them to the glory of eternal life' ('Se tu mi abbandoni ove anderò, che farò io, a chi chiamerò, a chi domanderò aiuto [...] e raccomandoti dolcissima Madonna l'anima del patre, e della madre mia, che tu per li tuoi meriti le traghi dalle pene del Purgatorio, e menale alla gloria di vita eterna'; ibid., cc. A6v e A7v).

17 'molte altre persone in numero infinito per li meriti di questa sacra Vergine, Dio liberò di tale infermità pestilentiale' (*La vita, et morte di Santa Caterina da Siena*, printed in Siena, 1580, c. B1v).

18 S.l., s.d., s.p.

19 Cf. above, ch. 4.

20 S.l., s.d., s.p.

transcription with the respective passages from the apocryphal Gospels on the basis of which the work was faithfully rewritten in summarized form:

The Transit of Our Lady. In Siena, s.d.	Transit from The Apocryphal Gospels, Marcello Craveri (ed.), Turin, Einaudi, 1969, pp. 405–72.[21]
Tell God the Father what I have told you / the Virgin answered and do not delay / the Angel departed and returned with delight, / and said, o woman, your every request / is satisfied by our Blessed Christ, / who can do by His Father whatever He wishes to do, / and while he was merrily speaking, there came into sight / St John the Evangelist. And on his knees to her with great love / he said, Blessed above all others, / Virgin Mother of Our Lord / from foreign lands have I come to you in haste / she took him by the hand, and Peter the shepherd / arrived too and knelt down / and he gently called before him / Jacobus the Elder, and the Younger also arrived. Then came Philip and Thaddeus, / Bartholomew, Simon, and Mathias, / and behind came Andrew and Matthew / and in front of the Virgin Mary, / who was near to the final Jubilee / and they knelt down.	[...] while Queen Mary was in her chamber. John the Evangelist and Apostle was immediately transported to Ephesus and entered the chamber of the Blessed Mary [...] And he knelt and begged forgiveness [...] And while she was about to ask him from where he came and why he had come to Jerusalem, lo! all the Lord's disciples [...] were transported by a cloud to the door of the Blessed Mary's chamber [...] James, Peter and Paul, Andrew, Philip, Luke, Barnabas, Bartholomew, Matthew, Mathias ..., Simon of Canaan
[...] Heaven triumphed when that / glorious immaculate soul entered therein / John the Evangelist related to Peter / that she was to be taken to be buried, / but the fell and evil Judaic people / were already all aroused, / John and Peter then prepared her / and toward the sepulcher made their way.	Meanwhile the Apostles [...] began to transport the Holy Body [...]. But halfway along their path, what should happen but a Jew called Ruben tried to throw to the ground the bier with the body of the Blessed Mary. But his hands withered up to the elbow and perforce he descended to the Valley

21 The Einaudi edition contains a transcription of the text of this passage from the apocryphal Gospel based on two fourteenth-century manuscripts kept in the Vatican Apostolic Library and the Ambrosian Library in Milan. Short devotional works like Transito had been popular since the Middle Ages and the literary contamination we are here referring to may have had its origins as far back as the fourteenth century; more research on the popularity of the apocryphal Gospels by the Pseudo-Joseph of Arimathea in the early modern era could however throw more light on the form and manner of this contamination. Regarding another well-known apocryphal work that frequently appeared on the Inquisition list, see E. BARBIERI, 'Un apocrifo nell'Italia moderna: la Epistola della domenica', *Monastica et Humanistica: scritti in onore di p. Gregorio Penco*, F. Trolese (ed.), 2 vols, Cesena, Badia di Santa Maria del Monte, 2003, vol. 2, pp. 717–32

And before the sacred bed / stood the palm tree that the angel had brought to her, / but a harsh and cursed Jew / seized the bed in his hand / but his hand stuck fast to the wood / and with the other he beat his breast / and became humble and meek in his fault, / at which his hand was free again.	of Jehosaphat, with cries and groans, because his hands were stiff beside the bier, and he could no longer draw them back. And he began to implore the Apostles to save him with their prayers so that he might become a Christian ... Forthwith he was healed and he thanked God [...].
Many Jews came nigh / and they knew not what to do, / for some were blinded, / and some dropped dead / and some were possessed by the devil, / and the earth seemed to sink / with great earthquakes, but the Apostles walked their way / and were protected by God, and they buried her.	[immediately preceding passage] [...] all the earth shook and [...] all the Knights of St John of Jerusalem [Gerosolimitani] began to think what they should do [...] But they were stricken with blindness and they beat their heads against the walls and knocked into one another [...].
And on the third day Mary rose again, / the pure Virgin, and was taken to Heaven, / the Angels and Saints kept her company, / and she was not far above the earth / when lo! St Thomas appeared, / and greeted her, and she gave him / a belt she had, and it is proven / that this is the belt displayed in Prato.	[...] the Apostles [...] laid the body in the sepulcher [...] the holy body was taken up to Heaven by the Angels. Then also the Most Blessed Thomas was transported suddenly to the Mount of Olives, [...] and he began to cry: O Holy Mother! Then the cloth in which the Apostles had bound the Most Holy Body was cast down from Heaven, [...] he took it and kissed it, rendering thanks to God [...].

'Books [...] which with false claims of spirituality and devotion contain inexact, false, apocryphal, and vain matter,' as Leoni, the Inquisitor of Bologna, declared a few decades later, but especially 'devotions containing some novelty' practiced by those who, 'fascinated by a certain spirit that is apparently full of pity but in fact is mere presumptuousness, shunned the massive, solid devotions of the past.'[22] It was therefore the meticulous Inquisitor of Bologna, a century after the publication of the first list of

[22] '[Libri] che sotto specie di spiritualità e divozione, contengono cose erronee, false, apocrife, pericolose, e vane,[...] divotioni che hanno del novitoso', praticate da coloro i quali 'affascinati da certo spirito d'apparente pietà, ma di vera presunzione, sdegnano l'antiche, massiccie, e sode [divozioni]'(*Breve raccolta d''alcune particolari operette spirituali proibite, Orazioni, e divozioni vane, e superstiziose, Indulgenze nulle o apocrife, et Imagini indecenti et illecite, che più frequentemente sogliono oggidì andare attorno. Fatta da F. Antonio Leoni Inquisitore di Bologna per commodo de suoi Vicari Foranei*; 2 February 1706, c. 4, in ACDF, Index, XXXVI/7). The same collection is in ACDF, Index, XXXVI/13b (*Raccolta di alcune particolari operette spirituali e profane proibite, in the appendix to Index librorum prohibitorum Innocenti XI P.M. iussu editus usque ad annum 1681. Eidem accedit in fine Appendix usque ad mensem Junii 1704; but cf. below, footnote 39*); in ACDF, Index XXXVI/14, ff. 403–517; and in ACDF, Index, XXXV/16.

Operette prohibite in Modena, who in 1706 reminded people of the Church authorities' original intentions and further clarified them. By publishing – for the first time in an autonomous edition – the now vastly extended list of *orationi et historiette prohibite* ('banned prayers and stories'), Leoni was doing no more than steering the Inquisitors' action back to the original project of creating liturgical and devotional uniformity, for which the only legitimate source of authority was the Holy See in Rome: 'Prayers or Devotions that are arbitrarily re-introduced by some particular person to be recited, or to have recited, publicly are marked as disapproved'.[23] No one, in other words, could claim the right to invent new devotional forms or practices, as this was the exclusive right of the Pope. The banning of any form of superstitious or apocryphal accretion,[24] as also of any undue mixing of the sacred and the profane,[25] thus received its proper historical and institutional recognition as

[23] 'Le Orazioni o Devozioni, che vengono nuovamente introdotte ad arbitrio di qualche Persona particolare, da recitarsi o farsi publicamente, appariscono disapprovate'(*Breve raccolta*, cc. 65–6). Cf. also where Leoni recalls that a ban had been placed on 'all Litanies except for the ancient and common ones that are to be found printed in the Breviaries, Missals and Rituals printed under due license, and for the Litanies of the Blessed Virgin, which are usually sung in the Holy House of Loreto' ('Litanie tutte fuori di quelle antiche, e communi, che si ritrovano stampate negli Breviarii, Missali, e Rituali impressi con le dovute licenze, e di quelle della Beata Vergine, che sogliono cantarsi nella santa casa di Loreto'; ibid., c. 53).

[24] Leoni returned to speak with great clarity on the subject of 'Prayers, not only invented ones or those that are blemished by dubious names and expressions, or in unknown tongues, but also others that are in themselves good and holy but it is ordered that they should be recited of necessity outside the normal practice of the Church, in some special way, or in some fixed number, without which it will not possible to achieve the desired effect, almost as if their virtue depended on the particular number or particular manner required, they contain something that is vain and superstitious, and if they are recited for improper purposes the abuse becomes all the more sortilegious and heretic, as is all abuse of anything sacred or blessed – as severally decreed by the Holy Office' ('Orazioni, non solo quelle composte, o depravate con nomi, e parole sospette, o incognite, ma anco l'altre per se stesse buone, e sante, se vengono prescritte da recitarsi necessariamente, fuori del commune uso della Chiesa, in qualche modo, o in qualche numero determinato, senza di che non possa conseguirsi l'effetto bramato, quasi che la loro virtù consista in detto numero, o modo singolare, hanno del vano, e del superstitioso, e se si dicano a qualche fine illecito, tale loro abuso diviene maggiormente sortilego, empio, ereticale, come è abuso di qualsiasi altra cosa sacra, e benedetta. Per più decreti del S. Officio'; ibid., c. 66). He also considered 'Prayers that were claimed to be good against arms, against enemies, to bear the torture of the cord, to make oneself loved, for childbirth, to escape dangers, and for other magic purposes, with abuse of the names of God and of the Saints, and holy or blessed things to be carried about one's person, either to be recited or to be swallowed, etc. As severally decreed by the Holy Office' ('l'Orazioni che si spaciano buone, contro l'Armi, contro i nemici, per sostenere la Corda, per farsi ben volere, per il Parto, per fuggire i pericoli, e per altri fini sortileghi, coll'abuso de' Nomi di Dio, de' Santi, e cose sagre, o benedette col portarle adosso, o recitarle, o inghiottirle etc. Per più Decreti del S. Officio'; ibid., c. 64).

[25] Leoni explicitly condemned 'Holy-profane prayers, be they Booklets, said to be famous but in fact infamous, in which words taken from Ecclesiastic prayers such as the

part of a cultural and religious project intended to ensure that the demands for the process of liturgic regularization and uniformity would culminate in the re-establishment of the unrenounceable authority of Rome.[26]

But while Leoni's considerations, on the one hand, helped to set some order among the multi-faceted aspects of the Church's offensive in the field of devotion, on the other, they also underlined the shortcomings of an operation that had shown its weaknesses ever since the beginning.

One of the key points to the whole matter had been lucidly focused on, some years before the publication of Leoni's short work, by Jean Baptiste Thiers, a devout, rigoristic French rationalist[27] who was the author of an imposing *Traité des superstitions*, published in 1679 and reprinted in 1697.[28]

Lord's Prayer, the Hail Mary, and the Credo or some Psalms or Hymns are mixed with offensive satires against some person, especially a Holy figure. As severally decreed by the Holy Office' ('l'Orazioni Sacro-profane, o siano Libelli, detti Famosi, ma realmente infami, ne' quali si framischiano alle parole dell'orazioni Ecclesiastiche, come del Pater, dell'Ave, del Credo, di qualche Salmo, o Inno, satire ingiuriose, contro qualche persona, specialmente Sacra. Per più decreti del S. Officio'; ibid., cc. 64–5).

26 This was a value that was even greater than the power of ecclesiastic tradition, as is evident, for example, from the observations cited by Leoni with reference to the delicate matter of indulgences. Recalling Clement VIII's constitution of 1604, he reiterated that 'when they are granted by some Archconfraternity or by any Order, Congregation, Society, the Society of Jesus, Chapter, or College, or by their Officers, Superiors, or other Persons, or other Person who may be specially and individually appointed, they shall have no value or force, unless they have been subsequently renewed and confirmed by the authority of the Pope in Rome' (ibid., c. 42). The same principle seems to be behind the prohibition of all forms of hereditary transmission of indulgences: 'The Indulgences granted by Supreme Popes to Chaplets, Rosaries, Beads, Calculi, Crosses, Medals, and Holy Images that they have blessed do not go beyond the person to whom the Supreme Pope himself granted them or to those to whom the said Chaplets, Medals, etc. were or will be distributed for the first time, nor may anyone lend the aforesaid Chaplets, Medals, etc., to others, [...] nor may anyone who has had one of these Chaplets, Medals, etc. and lost it replace it in any way with another' (ibid., c. 42).

27 M. Rosa, *Settecento religioso. Politica della Ragione e religione del cuore*, Venice, Marsilio, 2000, p. 233.

28 *Traité des superstitions selon l'Ecriture sainte, les decrets des Conciles, et les sentiments des Saints Pères, et des Théologiens, par M. Jean-Baptiste Thiers, Docteur en Théologie, et Curé de Vibraie. Seconde edition. Revue, corrigée, augmentée. A Paris Chez Antoine Dezallier, rue S. Jacque, à la Couronne d'or. 1697. Avec Approbation et Privilège du Roy* (4 tomes). I cite from this edition. Regarding this text, see F. Lebrun, *Le 'Traité des superstitions' de Jean-Baptiste Thiers, contribution à l'ethnographie de la France du XVII siècle*, in *Annales de Bretagne et des Pays de l'Ouest,* 1976, pp. 443–65; R. Chartier, J. Revel, *Le paysan, l'ours et saint Angustin*, in *La Découverte de la France au XVII siècle*, Paris, Cnrs, 1980, pp. 259–64; and B. Dompnier, *Les hommes d'Eglise et la superstition entre XVII et XVIII siècles*, in Id. (ed.), *La superstition à l'âge des Lumières*, Paris, Champion, 1998, pp. 13–47, in particular pp. 22–8.

From his observation point in France, Thiers remarked 'that Superstitions are as universally widespread in the Christian world',[29] drawing the reader's attention to the vast gap that had opened up between the strictness of the rules – the innumerable condemnations pronounced 'by the Scriptures, Councils, Popes, holy Fathers, Theologians'(*par l'Ecriture, les Conciles, les Papes, les saints Pères, les Théologiens*) – and the desolating reality of the capillary diffusion of superstitious practices. Man's intrinsic evilness, a characteristic feature of Thiers' theological and religious approach,[30] was not enough to explain a gap that was growing ever wider. This expanding gap drew its origin, according to Thiers, from the moral ambiguity and the corruption of the *pasteurs* ('priests'). The negligence and indolence shown toward their pedagogical and pastoral commitments[31] were nothing compared to their complacent toleration of superstitious practices and customs which they were supposed to combat: 'And often (it is painful to say) they [sc. superstitions] are either tolerated or authorized or observed by persons of distinguished character, by ecclesiastics, who with all their might and main ought to prevent them from taking root in the field of the Church, where the enemy sows them during the night, like tares among good wheat'.[32] Thiers' words – certainly a mature product of the religious

[29] 'que les Superstitions soient aussi universellement répandues dans le monde Chrétien' (ibid., c. A2r).

[30] Ibid., cc. A2r–v.

[31] The 'pasteurs' were directly guilty 'du peu de foi de la pluspart des Chrétiens, du peu des sentiment qu'ils ont de leur salut éternel, de la grandeur, de la puissance, de la fidélité de Dieu, du peu de connoissance qu'ils ont de sa Loi, du peu d'instruction qu'on leur donne sur la matiére des Superstitions' (ibid., c. A3r).

[32] 'Et souvent (ce qu'on ne sauroit dire sans douleur) elles [the superstitions] sont ou tolérées, ou autorizées, ou observées, par des personnes d'un caractère distingué, par des Ecclésiastiques, qui devroient empêcher de toutes leurs forces qu'elles ne prissent racine dans le champ de l'Eglise, ou l'ennemi les séme durant la nuit, comme l'ivroie, sur le bon grain' (ibid., c. A2v). The author returns to the same concept more specifically when speaking 'Des Exorcismes ou Conjurations, des Bénédictions ou Oraisons, pour guérir les maladies des hommes et des bêtes, pour les préserver de danger, pour chasser les rats et les souris, les taupes, les mulots, les serpents, les sauterelles, les chenilles, etc., pour détourner les orages, les vents, les tempétes, les ouragans, etc. Que ces Exorcismes sont de véritables charmes. Qu'ils sont condamnés par l'Eglise. Qu'il y a de la superstition à conjurer les bêtes, et à les excommunier' ('Of Exorcisms and Conjurations, of Blessings and Prayers, to cure the diseases of men and beasts, to protect them from danger to hunt rats and mice, moles, field mice, snakes, grasshoppers, caterpillars, etc., to divert storms, winds, tempests, hurricanes, etc. That such Exorcisms are real charms. That they are condemned by the Church. That it is superstition to conjure animals and to excommunicate them') – this is the full title of Book Six, Chapter II: 'Cependant', we read in this paragraph, 'combien y-a-t il de gens dans les villes et dans la campagne, qui se mêlent immunement de ce métier, et qui croient rendre de grands services à Dieu, à son Eglise, en s'en mêlant, soit parce qu'on ne les en reprend pas, ou qu'on ne les reprend que faiblement, soit même parce qu'ils trouvent quelquefois

polemics that invested French society at the time – sounded like an implicit act of condemnation of the continual reproposal of the Inquisition's censorship lists, which throughout the seventeenth century were full of titles of 'prayers and superstitious and apocryphal stories', pitilessly throwing light on the emptiness of the entire ecclesiastic operation. Leoni's volume, published around 1708, was merely the last act in a long sequence of censorship lists that had inherited the role of the Modena list compiled by the Inquisitor Arcangelo Calbetti. Just four years after the publication of that first list, in 1608 an almost identical version was published by his successor, Brother Michelangelo Lerri.[33] Very likely the same years are referred to in an undated list from the Inquisition list from Perugia now kept among the Protocols of the Archive of the Congregation of the Index.[34] In 1614 (1 October) the Inquisitor of Bologna completed the previous lists, issuing an edict to which he attached a list of 46 devotional works (the previous lists contained no more than 30 titles).[35] This last version served as the base for the list included in the *Syllabus seu Collectio librorum prohibitorum, et suspensorum a publicatione novi Indicis, iussu Sanctissimi ... Clementis Papae VIII de anno 1596* ('List or Collection of prohibited books, and suspended from publication of the new Index, by order of His Holiest ... Pope Clement VIII in the year 1596'), published in Bologna in 1618.[36] In the course of the century the list eventually reached the number of 64 titles, as can be seen in the second printing of the *Regole del Tribunale del Sant'Officio* ('Rules of the Tribunal of the Holy

des Ecclesiastiques assez ignorants pour approuver leur conduite, ou du moins pour n'y rien trouver à redire' ('However, how many people are there in towns and in country areas who ply this trade undisturbed? And who believe they are rendering great service to God and to His Church by so doing, either because they are not rebuked at all or then only mildly, or because they sometimes find ecclesiastics so ignorant that they approve of their conduct or at least do not find fault with it?') (ibid., v. I, c. 460). It is not difficult to imagine the negative reception which the rank and file in Rome must have given to such an invective. As it was not possible to draw a cloud of oblivion over such an imposing work, the stratagem employed by the church hierarchies was to send the accusations back to the sender, accusing him of contributing personally to the spreading of numerous superstitious practices, which he described in great detail in his voluminous work: this can be deduced from the opening pages which Thiers wrote for the second edition of the work (ibid., cc. A5r–v).

33 *Breve informatione del modo di trattare le cause del S. Officio Per li molto Reverendi vicarii della Santa Inquisitone, instituti nelle Diocesi di Modona, di Carpi, di Nonantola, e della Garfagnana, in Modona, at the printing-shop of Giulian Cassiani*, MDCVIII.

34 ACDF, Index, Protocols O, cc. nn.

35 Rome, Biblioteca Casanatense, Per. Est. 18.4 / 376bis.

36 *Syllabus seu Collectio librorum prohibitorum, et suspensorum a publicatione novi Indicis, iussu Sanctissimi ... Clementis Papae Vili de anno 1596. Additis etiam aliis libris, variis erroribus scatentibus, et suspectis, non legendis, neque retinendis, quo aduqsque expurgentur, aut permittantur a Sancta universali Inquisitione*, Bononiae, *apud* Sebastianum Bonomium, MDCXVIII.

Office'), which the Inquisitor of Ferrara, Tommaso Menghini, ordered to be printed.[37] Later, the list was officially included for the first time in the *Appendix* to a national Index at the beginning of the eighteenth century, in 1704, in the updated edition of the Index of Innocent XI, which had already been published in 1681.[38] Several years later Leoni's 'Raccolta' was copied by the editor of yet another edition of Innocent XI's Index (1734) in the appendix to the volume .[39]

The failure of the offensive that was intended to eliminate all elements of superstition from Catholic devotion can be considered to have been solemnly and officially sealed some decades later by the work of a leading figure of eighteenth-century Italian culture, Ludovico Antonio Muratori, when the cultural and religious climate was in many ways profoundly changed. For the year 1747 saw the publication of his celebrated treatise on *regolata devozione* ('regulated devotion').[40] In the rooms of the Vatican palaces his appeal for 'true and solid devotion' (*vera e soda divozione*) must have sounded like a full-scale *j'accuse* against the supporters and promoters of an 'empty and useless' (*vana et inutile*) baroque religiousness, marked by 'superficial devotions'(*divozioni superficiali*) that were beyond any doubt whatsoever characterized by their 'superstitious appearance and substance' (*apparenza e sostanza di superstizione*). The clear autobiographical references to the hostility with which his work had been greeted[41] did not nullify the ideal value of Muratori's criticisms of the 'excesses' (*eccessi*) that

37 *Regole del Tribunale del Sant'Officio, praticate in alcuni casi imaginarii da f. Tomaso Menghini d'Albacina, Inquisitore Generale di Ferrara, e suo Ducato, per lume de' Vicarii della di lui Giurisdizione. In questa seconda impressione corrette, ed ampliate,* in Ferrara, 1687, per l'erede del Giglio, stampatore del Sant'Offizio, ff. 108–11.

38 *Index librorum prohibitorum Innocentii XI P.M. iussu editus usque ad Annum 1681. Eidem accedit in fine Appendix usque ad mensem Iunii 1704,* Romae, Typis Rev. Ca. Apost., 1704, ff. 515–66. Regarding these prohibitions, see J.M. De Bujanda, *Index librorum prohibitorum 1600–1966*, vol. XI, 2002, pp. 440, 667–9.

39 *Breve raccolta d'alcune particolari operette spirituali proibite, Orazioni, e divozioni vane, e superstiziose, Indulgenze nulle o apocrife, et Imagini indecenti et illecite, che più frequentemente sogliono oggidì andare attorno* [printed after 1708]. Cf. E. Rebellato, *La fabbrica dei divieti. Gli indici dei libri proibiti da Clemente VIII a Benedetto XIV*, Milan, Sylvestre Bonnard, 2008, p. 77 e 354 (Appendice II, n. 170).

40 Regarding Muratori we will limit ourselves to pointing out F. Venturi, *Settecento riformatore. I: Da Muratori a Beccaria 1730–1764*, Turin, Einaudi, 1969; M. Rosa, 'L'"età muratoriana" nell'Italia del '700', Id., *Riformatori e ribelli nel '700 religioso italiano*, Bari, Laterza, 1969, pp. 9–47; *Atti del convegno internazionale di studi muratoriani*, Modena, I–IV volumes, 1972–1975. The work *Della regolata devozione* was recently published by Pauline Editions, Rome, 1990 with an introduction by Pietro Stella: it is from this edition that the following citations were taken. On Church censorship upon Muratori's work see P. Vismara, 'Muratori "immoderato". Le censure romane al *De ingeniorum moderatione in religionis negotio*', *Nuova rivista storica* LXXXIII, 1999, pp. 315–44.

41 L.A. Muratori, *Della regolata devozione*, p. 40; cf. also p. 195.

drove the faithful toward forms of what can accurately be defined as religious superstition, thus alienating them from the true objective of devotion, i.e. 'to worship and thank God' (*adorare e ringraziare Dio*). Muratori pointed his finger at the 'light-minded devotions' (*devozioncelle*) that were 'invented and promoted' for the sole purpose of 'obtaining from them some temporal profit',[42] i.e. the indefinite and variegated universe of 'medals, Agnus Deis, rosaries, scapulars, cassocks, cordons, images of saints, briefs, confraternities, and other similar visible pious inventions' in which 'simple ignorant folk' placed all their hopes of salvation, putting 'such faith [...] in them that they believe they are safe from various temporal ills, or they are convinced they cannot die in a state of disgrace with God, or that they can obtain some particular graces by reciting certain prayers for a certain length of time'.[43] These devotions, which had 'as their object the achievement or the increase of secular goods and commodities, or the liberation from the evils and preoccupations of which the temporal life of those who dwell in this world is full', were religious practices 'solely in appearance but not in substance'[44] that did not produce 'in us love of God and of our neighbor', and would not serve 'to correct our life and [...] and to make it conform to that of Jesus Christ'.[45] It was a sorry picture in which Muratori also saw a gradual weakening of religious tension upholding a firm doctrine that was faithful to the letter of the Gospels. The doctrinal degeneration which devotion to the saints and Marian piety had undergone during the seventeenth century, beyond any possible form of control, was a worrying menace for the future of the Catholic Church. His composed indignation was directed against the emotional outburst of those among the faithful who devoted themselves to the worship of Mary, reaching the point where 'they believed that it was she who forgave us our sins and saved us',[46] or to the worship of a chosen saint 'without any legitimate basis except in the mind of the common people',[47] to whom miraculous and exclusive virtues could be attributed.[48] Whatever the case, whether he was directing his criticism at

42 'inventate e promosse, per farne qualche traffico temporale' (ibid., p. 216).

43 'tal fiducia [...] in esse che si tenga sicuro di tali mali temporali, o si dia a credere di non poter morire in disgrazia di Dio, o di conseguir certe grazie determinate col recitar certe orazioni per determinato tempo' (ibid., p. 214).

44 'per oggetto il conseguimento o l'accrescimento dei beni e comodi del secolo, oppure la liberazione dai mali ed affanni dei quali abbonda la vita temporale di chi soggiorna nel mondo', sono pratiche 'di sola apparenza e non di sostanza' (ibid., p. 227).

45 'in noi l'amore di Dio e del prossimo', e non serviranno a 'emendare la vita nostra e [...] conformarla a quella di Gesù Cristo' (ibid., p. 227).

46 'a credere che a lei appartenga il perdonarci i peccati, il salvarci' (ibid., p. 197).

47 'senza legittimo fondamento nella sola testa del popolo' (ibid., p. 176).

48 Ibid.

degenerated forms of Marian piety and worship of the saints or referring to superstitious 'light-minded devotions'(*devozioncelle*) and to women who in public 'mutter' (*biascicano*) Lord's Prayers with a rosary in their hand, Muratori's objective coincided with those that ecclesiastic censorship had set itself in the second half of the sixteenth century. Muratori's continuous allusions to the Council of Trent and its 'purest of doctrines' (*purissima dottrina*), to the noble figure of Carlo Borromeo and the mass of punitive acts of censorship performed in that period, besides providing an ideal historical continuity between the 'Catholic Enlightenment' and the post-Council period, here come across above all as an implicit admission of the failure of that particular project and that particular offensive.

Regarding the reasons and dynamics behind this failure, it is necessary to pause in order to consider carefully and clarify where and how the interruption took place in the process inaugurated by the Roman hierarchies in the 1570s, which in the early 1600s still seemed to be offering its beneficial fruits. In order to answer these questions, we shall consider the following points: first, the impact achieved by the struggle against use of the vernacular (Italian); second, the slackening of the pressure exerted by censorship on superstitious and apocryphal accretions; and third, the form and manner of certain devotional activities proposed by some sectors of the Counter-Reformation ecclesiastic hierarchy, which in its attempt to obtain a tighter hold over the masses in no way disdained the use of elements which stirred the emotions but were at the same time expressions of extreme superstition.

Postponing the analysis of the second and third points to later paragraphs, our intention here is to underline how – within the context of an extension of the categories of Roman censorship intended to bring the entire cultural universe of the 'unlettered' closer to Counter-Reformation aspirations[49] – the struggle against the vernacular led to the elimination of texts that had played an important role in arousing the interest of the faithful in the theme of prayer and devotion. The Tridentine Index had

[49] During those years this process eventually led to the establishment by the Roman censors of a substantial state of equality between standard printed volumes and popular 'minor works'; a significant example of this is the invitation extended by Cardinal Borghese to the Inquisitor of Asti to 'use all possible diligence for its own sake and with the assistance of learned, zealous, and pious persons in the examination of books, and other minor works, and little stories, which every day are printed there, so that they shall not contain prohibited matter, in conformity with the Rules of the Index; nor shall any license to print be granted until the works have been attentively examined' ('usar ogni diligenza possibile per se stessa, e per mezzo di persone dotte, zelanti, e pie nel riveder li libri, e altre operette, o historiette, che alla giornata si stampano costì, accioché non contengano cose prohibite conforme alle Regole dell'Indice; né conceda licenza di stamparsi, che prima non siano reviste con ogni accuratezza'; Letter from Rome, 29 April 1605, in *Scriniolum*, f. 354).

triggered a progressive shifting of the objectives of ecclesiastic censorship toward the all-embracing category of 'immorality '. The preoccupation of safeguarding the ears of the 'childish populace' (*popolo fanciullo*) from any deviation from the rigid cultural Counter-Reformation models[50] had become one of the priorities of repressive action. While the Tridentine Rules – Rule VII in particular, prohibiting books 'that purposely deal with lewd or obscene matters'('qui res lascivas, seu obscenas ex professo tractant') and charging the bishops with the task of punishing anyone possessing them,[51] as also Rule IV regarding the question of the vernacular had provided the co-ordinates of this new offensive, the "maneuver"[52] derived its real substance from the censorship lists compiled in the 1570s and '80s in application of those rules. An emblematic testimony but also a fundamental theoretic legitimization of this new direction taken by Roman censorship was the publication in Rome in 1576 – coinciding precisely with the printing of the most important of the Inquisition lists – of the *Tractatio in qua cum de perfecta poëseos ratione agitur tum ostenditur cur abstinendum sit a scriptione poematum turpium, aut falsorum deorum fabulas continentium* ('Treatise dealing with the reasons for perfect poetry and the reasons for abstaining from writing poems that are lewd or contain stories of false gods') by Antonio Possevino.[53] The prohibition of all *Opere*

[50] See A. Biondi's essential'Aspetti della cultura cattolica post-tridentina'; the expression 'childish populace' was used by V. Frajese, *Il popolo fanciullo. Silvio Antoniano e il sistema disciplinare della Controriforma*, Milan, Franco Angeli, 1987.

[51] Applying this rule in 1573, during the third provincial Council, Carlo Borromeo gave forewarning of the imminent publication of an Index of obscene works (U. Rozzo, in *Index de Rome 1590, 1593, 1596*, cit., pp. 32–3; G. Fragnito, *La Bibbia al rogo*, p. 140). The Archbishop of Milan's intention very likely was 'thwarted' by the reduction of the margins of autonomy of the diocesan ordinaries, an intention that was implicit in the periodic dispatch of long lists of books of this kind from Rome to the peripheral Inquisition authorities (cf. G. Fragnito, *La Bibbia al rogo*, p. 140).

[52] We must not forget that these lists were part of the Inquisition's action aimed at extending the area affected by the prohibition of the vernacular in matters related to 'sacred material' through the revival of the much severer regulations contained in the Pauline Index regarding Rule IV of the Tridentine Index (see G. Fragnito, *La Bibbia al rogo*, pp. 130 et sqq.).

[53] Much of this treatise was later to reappear as chapter XVII of Possevino's *Biblioteca selecta*. Regarding this Counter-Reformation monument, cf. A. Biondi, 'La Biblioteca selecta di Antonio Possevino. Un progetto di egemonia culturale' *La 'Ratio studiorum': Modelli culturali e pratiche educative dei Gesuiti in Italia tra Cinque e Seicento*, G.P. Brizzi (ed.), Rome, Bulzoni, 1981, pp. 43–75; C. Carella, 'Antonio Possevino e la biblioteca "selecta" del principe cristiano', *Bibliothecae selectae. Da Cusano a Leopardi*, E. Canone (ed.), Florence, Olschki, 1993, pp. 507–16. Regarding Possevino, see S. Peyronel Rambaldi, 'Educazione evangelica e catechistica: da Erasmo al gesuita Antonio Possevino', *Ragione e 'Civilitas'. Figure del vivere associato nella cultura del '500 europeo*, D. Bigalli (ed.), Milan, Franco Angeli, 1986, pp. 73–92; L. Balsamo, 'Venezia e l'attività editoriale di Antonio Possevino (1553–1606)', *La Bibliofilia* XCIII (1991), pp. 53–93; Id., 'How to doctor a bibliography:

in versi di sacra scrittura così volgari come latini, li quali apportano gran danno ('Works in verse from the Holy Scriptures both in the vernacular and in Latin, which cause great damage') contained in the cited Index prepared by Giovanni di Dio,[54] proved in reality to be a mere change of rules with regard to the method of censorship described in the treatise. Thanks to a broad interpretation of this 'precept', vast portions of Italian literature, and not only that of the sixteenth century, ended up on these lists[55] together with many works of religious and devotional literature. We find collected together in the same categories of censorship the condemnation of minor devotional works intended for the humblest classes, such as *Confessione della Magdalena (in rima per Marco da Foligno)*; *Giardino della Nostra Signora Maria Vergine senza nome d'Auttore*; *Stanze in laude di M.V. di m. Gabriele Raineri*; *Medicina dell'Anima così per li sani, come per gli ammalati senza nome di stampatore et d'Auttore* ('Confession of Mary Magdalene (in rhyme for Marco da Foligno'; the

---

Antonio Possevino's practice', *Church, censorship and culture in early modern Italy*, G. Fragnito (ed.), Cambridge, Cambridge University Press, 2001, pp. 50–78.

54 GIOVANNI DI DIO, *Index Authorum*, cf. G. FRAGNITO, *La Bibbia al rogo*, p. 131; this prohibition was very likely related to a statement contained in a letter sent by Brother Damiano Rubeo to the Inquisitor of Bologna immediately after the Index was compiled, which stated that 'Psalms in the vernacular tongue are not permitted' and that 'the *Little flowers of the Bible* are to be removed' ('i Salmi volgari non si ammettono' and 'i *Fioretti della bibia si levano*'; Letter dated 25 April 1576, in A. ROTONDÒ, 'Nuovi documenti', pp. 156–7). This prohibition had already appeared in a printed *Aviso* a stampa *alli Librari che non faccino venire l'infrascritti libri, et ritrovandosene havere, che non li vendino senza licenza* ('Notice to Booksellers instructing them not to request the under-mentioned books and should they find any in their possession, they are not to sell them without license'), published in Rome on 22 May 1574 by Paolo Costabili, Master of the Sacred Palace, and distributed also without the City of Rome (*Scriniolum*, f. 87; and G. FRAGNITO, *La Bibbia al rogo*, p. 131; for more general information on this *Notice*, see U. ROZZO, *Index des livres interdits* vol. IX, pp. 26–7 and 39–40).

55 Regarding Italian literature and Church censorship, cf. V. CIAN, 'Un episodio della storia della censura in Italia nel secolo XVI. L'edizione spurgata del "Cortegiano"'. *Archivio storico lombardo*, s. 2, XIV, 1887, pp. 661–727; A. SORRENTINO, *La letteratura italiana e il Sant'Uffizio*, Naples, Perrella, 1935; P. PASCHINI, *Letterati ed Indice nella Riforma cattolica in Italia*, in ID., *Cinquecento romano e Riforma cattolica*, Rome, Edizioni liturgiche, 1958; N. LONGO, 'Fenomeni di censura nella letteratura italiana del Cinquecento', *Le pouvoir et la plume*, pp. 275–84; ID.,'La letteratura proibita', *Letteratura italiana*, vol. V, *Le questioni*, Turin, Einaudi, 1986, pp. 978–88; U. ROZZO, 'L'espurgazione dei testi letterari nell'Italia del secondo Cinquecento', *La censura libraria nell'Europa del secolo XVI*, U. Rozzo (ed.), Udine, Forum, 1997, pp. 219–71; ID.,'Italian literature on the index', *Church, censorship and culture in early modern Italy*, pp. 194–222; G. FRAGNITO, 'Aspetti e problemi della censura espurgatoria', *L'Inquisizione e gli storici: un cantiere aperto*, Accademia Nazionale dei Lincei, Rome 24–25 June 1999, Rome, Accademia dei Lincei, 2000, pp. 161–70; EAD., '"Li libbri non zò rrobba da cristiano": la letteratura italiana e l'indice di Clemente VIII (1596)', *Schifanoia*, 19, 1999, pp. 123–35.

anonymous 'Garden of Our Lady the Virgin Mary without author's name'; 'Stanzas in praise of M.V. Monsignor Gabriele Ranieri'; 'Medicine for the Soul, for the healthy and the sick, without printer's and author's name'), but also popular lay works that were generically classified as *Canzoni [e Comedie] dishoneste et lascive* ('Licentious and lewd Songs [and Comedies]'),[56]*Espositione d'Insogni, et ogni altro libro d'Insogni, Facetie, motti et Burle di diversi signori, Colloquio dishonesto di Damigelle, Historiette tutte, che non apportano giovamento né a buoni costumi né a dogmi della fede, Lettere amorose di vario tipo* ('Descriptions of Dreams, and every other book of Dreams','Pleasantries, witticisms and tricks by divers gentlemen', 'Damsels' licentious talk', 'Stories, none of which improves moral customs or dogmas of the faith', 'Love letters of various sorts'), *Madrigali cioè a tre voci, li quali sono moresche et altre sorte di Madrigali di simil sorte a quattro et a cinque voci, stampati in Venetia per Gironimo Scotto* ('Madrigals, that is to say with three voices, which are Moorish and other sorts of Madrigals and similar sorts with four or five voices, printed in Venice for Gironimo Scotto').[57] The introductory Rules of the Sistine Index later led to a further widening – but also to a more precise definition – of the category of heresy, which was subsequently

---

[56] This is the kind of prohibition that is visible in the action of the bishops in those years to which our attention is drawn by A. PROSPERI,'La Chiesa tridentina e il teatro: strategie di controllo del secondo '500', *I Gesuiti e i Primordi del Teatro Barocco in Europa*, Miriam Chiabò and Federico Doglio (eds), Viterbo-Rome, Centro Studi sul Teatro Medioevale e Rinascimentale-Torre d'Orfeo Editrice, 1995, pp. 25–6 and ID., *Tribunali della coscienza. Inquisitori, confessori, missionari*, Turin, Einaudi, 1996, pp. 342–9),who endeavored to be empowered to examine the texts of holy plays before they were first performed, as also in edicts like that of the Inquisitor of Pisa which prohibited 'all comedians' from 'acting anything taken from the Old or the New Testament and of sacred or holy scripture or any ecclesiastic or religious matter', or like the edict dated 21 May 1581 issued by the Archbishop of Florence, Alessandro de' Medici, which condemned 'comedies, tragedies, farces, tragicomedies and other spectacles whether portraying sacred or lay matter' (the last of these edicts was published by M. PLAISANCE in the appendix of his essay on 'Littérature et censure à Florence à la fin du XVI siècle', *Le pouvoir et la plume. Incitation, contrôle et répression dans l'Italie du XVI siècle*, Paris, Université de la Sorbonne Nouvelle, 1982, pp. 233–52; the text of the Edict is on pp. 249–50); cf. also G. FRAGNITO, *La Bibbia al rogo*, p. 132, footnote 52.

[57] An indication of the common intent of the compiler of the Index and the authorities that were institutionally in charge of censorship is provided by a letter, dated 21 March 1576, to the Inquisitor of Bologna and presumably to the other local Inquisitors, sent by the *socio* of the Master of the Sacred Palace, Brother Damiano Rubeo, in which he recommended that 'no stories, comedies or other vulgar books of love stories should be allowed to be printed, for alas the world is thus corrupted' ('né lassi stampare storie commedie et altri libri volgari d'innamoramenti, che pur troppo si vitia il mondo da se stesso'; A. ROTONDÒ, 'Nuovi documenti,' pp. 155–6).

confirmed in its general lines also by the Index of 1593.[58] In the course of the meetings of the Congregations of the Index it had been deliberated to extend the scope of the cited Rule VII of the 1564 Index to include 'also music books and lewd ditties, and pictures of this sort which, being silent, are not expressed in print, and books that purposely deal with lewd matter must be put on the Index',[59] and Sistus V's next action conclusively established the further extension of censorship to include books dealing with '*res amatorias*' as well as expressions of the written and oral 'unlettered' culture that had begun to be attacked in the 'long' lists: 'comedies, tragedies, and stories in the same vernacular tongue that contain similar matter including those that circulate in unpublished form thanks to charlatans, vagabonds, mimes, and strolling players'.[60] However, the

[58] The *Instructio* contained in the 1593 Index confirmed the massive offensive launched against the culture of the 'unlettered', vigorously stating all 'superstitions, sortileges, and divinations are to be condemned ... and writings that offend or violate church rites, religious orders, the State, human dignity, and individuals, as also jests and slander that are harmful and prejudicial to the good name and reputation of others; and also lewd and obscene pictures' ('superstitiones, sortilegia, ac divinationes [...] exempla, quae Ecclesiasticos ritus, religiosorum ordines, statum, dignitatem, ac personas, laedunt, et violant; facetiae etiam, aut dicteria in perniciem, aut praeiudicium famae, et existimationis aliorum iactata repudientur. Denique lasciva [...] obscenae imagines' ; *Index des livres interdits,* vol. IX, p. 860).

[59] 'etiam libros musices cantilenas obscoenas, vel eiusdem generis picture quae cum sint muti libri typis non exprimantur, et in Indice apponantur libri ex professo obscoena tractantes' (ACDF, Index, I/1, c. 19r, session of 16 April 1587; cf. also G. FRAGNITO, *La Bibbia al rogo*, p. 151).

[60] 'comoediae, tragediae, et fabellae fictae eiusdem idiomatis, quae similia continent, et quae etiam non scriptae a circumforaneis, vagis, mimis, histrionibusque circumferuntur'; Rule XIV of the Sistine Index of 1590, in *Index des livres interdits*, vol. IX, p. 797; cf. also G. FRAGNITO, *La Bibbia al rogo*, pp. 151–2. On the relationship between popular culture and Counter-Reformation Catholic culture, the paper by P. CAMPORESI, 'Cultura popolare e cultura d'élite tra Medioevo ed età moderna', *Storia d'Italia*, Annali 4, *Intellettuali e potere,* Turin, Einaudi, 1981, pp. 81–157 continues to be of fundamental importance. Also on this topic I permit myself to mention G. CARAVALE, 'Censura e pauperismo tra Cinque e Seicento. Controriforma e cultura dei senza lettere', *Rivista di Storia e Letteratura Religiosa*, 2002, 1, pp. 39–77. An indication of the final extent of the concept of heresy in the Sistine Index is provided by the fact it eventually included propositions defined as *male sonantes* ('ill sounding'); Rule XXI, *Index des livres interdits,* vol. IX, p. 799. Among the condemned works Rule XV also included treatises on dueling (ibid., p. 797; and G. FRAGNITO, *La Bibbia al rogo*, p. 154; on the prohibition of this kind of treatise writing, see the paper by C. DONATI, 'A project of 'expurgation' by the Congregation of the Index: treatises on duelling', *Church, culture and censorship in early modem Italy*, pp. 134–62). Other aspects of this culture were targeted in Rules XII e XIII. The first of these two concerned 'All books, treatises, and all Indexes of judiciary astrology, or of divination of possible future contingent matters, occurrences, and chance happenings, or of human actions depending on free-will are totally prohibited' ('Libri omnes, tractatus, et indices astrologiae iudiciariae, seu divinationum de futuris contingentibus, successibus, fortuitisque casibus, ac humanis actionibusì libero arbitrio pendentibus prohibentur omnino'), thus reproposing the prohibitions contained

aspect of the Inquisition's action in the field of censorship that better than any other revealed the reasons and sentiments behind this massive operation aimed at protecting the pious ears of the 'childish populace' was the violent offensive unleashed by the ecclesiastic hierarchies against the use of the vernacular in sacred matters. Although this offensive was destined to be institutionally codified in the form of concrete and definitive prescriptive rules, its confines and limits soon escaped the control of the Inquisition authorities in Rome. The elaborate process of codifying the rules and regulations that accompanied the activity of the Congregation of the Index and that of the Holy Office during the course of the second half of the sixteenth century, which Gigliola Fragnito reconstructed with great wealth of detail, culminated somewhat debatably in Rule IV of the Clementine Index and, above all, in the text of the *Observatio circa quartam Regulam* attached to it.[61] Together with the vernacular versions, the prohibition applied to 'other parts of the Holy Scriptures in both the Old and the New Testaments, published in whatever vernacular tongue, as well as summaries and compendia, including historic compendia of such Bibles or of books of Holy Scriptures, written in any vernacular tongue':[62] an outright declaration of war on all forms of direct enjoyment – i.e. without any ecclesiastic mediation – of the sacred by the broad sector of

in Rule IX of the Tridentine Index (on these prophetic and divinatory aspects of popular culture, cf. O. Niccoli, *Prophecy and People in Renaissance Italy*, Princeton, Princeton University Press, 1990 (first Italian edition: *Profeti e popolo nell'Italia del Rinascimento*, Rome-Bari, Laterza, 1987), as also 'any writing containing sortileges, poisons, magic spells, and incantations, all of which must be rejected' ('scripta quaecunque, sortilegia, veneficia, magiam, incantationesque continentia', which 'reiiciuntur omnino'; *Index des livres interdits*, vol. IX, p. 797). The second of the two Rules (number XIII) prohibited 'Epigrams, elegies, emblems, satires and poems; also offensive and denigratory books, defamatory pamphlets, apologies, and any writing with any title attacking the morality, customs, honor, and reputation of prelates, princes, or other persons, in whatever language thay may be written, including such that are anonymous'('Epigrammata, elegiae, emblemata, satyrae, et poemata; item libri iniuriosi, detractorii, libelli famosi, apologiae, et scripta quaecunque cuiuscunque sint tituli, honestati, bonis moribus, praelatorum, principum, aut aliorum honori, seu famae adver-santia, quocunque idiomate [...] etiam sine nomine auctoris'; ibid., p. 797); the text of the Rule did not refer exclusively – as we have seen – to forms of popular culture but did include them, as for example the genre known as 'Roman pasquinades', on which cf. the collection edited by V. Marcucci, *Pasquinate del Cinque e Seicento*, Rome, Salerno editrice, 1983, with a critical commentary by M. Firpo, 'Pasquinate', *Rivista storica italiana*, XCVI, 1984, pp. 600–621, and also the satires of Aretino.

61 *Index des livres interdits*, vol. IX, pp. 929–31.

62 'alias sacra scriptura tam novi, quam veteris testamenti partes quavis vulgari lingua editas; ac insuper summaria et compendia etiam historica eorundem Bibliorum, seu librorum sacra scriptura, quocunque vulgari idiomate conscripta' (ibid., p. 929; G. Fragnito, *La Bibbia al rogo*, pp. 182–3).

the population that was totally unfamiliar with the Latin tongue.[63] If the presence, among the titles of the *historie* ('stories') listed by the Inquisitor of Modena at the beginning of the seventeenth century, of the *Contrasto di Cicarello* and of the *Legenda devota del Romito de' Pulcini* ('The devout legend of the Romito de' Pulcini')[64] possibly represent the best testimony of a project that was primarily cultural rather than religious, a project intended to eradicate the most direct popular expressions of everyday life both of city dwellers and of peasants, either by adapting them or more simply by replacing them with terms and literary expressions of strictly Counter-Reformation origin,[65] it was the total mass of 'Modenese' titles –

---

[63] Although the text of the Clementine Rules included works in Latin verse, it was natural that the violent offensive against the use of the vulgar tongue in sacred 'scriptures' should find its complement in a massive campaign for the enhancement of Latin. In this regard, the contents of a letter sent to Rome in 1574 by Costabili to the Inquisitor of Bologna, are particularly eloquent: 'I desire our young people to improve at least their knowledge of the Latin tongue and I wish them to practice it for they will be much praised for it. The Jesuit fathers in this way acquire great renown. They have groups of twenty and fifteen men who recite prayers that are much celebrated in the chapel of Our Lord while for our young men months of time are not sufficient and they appear most inept' ('Vorrei che li nostri giovani attendessero alla peritia della lingua latina almeno e ve si esercitassero, che di qua potriano trarre molta laude. Li padri del Jesus con questo si acquistano molta reputazione. Hanno nomini che in 20 et 15 fanno orationi che riescono celebratissime in cappella di N.S. et a delli nostri non bastano li mesi di tempo che appaiono goffissimi'; A. ROTONDÒ, *Nuovi documenti*, pp. 153–4).

[64] The full titles of the works we have consulted are *El Contrasto di Cicarello da Cazan da contrastare in Maschera, e uno maridazzo di Toniolo e Menguosa, narrando tutte le virtù del sposo e della sposa, cosa piacevole e rediculosa*, and *Legenda devota del Romito et de Pulcini, cavata della vita patrum, e una Oratione del beato Simone da Trento devotissima.* It does not appear to be pure coincidence that there is no trace of either work in any Italian library: the two copies I cite I consulted in the British Library in London.

[65] The first of the two stories, for example, presents the colorful account of the violent quarrel between a peasant named Cicarel, and a farmer: the latter demanded to be compensated in money for a vulgar insult that Cicarel had dared to address to him; a regrettable episode that the reader hears about from the mouth of the farmer, who in broad Venetian dialect addresses a certain Bonsignor ('Mr Goodman'), the classic figure of the troubleshooter present in nearly all popular *contrasti* ('quarrels'), complaining about the peasant's insolence. In a climate of pressing economic refeudalization, and especially in the early Counter-Reformation period, any manifestation of peasant rebellion against the rigid social obligations imposed by the landowners, and any symptom of intolerance of the economic exploitation to which peasants were liable in times of famine and plague, was vigorously contested and skillfully transformed – in a matter of decades – into the image of a peasant who was happy with his country life and his social position (on these topics, particularly with regard to literary works concerning the theme of poverty, I take the liberty of referring to G. CARAVALE, 'Censura e pauperismo tra Cinque e Seicento. Controriforma e cultura dei senza lettere'). The Inquisition's condemnation of these two works should, however, also be attributed to the preponderant role that the protection of public 'morality' had taken on in the context of Counter-Reformation ideology. 'Unseemly' expressions –

all of them titles of short works in verse and in the vernacular – that inevitably fell into the cone of shadow cast by the Clementine rules and regulations: the simultaneous presence of these two elements (the vernacular and writing in verse) was often sufficient reason to attract the biased interest of censors and Inquisitors, far more than the careful analysis of the work in question.[66] If it is true, at least in part, that the compilation of the introductory rules of the Index corresponded to the logic of reducing the number of prohibitions contained in the Index, thus making it possible to avoid the condemnation of an excessive number of works,[67] in actual fact the application of the Clementine Index took quite a different turn.

It is known that in the late sixteenth and early seventeenth century the authorities in Rome – amid continual resistance from the congregations and

today we would define them as vulgar – such as those in *Contrasto* no longer found a place in the world of literature. The same consideration applies all the more so to unseemly and indeed harmful episodes meant to be listened to, such as those narrated in the *Legenda divota del Romito*: although the 'moral' of the story contained in it was perfectly consistent with the rigid canons of the Counter-Reformation ('two things cause loss of glory / one is pride / and the other is vainglory'), the episode through which the anonymous author attempted to attain his objectives was not quite so orthodox. The protagonist of the *Legenda* was a peasant, a good and faithful Christian, sorrow-stricken because he could not have a child by his wife. However, his repeated heartfelt prayers succeeded in obtaining the much-desired conception. But once they had obtained what they had so ardently desired, the peasant and his wife concentrated all their attention on the child and began to neglect their pious practices of giving charity and their customary dialogue with God. To punish the man's ingratitude, God decided to send a clear signal in order to bring him back on the straight path. Up to here, we may agree, everything came within the rules of an edifying Counter-Reformation message. The 'thunder' that 'God sent him / to make him return to the straight path', was, however, intended to frighten the credulous and uneducated readers of such stories. Although the strategy of the constant inducement of the fear of some cruel divine punishment still had its recognized place in the Counter-Reformation armamentarium, the devouring of a child by a wild animal was evidently too brutal a method in the eyes of the churchmen, who had by now learned to appreciate the advantage of gently persuasive methods such as confession and other methods that caught people's attention, used in the course of their ever more frequent popular missions.

66 A good example of this is provided by the story related in Gabriele Fiamma's *Rime spirituali*, which were included in the Index of Giovanni di Dio and later in that of Parma in 1580. Rather than mystic outbursts, the doctrine of *quieto travaglio* ('quiet work'), and allusions to the weakness of the human flesh, which can be overcome only by the grace of God and with the 'benefit of Christ', one of the reasons for the condemnation of this text must have been the genre to which it belonged and its little-concealed defense of popular versions of the Bible. (cf. C. Ossola, '"Queto travaglio" di Gabriele Fiamma', *Letteratura e critica. Studi in onore di Natalino Sapegno*, vol. III, Rome, Bulzoni editore, 1976, pp. 239–86, in particular pp. 246–7, 251–3, 257–9). Ossola also stresses the significant action of the adaptation, in Counter-Reformation style, that Fiamma realized in the preparation of his later literary works in order to escape the censorship of the Roman hierarchies (ibid., pp. 252 et seqq.).

67 Cf. G. Fragnito, 'Li libbri non zò rrobba da cristiano', p. 127 and footnote 32, p. 132.

religious orders which, clinging to their traditional network of privileges and exemptions, showed their reluctance to provide the Congregation of the Index with complete lists of the prohibited or suspended books kept in their libraries – obtained from the Fathers Superior of each individual institute complete lists of all the titles of volume in their libraries (and therefore not only of those that had been prohibited).[68] Besides the celebrated precious series of Vatican Codices containing the results of this impressive operation of book cataloging, it is possible today to consult a series of lists kept in the archive of the Congregation of the Index which gives the titles of suspended or condemned books or books that were confiscated and kept in the archives of the convent where the Inquisitors or their deputies normally lodged. These lists enable us to extend the scope of our vision to the titles of books owned before the Clementine Index came into force and before the books were handed over to the Inquisition authorities by booksellers, ordinary citizens, or members of the secular clergy.[69] In other words, these papers permit a first survey of the actual effect of the Clementine Index, with particular reference to the broad and vague indications contained in the *Observatio circa quartam regulam*, which, as said, contained a generic prohibition of nearly any writing containing material in the vernacular derived from the Holy Scriptures.[70] Limiting ourselves to the theme of prayer, the presence of clearly heretic works or others suspected of being so, such as *Espositione pia di Antonio Brucioli nei precetti, nel Credo, et Oratione Domenicale* ('Pious Exposition by Antonio Brucioli regarding the Precepts, the Credo,

---

68 G. Fragnito, 'L'applicazione dell'indice dei libri proibiti di Clemente VIII', *Archivio storico italiano*, CLIX (2001), 1, pp. 107–49, in particular pp. 126–30, corrects the interpretation commonly accepted by historiographers according to which previously discussion had revolved around a 'great inquiry' into the libraries owned by religious orders. Regarding this important cataloging operation, see the catalog of codices edited by M.M. Lebreton and A. Fiorani, *Codices Vaticani Latini. Codices 11266–11326. Inventari di biblioteche religiose italiane alla fine del Cinquecento*, Rome, Biblioteca Apostolica Vaticana, 1985; cf. also R. De Maio, *I modelli culturali della Controriforma. Le biblioteche dei conventi italiani alla fine del Cinquecento,* in Id., *Riforme e miti nella Chiesa del Cinquecento*, Naples, Guida, 1973, pp. 365–81; A. Barzazi, *Ordini religiosi e biblioteche a Venezia tra Cinque e Seicento,* in 'Annali dell'Istituto storico italo-germanico in Trento', 21, 1995, pp. 141–228; M. Dykmans, *Les bibliothèques des religieux d'Italie en l'an 1600,* in 'Archivum Historiae Pontificiae', 24 (1986), pp. 385–404; M. Rosa, '*Dottore o seduttor deggio appellarte*'. *Note erasmiane*, in 'Rivista di storia e letteratura religiosa', 26 (1990), pp. 5–33. For a more detailed bibliography on the matter, and also for a general picture and a careful reconstruction of the event, see G. Fragnito, *La Bibbia al rogo*, pp. 241 et seqq., in particular footnote 36, pp. 245–6.

69 G. Fragnito, *La Bibbia al rogo*, pp. 246 et sqq.

70 The works contained in these lists were amply dealt with by G. Fragnito (*La Bibbia al rogo*, pp. 246–313), to which we refer the reader for an overall picture.

and the Lord's Prayer'),[71] *Forma delle orationi eclesiastiche, et il modo di amministrare i sacramenti, et di celebrare il santo matrimonio Calvini ut creditur* ('The form of ecclesiastic prayers and the manner of administering the sacraments and celebrating the Holy Matrimony by Calvin *ut creditor*'),[72] and *Meditationi sopra il Pater nostro senza authore* ('Meditations on the Lord's Prayer, anonymous')[73] was merely a final tardy testimony of a battle that by now was over. The appearance of titles of what were known as *offitioli* ('little offices'), compendiums of prayers, collections of unauthorized litanies, such as *Hortulus Animae* ('Garden of the Soul'),[74]*Hore della gloriosa vergine* ('Hours of the Glorious Virgin'),[75] *25 Offitioli della Madonna antichi* ('25 Ancient Offices of Our Lady'),[76] *Silva Orationum Venetiis 1589* ('Forest

[71] ACDF, Index, XVIII (one volume), c. 44r, 'Libri prohibiti e sospesi, mandati dal vescovo di Lucca alli 8 di ottobre' ('Prohibited and suspended books, sent by the Bishop of Lucca on 8th October').

[72] Ibid., c. 59v, 'Cathalogus librorum partim damnatorum, partim expurgandorum in civitate Parmae repertorum, et ad novi Indicis publicationem S.to officio praesentatorum' ('Catalog of books to be found in the city of Parma, some of which are to be condemned, and some to be expurgated, presented to the Holy Office following the publication of the new Index'); note from the Inquisitor of Parma received in Rome on 10 September, cf. ibid., c. 60v.

[73] Ibid., c. 63r, 'Libri prohibiti et suspensi qui habentur in sancto offitio Veronae' ('Prohibited and suspended books to be found in the Holy Office of Verona').

[74] Ibid., c. 39r, 'Index librorum [...] Curiae Archiepiscopensis Neapolitanae' ('Index of books in the Archiepiscopal Curia of Naples'); ibid., c. 40r, 'Bibliotheca Iosephi Pelusi' ('Giuseppe Pelusi's Library'); ibid., c. 44v, 'Libri prohibiti e sospesi, mandati dal vescovo di Lucca alli 8 di ottobre' ('Prohibited and suspended books, sent by the Bishop of Lucca on 8th October'); ibid., c. 70v, 'Index librorum prohibitorum qui reperiuntur penes librarios Bononiae'; ibid., c. 77v, 'Index librorum suspensorum et Prohibitorum, qui sub facultate Inquisitionis Florentiae inveniuntur' ('Index of suspended and prohibited books to be found by the Inquisition of Florence'); ibid., c. 84v, 'Lista di libri prohibiti, che si ritrovano nella Cancelleria della S. Inquisitione di Pisa' ('List of prohibited books to be found in the Chancellery of the Holy Inquisition in Pisa').

[75] Ibid., c. 84v, 'Lista di libri prohibiti, che si ritrovano nella Cancelleria della S. Inquisitione di Pisa' ('List of prohibited books to be found in the Chancellery of the Holy Inquisition in Pisa').

[76] Ibid., c. 79r, 'Libri abruciati da dui some in circa, da me fra Antonino Topi da Montepulciano, Vicario del Sant'Officio, di commissione del Molto Reverendo Padre Inquisitore di Fiorenza, cioè la quarta domenica d'Agosto 1598 la mattina mentre si celebravano le messe, avanti la porta della Chiesa di San Francesco; nota de libri abruciati mandata dal Vicario di Montepulciano a 27 d'ottobre' ('Books, about two loads, burned by me, Brother Antonino Topi da Montepulciano, Vicar of the Holy Office, by order of the Very Reverend Father Inquisitor of Florence, on the fourth Sunday in August 1598 in the morning while Mass was being celebrated, outside the door of St Francis' Church; list of burned books sent by the Vicar of Montepulciano on 27th October'), cf. c. 79v; see also ibid., c. 82r: *Officii diversi lattini vecchi et vulgari*, in 'Libri proibiti et sospesi che si ritrovano nella santa Inquisitione di Siena' ('Prohibited and suspended books to be found at the Holy Inquisition in Siena').

of Venetian Prayers 1589'),[77] *Compendium orationum* ('Compendium of Prayers'),[78] and *Precationes piarum enchiridion Antuerpiae* ('Enchiridion of pious prayers published in Antwerp'),[79] continued to represent a project – that of the creation of liturgic uniformity – which, despite all the practical difficulties, was still pursuing its original aims. Finally, the frequent presence of some of the most widespread popular devotional texts in the vernacular (such as *Giardino d'orationi*,[80] *Il Monte delle orationi volgari sine auctore*,[81] and *Specchio di orationi*) asked the question of the extent of the effect of the Church's offensive on the relationship between the faithful and inward devotion. Through these texts, in the course of the century, large numbers of *semplici et idioti* ('simpletons and idiots') had had the chance of approaching the practice of praying inwardly and thus of gaining confidence with the theme of mental prayer, shunning intellectual sophisms and the mystic outbursts of a certain form of spiritual literature intended for 'the better educated' but at the same time avoiding the dangers of the mechanical *biascicamento* ('muttering') of Lord's Prayers and the superstitious repetition of outward acts devoid of any true feeling. The *Libro devoto e fructuoso a ciaschaduno chiamato Giardino de Oratione* ('Devout and to everymen fruitful book called Garden of Prayer'),[82] which was reprinted in the first half of the

77 Ibid., c. 67r, 'Libri prohibiti et suspecti qui reperiuntur in Sancto Officio Inquisitionis Bononiae' ('Prohibited and suspect books to be found here in the Holy Office of the Inquisition of Bologna'); list sent 6 September, cf. ibid., c. 68v.

78 Ibid., c. 48v, 'Lista di libri prohibiti et sospesi che si trovano nell'Inquisitione di Ancona' ('List of prohibited and suspended books to be found at the Inquisition of Ancona'). ibid., c. 59r, 'Cathalogus librorum partim damnatorum, partim expurgandorum in civitate Parmae repertorum, et ad novi Indicis publicationem S.to officio praesentatorum' ('Catalog of books in part to be condemned in part to be expurgated to be found in the city of Parma and presented after the publication of the new Index by the Holy Office'), note from the Inquisitor of Parma received in Rome on 10 September, cf. ibid., c. 60v); ibid., c. 61v, 'Libri prohibiti et suspensi qui habentur in sancto offitio Veronae' ('Books prohibited and suspended to be found in the Holy Office of Verona'); ibid., c. 86r, 'Catalogus librorum prohibitorum, qui post novi Indicis publicationem, a diversis presentati fuerunt S. Officio Inquisitionis Comi, et adhuc inveniuntur in camera R.P. Inquisitoris' ('Catalog of prohibited books which after the publication of the new Index were presented to the Holy Office of Como, and now to be found in the office of the Reverend Father Inquisitor').

79 Ibid., c. 48r, 'Lista di libri prohibiti et sospesi che si trovano nell'Inquisitione di Ancona' ('List of prohibited and suspended books to be found at the Inquisition of Ancona').

80 Ibid., c. 81r, 'Libri proibiti et sospesi che si ritrovano nella santa Inquisitione di Siena' ('List of prohibited and suspended books to be found at the Holy Inquisition of Siena').

81 Ibid., c. 48r ('List of prohibited and suspended books to be found at the Inquisition of Ancona' ('List of prohibited and suspended books to be found at the Inquisition of Ancona'); ibid., c. 63r, 'Libri prohibiti et suspensi qui habentur in sancto offitio Veronae' ('List of prohibited and suspended books to be found at the Holy Office of Verona').

82 Novamente stampato. In Venetia per Bernardino de Viano de Lexona, 1521, adì XXV Marzo.

sixteenth century at least ten times,[83] was in actual fact a genuine manual on the *excellentia* ('excellence') and *virtude singulare et specialissima* ('singular and very special virtue') of prayer for 'unlearned' readers. This felicitous little work taught the 'unlettered' to respect the 'most ancient institution' (*antiquissima institutione*), the 'most singular representation' (*singolarissima representatione*) and the 'most useful devotion' (*utilissima devotione*) of 'vocal prayer' (*oratione vocale*) and 'psalmody'(*psalmodia*),[84] recalling at the same time that 'prayer [...] said with the mind extended toward God out of pitiful and humble affection [...] brings the soul closer to God',[85] thus introducing his devout readers to the 'greatness and usefulness of divine contemplation' (*grandecia e utilità della contemplazione divina*). Some sensitive guardians of the strict rules of monastic and convent life may have been shocked by the criticisms made by the anonymous author of *Giardino* of those who 'say the office in chorus because they have some temporary benefice of which they are slaves and they do not have enough freedom to hear the sweetness of the psalmody'[86] or by those who 'say the psalms and the office because the Church obliges them, or because they have benefits, or because they hold holy office'.[87] Likewise, we cannot exclude the possibility that the philological sensitivity of some censors may have been disturbed by the occasional presence of brief holy narratives derived from apocryphal writings such as *Purgatorio di San Patrizio* or *Transito di San Girolamo*.[88] What, however, must have put the Inquisitors and censors on the tracks of the *Giardino di orazione*, thus causing its sudden disappearance from the hands of the faithful, was the clear affirmation of the superiority of the vernacular, which was the only language that 'simple folk' could understand, as also the presence of passages from the scriptures presented directly in the vernacular. With a proud declaration of his intentions the anonymous author in fact began his 'narrative' with the following statement:

---

83 On this work, edited for the first time in Venice by Bernardino Benali, see the paper by S. DA CAMPAGNOLA, 'Giardino di orazione" e altri scritti di un anonimo del quattrocento. Un'errata attribuzione a Niccolò da Osimo', *Collectanea franciscana*, 41 (1971), pp. 5–59; and also C. GINZBURG, 'Folklore, magia, religione', pp. 633–4. A.J. Schutte drew our attention to six editions printed between 1494 and 1543 (*Printed vernacular Italian books*, pp. 302–3).

84 *Libro devoto e fruttuoso a ciaschaduno chiamato Giardino de Oratione*, cc. Blr et seqq.

85 'oratione [...] è una intentione di mente verso Dio per pietoso et humile affecto [...] quella che fa più venir l'anima con Dio' (ibid., c. A2v).

86 'dicono lo officio in choro perché hanno alcuna provisione temporale e questi sono servi di quella provisione e non hanno la libertà perché non possono sentire la dolcezza della psalmodia' (ibid., c. C2v).

87 'dicono li psalmi e l'officio perché secondo la chiesa sono obligati, o perché hanno beneficii, over perché son in ordine sacro' (ibid.). Cf. also ibid., c. C3r.

88 S. DA CAMPAGNOLA, 'Il "Giardino di orazione"', p. 28.

> I myself am a rough and ignorant fellow, but when I consider my poverty and that of many other men and women who have little knowledge and cannot understand books of literature and science yet seek to come close to God and I also consider that the kingdom of Heaven is also made for them and that it is perhaps for them, rather than for those who are proficient in the great sciences, that I have thought to compose this work and this treatise on prayer in the vernacular, so that these simple, ignorant souls may understand prayer and practice it: and as ignorance is more important than knowledge: science makes the soul proud and I wish to do something more useful than satisfying the vanity and curiosity of those who seek speech that is ornate, Rhetorical and exquisite.[89]

What may have seemed to most people in the mid-fifteenth century (the first edition of the work dates from 1454) a useful and 'fruitful' devotional text must, a century and a half later, have looked like a risky editorial venture – all the more so if one considers, as has been suggested, that the impassioned apology of the ignorance of the common people and the exaltation of the vernacular as the only language that simple folk could understand were accompanied by what the Inquisitors must have considered to be, in the light of the strict rules of the Clementine *Observatio*, a genuine admission of guilt: 'I put nothing of my own', the anonymous author had said in all serenity, 'but only what I have found in the Holy Scriptures and the books of the doctors of the Church'.[90] The less-educated devout Catholics were thus deprived of a text that for many had represented the symbol of an accessible and fertile synthesis of the demands of an inward sense of religiousness based on an appeal to imitate Christ and the needs of an outward religiousness based on 'fasting and almsgiving' (*digiuno et elemosina*).

During the course of the century the *Giardino d'orazione* had become very popular, but the renowned *Specchio di oratione* by the Capuchin friar, Bernardino da Balvano – which first appeared in Messina in 1553 and was reprinted no fewer than fourteen times in the course of the following

89 'io indocto e grosso considerando la indigentia di me stesso e de molte altre persone maschi e femine le quale hanno pocha scientia, e non possono intendere li libri literali e scientifici e nondimeno anche lor cercano de acostarsi a Dio e per lor anche è facto il regno del cielo: e forsi più tosto che per li superbi delle grande scientie mi ho pensato di componere questa opera e questo tratato de l'oratione in vulgare: acciò che queste anime idiote e simplice possano havere intendimento di questa oratione e in essa exercitarsi: havendo più la vanità della scientia: la qual fa l'anima insuperbire e volendo più presto fare utilità che satisfare alla vanità e curiosità di quelli che cerchiano pur de haver parlamenti ornati Rhetorici e exquisiti' (*Libro devoto e fructuoso*, cc. A2v–A3r).

90 'Non pongo alcuna cosa da me ma quello che ho trovato nelli sancti libri de la scriptura e per li santi doctori' (ibid.).

century and a half[91] – was perhaps at the end of the sixteenth century the best-seller of all popular devotional titles of the day. This editorial success was clearly due to the clarity, the fervor, and above all the simplicity with which this little work handled the theme of inward prayer. Belonging to a rich literary tradition – that of the Franciscans and the Capuchins – which on the subject of mental prayer was destined to produce (and had already in part produced) some of the most intense writings of sixteenth-century spirituality, the *Specchio di oratione* distinguished itself by its essentially practical nature. The essential theoretic indications were directly redrafted as a number of concrete and convincing exercises that could be immediately taken in by the reader: in the editorial panorama of the sixteenth century it was one of the texts that the 'unlearned' faithful found easiest to use. Even the well-known *Pratica dell'orazione mentale* by Bellintani, a text published twenty years later and often considered a symbol of sixteenth-century Capuchin spirituality when compared with Balvano's spiritual little work, 'may have seemed suited to educated readers' (*poteva parer cosa per letterati*).[92] Balvani's text, which without detracting in any way from *Prattica*'s spiritual and religious intensity, placed itself entirely at the service of 'simple folk', as the author explicitly declared at the beginning of the work: 'And since this is written for the consolation of simple folk, in order that those who are unskilled in reading may practice this more easily according to their needs at various times and to their level of attainment, we will give a model example of each of these types concerned'.[93] Lest this

[91] *I Frati Cappuccini. Documenti e testimonianze del primo secolo*, C. Cargnoni (ed.), III/l, p. 556.

[92] Writing in August 1594 to Orazio Mancini, Bellintani – in the wake of the anti-vernacular current that was beginning to affect all sixteenth-century devotional editorial publications (the remark added by the Capuchin friar, clearly alluding to the editorial difficulties encountered in those years by vernacular writings, i.e. 'if they were authorized to be published', is particularly significant) – admitted, at least implicitly, that his *Prattica* 'may have seemed to be suitable for educated readers': 'I do not put them in Latin for two reasons: one is that in Latin I cannot avoid using too many words, which I can do in the vernacular. [...] The other reason is that although at first they may seem to be suited to educated readers, nonetheless, if they were authorized to be published, experience (I am sure) would show that the ordinary language of the people would make them more popular, and they would be useful to simple folk' ('Non gli faccio latini per dui rispetti: l'uno è che nel latino non posso temperarmi dalle molte parole, come faccio nel volgare. [...] L'altro è che quantunque paia al principio che siano cose per letterati, nondimeno, se si lasciassero uscire, la sperientia (son sicuro) farebbe vedere che la lingua volgare volgarebbeli più, et al volgo anchora servirebbono'; Letter to Orazio Mancini, Brescia, 3 August 1594, *I Frati Cappuccini*, III/1, p. 121).

[93] 'E perché questo si scrive a consolazion di semplici, acciò sappiano quelli che son poco prattici più leggermente essercitarsi a questo, secondo sarà di bisogno a diversi tempi e vari gradi si ritroveranno, daremo per modello uno essempio a ciascheduno di questi affetti sopra detti' (ibid., p. 567).

might remain merely a vain promise, Balvano thus promised his readers concrete 'examples' (*essempi*) to guide them in the 'exercise' (*essercitatione*) of the 'mysteries' of prayer: 'And so that the faithful who are new to praying may find the way thereto open, we shall give a short example as a model for them to practice in the mysteries that are acts of holy prayer, so that those who dedicate themselves to it with fervor shall with experience feel the wondrous fruits of holy prayer'.[94] All this was, therefore, not only related to the clear and simple language in which Balvano described the central nature of the Son of God's message of love;[95] it was also related to the author's particular skill in adapting his inward spiritual teaching to people's everyday rhythms and habits, with explicit references to the concrete occupations of the faithful. 'Rise every day one or two hours before you wish to go about your business', the Capuchin friar advised for the hours of the morning, 'go to your place of prayer in the oratory or to your private room; kneel down and with true devotion invoke the name of the Most Holy Trinity, cross yourself three times in the name of the Father, the Son, and the Holy Ghost and, having said the Credo to testify your faith, briefly consider what you have to do during the day, whether it is good or bad.'[96]

'In the evening', Balvano concluded, 'when you have returned home, you must, in your customary place of prayer, and after attending to your personal matters and before taking to your bed, make a careful examination of all you have done during the day, of your thoughts, your words, and all else.'[97] Between these two cardinal points, the author of *Specchio* carefully selected the most significant 'business activities' (*negoci*) of a potential reader's routine working day, presenting for each of them a literary metaphor capable of impressing on the mind the 'spiritual concepts' (*li spirituali concetti*) of prayer: 'If a tree fails to produce fruit', we read,

---

94 'E acciò che gli fideli all'orar novelli abbiano di ciò il cammino aperto, daremo per modello un breve essempio, come essercitar s'hanno nelli misteri essi atti della sacrosanta orazione, alla quale chi al spesso darà opera con fervore, sentirà con esperienza del sacro orar gli meravigliosi frutti'(ibid., p. 575).

95 'The most effective remedy for all the treacheries of one's worst enemy is to carry Sweet Jesus alive in one's thoughts and to delight in Him with intimate love' (ibid., p. 583).

96 'Ogni giorno levati una o due ore per tempo dinanzi che vorai andare alli tuoi negoci; va al luogo della tua orazione, nell'oratorio o camera secreta; posto in genocchioni, devotamente invocando il nome della santissima Trinità, ti segnerai con la croce tre volte, nel nome del Padre, del Figliuolo e Spirito Santo, e detto il Credo per confession della fede, considera per un poco quello che hai da fare il dì, s'egli è cosa buona o mala' (ibid., p. 632).

97 'La sera, ritornato a casa, nel consueto luogo dell'orazione, dopo acquietato le tue facende, primo che vai riposarti, diligentemente essamina quello tutto che hai fatto il giorno, li pensieri, le parole e ogn'altra cosa' (ibid., p. 634).

'a farmer's labors are in vain; and if the soul fails to produce the acts of mental prayer, reading and writing are scarcely fruitful'.[98] We also read:

> The good son [who] every day attends to his lessons knows nothing at first but by attending he becomes learned. Just as drops of water, however insubstantial, will leave their mark on the hardest of stone. In the same way, a spiritual person, by continually acting in the field of prayer and of these mysteries, although in the beginning he may be rough and lacking in skill, will by faithful perseverance and with the grace of the Lord become a learned master.[99]

Thus, the final result was a decisive mixture of Catholic precepts and of practical teaching based on the experiences of everyday life that is well synthesized in the following passage:

> Thus to find pardon with God, you shall confess to the best confessor you can find all your sins in their entirety, and when from him you have received absolution and you have returned to your neighbor all that you owed, make provisions and prepare yourself, your house, your family, and all your business in such a way that you find nothing that can prevent you from being in the grace of God. And it would also be right and proper to make a will and dispose of your estate when you are in good health, so that if illness should come you are not oppressed by thoughts of your business and the anxieties of this world.[100]

This, like *Giardino di orazione*, was another text fated to fall into the net of the local Inquisitors, the executors of the Clementine *Observatio*. In a letter to the Inquisitor of Messina, written on 6 May 1553 as he completed the work, Balvano himself declared – when the use of passages from the Scriptures in the vernacular was evidently no longer a reason for condemning a text – that he had collected together, after a week's study of

---

98 'Se l'arbore non pervene a gli frutti, invano sono le fatiche dell'agricoltore; e se l'anima non produce gli atti della mentale orazione, il leggere e meditare è di poco frutto' (ibid., p. 570).

99 'Il figliuolo [che] ogni giorno frequenta la lezione, benché prima non sapesse, per il continuare diventa dotto. E la gocciola dell'acqua, quantunque molle, al spesso cascando cava il duro sasso. In tal modo la persona spirituale di continuo essercitandosi nell'orazione e a questi misteri, conciosia cosa che al principio sia rozza e poco esperta, diventerà con grazia del Signore (perseverando fedelmente) d'essa dotta e maestra' (ibid., p. 630).

100 'Dunque per trovar venia appresso a Dio, al miglior confessore che potrai avere confesserai tutti interamente i tuoi peccati, e ricevuta da lui l'assoluzione e sodisfatto al prossimo quel tutto che dovevi, disponi e ordina te stesso, la casa e la famiglia, e tutti tuoi negoci per modo che non ti ritrovi cosa alcuna la quale t'impedisca dalla grazia di Dio. E sarebbe anco bene farti un testamento e disponere le cose tue quando stai sano, per modo che, occorrendo l'infirmità, non ti suffochino gli pensieri delli negoci e ansietà di questo mondo' (ibid., pp. 631–2).

the Holy Scriptures, everything that dealt with the topic of prayer and that he had presented it as a 'mirror' in the pages he had written.[101] Citations from the work of St Basil, St Augustine, St Ambrose, and St Bernard were interspersed with faithful transcriptions of passages taken from the Book of Genesis, the Psalms of David, the Letter to the Corinthians, and other Old and New Testament books. Everything was faithfully presented in the vernacular, which was sufficient to condemn this precious little book to vanish from the universe of seventeenth-century devotional literature. Mattia Bellintani's *Pratica dell'orazione mentale* ('Practice of mental prayer') – deliberately devoid of passages from the Scriptures in the vernacular – continued to circulate, more or less undisturbed, throughout the seventeenth century, but nevertheless one cannot forget that the 'simple and unlearned faithful' had at the same time been deprived of a devotional instrument that was far better suited to their humble daily demand for religion than Bellintani's text.

With regard to the 'deprivations'(*privazioni*) to which 'simple folk' were exposed within the framework of the application of the Clementine Index, it has been shown in crystal-clear fashion that 'the ban that compelled them to do without texts which previously they had used in the home (and often also at school), or else to follow sermons and the liturgy in Latin, thus helping to foster their piety, was – and the relevant sources are explicit on the point – truly traumatic. The trauma was of two sorts since it meant not only renouncing familiar books but also, very likely, the need to get accustomed to new texts.'[102] This traumatic 'shock to good and simple folk'[103] was in fact the inevitable price imposed by an overall political and religious strategy set in motion by the church hierarchies; a strategy designed to reduce the spaces and times for individual piety, replacing them with opportunities for devotional practices that were easier for the severe and attentive 'eye of the Father'[104] to keep under control.

101 Ibid., p. 556.

102 G. Fragnito, 'Dichino corone e rosari: censura ecclesiastica e libri di devozione,' *Cheiron*, XVII, 2000, pp. 135–58, in particular p. 153. In a letter to Cardinal Valier cited by Fragnito, Cardinal Tolomeo Gallio, Bishop of Osimo, remarked that 'the effect of this new Index was most serious on nuns and other simple folk, who were left without most of the books of the Holy Scriptures written in the vernacular' ('l'essecutione di questo nuovo Indice a nessuno è stata più grave che alle monache et altre persone semplici, che restano private della maggior parte de libri volgari della sacra scrittura'; letter from Cingoli, 12 September 1596; ibid., p. 138).

103 Letter from Antonio Benivieni, Vicar of the Archbishop of Florence, to the Reverend Lionardo, a Florentine canon in Rome, Florence 26 October 1596, cited by G. Fragnito, 'Dichino corone e rosari', p. 139.

104 The expression is borrowed from the title of a book by A. Turchini, *Sotto l'occhio del padre. Società confessionale e istruzione primaria nello Stato di Milano*, Bologna, Il Mulino,

Without wishing to dwell overlong on aspects of historiography that have already been adequately considered and are in any case beyond the scope of the present work, it is necessary to underline how, on the one hand, the elimination of widely popular texts used by the common people, such as *Giardino d'Orazione* and *Specchio d'Oratione* ('Mirror of Prayer'), and, on the other, the corresponding Counter-Reformation policy of establishing a firm hold over the mass of the faithful by using emotionally stimulating devotional instruments that doctrinally speaking were not entirely orthodox, had their counterpart in a gradual but irreversible slackening of the tension of censorship with regard to the most variegated forms of devotional superstition. Leafing through the great mass of expurgatory documents sent in by local Inquisitors and censors in the late sixteenth and early seventeenth centuries in application of the generic Clementine Rules, documents that continued to pile up untidily on the desks of the ever busier members of the Roman Congregation Index, one can form a clear view of this complex process.[105]

1996. More in general, regarding the lines of Counter-Reformation devotional strategy, cf. M. Rosa, 'Pietà mariana e devozione del Rosario nell'Italia del Cinque e Seicento', *Religione e società nel Mezzogiorno tra Cinque e Seicento*, Bari, De Donato, 1976, pp. 217–43; Id., 'La Chiesa meridionale nell'età della Controriforma', *Storia d'Italia*, Annali 9, *La Chiesa e il potere politico*, Turin, Einaudi, 1986, pp. 291–345; Id., 'L'onda che ritorna: interno ed esterno sacro nella Napoli del '600', *Luoghi sacri e spazi della santità*, S. Boesch Gajano and L. Scaraffia (eds), Turin, Rosenberg & Sellier, 1990, pp. 397–417; C. Russo, 'La religiosità popolare nell'età moderna: problemi e prospettive', *Problemi di storia della Chiesa nei secoli XVII–XVIII.* Atti del V Convegno di Aggiornamento (Proceedings of the Fifth Refresher Meeting) (Bologna 3–7 Sept. 1979), Naples, Edizioni Dehoniane, 1982, pp. 137–90; *Devozioni e pietà popolare fra Seicento e Settecento: il ruolo delle congregazioni e degli ordini religiosi*, S. Nanni (ed.), *Dimensioni e Problemi della Ricerca Storica*, 2 (1994), pp. 5–290; A. Prosperi, *Tribunali della coscienza*, in particular part III: *I missionari*, pp. 551 et sqq.

[105] We are referring to the numerous notes of censorship sent by the local authorities, which frequently organized themselves in what were in effect local congregations of the 'Index', in application of the broad and generic Clementine rules. Once the correction of the text had been carried out according to the rules imposed by the Roman Congregation itself, the text of these censures had to be sent to Rome for further investigation and for the much-desired (but never achieved) creation of the uniformity of texts. In actual fact this mass of documents soon became unmanageable for the Roman Members of the Congregation, with censorship activity unable to maintain the pace. Only a minimum number of these documents were made to conform and were organized within an expurgatory Index. This was published in 1607 but then immediately suspended. On these topics, cf. Gigliola Fragnito's numerous contributions, including 'L'applicazione dell'indice dei libri proibiti di Clemente VIII'; Ead., 'In questo vasto mare de libri prohibiti et sospesi tra tanti scogli di varietà et controversie'; Ead., 'Aspetti e problemi della censura espurgatoria'; Ead., 'Li libbri non zò rrobba da cristiano'.

CHAPTER 11

First Signs of Surrender

A trial in the mid-1580s conducted by the Inquisitor of Udine, Brother Girolamo Asteo, against a miller, Domenico Scandella, known as Menocchio, was made famous by research carried out by Carlo Ginzburg. The trial had already provided a significant testimony of the line of approach followed by the Church hierarchies: an important aspect, possibly the most significant, of the Udine trial (Udine is in the province of Friuli) consisted in a careful examination of the books possessed and read by the accused, the purpose of which was to identify the sources from which he had learned the heretic 'opinions ... [that] came out of his head' (*opinioni ... cavate dal suo cervello*). The vast gap between the actual letter of the text and the miller's far-fetched conclusions, regarding which Ginzburg produced some of the finest pages of his work,[1] immediately appeared to the Friuli authorities to be clear evidence of the doctrinal and theological misinterpretations to which the Gospel text was potentially liable if left in the hands of an inexpert reader, without the intermediation of the Church. The texts discovered in the house of Menocchio or in those he cited to justify his 'opinions' included, in addition to the bare text of the Bible in Italian, many of the devotional texts and short works in Italian that during recent decades had nourished the religious piety of 'simple folk and idiots' and directed their devotional preferences, regardless of the strict limits imposed by the Church authorities, i.e. works like *Fioretto della Bibbia, Rosario della gloriosa Vergine*, *Vita della Madonna,* and *Historia del giudicio*. Simply by reading an excerpt from *Fioretto della Bibbia* – the miller from Friuli had confessed – he had come to the conclusion that Christ was St Joseph's carnal son, that Mary's virginity was a fanciful invention of some father of the Church, and that Christ was therefore merely a man like any other:[2] an 'opinion' of which Menocchio had found indirect confirmation in another currently very popular devotional text that he had read, entitled

---

1 C. Ginzburg, *The Cheese and the Worms. The Cosmos of a Sixteenth-Century Miller*, translated by J. and A. Tedeschi, Baltimore-London, Johns Hopkins University Press, 1980 (first Italian edition: *Il formaggio e i vermi. Il cosmo di un mugnaio del '500*, Turin, Einaudi, 1976), in particular pp. 32–3; the trial proceedings were edited by Andrea Del Col: *Domenico Scandella known as Menocchio: his trials before the Inquisition (1583–1599)*, translated by John and Anne C. Tedeschi, Binghamton, N.Y., Medieval & Renaissance Texts & Studies, 1996 (first Italian edition: *Domenico Scandella, detto Menocchio. I processi dell'Inquisizione (1583–1599)*, a cura di A. Del Col, Pordenone, Edizioni Biblioteca dell'Immagine, 1990).

2 C. Ginzburg, *Il formaggio e i vermi*, cit., p. 28.

Rosario della gloriosa Vergine Maria. As the miller Scandella had explained to the ever-more-perplexed Inquisitor of Friuli, 'Mary was called the Virgin because she had been in the Temple of the Virgins – there was a temple where twelve virgins were kept and married off as and when they grew up. All this I read in a book called *Lucidano della Madonna*'.[3] 'Christ', he would confidently declare, 'was a man like any other, born to St Joseph and the Virgin Mary'. Or again, citing a very popular work entitled *Vita della Madonna* – identified by Ginzburg as the *Legendario de le vite de tutti i santi* by Iacopo da Varagine[4] – he declared his conviction that the Virgin Mary did not deserve any particular honors on this earth from the faithful.[5] Worse still, having examined some 'rough octaves clumsily copied from a passage in the Gospel of St Matthew', he had even gone so far as to deduce 'that it is a greater rule to love one's neighbor than to love God'.[6] The problem that the Inquisitors in Friuli had to

---

[3] Ibid., p. 34. Ginzburg cites the words that Menocchio might have read in this book: 'Contemplate here, zealous soul, how after making an offering to God and to the priest, St Joachim and St Anne left their most precious daughter in the temple of God, where she was to be cared for with the other virgins who had been dedicated to God. In that place she dwelt in sublime devotion contemplating divine things, and she was visited by the Holy Angels, as though she were their queen and empress, and she was always engaged in prayer' (ibid., p. 34). Ginzburg commented: 'He changed the significance without actually distorting the literal meaning. In the text, the appearance of the angels set Mary apart from her companions, conferring a supernatural aura upon her. But in Menocchio's mind, the significant element was the presence of "the other virgins," which explained in the simplest manner the title given to Mary by linking her with her companions. Thus, what was originally a detail ended by becoming the central issue, thereby altering the general sense' (ibid., p. 34).

[4] In particular, this must have been related to the chapter entitled *De l'assumptione de la beata Vergine Maria*, which was a re-elaboration of 'a certain apocryphal booklet ascribed to St John the Evangelist' (ibid., p. 35).

[5] Cf. ibid., pp. 34–6.

[6] Ibid., p. 37. 'Because I read in a *Historia del Giudicio* [*Opera nuova del Giudicio universale. Nel qual si tratta della fin del mondo, cioè quando Gesù Christo verrà a giudicar i buoni, et i rei; Con la venuta d'Antichristo*] that when judgment day comes, [God] will say to that angel: "You are wicked, you have never done a good deed for me;" and that angel replies: "My lord, I have never seen you so that I could do you a good deed." [And God said] "I was hungry and you did not feed me, I was thirsty and you did not give me drink, I was naked and you did not clothe me, when I was in prison you did not come to visit me." And because of this I believed that God was that poor neighbor, because he said "I was that beggar"' (ibid.; this short work already appeared among the titles of forbidden *historiette* in Calbetti's list in 1604). Ginzburg identified the octaves on the basis of which Menocchio had founded his convictions: 'Christ will reply with joyful countenance: / "That beggar who came to the door / famished, afflicted, and overcome / Was asking for charity in my name, / He was not driven off or cut down by you, / But he ate and drank of what was yours, / To him you gave for love of God: / Know now I was that beggar"', and he comments as follows on the peculiar use of the text made by the accused party: 'While distortion of the meaning in the preceding cases had occurred essentially by way of omissions, the procedure here is more complex. Menocchio takes one more step in respect to the text that, though small

resolve was certainly not that of verifying whether or not the texts Menocchio had read were apocryphal, nor was it a question of deploying scrupulously meticulous philological scholarship to trace the incriminated passages and thus assess the manner and the extent of the accused party's twisting of the text:[7] it was instead necessary to establish whether it was true, as was widely believed, that an uneducated person with little knowledge of doctrine like the miller of Friuli was unable to reflect autonomously on sacred matters without running the risk of falling into heresy.

Ginzburg wrote with reference to the miller's manner of proceeding, 'we shouldn't be surprised by Menocchio's use of passages in the *Legendario* and the *Fioretto*, taken from the apocryphal gospels. In view of the contrast he drew between the laconic simplicity of God's Word – "four words" – and the immoderate growth of Scripture, the very notion of apocryphal had to be abandoned. Apocryphal and canonic gospels alike were placed on the same level and were regarded as purely human texts'.[8] In precisely mirror fashion, the Inquisition authorities, blinded by the danger of too direct an access to the Holy Texts, tended to downplay and indeed deny the distinction between apocryphal texts (and therefore potentially dangerous) and canonic texts. In other words, although the writings were for the most part apocryphal and superstitious, the short devotional works cited by Menocchio in the course of his Inquisition trials were judged by the Inquisition authorities to be dangerous only insofar as they were vehicles of the sacred that were too easily accessible to anyone ignorant of Latin.[9]

in appearance, is actually enormous: if God is our neighbor, 'because he said "I was that beggar," 'it's more important to love our neighbor than to love God' (ibid., p. 38).

7 On *Fioretto* and Menocchio's twisted reading, cf. ibid., pp. 52–3, 60–61 and 72–3.

8 Ibid., p. 37.

9 It is no coincidence that many of the titles mentioned by Menocchio are to be found on the lists of books confiscated at the end of the century. The lists were sent to Rome by the local Inquisition authorities as prescribed by the Clementine Rules (on which cf. above, ch. 10): starting with *Fioretti della Bibbia*, in ACDF, Index, XVIII (*vol. unico*), c. 61v, 'Libri prohibiti et suspensi qui habentur in sancto officio Veronae' ('Prohibited and suspended books to be found in the Holy Office of Verona'); and ibid., c. 80v, 'Libri proibiti et sospesi che si ritrovano nella santa Inquisitione di Siena' ('Prohibited and suspended books to be found in the Holy Inquisition of Siena'); passing then to *Vita della Madonna*, in ibid., c. 48v (the title appears twice in the 'Lista di libri prohibiti et sospesi che si trovano nell'Inquisitione di Ancona'; 'Lists of prohibited and suspended books to be found in the Inquisition of Ancona'); and concluding with *Fior di virtù*, frequently mentioned by Menocchio, in ibid., c. 80v, 'Libri proibiti et sospesi che si ritrovano nella santa Inquisitione di Siena' ('Prohibited and suspended books to be found in the Holy Inquisition of Siena'); or to similar works like *Vita di Cristo*, in ibid., c. 48v, 'Lista di libri prohibiti et sospesi che si trovano nell'Inquisitione di Ancona' ('List of prohibited and suspended books to be found in the Inquisition of Ancona'); and c. 85r, 'Lista di libri prohibiti, che si ritrovano nella Cancelleria della S. Inquisitione di Pisa' ('List of prohibited books to be found in the Chancellery of the Holy Inquisition of Pisa').

The uncontrolled spreading of the struggle against use of the vernacular therefore reflected the beginning of a slackening of the tension of censorship *vis-à-vis* apocryphal and superstitious material. If we concentrate our attention on the felicitous genre of Marian devotion,[10] it is possible however to observe a further development, i.e. the existence of clear albeit fragmentary signals of a doctrinal 'relaxation' that was destined to have long-term consequences.

Indeed, considering that even the constantly watchful Inquisitor of Modena, Brother Arcangelo Calbetti, chose to downplay his collaborators' alarmed warnings regarding the attribution of beatifying and sanctifying powers to the figure of the Blessed Virgin contained in the well-known *Rosario della Madonna* by Capoleone Ghelfucci,[11] we can hardly be surprised by the

---

[10] On which cf. the essay by Mario Rosa, 'Pietà mariana e devozione del Rosario nell'Italia del Cinque e Seicento'; on the Marian cult, see also P. Scaramella, *Le Madonne del Purgatorio. Iconografia e religione in Campania tra rinascimento e controriforma*, Genoa, Marietti, 1991.

[11] Calbetti, describing the case in question to the Secretary of the Congregation of the Index, Paolo Pico, expressed himself in the following terms: 'My only reason for writing to you in Rome was that certain God-fearing persons who are guided by their scruples told me it would be right to have this book revised because it contained certain things that might offend a Christian reader; but when I tried to find them, all they could tell me was that they concerned two points in the first canto. These were, in the first canto, when discussing the mystery of the Incarnation he pretends poetically that the Everlasting Father, wishing to achieve the Incarnation of the Word, first asks the Senate and the Consistory of Angels for advice, because in the 29th stanza He says: "Courage my daughter, courage, unfold your wings, and spread / your wingèd path / through the everlasting air; / and from all Heaven bring the general Senate all together in one place for *consultation*", which (according to the above-said persons) is contradictory to God's infinite wisdom; and in the same canto, when the Senate has assembled, He appears to ask the Angels for their consent to work this Incarnation [...]. They also declared to me that they disliked those words expressed in such absolute terms in canto 3 stanza 58 and in canto 4 stanza 11, in which he attributes to the Blessed Virgin the power of beatification and sanctification; in the first he says: "You are blessed, *and you can / with your blessedness bless whom you wish*", while in the second he says: "Lo! As soon as your greeting / brought to my ears the vital air [in the 1603 edition that I consulted the term used to describe the air was not vital but vocal] / for my sweet child enjoyed this, and while / *you make Him a Saint*, He exulted in Your belly" [...]. When I heard these reasonings, I began to revise the book, but having discovered nothing important I gave it up, because (so it seems to me) the above-said things can be taken in a good and positive sense; and, as for me, I noticed no other mistakes, except for those pointed out by these God-fearing people who acted in all good zeal; that is what I can tell you' ('Non per altro vi scrissi a Roma per il *Rosario* del Ghelfucci, se non perché alcune persone scrupolose, e timorate mi dissero che sarebbe stato bene a far riveder detto libro, perché v'erano alcune cose, che havrebbono potuto offendere il christiano lettore; e ricercando io quali fussero, non mi seppero dir altro se non due luoghi nel primo canto, e son questi: che nel primo canto suddetto ragionando del mistero dell'incarnatione finge poeticamente che il Padre eterno volendo far l'incarnation del Verbo, prima ne dimandasse consiglio al Senato e concistoro degli Angioli, perché dice così nella stanza 29: "Su figlia su, movi le piume, e stendi / per l'aure eterne il tuo camino alato; / da tutto '1 Cielo a *consultar* mi rendi / tutto in un punto il general

easy-going attitude shown by Anastasio Bresciano, a monk from Cassina, and of Friar Raffaello Riva, 'a Venetian of the Order of Preachers' (*venetiano dell'ordine de' predicatori*), to the statements in the *Discorsi Spirituali* by Canon Angelo Gaucci.[12] Both censors had prefaced their notes with words of praise for the work that they were about to correct. Bresciano's gloss contained the following remarks: 'In my opinion, in order both to cast great light and to urge souls toward virtue – and not only those of simple folk owing to its being in the vulgar tongue but also of all ranks of persons – and also for the reasons given below, it merits admission and approval',[13] and Riva echoed him as follows: 'Everyone and in particular simple folk can derive from this reading consolation and spiritual benefit'.[14] It was therefore clear, from the very first moment, that the attitude of the two censors to the author and the text was benevolent: each of the critical remarks they made was followed by a comment that tempered its polemic impact. Immediately after underlining

---

Senato", il che (dicevano i sopradetti) ripugna alla infinita sapienza di Dio. E nel medesimo canto, congregato poi il soprascritto senato, par che finga che ne domandi il consentimento a gli Angioli per far quest'incarnatione [...] M'accennarono anchora che dispiacevano quelle parole così assolutamente poste nel Canto 3 stanze 58 et nel canto 4 stanza 11, nelle quali attribuisce il beatificare e santificare alla beata Vergine; e nel primo luogo dice così: "letto d'honore, e sei beata, e *puoi / di tua beatila bear chi vuoi*', nel secondo dice": "Ecco che a pena il tuo saluto in tutto / porta all'orecchie mie l'aura vitale [nell'edizione del 1603 da me consultata 'l'aura' è 'vocale' / che il dolce infante mio gioinne, e mentre / *tu lo fai santo,* ei n'essultò nel ventre" [...] Sentendo io questi motivi cominciai a rivedere il libro, ma poiché non scopersi cosa di rilievo tralasciai, poiché (per quanto par a me) le soprascritte cose si possono prendere in buon senso; et quanto a me, non ho altri errori notati, se non queste cose che mi furono accennate da queste persone timorate che si movevano per buon zelo; questo è quanto posso dirle'; letter from Modena, 10 April 1604, in ACDF, Index, Protocolli N, cc. 475r–v and 487r). The full title of Ghelfucci's work was: *Il Rosario della Madonna Poema Eroico del sig. Capoleone Ghelfucci da Città di Castello, dato alle stampe dai figliuoli dopo la morte dell'Autore. A divotione dell'Illustrissimo Signor Cintio Aldobrandini Cardinale di San Giorgio. Agiuntovi nuovamente gli Argumenti a ciascun Canto.* Con privilegio. In Venetia, appresso Nicolò Polo, 1603.

12 'Censura della prima parte delli Discorsi spirituali di messer Angelo Gaucci Canonico di Macerata stampata in Macerata 1596 fatta per Anastasio di Brescia monaco cassinense' ('Censure of the first part of the Spiritual Discourses of Messer Angelo Gaucci, Canon of Macerata, printed at Macerata 1596, done for Anastasio di Brescia, monk of Cassino'; ACDF, Index, Protocolli O, cc. 226r–228r); and 'Giudicio sopra la prima parte de discorsi di M. Angelo Gaucci, canonico di Macerata, stampati nella medesima Città l'anno 1596 di Fr. Rafaello Riva Venetiano de Predicatori' ('Judgment of the first part of the discourses of Messer Angelo Gaucci, Canon of Macerata, printed in the same City, year 1596, by Brother Rafaello Riva Venetiano de Predicatori'; ibid., cc. 230r–232v).

13 'Giudico che sia per apportar gran lume, et anco mover le anime alla virtù non solo de semplici per esser l'opera volgare, ma anco d'ogni conditione di persona, et che per ciò con le infrascritte osservationi sia degna d'essere admessa et approvata' (ibid., c. 226r).

14 'Ogn'uno e particolarmente il semplice può cavare da questa lettione consolatione e utilità spirituale' (ibid., c. 230r).

three of Gaucci's 'propositions' (*propositioni*) regarding the fanciful legend of the 'Holy House of Loreto' – 'propositions' which, as the censor himself recognized, possessed 'the weakest of foundations' (*debolissimi fondamenti*) – the monk from Cassino for example hastened to justify the author, pointing out that 'it is indeed true that these propositions are not absolutely as true as the author may say but are proposed and confirmed only by simple and private contemplation'.[15] In the same way the second censor first reacted disdainfully to Gaucci's ill treatment of the miracle of Christ's sacred blood – 'With these three drops of blood, it seems to me that one is too much tied to his long and yet not ungrateful simile, because if we wish to avoid a multiplication of miracles, it is advisable that a greater number than three drops of blood should be part of the matter that forms the body of Our Lord'[16] – and then he made a point of offering an interpretation that justified his affirmations.[17] The signal that thus reached the authorities in Rome from the outlying areas was one that indicated a re-evaluation of the potential danger of superstitious and miracle-working elements, if not indeed an invitation to accept them benevolently. It is difficult to imagine the reaction in Rome of the consultors and the cardinals to a message of the sort: the lack of specific documentation on the subject suggests that the vast backlog of work they had to cope with prevented them from ever viewing the text of the censures. However, some indications as to the reactions of Rome and to the position it took up can be obtained thanks to another case that was dealt with in those years, a case that was similar both in its general contents and in its specific themes; it is also better documented than the previous work. The document we are referring to is 'Nota delle cose che sono parse degne di censura nel libro intitolato Giglio Angelico di Francesco Cortese minore osservante' ('Note of points appearing to require censure in the book entitled Giglio Angelico di Francesco Cortese, Minor Observant'), the author of which was the well-known Inquisitor of Genoa, Eliseo Masini.[18] Masini's remarks on

15 'ben è vero che queste propositioni non sono assolutamente come vere dette dall'Authore, ma proposte et confermate solo come semplici et private contemplationi' (ibid., c. 230v).

16 'Con le tre goccioline di sangue, parmi troppo si sii ubligato a quella sua lunga e peraltro non ingrata similitudine, perché se non vogliamo multiplicare miracoli, conviene che maggior numero di tre goccie di sangue concorresse come materia della formatione del corpo di N.S' (ibid., c. 230v).

17 'This matter of the three drops of blood is something quite new, as the author himself appeared to have noticed when on the next page […] he says that blood was one of the things that contributed to the making of a savior of the world' ('Il perché par nuovo questo di tre goccioline, il che forse meglio considerò lo stesso auttore, quando nella seguente carta[…] disse che il sangue era di quelle cose che concorrevano a far un salvatore del mondo'; ibid.).

18 ACDF, Index, Protocolli Z, cc. 85r–86v. The complete title of the work is *Giglio Angelico esposto con alti sensi in sette Lettioni, ne sette Sabbati di Quaresima. Con una*

censorship showed his doctrinal and philological sensibility. 'At page 39'he noted, 'he says that the Virgin generated with God; although he subsequently clarifies his thought, at first sight such words offend the ear.'[19] Immediately afterwards, on the same wavelength, he noted: 'At page 40, he attributes to the Virgin knowledge of all visible and invisible creatures, and says that she has known all the species, and the virtues of the stars, of the Heavens, of the elements, and of all things.'[20] But the Inquisitor of Genoa was not alarmed only by the doctrinal ambiguity of these statements. In the entire work – the censor maintained, providing an abundance of details – Cortese 'makes the Holy Writ mean whatever he likes, twisting its authority as he pleases, and the concepts expressed are for the most part worthless'.[21] However, faced with a statement like this, coming from the pen of a respected and authoritative Inquisitor, the Congregation of the Index had the whole matter hushed up and dismissed Masini's remarks as 'matters of no moment' (*parvi momenti*), putting an end to all possible discussion with a sharp *liber utilis permittatur* ('useful book, permitted').[22]

It is, therefore, no surprise to discover that these signs of doctrinal relaxation and this widening of the censors' restrictions were accompanied by a progressive cheapening of the quality of the actual act of censorship. The cardinals who were members of the Index spent all their energy on discussions regarding the utility of unimportant adverbial expressions, devoting days on end to the production of lexical and grammatical declarations of little account. The censures of the Latin version of one of the most popular texts among the clergy (but also among lay folk) such as Antonio Rampegolo's *Figure della Bibbia* – censures and comments that were later inserted into the only expurgatory Index published in the course of the century, i.e. that edited by Giovanni Maria Guanzelli da Brisighella[23] – offer in this sense a significant

breve inventione, e morale dichiaratione del Vangelo corrente nelle seconde parti. Lette nel MDCVIII con maggiori misteri a Padova, da Fra Francesco Cortese da Montefalco, Teologo, e Predicatore Generale de Menori osservanti. Con tre tavole dell'Autori citati. Dell'autorità da quali sono cavati i concetti. E delle cose più notabili. With privilege, in Venice in the Sign of Hope, 1608, With licence of the superiors. On Eliseo Masini, see A. Errera, *Processus in causa fidei*, pp. 263–9 and J. Tedeschi, *The Prosecution of Heresy, ad indicem.*

19 'A car. 39 dice, che la Vergine generò con Iddio; et se ben poi si dichiara, tutta via simili parole a primo scontro offendono l'orecchie' (ACDF, Index, Protocolli Z, c. 85r).

20 'A car. 40, attribuisce alla Vergine la cognitione di tutte le creature visibili, et invisibili, et dice, ch'ella ha conosciuto tutte le specie, le virtù delle stelle, de' Cieli, de gli elementi, et di tutte le cose' (ibid.).

21 'fa dire a suo modo la Divina scrittura torcendo le autorità di essa come a lui pare et i concetti per lo più sono di cartocci' (ibid., c. 86v).

22 ACDF, Index, Protocolli S, c. 96v.

23 *Indicis librorum expurgandorum in studiosorum gratiam confecti. Tomus primus. In quo quinquaginta auctorum libri prae caeteris desiderati emendantur. Ver Fr. Io. Mariam Brasichellense Sacri Palatii Apostolici Magistrum in unum corpus redactus, et publicae*

testimony. Dealing as it does with a collection of writings from the Scriptures, i.e. with a compendium of edifying episodes taken from the Old and the New Testaments, the version in the vernacular turned out to be, in the rigid regime imposed by the Clementine *Observatio*, one of the texts most often reported by the local authorities in the lists of impounded books sent to Rome at the end of the century.[24] Therefore, while the vernacular version was destined to disappear from the editorial market, the Latin version, was condemned, *quamdiu corrigetur*, in the 1596 Index[25] and subjected to minute expurgation. In many cases it was a question of replacing a simple and harmless noun with another that was linguistically or grammatically more appropriate, without altering in the slightest way the overall meaning of the sentence where it was to be found. Thus, the word *latriam* was replaced by *idolatriam*: 'Noun *Avaritia* (Greed). *Simulachra gentium, argentum, et aurum,* Paulo infra initium, fol 63, habetur, *Diabolus cognoscens humanum appetitum esse pronum ad simulachra, et ideo latriam*, corrected thus: *Diabolus cognoscens humanum appetitum esse pronum ad simulachra et idolatriam*';[26] or the adjective *clarissimi* became *charissimi*: 'Word, eodem. *Qui de terra est de terra loquitur,*

---

commoditati aeditus. Rome, Ex Typographia R Cam. Apost. 1607, superiorum permissu, ff. 26–36. On the vicissitudes leading up to the publication of this expurgatory Index, see also the peculiar episode that led to its immediate suspension, cf. G. FRAGNITO, 'In questo vasto mare de libri prohibiti', p. 31.

24 ACDF, Index, XVIII (vol. unico), c. 38v, 'Index librorum [...] Curiae Archiepiscopensis Neapolitanae' ('Index of books [...] in the Archbishop's Curia in Naples'); ibid., c. 40r, 'In biblioteca Hectoris Soldanelli quod dicitur della gatta' ('In the library of Ettore Soldanelli, commonly called *della gatta ['the she-cat's*'); ibid., c. 40r, 'Bibliotheca Iosephi Pelusi' ('In the library of Giuseppe Peluso'); ibid., c. 44r, 'Libri prohibiti e sospesi, mandati dal vescovo di Lucca alli 8 di ottobre' ('Prohibited and suspended books sent by the Bishop of Lucca on 8 October'); ibid., c. 48r, 'Lista di libri prohibiti et sospesi che si trovano nell'Inquisition di Ancona' ('List of prohibited and suspended books to be found in the Inquisition of Ancona'); ibid., c. 55r (List lacking indication of origin); ibid., c. 59r, 'Cathalogus librorum partim damnatorum, partim expurgandorum in cavitate Parmae repertorum, et ad novi Indicis publicationem S.to officio praesentatorum' ('Catalog of books to be either condemned or expurgated which can be found in the city of Parma and were surrendered to the Holy Office following the publication of the new Index'), note from the Inquisitor of Parma received in Rome on 10 September, cf. ibid., c. 60v; ibid., c. 65v, 'Libri prohibiti et suspecti qui reperiuntur in Sancto Officio Inquisitionis Bononiae' ('Prohibited and suspended books found in the Holy Office of the Inquisition of Bologna'), sent on 6 September, cf. ibid., c. 68v; ibid., cc. 68v and 70r, 'Index librorum prohibitorum qui reperiuntur penes librarios Bononiae' ('Index of prohibited books found at booksellers in Bologna'); ibid., c. 75r, Inquisitionis Genoae' ('Inquisition of Genoa'); ibid., c. 77r, 'Index librorum suspensorum et Prohibitorum, qui sub facilitate Inquisitionis Florentiae inveniuntur' ('Index of suspended and prohibited books that were found in the Inquisition of Florence').

25 *Index des livres interdits*, vol. IX, p. 463.

26 The difference between the two similar words (latria and idolatria, i.e. greed and idolatry) is hard to render in English: 'Noun, Greed. *Images of progeny, of silver, and of gold.* Just after the beginning, at page 63, we read: *The Devil knows that man has an appetite for*

quae est figura O, in fine habetur, *si consideremus fratres clarissimi*, legatur, *fratres charissimi*;'[27] the grammatically incorrect *peccarum* was changed to *peccatorum*: 'Noun, Beatitude. *Qui biberit ex hac acqua*, quae est figura B, in fine habetur *ex gratiae largitale peccarum*, corrigatur, *ex gratiae largitale peccatorum*';[28] and again, the insertion of *venit* was clearly functional to a more fluent reading of the phrase without however modifying its contents by as much as a comma: 'Word, eodem. *Inebriabuntur ab ubertate*, quae est figura C, fol. 80, habetur paulo infra initium folii, *quia tertio anno Imperii sui, primus annus fuit*, legatur, *quia tertio anno Imperii sui venit, primus annus fuit*'.[29] It is not my desire to bore the reader with repeated citations and it will be sufficient here to point out how the censors, maniacally caught up in this work of minute and fruitless rewriting, often ended up reproposing – after announcing yet another act of linguistic precision – exactly the same expression that it was their purpose to correct: 'Word, eodem [Avaritia], fol. 67. *Aquae multae, populi multi*, quae est figura N, circa medium, habetur, *percipiet quantum anima in eisdem erat sterilis, et fine bono*, corrigatur, *percipiet quantum anima in eisdem erat sterilis, et fine bono*',[30] thus running the risk of confounding their role as censors with the much humbler one of proofreader: 'Verbo eodem, fol. 80 – they noted among their papers – legitur, *observavit igitur, quod veniret temporis plenitudo, etc. et fugaret peccati emendam*, corrigatur, *et fugater peccati mendam*'.[31] These are just a few short examples that do not exhaust the overall meaning and value of the censures published by Brisighella at the beginning of the seventeenth century; they are, however, significant examples that provide a measure of a kind of Church censorship which –

images and for adulation, to be corrected thus: *The Devil knows that man has an appetite for images and for idolatry*' (*Indicis librorum expurgandorum*, c. 28).

27 'Same word. *Whoever is of the earth speaks of the earth*, which corresponds to the allegory O, at the end we have: [...] very famous brothers, to be corrected: very dear brothers' (ibid.).

28 'Word, Beatitude: *Whoever drinks of this water*, which corresponds to allegory B, at the end we read: *ex gratiae largitale peccarum*, to be amended: *ex gratiae largitale peccatorum*' (Ibid., c. 28–29).

29 'Same word, They will be inebriated by the great abundance, which is allegory C, page 80 just after the beginning of the page, we read: *since in the third year of his reign, it was the first year*, to be corrected thus: *since it came in the third year of his reign, it was the first year*'; ibid., cc. 29.

30 'Same word [greed], page 67. Many waters, many peoples, which is allegory N, about halfway, we read: let it be perceived how sterile the soul was, and to good purpose, to be emended: let it be perceived how sterile the soul was, and to good purpose'; ibid., c. 28.

31 The difference of meaning between *menda* and *emenda* is might be rendered in English as follows: 'Same word, page 80 – they noted among their papers – we read, he therefore watched for the fullness of time to come etc. and for the error of sin to be mended, to be corrected thus: and for the error of sin to be amended'; ibid., c. 29.

ever more lost among contingent meanings and linguistic interpretations of individual words and single adjectives – risked losing sight of its intention to keep superstitious devotion in check and of the rigorous definition of the doctrinal and theological boundaries of Catholic orthodoxy.

It was no coincidence that in the early 1600s the editorial market for devotional publications saw the success of texts like *Rosario della Beata Vergine* ('The Blessed Virgin's Rosary') by Archangelo Caraccia, or *Trattato dell'angelo custode* ('The Guardian Angel's Treatise') by the Jesuit Francesco Albertini. First printed in 1614 and republished more than ten years later, in 1627, Caraccia's work demonstrated how popular the Marian Rosary had become among the common masses.[32] The fact was that, reading Caraccia, one came across statements which for nearly half a century the censorship authorities had been endeavoring – as we have seen – to eliminate: 'Whoever carries the blessed Rosary on his person gains two hundred years, and two hundred and forty quarantines of indulgences. Much it does against Demons, as will be said in Part Four'.[33] It may also be that the Company of the Most Holy Rosary was in fact authorized to grant precisely these indulgences which it promised to its faithful followers,[34] but this was not the point. What is remarkable is the

32 *Rosario della Beata Vergine, con l'indulgenze e privileggi concessi alla Compagnia. Raccolto dal P. Maestro F. Argangelo Caraccia da Rivalla, dell'Ordine de' Predicatori. Di nuovo ristampato con la Gionta d'alcune divote considerazioni fatte dall'Autore*. In Rome, for Guglielmo Facciotti 1627. Licensed by the Superiors. We cite from the second edition of the work – an edition which according to the author was more reliable and closer to the real original intentions because it had been 'purged of certain things that had been added to it [in the first edition] without his knowledge' (ibid., f. 2r). On this text see the observations of Mario Rosa, who placed it in the context of the evolution of the rich genre of Marian Piety in the latter part of the sixteenth century and the early part of the seventeenth (M. Rosa, 'Pietà mariana', pp. 228–31).

33 'Chi porta il Rosario benedetto adosso guadagna duecento anni, e ducente quarantene d'Indulgenza. Molto vale contra i Demoni, come si dirà nella Quarta Parte' (*Rosario della Beata Vergine*, p. 89).

34 'Whoever attends the Salve Regina which is sung on Saturday evenings, and on festivities at the Altar of the Most Holy Rosary, will have forty days' indulgence. Whoever says, or causes others to say, or hears the Mass of the Most Holy Rosary gains all the indulgences that are gained by reciting the whole Rosary. Every day, visiting the Altar of the Most Holy Rosary and praying for the exaltation of the Holy Faith will gain one hundred days' indulgence. Whoever accompanies the Procession, one hundred days. Whoever accompanies the Standard when it is carried for the Dead, one hundred days' ('Chi sta presente alla Salve Regina, che si canta la sera de' Sabbati, e giorni festivi all'Altare del Santissimo Rosario, ha 40 giorni d'indulgenza. Chi dice, fa dire, et ode la messa del Santissimo Rosario, guadagna tutte l'Indulgenze, che si guadagnano in dire tutto il Rosario. Ogni giorno visitando l'Altare del Santissimo Rosario, pregando per l'essaltatione della Santa fede, si guadagnano cento giorni d'Indulgenza. Chi accompagna la Processione, cento giorni. Chi accompagna il Stendardo quando si porta alli Morti, cento giorni'; ibid., p. 89).

miracle-working culture within which these indulgences were presented to the faithful, as for instance the invitation frequently repeated to the reader to carry with him 'the blessed Rosary round his neck' (*il Rosario benedetto al collo*),[35] votive images of our Lady,[36] or even 'oil of the lamp' (*l'oglio della lampada*),[37] i.e. the same magic-superstitious ritual and sacramental armamentarium used by the *donnicciole* ('rough women of the people') that for some time the Inquisitors had been putting on trial on charges of *maleficii* ('laying on curses') and *strigarie* ('witchcraft').[38] This amounted to offering forms of devotion that gave the reader no real way out other than a harsh choice between, on the one hand, the miracle-working virtues promised to faithful adherents of the Company,[39] and, on the other, the threats of the cruelest of punishments for its opponents.[40] In other words, it was a proposal that was perfectly suited to the sectarian mentality and exclusivistic needs of those who employed Catholic rites and practices for magic and superstitious ends.

---

[35] 'Miracle VII', dedicated to 'some persons freed from the Demon by the Blessed Rosary', spoke 'of a man much troubled by the Demon' who 'when wearing the Blessed Rosary round his neck was not troubled but when he took it off he was immediately afflicted again' ('d'un huomo molto travagliato dal demonio» il quale «mentre, che haveva il Rosario benedetto al collo, non era travagliato, e come lo levava, subito era tormentato'; *Rosario della Beata Vergine*, p. 160); but cf. also 'Miracle XI,' ibid., p. 164.

[36] Cf. 'Miracle XVIII', entitled 'Many freed from the plague thanks to the Rosary', where it was possible to read: 'In the year 1494, in the city of Lisbon, there was a great pestilence, and Father Master Alano tells of a woman who on the point of death recommended her soul to Our Lady of the Rosary, holding in her arms an Image of the Blessed Virgin. She fell asleep, and soon afterward awoke safe and sound. This was on 24th August' ('L'Anno 1494 nella città di Lisbona [ci] fu una gran pestilenza, et il Padre Maestro Alano narra di una Donna, che già si moriva, si raccomandò alla Madonna del Rosario, tenendo nelle sue braccia un'Imagine della Beata Vergine. Si addormentò, e poco dopo si svegliò sana e salva. Fu questo alli 24 di Agosto'; ibid., p. 172).

[37] 'In the same city [...] another woman was about to die, her soul was recommended by her husband to Our Lady and he anointed the sore with oil from the lamp of the Rosary and immediately she was healed' ('Nella medesima città [...] un'altra Donna [che] stava per spirare, fu raccomandata dal Marito alla Madonna del Rosario et unse la piaga con l'oglio della lampada del Rosarioe subito restò sana'; ibid., p. 172).

[38] On these topics, in addition to the cited essay by M.P. Fantini, 'L'orazione di Santa Marta',see also G. Romeo, *Inquisitori, esorcisti e streghe nell'Italia della Controriforma* Florence, Sansoni, 1990.

[39] The reader was skillfully attracted by the promise of 'benefits' which could even reach the point of altering the inevitable fate of death; cf. for example 'Miracle XVI', ibid., pp. 169–70.

[40] The figure of the Blessed Virgin that was presented to the faithful was one of a vindictive person who was cruel to anyone who dared to oppose her will; see, for example, the 'grave infirmity, which caused great pain' (*la grave infirmità, che dava grandissima pena*) that was inflicted upon anyone who refused to be carried away by the fascinating power of the 'Most Sacred' Rosary, 'Miracle II', ibid., pp. 141–3.

Published just two years before, in 1612, *Trattato dell'angelo custode* by the Jesuit Albertini presented a number of analogies with Caraccia's text.[41] The angel here replaced the Rosary as the provider of 'bodily benefits and worldly goods' (*benefici nel corpo e ne beni temporali*) while, in a language that seemed to draw its inspiration from the numerous versions of *incantationes ad amorem* which then circulated, Albertini promised consolation and solutions for everyone: for 'those who wished to get married, [for whom] the Guardian Angel will find the good and faithful companion of their life',[42] for those who are 'locked up in prison' (*restretto in carcere*),[43] for weary travelers,[44] for the sick, and for those possessed by the devil.[45] The Jesuit did not limit himself to breaching the Clementine ban on publishing litanies other than those officially listed in the 1601 decree,[46] and he also risked going beyond the limits of doctrinal orthodoxy by attempting to calculate the speed of angels and by advancing some rather unlikely explanations concerning the gift of ubiquity traditionally attributed to the Angels in the Holy Scriptures and in the writings of the Fathers of the Church:

> the swiftness of movement of the Angels passes our imagination, so that we who admire the rapidity of the flight of a Hawk, of the leap of a Pard, of the swimming of a Dolphin, the flight of an arrow, and the fall of a thunderbolt

---

41 *Trattato dell'angelo custode del R.P. Francesco Albertino da Catanzaro della Compagnia di Giesù. Con l'Offitio dell'angelo custode, approvato da N.S. Papa Paolo Quinto. Et un altro trattato utilissimo alla devotione verso la Beatissima Vergine. Fatto da un Sacerdote Napolitano Dottore in Teologia* ('Treatise of the Guardian Angel by Reverend Father Francesco Albertino of Catanzaro of the Company of Jesus. With the Office of the Guardian Angel, approved by Our Lord Pope Paul V. Together with another most useful treatise for devotion to the Most Blessed Virgin. By a Neapolitan Priest and Doctor of Theology'), Ad istanza del Signor Gioseppe Scotto. In Roma, per Guglielmo Facciotti, 1612. Con licenza de' superiori. Si vendono alla bottega di Nicolò de Ludi. All'arco di Camiliano. Con Privilegio. Regarding this treatise, cf. L. Fiorani, 'Astrologi, superstiziosi e devoti nella società romana del Seicento', *Ricerche per la storia religiosa di Roma. Studi, documenti, inventari*, 2 (1978), Rome, Edizioni di storia e letteratura, pp. 147–50. Regarding Albertini, see C. Sommervogel, *Bibliothèque de la Compagnie de Jesus*, I, Brussels-Paris, tome. I, 1891, coll. 127–8.

42 'quelli che vogliono accasarsi, [a cui] l'Angelo custode trova chi habbia ad essere della sua vita buono, e fedel compagno' (*Trattato dell'angelo custode*, p. 169).

43 Alberini presented the Angel as a kind of benevolent prison guard who was ready to turn a blind eye on the guilty but penitent prisoner he was in charge of; ibid., p. 173.

44 'If you happen to be traveling and are beset by dangers, turn to the Angel' ('Se vi ritrovate in viaggio, assaliti da pericoli, ricorrete all'Angelo'; ibid.).

45 'For three days, setting aside all pleasures, you must attend to your prayers together with your wife, and in this way you will be freed from danger and from the hands of the demon' ('Per tre giorni, lasciando da parte i diletti, hai da attendere all'oratione insieme con tua moglie, et in questo modo restarete dal pericolo, e dalle mani del demonio liberati'; ibid., pp. 170–72).

46 L. Fiorani, *Astrologi, superstiziosi e devoti*, p. 149 and footnote 117.

> admit defeat when we consider a single revolution of the Firmament, which in an hour, some say, advances as far as a man who travels every day forty miles could journey if he walked continuously for two thousand nine hundred and four years; or, according to others, as far as it would take to surround all the earth from East to West [...] for us, who as I say are fearful when we hear of such movements, greatly exceeded by the speed of Angels, no example or similitude remains that can help us to conceive of the speed of the movement with which an Angel descends from Empyreal Heaven, from a distance that is little less than infinite, to succor us.[47]

Only thanks to their 'swiftness' (*prestezza*) – Albertini continued without the slightest hesitation – 'can the Angels be present everywhere; for verily so great is the swiftness of their movement that although they cannot be in the same instant in more than one place, they can however in fact be present in a very short space of time in all parts of the world'.[48] This conclusion reached by his fanciful reconstruction was the most symptomatic testimony of a devotionalism that was now beginning to find it difficult to remain within the doctrinal bounds of the past.

These were not isolated, marginal editorial cases. Nor were they texts that were extraneous to the devotional panorama of the age.[49] They were symptomatic expressions of a pedagogic trend in religion whose main object was the conquest of the masses of believers by proposing and providing an image of the sacred that could satisfy their most instinctive and concrete daily demands much better than strict observation of the rigorous canons of theological correctness and doctrinal purity. Therefore, statements which were extravagant from the religious point of view and misleading from that of doctrine, and which were very similar to the most widespread 'superstitious' expressions and practices of the time, were not the fruit of

---

47 'Avanza tutte le nostre imaginationi la prestezza dell'Angelico moto, si che a noi, che ammiriamo la velocità del volo d'un Falcone, del salto d'un Pardo, del nuoto d'un Delfino, il corso d'una frezza, la caduta d'un fulmine; a noi, che ci rendiamo per vinti nel considerare un giro solo del Firmamento, ch'in un hora, dicono alcuni, camina tanto, quanto viaggio farebbe un huomo, se facendo ogni giorno quaranta miglia, continuamente caminasse per dua mila nove cento, e quattro anni; o secondo altri tanto, quanto ci vorrebbe a circondar tutta la terra dall'Oriente fino all'Occidente [...] a noi dico che restiamo spaventati udendo ragionar di così fatti movimenti, i quali sono di gran lunga avanzati dall'Angelica velocità; non resta essempio, o similitudine alcuna, che ci possa aiutare a concepire la fretta di quel moto, con che un Angelo discende dal Cielo Empireo, di lontananza poco meno che infinita, per nostro aiuto' (*Trattato dell'angelo custode*, pp. 104–5).

48 'gli Angioli sono presenti in ogni luogo; perché invero tanto grande è la prestezza de' movimenti loro, che se bene non possono in un medesimo istante ritrovarsi in più d'un luogo, possono tuttavia in brevissimo spatio di tempo a tutte quante le parti del mondo esser realmente presenti' (ibid., pp. 105–6).

49 Cf. the considerations of L. Fiorani, 'Astrologi, superstiziosi e devoti', and see also below, the emblematic case of Niccolò Riccardi, the Master of the Sacred Palace.

the personal inventiveness of some disrespectful writer or preacher but the result of the political and religious action of the Church hierarchies, which seemed to have totally given up combating all forms of superstition.

It was clear that a fracture that was hard to recompose had occurred between the Tridentine project of rules and regulations, on the one hand, and the reality of what was proposed by Counter-Reformation devotion, on the other – between the mass of repressive censorship measures, which from the late 1560s had regularly accompanied the policy of resisting any superstitious and pagan infiltrations that corrupted the texts and rites of Catholic religious belief, and a cultural and religious practice that in both the short and the medium term answered needs of a decisively different order.

It was a fracture between rules and reality that a Venetian Servite, Paolo Sarpi, was soon to describe, lucidly and precisely, following the example of the attentive considerations published a few years before by an English writer named Edwin Sandys. First published anonymously in English in London in 1605,[50] *A Relation of the state of Religion* by Sandys appeared in Geneva in Italian twenty years later, in 1625.[51] The promoter of this initiative was Paolo Sarpi, who – captivated by Sandys' irenic inspiration – decided to expand the text himself with a series of significant additions. [52] In particular, Sarpi carried out an in-depth study of what he considered to be one of the English author's most felicitous intuitions: as an acute observer of the Italian religious scene, Sandys had noticed an irreparable breach between Catholic doctrine as taught in the 'schools' (theory) and the religious exercise of the faithful (practice): 'This religion', he wrote, 'seemeth notwithstanding at this day, not so corrupt in

[50] *A Relation of the state of religion: and with what Hopes and Policies it hath beene framed, and is maintained in the severall states of these western parts of the world*, London, Printed for Simon Waterson dwelling in Paules Churchyard at the signe of the Crowne, 1605. In actual fact it was written some years before, on the occasion of the author's visit to Italy in 1599; the work was published in England without his knowledge. Regarding this work and its vicissitudes, see G. Cozzi, 'Sir Edwin Sandys e la "Relazione dello Stato della Religione"', *Rivista Storica italiana*, LXXIX (1967), pp. 1095–1121.

[51] *Relazione dello stato della Religione, e con quali dissegni et arti ella è stata fabricata e maneggiata in diversi stati di queste occidentali parti del mondo*, in Paolo Sarpi, *Lettere a Gallicani e Protestanti, Relazione dello Stato della Religione, Trattato delle materie beneficiarie*, Gaetano and Luisa Cozzi (eds), Turin, Einaudi, 1978 (this edition 'contains a precise reproduction of part of volume 35, tome I, of the series "La letteratura italiana, Storia e testi"', Riccardo Ricciardi editore, Milan-Naples, published in 1969), pp. 51–88.

[52] Regarding Paolo Sarpi, in addition to Gaetano Cozzi's studies, see V. Frajese, *Sarpi scettico. Stato e Chiesa a Venezia tra Cinque e Seicento*, Bologna, Il Mulino, 1994, and the bibliography cited therein; also of fundamental importance is Corrado Vivanti's introduction to his edition of *Istoria del Concilio tridentino* by Paolo Sarpi, as also *Vita del padre Paolo* by Fulgenzio Micanzio, Turin, Einaudi, 1974, and the introduction by the same author to Paolo Sarpi's *Opere*, C. Vivanti (ed.), Rome, Istituto poligrafico e Zecca dello Stato, 2000.

the very doctrine and in their Schooles [...] as it is in the practise thereof, and in the usage among themselves'.[53] Rereading these pages some years after they were originally written, Sarpi must have realized that Sandys' simple but effective observation was even more apposite than it had been at the turn of the century. All he had to do was to pick up the threads of the discourse where Sandys had left off. In the opinion of the Venetian Servite – in line with his characteristic approach in matters concerning jurisdiction – the causes of this irreparable breach lay in the usurpation of temporal power by the Roman pontiffs in medieval times.[54] However, over and above the massive attack on the papacy, it was Sarpi's lucid observation of daily religious practice – constantly compared with the official rules and regulations of the Church – that enabled him to pronounce his withering diagnosis. From the topic of prayer to the delicate question of indulgences, the verdict was always the same: in theory, doctrinal rigor and inwardness but, in practice, superficiality and outwardness: '*In the schools* it is conceded that prayer pleases God, only if the heart is all attentive: and *in practice* prayers, both public and private, are recited with the voice alone and people are convinced that in this way they have satisfied their debt'.[55] His considerations on the concession of indulgences were analogous:

> *In the schools* they say that indulgences are worthless, if the person dispensing them does so with excessive prodigality, or when the cause is not right and proper, or when the person seeking them is not in a state of grace with God. *In practice* things are quite the opposite – it would go against religion to say that there is no value in plenary indulgence, with liberation of the soul from Purgatory, granted to those who wear, and kiss, and keep a medal, or else granted to obtain money or some favor from some gentleman or some lady.[56]

53 E. Sandys, *A Relation of the state of religion*, p. A3v.

54 P. Sarpi, *Relazione*, pp. 55–6.

55 '*Nelle scuole* non si concede che l'orazione sia grata a Dio, se non con l'attenzione del cuore: et *in prattica* le orazioni così publiche, come private si recitano con la voce solamente, e le persone si tengono così d'aver sodisfatto al lor debito' (ibid., p. 56).

56 '*Nelle scuole* si dice che le indulgenzie non vagliono, quando chi le dispensa usi in ciò troppa prodigalità, o che la causa non sia pia, o chi le vuol ricevere non si truovi in grazia di Dio. *Nella prattica* tutto il contrario, sarebbe impietà a dire che non fosse valida una indulgenza plenaria, e con liberazione d'anime del purgatorio, concessa a chi porterà, baderà, guarderà una medaglia, concessa per cavar denari, o per favorire qualche signore overo qualche dama' (ibid.). Sarpi returned to the practice of indulgences later on in a number of subtly ironic pages: 'Nevertheless many contradictions remain even in the present expressions. I have seen a medal blessed by the Pope, with a printed record of its virtues, among which I noticed two in particular, the first saying that whoever said seven Lord's Prayers and seven Hail Maries, for the conversion of the Philippine Islands, would save a soul from Purgatory, while the second said that whoever recited five Lord's Prayers and five Hail Maries, for the exaltation of the Church and the preservation of the Pope, would likewise save a soul from

This gap between the orthodox doctrine of intercession and the superstitious abuse of the religious practice of the faithful appeared to Sarpi even more evident when he began to examine the topic of 'recourse to saints' (*ricorso a' santi*):[57]

> *In the schools* it is permitted to have recourse to the saints, as also to the givers of grace, but only insofar as they intercede with God: *in practice* however they ask for grace directly from them, and indeed there are many who one might think were unable to obtain them from God, but only from the particular saint who performs this office: and consequently they have shared out the power of working miracles, attributing to some the power of curing teeth, to others the neck, to other the breasts, to others fever, and to others the plague [...]. Thus they have split into factions, each exalting its own saint above all others in the various devotions, in competition: for which reason it comes about that modern saints cloud the memory of those of olden times and exclude them from all honors.[58]

Purgatory. And I marveled that anyone could be found who wished to obtain with seven what he could obtain with five' ('Restano nondimeno eziandio nelle formule presenti molte contradizioni. Ho veduto una medaglia benedetta dal papa, col registro stampato delle sue virtù, tra le quali ne osservai due, la prima, chi dirà sette *Pater nostri* e sette *Ave Marie* per la conversione dell'Isole Filippine, caverà un'anima del purgatorio. La seconda, chi dirà cinque *Pater nostri* e cinque *Ave Marie* per la esaltazione della Chiesa e conservazione del papa caverà un'anima del purgatorio. E mi maravigliai come si potesse trovare alcuno che volesse far con sette quello che si poteva far con cinque'; ibid., pp. 71–2).

[57] This was a theme regarding which the author was keen to underline his complete Catholic orthodoxy – thus making his polemic outburst even more forceful: 'One must not deprive saints of the honor and veneration that are their due: but only that part that has been wrongly added contrary to the honor due to God, from whom we must hope to receive only health' ('Non si deve levare a' santi l'onore e la venerazione debita: ma quel solo che per abuso è introdotto contro all'onore debito a Dio, dal quale solo si dee sperare la salute'; ibid., p. 58.)

[58] '*Nelle scuole* si concede il ricorso a' santi, come a datori della grazia, ma solo come intercessori appresso Dio: *nella prattica* però le grazie si domandano a loro, anzi ce ne sono molte che non si reputerebbe poterle ottener da Dio, ma sol da quel santo ch'è proposto a tale ufficio: imperciò che hanno divisa la podestà di far miracoli, ascrivendo ad alcuni la cura sopra i denti, ad altri sopra il collo, sopra le mamelle, sopra la febbre, sopra la peste [...]. Dividendosi anco in fazzioni, per le varie divozioni, essaltando ciascuno il suo santo sopra gli altri, a concorrenze: da che anco nasce che i santi più moderni offuscano la memoria de' vecchi e gli escludono dagli onori' (ibid., p. 57). In his polemic Sarpi included not only worship of the saints but also that of the Virgin: 'And as for the Blessed Virgin [...] the honor they show to her is usually double that which what they show to our Savior' ('E quanto alla Beata Vergine [...] l'onore che danno a lei è doppio per lo più di quello che fanno al Nostro Salvatore'; ibid.); and again: '*In the schools* they distinguish the honor that is due to God and that due to persons, calling the one *dulia* and the other *latria*: but *in practice* this distinction is not to be found. Consequently the same signs of reverence are made to God and to the saints in equal measure' ('*Nelle scuole* si distingue l'onor dovuto a Dio, e quello che si rende alle creature, chiamando

The picture that comes out of the pages written by Sarpi – which inevitably included a violent attack on the Church's rules and regulations against the use of the vernacular[59] – was, therefore, one of a clean gap between the objectives announced and those achieved (or pursued) by the Catholic authorities. Without entering into the merits of Sarpi's opinions – in which it is no exaggeration to say that one may read an explicit accusation of duplicity directed against the Church hierarchies – we can say that his analysis appears above all to be a testimony of the failure of the project to control devotions and superstitions, of the ineffectiveness of the regulations regarding censorship, and of its incapacity to make any mark on reality and to measure its objectives against the real state of things.[60] But this is not the main point. To the more sensitive intellects of the day,

questo dulìa e quello latria: ma *in prattica* questa distinzione non si trova. Imperò che gli stessi segni di riverenza si rendono a Dio et a' santi ugualmente'; ibid., p. 57).

59 'The holy offices, not being understood by the people, do not have the power to keep them absorbed in any form of spiritual contemplation: whence, to overcome this failure they hold their attention with the reciting of rosaries and chaplets, as if they were magic spells' ('I loro uffici divini, come dal popolo non intesi, non hanno forza di trattenerli occupati in alcuna contemplazione spirituale: laonde, per supplire a questo mancamento, gli trattengono fra tanto a recitare, a guisa d'incantesimi, rosari e corone'; ibid., p. 58). 'It happens that the common people [...] receive no instruction in matters of faith nor do they understand in their prayers what they are asking of His Divine Majesty: indeed, very often what people have in their mind when they pray to God is the opposite of the words they pronounce: and the common folk recite prayers in Latin so barbarously that very often the meaning is the opposite and instead of praying, they blaspheme, and they will recite to one the prayers meant for another, so that when kneeling before St Catherine they will say *Pater noster qui es in coelis*, and with great devotion they will stand before a crucifix and say *Ave Maria gratia plena*' ('Avviene che il popolo [...] non riceve instruzzione alcuna nella fede, né sa quello che nelle orazioni dimandi alla Maestà Divina: anzi bene spesso quello ch'egli ha nell'animo suo di pregare Dio è contrario alle parole che pronuncia: et il vulgo così barbaramente recita le orazioni in latino, che ben spesso gli dà contrario senso, et invece d'orare, bestemmia, e reciterà ancora le orazioni ad uno inviate ad un altro, inginocchiandosi a S. Caterina dirà *Pater noster qui es in coelis,* e con gran divozione si metterà inanzi ad un crocefisso, e dirà *Ave Maria grafia piena*'; ibid., p. 60).

60 No attempt at self-critical consideration regarding these themes is apparent in the text of the censures ordered by the Congregation of the Index following the publication of the Italian translation of *Relazione sullo stato della religione*, following which, on 26 July 1626, the book was banned: Censure del libro intitolato Relazione dello stato della religione tradotto dall'inglese in linguaggio italiano del Cavalier Edoino Sandio ('Censures of the book by Sir Edoino Sandio (sic) entitled *Relazione dello stato della religione* translated from English into Italian'), in ACDF, Index, Protocols A2 (23), cc. 653r–658v. The censor limited himself to listing the contents of the work with scarcely any critical intervention, highlighting above all the criticisms and accusations directed by the author against the Catholic Church, and then, only secondarily, referring to Sandys' benevolent observations regarding the Roman theological and liturgic system. There was no attempt whatever to make any in-depth study of the double level which, Sandys and Sarpi insinuated, did exist – a study that evidently would have required a questioning of the entire matter of Counter-Reformation strategy.

Sarpi's message must have sounded like a full-scale rejection of the theoretic distinction between the two levels of devotion, public and private, which the political and religious strategy of the Counter-Reformation Church set such store by. It was precisely this distinction – explicitly theorized in the 1601 decree on litanies, but not only on that occasion – that over the years was to become the key to understanding the failure of the censorship practiced by the Roman ecclesiastic hierarchies in the field of devotion.

Without a constant and rigorous control over the doctrinal purity of devotion, the principle of a distinction between the public and the private spheres was beginning to become just a convenient and practical way of attaining repressive objectives as and when required. Thus, the proposal advanced a few years previously by Pope Clement VIII to admonish in private authors whose work it was considered necessary to expurgate (thus not proceeding officially with a formal suspension by the Congregation) – a proposal that was very likely intended to create a sense of individual responsibility among authors, and among the faithful in general, in addition to cutting down the not inconsiderable backlog of bureaucratic procedures awaiting settlement – was destined to be replaced over the years by the ever-more-frequent practice of communicating directly ('in private') to the booksellers the banning of a dangerous text, thus avoiding a public scandal and guaranteeing greater effectiveness to the ban itself.[61]

---

61 'By order of His Holiness Our Lord, I hereby inform Your Reverence that you shall suspend sale of this book and withdraw all copies thereof to be found in bookshops or in the possession of ordinary persons, this to be done *in private* without pronouncing any edicts and without revealing that you have received such orders from here' ('[D]i ordine della Santità di N.S. fo sapere a V.R. ch'ella sospenda la vendita di tal libro et raccoglia gli essemplari di essi che si trovano appresso li librai o private persone et il tutto esseguisca *privatamente* senza formare editti';letter from Cardinal Arrigoni to the Inquisitor of Bologna Rome, 18 June 1605, in A. Rotondò, 'Nuovi documenti', p. 182, my emphasis; 'I inform Your Reverence by order of our Lord that you shall *in private*, without pronouncing any edict, as if by yourself, proceed to withdraw all examples of the said books without revealing that you have received any orders from here' ('Fo sapere a V.R. per ordine di N.S. ch'ella *privatamente*, senza pubblicare editto, come da sé procuri di raccogliere gli essemplari di detti opuscoli senza mostrare d'haverne ordine di qua'; letter from Cardinal Arrigoni to the Inquisitor of Modena, Rome, 12 May 1606; ibid., p. 182, my emphasis). Instructions in the same tone can be read in a letter dated 16 July 1609 from Cardinal Arrigoni to the Inquisitor of Modena: 'You must notify *in private* the booksellers under your jurisdiction' ('Ella *privatamente* notifichi a i librari della sua giurisdittione'; ibid., p. 186, my emphasis); and in a letter dated 26 July 1614 from Cardinal Bellarmino again to the Inquisitor of Modena: 'Without however making any announcement, but *in private* you shall command all booksellers in your Diocese or others who order books' ('Senza però far bando ma *privatamente,* commanderà a tutti gli librari che sono nella sua Diocesi o ad altri che fan venir libri'; ibid., p. 197, my emphasis). This is merely a partially representative example of the correspondence exchanged between the central organs in Rome and those in outlying areas, but the dates when the letters were sent (the first just after the election of the new Pope on 16 May 1605) allow us to suppose that this practice was inaugurated by Paul V, in direct opposition to that followed by his predecessor Clemente VIII.

The 1601 decree was therefore destined to remain merely a testimony of the forced surrender of the Church hierarchies, a disconsolate coming to terms with the impossibility of exercising any close control of the entire devotional universe of the time.[62]

---

[62] A similar degeneration of the distinction between the public and the private sphere seems likewise to have occurred in the context of the 'politics of sanctity' conducted in those years by the Roman hierarchies. The compromise proposed by Bellarmino and Baronio was animated by the noblest of intentions but it was not destined to survive the death of its promoters. It was only in the mid-1620s and in particular with the second and final version of Urban VIII's decrees on the cult of of persons who died in the odor of sanctity that it became possible to understand what the destiny of this important distinction between public and private would be. Correcting a plainly too rigorous previous version of the decree, the Cardinals of the Congregation of the Holy Office in 1625 established that the collection of donations, images, and ex-votos dedicated to those who died in the odor of sanctity would be tacitly authorized so long as it was done 'in secret', without 'infringing the decorum of public authority', until the canonization procedure got under way. The public/private distinction thus appeared to be losing much of the ideal charge it had in Bellarmino and Baronio's original intentions and to have become (at least to a certain extent) subject to a stifling logic of financial profit in which tacit assent to private worship became above all an expedient to avoid losing the income derived from cults that had not yet been officially approved (cf. M. Gotor, 'La fabbrica dei santi: la riforma urbaniana e il modello tridentino', in particular pp. 679 and 725; Id., 'La riforma dei processi di canonizzazione dalle carte del Sant'Uffizio', *L'Inquisizione e gli storici: un cantiere aperto*, Rome, Atti dei Convegni Lincei, 2000, pp. 279–88; and Id., *I beati del papa*, pp. 127 et sqq.)

CHAPTER 12

Roberto Bellarmino and Tommaso Campanella: An Unexpected Encounter

A solid but belated testimony of a battle that by now was lost: that is how the last act of a career characterized by doctrinal rigor and philological precision was destined to appear. Scarcely a year before he died Cardinal Bellarmino left among the papers of the Congregation of the Holy Office the legacy of a *modus iudicandi* that no one else was able to take up. In 1621 he had been given the task of investigating a book of litanies, printed in various editions by the Duke of Bavaria, which circulated not only in Italy but also in Poland and Spain. This collection of prayers – to be more precise, the second 'larger and more widely known' (*più copiosa, e più volgata*) edition of this collection – had been on the list for inspection since 1610, when the Papal nuncio at Graz, the Bishop of Troia, had drawn its existence to the notice of Cardinal Millini, pending instructions from Rome.[1] Some months later, probably on the request of Millini himself or some other member of the Congregation of the Holy Office, the nuncio sent a copy of the second edition of the book to Rome. Despite the discouraging picture of devotional anarchy drawn by the nuncio in a letter to Cardinal Arrigoni – a picture which, although it applied only to the

---

1 'It behoves me to advise your Most Illustrious Lordship that the Duke of Bavaria has had a book of his litanies printed three times in Munich, but only the third impression of 1607 was reviewed and approved by this Sacred Congregation. In this, many litanies that appeared in the second impression were missing. The title is *Fasciculus sacrarum litaniarum ex sacris scripturis, et Patribus*, Munich, Jubilee Year 1600, and nonetheless this second impression is more copious, more widely known, and more used not only here but also, as I have heard from the Jesuit Fathers, and also in Poland, in Spain and in Florence. I judged I should do no more in this matter, and I shall await orders from this Sacred Congregation. To Your Most Illustrious Lordship I make the humblest of bows' ('[M]i par d'avvisare a V.S. Ill.ma che havendo il Duca di Baviera stampato in Monacho tre volte un suo libro di litanie, solo la terza impressione del 1607 è stata revista et approvata da cotesta Sagra Congregatione, in cui mancano molte litanie di quelle ch'erano nella seconda impressione, il titolo della quale è *Fasciculus sacrarum Utaniarum ex sacris scripturis, et Patribus,* Monachii, anno Iubilei 1600, e non di meno questa seconda, come più copiosa, e più volgata, et adoprata non sol qui, ma per quant' ho inteso da Padri Giesuiti anco in Polonia, in Spagna, et in Firenze. Non ho giudicato dover fare altro da me in questo negotio, attenderò l'ordine di cotesta Sagra Congregatione et a V.S. Ill.ma fo humilissima riverentia'; Letter dated 13 December 1610, in ACDF, St. St. TT-1 a, s.n.p.).

territories of the German Empire of which he had direct knowledge, could easily have been extended also to Italy[2] – the work in question that was given to the Master of the Holy Palace to verify[3] had long been forgotten. It was the pressure exerted by the Duke of Bavaria, who could not use the text without the approval of the Congregation,[4] that persuaded the Master of the Holy Palace to restart the machinery of censorship. The indifference of the Roman censorship authorities with regard to the subject of litanies – well exemplified by the ten long years of waiting – contrasts very sharply with the haste with which Bellarmino, having been charged with the task of examining the work, rapidly presented the results of his labors to the Congregation of the Inquisition.[5] In what for the authoritative Cardinal must have represented the last opportunity for him to repeat to an audience of colleagues the original spirit of a long-matured decree – the decree promulgated at the start of the century regarding the question of litanies – and the validity of a public/private dialectic supported by meticulous philological verification of the purity of all devotional forms, Bellarmino was stimulated to act by an invocation addressed by the author of the booklet to the founder of the Company of Jesus, Ignatius di Loyola. As is known, the official position of the Church prescribed the total prohibition of the worship of saints who had not yet been canonized; consequently, Bellarmino necessarily declared himself to be in favor of elimination of

---

2 'In performance of the order given to me by Your Most Illustrious Lordship in your letter dated 19 of last month, by order of the Sacred Congregation of the Holy Office, I herewith send you the book of litanies printed in Munich. I take this opportunity to report to Your Most Illustrious Lordship that in these countries nearly every Saint has his own special litanies, which in their festivities they are accustomed to recite, even though they have not been approved, as I myself heard one day when I was with His Highness here in St Paul's, whose festivity it was. However, as this is an ancient and popular custom, I think it will be almost impossible to abolish it and I believe it would cause much disturbance. Nevertheless I shall await the orders of Your Most Illustrious Lordship, before whom I most humbly bow' ('In essecutione del commandamento datomi da V.S. Ill.ma nella sua de 19 del passato d'ordine della Sacra Congregatione del S. Officio, le invio l'allegato libro di litanie stampato in Monaco. Con questa occasione mi par di dar conto a V.S. Ill.ma che in questi Paesi quasi ogni Santo ha le sua litanie particolari, et nelle lor feste si soglion recitare, ancorché non siano approvate, havendole sentite io stesso un giorno, che mi trovai con S.A. qui in S. Paolo, la cui festa all'hora correva. Però essendo questo costume antico, et generale, credo che sarebbe quasi impossibile il torlo, et dubito che ne seguirebbe gran disturbo. Attenderò nondimeno gli ordini di V.S. Ill.ma alla quale fo humilissima riverenza'; Letter dated 14 March 1611 from Graz, in ACDF, St St TT-1 a, s.n.p.).

3 'The book which has been mentioned in the letters is to be revised by the Master of the Sacred Palace' ('Liber, de quo in literis videatur a Maestro sacri palatii'; ibid.).

4 ACDF, Index, I/2,c. 200r, meeting of 1 August 1620.

5 ACDF, Inquisizione, Censurae Librorum, vol. II, folder 14 (1621), ff. 615r–v: *Censura brevis ad litanias, quas misti Serenissimus Dux Bavariae Gulielmus*; published by P. GODMAN, *The saint as a censor. Robert Bellarmine between Index and Inquisition*, pp. 308–10.

the invocation (*putarem esse omittendam hanc invocationem*: 'my opinion is that this invocation is to be omitted'), in obedience to the precise and specific Papal indication in this field communicated some years before by Cardinal Pietro Aldobrandini.[6] However, by virtue of a daily practice that seemed to have substantially adopted the moderate solution (in favor of allowing in private devotional acts that were prohibited in public) which he himself, together with Baronio, had suggested during the heated discussion which since the beginning of the century had occupied the members of a temporary Congregation of the Blessed,[7] Bellarmino felt he was authorized to declare that 'it may perchance remain, because these litanies cannot be recited except by individual persons in private. It is therefore permitted to invoke in private those we believe to be saints'.[8] The process of making the faithful themselves individually responsible within the framework of private devotional practice had to advance together with a precise observation of ecclesiastic prescriptions in the framework of public devotional practice. However, this devotional dualism – and this was the aspect Bellarmino most insisted on – achieved some intrinsic validity of its own only in the context in which he inserted it within his censorship notes. Only by maintaining a high threshold of philological and doctrinal watchfulness with regard to the sundry forms of popular devotion was it possible – in his view – to guarantee the sensible application of the principle that defined a hiatus between private devotion and public devotion, which otherwise would have heralded an uncontrolled proliferation of superstitions. Consequently, the philological reliability of the text had to be verified; whenever there were accounts or passages that were difficult to assign to a definite source in the Scriptures or passages containing obvious historical inaccuracies, it was necessary to act with zeal: 'The seven sleeping saints – he noted – such things could be omitted because of their historical uncertainty';[9] and a little

---

6 'Received news of a printed booklet containing various prayers and litanies of saints, including one bearing the name of Father Ignatius. A report of this was made to His Holiness, who ordered that the booklet should be corrected and that when it was printed again in the future the memory of Father Ignatius should not be placed among the saints' ('Avuto notitia di un libretto stampato di varie orationi et litanie de santi, tra quali vien'anco posto il nome del padre Ignatio, ne fu fatta relatione a S. S.tà, la quale ordinò che il libretto si corregesse, et che stampandosi in l'avvenire non vi si mettesse fra santi la memoria di detto padre'; Letter from Cardinal Aldobrandini, Rome 8 October 1602, in I. de Récalde, *Les jésuites sous Aquaviva*, Paris, Librairie Moderne, 1927, pp. 293–4).

7 Cf. M. Gotor, *La fabbrica dei santi*, p. 701.

8 'forte possit manere, quia hae litaniae non possunt recitari nisi privatim a singulis. Privatim autem licet invocare eos, quos pie credimus esse sanctos.' In particular, Bellarmino was reflecting on the case of the founder of the Jesuit Order Ignatius of Loyola (ACDF, Inquisition, Censurae librorum, vol. II, cit., c. 615v; P. Godman, *The saint*, p. 309).

9 'p. 345: *sancti septem dormientes*', he noted 'Ista potuissent omitti propter incertitudinem historiae'; ibid., c. 615v; P. Godman, *The Saint as a Censor*, p. 310.

further below: 'Page 396: *For your sweet heart transfixed on the Cross for us*. It does not seem sure that the soldier's spear transfixed Jesus' heart. The Gospel account says only that Christ's side was pierced by a spear; there is no mention of the heart being transfixed',[10] and a little further on: 'Page 300: *Litanies to the holy virgins and widows*. This should read more correctly: 'to women saints', because in these litanies there are some women saints who are neither virgins nor widows, such as St Mary Magdalene, St Mary of Egypt, and others'.[11] Historical inaccuracies like these, as also inventions and mistakes of content, might lead 'simple folk' off the straight path of faith by creating confusion and doubt: 'Page 348: *For your manger, free us, o Lord*. This supplication is totally inappropriate, as is also: "for your seamless robe", "for the table where you dined", and yet others that could be omitted'.[12] Sometimes a single noun wrongly added to the text could arouse the fancy of the masses: 'Pages 103 and 117: *having drunk gall and vinegar on the Cross*. The pages of the Gospel make no mention of Christ drinking gall and vinegar on the Cross, but only vinegar. Before the crucifixion, according to St Matthew, Christ drank wine mingled with gall, while Mark spoke only of wine mingled with myrrh. In the *Psalms* we read: "They gave me also gall for my meat; and in my thirst they gave me vinegar to drink". Therefore it should say: "Having drunk vinegar on the Cross", because only that is to be found in the *Gospels* and in the *Psalms*'.[13]

Lastly, Bellarmino went on, there were some cases where linguistic uncertainties or unintentional oversights risked causing dangerous errors of doctrine, such as the possible degenerations of the Marian cult: 'Page 20: *Jesus, star of the sea, have mercy on us*. This term, star of the sea, we read among his notes, is usually attributed to the Blessed Virgin. It might be better, when referring to Christ, to say 'the bright and morning star', as

---

10 'F. 396: *Per dulce cor tuum pro nobis in cruce transfixum*. Non videtur esse certum quod lancea militis transfixerit cor Christi. Solum enim in Evangelio habetur latus Christi lancea fuisse apertum; de transfixione cordis nulla fit mentio'; ibid., p. 310.

11 'F. 300: *Litaniae ad sanctas virgines et viduas*. Rectius diceretur: "ad sanctas mulieres", quia in his litaniis ponuntur aliquae sanctae, quae non sunt neque virgines neque viduae, ut Sancta Maria Magdalena, Sancta Maria Aegyptica et aliae'; ibid., p. 309.

12 'p. 348: *Perpraesepe tuum libera nos, Domine*. Petitio est valde impropria, ut etiam illa: "per vestem inconsutilem", "per mensam, in qua caenasti", et aliae similes, quae potuissent omitti'; ibid., p. 310.

13 'Ff. 103 et 117: *felle et aceto in cruce potate*. Non habetur in *Evangeliis* Christum in cruce felle et aceto fuisse potatum, sed solum aceto. Ante crucifixionem, scribit Sanctus Matthaeus, Christum fuisse potatum vino cum felle mixto, pro quo Marcus dicit vino myrrato fuisse potatum. In *Psalmis* dicitur: "dederunt in escam meam fel et in siti mea potaverunt me aceto". Itaque dici deberet: "Aceto in cruce potate", quia hoc solum habetur in *Evangeliis* et in *Psalmo*'; ibid., c. 615r; ibid., p. 309. We hypothesize that Bellarmino's modification was determined by his fear of what an 'unlearned' reader might imagine, with regard to the death of Christ, when reading or – more likely – hearing this harmless expression (*felle* =poison).

in the last chapter of *Revelation*. For the star of the sea is the North star, which is of limited size. The bright and morning star, which astrologers call the star of Venus, outshines any other star'.[14] It is not hard to discern behind this observation a precise reminder not to confuse the attributes of Christ with those of the Virgin Mother, nor to attribute to Our Lady the image full of 'splendor' and 'power' that belonged, both by tradition and by doctrine, to the Son of God: 'Page 179: *Holy Mary, Mother of God the Father*. The unlearned do not understand this. And some may think that the Blessed Mary is the Mother of God the Father. To avoid any ambiguity it would be better to say: "Holy Mary, Mother of the Son of God". This expression is perfectly consistent with the expressions before and after, for the one before says that Mary is the "daughter of God the Father," and this is perfectly consistent with the one that comes after: "Mother of the Son of God", and with the third: "Spouse of the Holy Spirit"'.[15] The Blessed Virgin was 'only' the Mother of the Son of God and that was what she had to remain. It was totally misleading to attribute to her theological functions or positions to which she had no right. Behind the question of terminology Bellarmino could see the risks of a cult that threatened the theological and doctrinal pillars of the theology of redemption, by recognizing in the figure of the Virgin Mother the salvific power of humanity, which only the Son of God, pitifully sacrificed on the Cross, could legitimately hold.[16] Never had an act of censorship been so precise and opportune. Never, however,

---

14 'F. 20: *Iesu stella maris, miserere nobis*. Haec appellatio stelle maris', we read among his notes, 'tribui solet Beate Virgini. Fortasse melius de Christo diceretur "stella splendida et matutina", ut dicitur in *Apocalypsi* capite ultimo. Nam stella maris est stella polaris, quae exigua est. Stella splendida et matutina est stella omnium fulgentissima, quae ab astrologis dicitur stella Veneris'; ibid., c. 615r; ibid., p. 309.

15 'F. 179: *Sancta Maria Mater Dei Patris*. A rudioribus non intelligetur. Et fortasse aliqui putabunt Beatam Mariam dici matrem Dei Patris. Ad tollendam ambiguitatem, melius diceretur: "Sancta Maria, mater filii Dei". Et hoc optime coheret cum precedenti et sequenti sententia. Nam in precedenti dicitur Maria filia Dei Patris, cum qua sententia optime cohaeret sequens: "Mater filii Dei" et tertia: "Sponsa Spiritus Sancti"'; ibid.

16 Bellarmino's activity with regard to the subject of prayer was not limited to this one action. On other occasions he took pains to state his point of view, as for example when he found himself obliged to correct and reprimand a certain Petilius, the overhasty compiler of a censure of *Vita della Beata Vergine* by a Neapolitan theologian by the name of Lorenzo Masselli. In Bellarmino's view, Petilius was guilty of drawing a number of summary and erroneous interpretations regarding doctrinally delicate matters such as the approval or otherwise of visions of the devil and, above all, regarding the topic of prayer: 'In book 2 chapter 16, something has been added to the prayer of St Joseph's Church. It is a great sin if something is modified when the prayer is recited publicly, while there is nothing wrong if something is added in a private prayer in one's own room, in order to achieve deeper involvement' ('Notat lib. 2, cap. 16, additum aliquid ad orationem Ecclesiae et Sancti Ioseph. Hoc magnum esse peccatum, si mutaretur orario publice recitanda, at quod privatim in cubiculo aliquid addatur ad augendum affectum, nullum est malum'; ACDF, Index, Protocolli

was an act of censorship so unheeded. In 1626 Niccolò Riccardi published *La prima parte dei ragionamenti sopra le Letanie di Nostra Signora*:[17] a voluminous work which, three years later with Riccardi's appointment to one of the most prestigious positions in the entire ecclesiastic repressive system, that of Master of the Holy Palace, obtained, albeit indirectly, an official recognition from the Roman hierarchy.

What Riccardi offered in his book was not merely a belated and enthusiastic (though indirect) encomium of Albertini's *Trattato dell'angelo custode*. The Jesuit Albertini's bold attempt to calculate the speed of the angels received its complete legitimization in the pages of the future censor: the complex and detailed pseudo-scientific calculation with which the loquacious Dominican preacher strove to reckon the exact overall number of angels inhabiting the sphere of Heaven outdid, in its imagination and creativity, the results obtained by the Jesuit's improvisations. As if challenging the authority of St Thomas, who rhetorically dared to declare that 'our minds lack the algorithm and the numbers to count the angels', Riccardi plunged stubbornly into a calculation which in many points verged on mathematical delirium. The following page is worth reproducing in full:

> The Angels are so numerous that they exceed the number of all bodily substances, the sands in the Sea, the atoms of the Sun, the leaves of the trees; all living and nonliving creatures, and even the stars in the sky: this is proved by St Thomas with the authority of St Dionysius, *Multi sunt Beati exercitus supernarum mentium, infirmum, et angustum nostrarum mentium numerum superexcedentes* (*Many are the blessed in the army of higher minds, many more than the weak and limited number of our own minds*). St Thomas declared that our minds lack the algorithm to be able to count the armies as also the soldiers of sovereign and separate substances. Angelical substances exceed (says the Angel of Doctors) all corporal things both in multitude and in magnitude, and in corpulence, and incorruptible bodies exceed corruptible and sublunar bodies, which compared to them are nothing. And it is possible to consider this a not improbable way of reasoning, because if we consider that the Angels are distributed in nine orders, and the more soldiers, or singers, in each battalion

S, c. 231r; see also P. Godman, *The Saint as a Censor*, pp. 303–4). Cf. the text of Petilius' censures in ACDF, Index, Protocolli S, cc. 229r–v and 232r.

17 *La prima parte dei ragionamenti sopra le Letanie di Nostra Signora del padre Maestro Fra Nicolò Riccardi dell'ordine de' Predicatori, e Reggente della Minerva in Roma*. Genoa, for Giuseppe Pavoni. 1626. Licensed by the Fathers Superior. On Riccardi, see V.M. Fontana, *Syllabus magistrorum Sacri Palatii Apostolici*, Rome, ex typ. N.A. Tinassii, 1663, pp. 160–62; G. Catalano, *De magistro Sacri Palatii Apostolici Libri duo. Quorum alter originem, praerogativas, ac munia, alter eorum Seriem continet, qui eo munere ad hanc usque diem donati fuere*, Rome, Typis Antonii Fulgoni apud S. Eustachium, 1751, pp. 158–60; and especially A. Eszer, 'Niccolò Riccardi, O.P. – "padre Mostro" (1585–1639)', *Angelicum*, LX, 1989, pp. 458–61.

or choir, the more noble and sublime they are in their abundant perfection; so that there are more Seraphim than Cherubim. And as for example the excess of the elements is calculated to be tenfold in proportion, such that fire is ten times greater than air, and air than water; so it is known that for each one of the Angels in the lowest choir there are ten Archangels, one hundred Principalities, one thousand virtues, ten thousand Powers, one hundred thousand Dominations, one million Thrones, ten million Cherubim, and one hundred million Seraphim; so that for each Angel of the lowest orders, it will be necessary to multiply them by the other one hundred and eleven million one hundred and eleven thousand one hundred and ten choirs; one must then consider that in the last choir of angels there is at least a number so great that it is sufficient to guard all men who are, who were, and who will be: thus each reasonable soul, except that of Christ, has its Angel, without one guarding two, either together or at different times; whence it follows that there are as many guardian angels as there are in all men assembled, who will appear on the fearful day of judgment; let us make thereof a rough reckoning that there are ten million souls regularly in the universe, which is a very small number, putting one century after the other and considering that every hundred years all men are renewed, and the age of the World must be sixty centuries, as is said by those who declare that the age of the World is six thousand years, and the number of men will thus come to six hundred millions: having multiplied this number by the Angels up to the level of the Seraphim, we reach the number to be seen in the following calculation: 60,000,000,000. Six million million million six hundred and sixty-six thousand six hundred and sixty-six million million six hundred and sixty thousand million angels; let us take this number which is so large compared to us and so small compared to the other number we are attempting to calculate that not even a thousand of these distances reaches it.[18]

---

[18] ‘Gli Angioli sono in tanto numero, che vincono il numero di tutte le sostanze corporee, le arene del Mare, gli atomi del Sole, le foglie de gli alberi; tutti i viventi, e non viventi, et infino le stelle del Cielo: lo prova S. Tomaso con l’autorità di San Dionigi, *Multi sunt Beati exercitus supernarum mentium, infirmum, et angustum nostrarum mentium numerum superexcedentes,* affermando cioè che manca l’algorismo, et il numero alle nostre menti per poter annoverar gli eserciti, non che i soldati delle sovrane e separate sostanze. Eccedono (dice l’Angiolo de’ Dottori) le sostanze Angeliche tutte le corporee nella moltitudine, come nella magnitudine, e corpulenza sorvanzano i corpi incorruttibili questi corruttibili, e sublunari, che a suo ragguaglio sono un niente. E se ne può fare non improbabile discorso, considerando che essendo gli Angioli distribuiti in nove ordini, ci sono tanto più soldati, o cantori in ciascheduna squadra, o coro, quanto è più nobile e sublime, per abbondare in loro la perfezione; si che ci sono più Serafini che Cherubini. E si come, per esempio, l’eccesso de gli elementi si calcola, che sia in proporzion decupla di maniera che dieci volte sia maggiore il fuoco che l’aria, l’aria che l’acqua; cosi intendesi che per ogn’uno de gli Angioli dell’infimo coro ci siano dieci Arcangioli, cento Principati, mille Virtù, dieci mila Potestadi, cento mila Dominationi, un mi-lion di Troni, dieci milioni di Cherubini, e cento milioni di Serafini; si che per ogni Angiolo de’ più bassi bisognerà multiplicarne per gli altri cori cent’undeci milioni, cento undeci mila, e cento dieci; bisogna poi considerare, che nell’ultimo coro d’Angioli ce n’è tanto numero almeno, quanto basta a custodire tutti gli huomini che sono, fumo, e saranno, havendo ciascheduna anima ragionevole, fuor di quella di Christo, il suo Angiolo, senza che uno ne custodisca due, o insieme, o in tempi differenti; di onde nasce, che almeno

Sixty billion Angels floating above our heads – that was the final number which, by his scientific and philological reasoning, Riccardi demonstrated could be calculated.

The frenzied pages of the future Master of the Sacred Palace do not only provide confirmation of the popularity of the devotional model emerging from the texts of Caraccia and Albertini: they also reflect the extent of the final abandonment of all attempts by Church censorship to purify religious and devotional practices of all superstitious accretions and pagan reminiscences. This cannot in fact have been a momentary and unwanted oversight. The complex calculation of the number of angels fitted perfectly well into the economy of those pages, showing itself to be completely functional to his *reasonings on Our Lady's Litanies*. 'If the Holy Virgin', Riccardi proceeded in his bold reflection, 'possessed in the first instant of her grace much more grace than the supreme Angel possesses now, what immensity of grace had he who exceeded by far the number of the above said millions, who had so much grace, which could not be written even with nineteen figures?'[19] What was being presented step by step in Riccardi's work was a complete and organic theological reflection which – with the successive comments and interpretations provided on the basis of the numerous *incipit*s of the Marian litanies – was intended to offer the readers a deifying image of the Virgin Mary. The first words were extremely explicit: 'The Virgin [is] so well placed between God and man, as lukewarm is between hot and cold, that one might say she is, if the word were not too much of a profanity, a *semi-goddess*'. This 'semi-goddess', explained Riccardi, 'is half one might say a created God; a finite infinity; an almighty weakness; [...] worth as much as a created God, a God that is lame, reduced by half, a God come out of himself and

tanti Angioli custodi ci sono, quanta è tutta la radunanza de gli huomini, che nel tremendo giudizio comparirà; Facciamone un conto all'ingrosso, che ci siano dieci milioni d'anime nell'universo regolarmente, che è pochissimo numero, mettendo un secolo con l'altro, e che di cento in cent'anni si rinovino tutti gli huomini, che debbano essere i secoli del Mondo sessanta, come vogliono quelli, che definiscono la durazione del Mondo a sei mila anni, verranno gli huomini ad essere sei cento milioni: multiplicati sopra questo numero gli Angioli fino a Serafini, fanno come si vede nel seguente conto: 60000000000. Sei milioni di millioni di millioni sei cento sessanta sei mila sei cento sessanta sei millioni di millioni, e seicento sessanta mila millioni di Angioli; prendiamo questo numero tanto grande a noi, e tanto picciolo a quel, che pretendiamo misurare, che non ci arriva con mille di queste distanze' (*La prima parte dei ragionamenti sopra le Letanie*, pp. 208–10).

19 'Se la Vergine Santa – così il Riccardi continuava la sua ardita riflessione – hebbe nel primo istante della sua grazia, più grazia assai che l'Angiolo supremo s'habbia adesso, quanta immensità di gratia hebbe chi superò di gran lunga il numero delli millioni sopradetti, che haveva di grazia, li quali con dieci nove caratteri numerali non potevano descriversi?' (ibid., p. 211).

mixed with imperfection'.[20] Proceeding further in a linguistic ascent that was hard to control, Riccardi soon reached the point of no return: 'Mary halfway between God and living creature, and God made into a creature, or creature made into God', he rashly declared.[21] Thus, once having come so close to the peaks of deification, Riccardi's exalted Marian glorification no longer encountered any obstacle in its path or anything else to inhibit it. From the proclamation of the Virgin's omnipotence, only partially tempered by the later afterthought 'with the Lord's participation',[22] it was no great distance to an improbable and theologically unusual inversion of roles. The almighty divine figure was relegated in a flash to the humbling condition of a Marian subject: 'God exchanges titles with his Mother, she becomes a Goddess and He a mere creature and vassal [...] in the Virgin is placed a prudence that does not reign over empires but commands God, her subject: *Erat subditus illi*' ('*He was subject to Her*').[23]

If temporal power was also totally subordinate to the 'Sovereign Empress' (*Sovrana Imperatrice*) – the destiny of all nations was in her hands, Riccardi argued in one of his countless outbursts, just as the health and the future of Princes and sovereigns depended on her changing moods[24] – it was evident that this 'infinite and incomprehensible almighty' Virgin was 'much more admirable than the Son'.[25] Riccardi's Mary, whose virtues and powers were repeatedly compared to the figure of God, was

20 'La Vergine [è] così a punto fra Dio, e l'huomo, come il tepido fra il caldo el' freddo, che si potrebbe dire, se il vocabulo non fusse troppo profano, *semidea*.' Tale 'semidea è mezzo, come dire un Dio creato; un finito infinito; un omnipotente debolezza; [...] tanto vale, quanto un Dio creato, Dio zoppicante, dimezzato, un Dio fuoruscito di se stesso, e mescolato con l'imperfezione';ibid., pp. 56–7).

21 'Maria mezzo tra Dio, e le creature, e Dio increaturito, o creatura deificata' (ibid., p. 323).

22 'Not only is she powerful but *in a certain manner, one may say, she is almighty* with the participation of the Lord, who shows Himself to be so liberal a communicator of his greatness toward her' ('Non solamente è potente, ma *in certa forma anche si può dire onnipotente* con participazione di quel Signore, che delle sue grandezze verso di lei comunicatore cotanto liberale si mostra'; ibid., p. 388).

23 'Dio cambia i titoli con sua madre, essa si fa dea e lui creatura e vassallo [...] nella Vergine si pone una prudenza non regnativa d'Imperii, ma commandatrice di Dio sogetto: *Erat subditus illi* [sic]'; ibid., pp. 354–5).

24 'Your hand holds the overthrow of nations, their transportation, the freedom and the service of men; the slavery of kings, the reign of slaves, the birth and the end of Republics and Monarchies. All is under your jurisdiction' ('In tua mano sta lo spiantar a fatto le nationi, lo transportarle, la Berta e servato degli huomini; la schiavitudine de' re, lo regnar de' schiavi, la nascita e fine delle Republiche e delle Monarchie. Tutto è sua giurisditione'; ibid., p. 403).

25 'questa "infinita et inc[om]prensibile onnipotente" Vergine "[è] molto più ammirabile, che il Figlio"' (ibid., p. 304; cf. also p. 155).

therefore destined to take the place of Christ in every possible way.[26] A previously unknown 'benefit of Mary' symbolically took the place of the sixteenth-century 'benefit of Christ', decisively assuming a central position on the doctrinal scene designed by the future Master of the Holy Palace: 'All merits derive from Mary,' Riccardi proclaimed: 'gifts, graces, prerogatives, privileges, helps, invocations, inspirations, sacraments and good desires'.[27] In other words everything came down from her and nothing happened without her approval. This unchecked exultation of her taumaturgic powers must thus have been, in the eyes of her followers, the surest guarantee of the infallibility of their prayers: 'The *invincible strength of prayer* does as it will and achieves whatever it wants'.[28] Faced by her requests, God – both her subject and her debtor – could only accept with enthusiasm and grant her every wish:

> *Christe eleison* is such an effective prayer that He cannot deny grace: because *the Blessed Virgin is God's creditor*, as she gave him all the body of mercy and the metal of money with which He pays satisfactorily, and meritoriously *ad infinitum*, and the debt can never be paid, *and therefore in justice the request is made in the name of the Virgin, as she is the creditor of an insoluble and infinite debt.*[29]

The circle drawn by Riccardi could therefore be considered complete. The unconditional guarantee of success in temporal and spiritual matters was what the future censor assured to the ordinary believer in exchange for an equally unconditional individual abandonment to Mary's miraculous power.[30]

---

26 On the Marian cult, besides the texts cited above, ch. 11, cf. S. De Fiores, 'Il culto mariano nel contesto culturale dell'Europa nei secoli XVII–XVIII,'*De cultu mariano saeculis XVII–XVIII. Acta congressus mariologici mariani internationalis in Republica Melitensianno 1983 celebrati*, vol. 2, Rome, PAMI, 1987, pp. 1–58. On the seventeenth-century degenerated expressions of this cult, see R. Laurentin, 'La Vierge Marie comme signe de contradiction au XVII–XVIII siècle', *De cultu mariano*, pp. 102–5; S. De Fiores, 'Mariologia inculturata in Italia tra passato e futuro', *Theotokos*, 1 (1993), pp. 19–22.

27 'Da Maria vengono tutti meriti, doni, gratie, prerogative, privilegii, ausilli, invocationi, l'inspirationi, li sacramenti, e li desiderii buoni' (*La prima parte dei ragionamenti*, p. 344).

28 'La *forza invincibile dell'orazione* ne fa a suo modo, e gli fa fare tutto ciò che vuole' (ibid., p. 89; my emphasis).

29 '*Christe eleison* è un pregare tanto efficace, che non può negare la gratia: perché *la B. Vergine è creditrice di Dio* havendoli dato il corpo tutto della misericordia, et metallo della moneta, con che paga satisfattoriamente, et meritoriamente in infinito, tanto che non si può estinguere mai il debito, *e però per giustitia si dimanda a nome della Vergine, essendo ella creditrice di debito insolubile, et infinito*' (ibid., p. 22).

30 In light of these considerations there is no reason to be surprised by the proliferation of seventeenth-century publications of works dedicated to the 'slaves' of Mary or Joseph

While elsewhere the long lists of condemnations of superstitious prayers were reproposed – evidently mechanically and unsuccessfully – the future Master of the Holy Palace officially testified the failure of the battle by proudly reproposing the same message that only a few decades before the Church hierarchies had proposed to cancel from the devotional practices and the minds of the faithful. In exchange for total unconditional submission to the authorities in Rome, the faithful were presented with a code of magic formulae with which they could realize all their material and earthly desires, even before those of the spirit.

Thus, as if by some mocking stroke of destiny, the man now dressed in a censor's official garb, the holder since 1629 of one of the highest positions in the Roman Church's system of repression, and officially responsible for the defense of Catholic morality,[31] became the easy target of one of the most illustrious victims of the Inquisitors and the Church censors, who had suddenly himself become – for the occasion – an implacable censor: Tommaso Campanella. It is undeniable that behind the compilation of the detailed *Censure sopra il libro del Padre Mostro: 'Ragionamenti sopra le litanie di Nostra Signora'* ('Censures of the Litanies of the Patermonster: "Comments on the Litanies of Our Lady")[32] by this philosopher of Stilo there was above all a strong desire for revenge. Freed from the Holy Office prison in Rome in July 1628 thanks to the good offices of Urban VIII and transferred to the convent of Santa Maria sopra Minerva, in the course

or other saints. Until specific research is carried out in this field, we must limit ourselves to observing, to this regard, that the offensive launched by the Inquisition Authorities in the second half of the seventeenth century against this type of writing was decidedly tardy and unrealistic; cf. the decree of the Congregation of the Holy Office in 1673, which prohibited 'Libelli omnes, et folia impressa, et Imagines incisae ubi representantur homines penduli a Christo, a sacra Pixide, a Beatissima Virgine, a S. Iosepho, et a quovis alio Sancto, et ubi de hac captivitate, vel vulgari lingua Schiavitudine agitur; et in specie prohibentur infrascripti libri de supradicta captivitate tractantes' ('All books and printed matter, as well as engraved images, containing representations of men who depend on Christ, the Holy Chalice, the Most Blessed Virgin, St Joseph, and any other Saint, and any such works dealing with this captivity, or slavery as it is vulgarly called, and in particular the following books dealing with the said captivity'); and the long list of condemned works, most of which were named after the 'Schiavi della Santissima, e Immaculata Regina del Cielo Madre di Dio' ('Slaves of the Most Holy, and Immaculate Queen of Heaven Mother of God'; ACDF, St St O3-e, one volume, f. 579; the entire code is however full of manuscript and printed texts of this kind of short work produced in the first half of the seventeenth century and now condemned by the Holy Office).

31 On the Master of the Sacred Palace's growing role in the field of censorship, well beyond the limits of his traditional jurisdiction, cf. G. Fragnito, 'In questo vasto mare de libri prohibiti et sospesi', p. 35.

32 Tommaso Campanella, *Censure sopra il libro del Padre Mostro: 'Ragionamenti sopra le litanie di Nostra Signora'*, A. Terminelli (ed.), Rome, Edizioni Monfortane, 1998. There is a critical commentary of the text by G. Ernst, *Tommaso Campanella. La vita, le opera*, Rome-Bari, Laterza, 2002, pp. 216–17.

of the following year Campanella was finally cleared of all charges by the highest echelons of the Roman Inquisition. The accumulated rage and rancor toward his previous persecutors were, however, hard to overcome. And the opportunity was one that he could not let go. Thus, in the closing months of 1630 Campanella set to work. The desire to get his clear revenge, on the moral level even before that of doctrine, on one of the most intransigent censors of his *Atheismus triumphatus* and his *De sensu rerum*, did not however detract anything from the quality of his observations. These censures, destined to remain in manuscript form, were to bring further complications into the life of the philosopher from Stilo. Yet they represent an irreplaceable testimony of the doctrinal and other degenerations which affected the Marian cult in the early decades of the seventeenth century.

The insinuating 'murmurings against [Riccardi's] sermons and his book' (*murmurationi contra le prediche e libro [del Riccardi]*)[33] of which Campanella had been informed, surprisingly found unexpected confirmation in Riccardo's own words. It was said that he had admitted his guilt fairly openly: 'You are unable to write. I say a thousand heresies when I preach, but I say them with such a skill that I make them appear to

33 'Having heard in Naples and in Rome', Campanella explained, not without a certain ill-concealed satisfaction, 'loud murmurings against the sermons and the book of Father [...] who boldly criticizes and sneers at God, at the sacraments, and at the saints, and – although a Doctor of the Church – confuses the terms of Holy Theology. A sonnet from it was recited to me, [...] he said that if it had been possible, he would have burned St Catherine of Siena and St Brigida, because they did not agree on the *conceptione B. Virginis*, and therefore their revelations are not divine. [...] Likewise, preaching in Naples, he said that ashes are more powerful than God: for God is fire, *ignis consumens est,* and ashes resist fire. Likewise, preaching at the Minerva, he said that Seraphim are the pestilence and poison of Paradise because in the Book of Numbers we can read: *Misit Deus ignitos serpentes* (*And the Lord sent fiery serpents*)[...] Likewise he said the Mother of Christ is ignorant: and when he saw his listeners' amazement he said: "I will prove it to you with the Song of Songs: *Si ignoras te, o pulcherrima*'" ("*if thou know not, o thou fairest among women*"); 'Havendo inteso in Napoli, et in Roma – spiegava, non senza un malcelato compiacimento, Tommaso Campanella – gran murmurationi contra le prediche e libro del P. [...] che audacemente sparla e motteggia contra Dio, contra i sacramenti, contra i santi, e dottor della Chiesa et confonde i termini della S. Theologia, del che mi fu recitato un sonetto, [...] disse che se lui poteva, haveria brugiato S. Catherina di Siena e S. Brigida, perché sono contrarie nella materia della *concepitone B. Virginis,* et però le loro rivelatione no[n] sono divine. [...] Item predicando in Napoli disse che la cenere è più potente di Dio: perché Dio è fuoco, *ignis consumens est,* e la cenere resiste al fuoco. Item alla Minerva predicando disse che li Serafini sono peste e veneno del Paradiso, perché nel libro dei Numeri è scritto: *Misit Deus ignitos serpentes* [...] Item disse la Madre di Christo è un'ignorante: e stupendosi gli ascoltatori, disse: "Vi lo provo con la Cantica: *Si ignoras te, o pulcherrima*"'; T. CAMPANELLA, *Censure sopra il libro del Padre Mostro,* pp. 29–30.

be Holy Doctrine', he is reported to have said, rather too spontaneously.[34] What, however, most mattered to Campanella was the fact that these malevolent rumors found their unequivocal confirmation in his weighty volume.[35] Leafing through the numerous pages of the Marian work by the Master of the Holy Palace, Tommaso Campanella began to note down and comment in detail on every 'extravagant' (*stravagante*) or, worse still, every doctrinally heretic, remark that his attentive eyes picked out: 'And yet', he wrote with satisfaction at the end of his labors, 'I derived the following propositions: whence it can be seen from this book that it is possible to prove Paganism, part of Mohammedanism, and the Talmud, and that heretics of the present day can be used to prove that what Calvin and Luther and Wycliff write against the Roman Church is true, and all the more so now that this abomination is *in loco santo*'.[36] If some ridiculous and fanciful expressions used by Riccardi, such as 'half Goddess' (*mezza Dea*) or 'coming out of himself' (*fuoriuscito da se stesso*), appeared to the philosopher to be an amusing bequest of paganism, which the Tridentine Church had resolved to fight,[37] Campanella was above all preoccupied by heretic affirmations that were destined to provide posthumous legitimization of the violent accusations directed by the transalpine heresiarchs against the Church hierarchies and, above all, to mislead the ingenuous reader away from a correct and orthodox interpretation of Catholic Mariology: 'It is heresy to say' the philosopher for example emphasized, 'that Mary is a God made into a created being, for He was not changed into the substance of Mary nor did He grant to Mary the status of unity of person, which He did only with Christ the Man'.[38] Campanella's method was to carry out both a philologically rigorous reading of the definitions provided by Riccardi and also, in particular, a punctilious analysis of the doctrinal consequences and theological postulates that these rash definitions bore

---

[34] 'Tu non sai scrivere. Io dico mille heresie, quando predico, ma con tal destrezza, che li fo' parer dottrina santa' (ibid., p. 30).

[35] Campanella himself declared that he was not the only one to notice the peculiarities of this publication: 'Certain PP. NN. [Jesuits] said: If you want to see P.M. [*Padre Mostro*, Father Monster]'s lack of religion and intelligence [...] read his book about litanies' ('Vidi poi trattando seco peggio, et perché certi PP. NN. [Gesuiti] dissero: Se volete vedere l'empietà, et poco cervello del P.M. [...] leggete il suo libro sopra le litanie'; ibid., p. 30).

[36] 'E però ne cavai le seguenti propositioni: onde si vede che da questo libro si può provar il Gentilismo, parte del Mahomettismo e del Talmud et che gli heretici di questo tempo si ponno servire a provar, che sie vero quanto scrive Calvino, et Lutero, et Uvicleffo contra la Chiesa Romana, massime hora che sta l'abominatione *in loco santo*' (ibid., pp. 30–31).

[37] Ibid., pp. 64–5.

[38] 'Haeresis est, dicere Mariam *Dio increaturito*, non enim conversus est in substantiam Mariae; neque assumpsit Mariam ad unitatem personae, sed hominem Christum tantummodo' (ibid., p. 98).

in nuce: to maintain that Mary is a 'God made into a creature' (*Dio increaturito*), the philosopher explained, would presuppose that God had been converted *in substantiam Mariae* or at least that Mary had been called upon to replace Christ as the third person in the Most Holy Trinity. Equally easily to demonstrate was the doctrinal error of another statement by Riccardi, to the effect that all man's merits, gifts, graces, desires, and inspirations derive from the virtues of the Blessed Virgin: 'It is heresy if it is meant physically; for these things come from God', Campanella insisted, 'if it is meant morally and for the purpose of evocation, he is lying because many of these come from the Angels and Saints. With regard to inspirations and desires, it is heresy to affirm this, unless one is referring to God. For God alone insinuates His way into our souls, only He creates prophets, moves human will, and grants gifts and grace. And of such matters He said "And to no one shall I give my honor"'.[39]

Whereas in some cases a careful rereading of the sources used by Riccardi to support his arguments was sufficient to reveal the exaggerated nature of his interpretations and the misleading conclusions he drew from them,[40] in others a direct reference to the wording of the holy texts was sufficient to belie the bold observations of the future Master of the Holy Palace. Recalling that the 'qualities' (*attributi*) of the Son of God cannot be in any way considered inferior to those of the Virgin Mary, Campanella underlined that, unlike the figure of Christ, Mary has no part whatsoever in the divine nature.[41]

It was therefore necessary to restore Mary to her proper theological and religious dimension, purifying her of the high-sounded title of *principium omnium honorum* ('source of all honors'), which had been unduly attributed to her and restoring her to the more appropriate role of 'minister of frail mankind, for which God was made human and sacrificed Himself'.[42] The Mother of God's fullness of grace certainly manifested itself in a special way in her mercy toward persons in need of salvation, exhibiting itself in an action of intercession and propitiation at the throne of God. But the Virgin's mercy was simply a reflection of the goodness

---

[39] 'Haeresis, si physice intelligat; sunt enim haec a Deo, si moraliter, et suggestive, mentitur, quoniam sunt multa ab Angelis, et a Sanctis. De inspirationibus, et desideriis haeresis est id affirmare, praeter quam de Deo. Solus enim in animas illabitur; solus et facit prophetas, movet voluntates, dat dona et gratias. Et de his dixit: "Honorem meum nemini dabo"' (ibid., pp. 101–2).

[40] Ibid., p. 103.

[41] Ibid., p. 94.

[42] 'ministra humanitatis fragilis, per quam satisfacturus erat Deus humanatus' (ibid., p. 102).

and love of the Father.[43] Therefore, just as the proclamation of Mary's omnipotence led Riccardi to fall into grave doctrinal error,[44] so also the stratagem he employed in order to escape Inquisition control – in the words of this worldly-wise philosopher –was of little avail. Even the mere attribution to the Virgin of the power to 'take part' (*partecipare*) in God's omnipotence would have meant, in all cases, attributing to the Mother of Christ the power to create new worlds, to remit sins, to redeem mankind, and to possess other powers that belonged exclusively to God and His venerated Son.[45]

A form of very special attention to the subject of prayer was beginning to emerge from Campanella's censure. Considering this matter's central importance in Riccardi's work, it could perhaps hardly have been otherwise. Faced with the Master of the Holy Palace's 'scandalous' affirmations concerning the 'invincible power of Marian prayer' (*forza invincibile dell'orazione mariana*), Campanella reacted with genuine indignation. If it were true, he wrote, that the Mother of Christ 'makes Him [God] do what she wants' (*gli fa fare tutto ciò che vuole*), the Virgin's prayers would consequently have the power to condemn to eternal death a man predestined to salvation or to save the soul of a reprobate.[46] To allow 'simpletons and idiots' to believe that in the name of the Virgin any request they might make could be granted and satisfied was the most heretic thing he had ever heard: 'This is plain heresy, because he says that nothing that is sought in the name of the Virgin can be denied, and yet there are many who seek things in the name of the Virgin but are not answered. [...] Christ said: "Whatever you seek in my name shall be given to you", and not in the name of the Virgin', Campanella specified.[47] Only by vigorously reaffirming the centrality of devotional Christocentrism[48] would it be possible to restore the correct measure and proper value to the Blessed Virgin Mary's intercessory prayer.[49]

The unlucky fate of Campanelli's censures – destined not only, as said, to remain in manuscript form but also to provoke an unexpected and unpleasant Church offensive toward some of the most important of his

---

43 Ivi, p. 47.

44 Ibid., p. 106

45 Ibid., pp. 106–7.

46 Ibid., p. 107.

47 'Manifesta haeresis, quoniam in nomine Virginis nihil petitum posse negari dicit, et tamen multi rogant in nomine Virginis, et non exaudiuntur. Christus dixit: "Quaecumque petieritis in nomine meo, dabit vobis," et non nomine Virginis' (ibid., p. 51).

48 Ibid., pp. 50–51.

49 Ibid., f. 306.

philosophical and religious writings[50] – was now only the last of the signals of a clear act of surrender by the Roman hierarchies to the deviations that were characteristic features of seventeenth-century devotional literature.

The same mocking trick of destiny that had favored the clamorous inversion of roles between censor (Riccardi) and victim (Campanella) ended by presenting the image of an unsuspected 'elective affinity' between two traditional enemies in the history of those years: the heretic Tommaso Campanella and the Inquisitor Cardinal Roberto Bellarmino, brought together – even though only for a brief moment – by a battle, now lost, in the name of the purity of doctrine and devotion,[51] a battle for doctrinal purity and rigor which perhaps – now that the danger of Lutheranism had finally been driven off – was no longer worth fighting.

---

50 A. TERMINELLI, *Introduzione* to T. Campanella, *Censure*, p. 14.

51 On the esteem and reciprocal respect which, despite the diversity of their positions, characterized the relationship between these two important figures in the culture of the age, cf. G. ERNST, 'Il ritrovato Apologeticum di Campanella al Bellarmino in difesa della religione naturale', *Rivista di storia della filosofia*, 1992, n. 3, pp. 565–86 and in particular pp. 566–7.

Bibliography

Primary Sources

ALBERTINI, FRANCESCO, *Trattato dell'angelo custode del R.P. Francesco Albertino da Catanzaro della Compagnia di Giesù. Con l'Offitio dell'angelo custode, approvato da N.S. Papa Paolo Quinto. Et un altro trattato utilissimo alla devotione verso la Beatissima Vergine. Fatto da un Sacerdote Napolitano Dottore in Teologia*, Ad istanza del Signor Gioseppe Scotto. In Roma, per Guglielmo Facciotti, 1612. Con licenza de' superiori. Si vendono alla bottega di Nicolò de Ludi. All'arco di Camiliano. Con Privilegio

BATTISTA DA CREMA, *Specchio interiore opera divina per la cui lettione ciascuno devoto potrà facilmente ascendere al colmo della perfettione*, Milan, apud Calvo, 1540

BATTISTA DA CREMA, *Opera utilissima de la cognitione et vittoria di se stesso ... Composta per il reverendissimo Battista da Crema maestro di scientia spirituale pratica et perfettione, christiano rarissimo* (first edn, Milan, 1531), Venice, Nicolò Bascarini, 1545

BATTISTA DA CREMA, *Philosophia divina di quello solo vero maestro Iesu Christo crucifixo, Milan, Gotardo da Ponte, 1531*

BATTISTA DA CREMA, *Della devotione*, contained in the volume *Via de aperta verità*, Venice, Bastiano Vicentino, 1532 (first edn Venice, 1523)

BELLINTANI DA SALÒ, MATTIA, *Prattica dell'oratione mentale, di f. Mathia Bellintani da Salò, dell'Ordine de' frati di S. Francesco Capuccini. Opera molto utile per quelle divote persone, che desiderano occuparsi nell'oratione con frutto e gusto*. Con privilegio dell'Illustrissimo Senato di Milano per anni dieci. In Brescia, appresso Vincenzo Sabbio, 1573, in *I Frati Cappuccini. Documenti e testimonianze del primo secolo*, C. Cagnoni (ed.), III/l, Letteratura spirituale ascetico-mistica (1535–1628), Perugia, EFI Edizioni Frate Indovino, 1991, pp. 665–736

BELLINTANI DA SALÒ, MATTIA, *Pratica dell'orazione mentale di fra Mathia Bellintani da Salò dell'Ordine dei Frati di S. Francesco Capuccini. Parte prima: Di nuovo dallo stesso autore riveduta, corretta, ed in alcune parti ridotta a miglior forma. Parte seconda: Nuovamente posta in luce*, Venice, apud Pietro Dusinello, 1584, critical edition by Father Umile da Genova, O.M.C. (Order of Capuchin Minors), Assisi, Collegio S. Lorenzo da Brindisi dei Minori Cap., 1931

(*La*) *Benedittione di Nostra Donna*, In Siena, 1578

BERNARDINO DA BALVANO, *Specchio di oratione*, Messina, per Pietro Spira, 1553

BONGIORNO, FERDINANDO, *Il bongiorno overo orationi delle quaranta hore*, 1601

BORROMEO, CARLO, *Lettera pastorale ed instituto dell'orazione comune*, Roma, appresso gli heredi d'Antonio Blado, 1574

Concilium Tridentinum. Diariorum, Auctorum, Epistolarum, Tractatuum nova collectio, vol. V, Freiburg, Brisgoviae, B. Herder, 1911

La confessione di santa Maria Maddalena, In Venetia, dalla bottega del Guadagnino, al segno dell'Hippogrifo, 1585

Confitemini della Madonna con le Litanie, Venetia, per Augustino Bindoni, 1553

CAMPANELLA, TOMMASO, *Censure sopra il libro del Padre Mostro: 'Ragionamenti sopra le litanie di Nostra Signora'*, A. Terminelli (ed.), Rome, Edizioni Monfortane, 1998

CARACCIA, ARCANGELO, *Rosario della Beata Vergine, con l'indulgenze e privileggi concessi alla Compagnia. Raccolto dal P. Maestro F. Argangelo Caraccia da Rivalla, dell'Ordine de' Predicatori. Di nuovo ristampato con la Gionta d'alcune divote considerazioni fatte dall'Autore*. In Roma, per Guglielmo Facciotti 1627

(*El*) *Contrasto di Cicarello da Cazan da contrastare in Maschera, e uno maridazzo di Toniolo e Menguosa, narrando tutte le virtù del sposo e della sposa, cosa piacevole e rediculosa*, s.d., s.l.

CORDONI DA CITTÀ DI CASTELLO, BARTOLOMEO, *De unione animae cum supereminenti lumine. Opera nuova et utile ad ogni fidel Christiao. Composta per il Reverendo padre frate Bartolomeo da Castello de l'ordine de l'observantia*, Perugia, per gli Cartolari, October 1538

CORDONI DA CITTÀ DI CASTELLO, BARTOLOMEO, *Dyalogo dell'unione spirituale de Dio con l'anima*, Milan, per Francesco Cantalupo et Innocentio da Cicognara, 1539

CORDONI DA CITTÀ DI CASTELLO, BARTOLOMEO, *De vnione anime cum Deo*, Perugia, per Girolamo Cartolaro, 1538. Ristampata in Bologna per Fausto Bonardo, 1589

CORTESE, FRANCESCO, *Giglio Angelico esposto con alti sensi in sette Lettioni, ne sette Sabbati di Quaresima. Con una breve inventione, e morale dichiaratione del Vangelo corrente nelle seconde parti. Lette nel MDCVIII con maggiori misteri a Padova, da Fra Francesco Cortese da Montefalco, Teologo, e Predicatore Generale de Menori osservanti. Con tre tavole dell'Autori citati. Dell'autorità da quali sono cavati i concetti. E delle cose più notabili.* Con privilegio, in Venezia, al segno della Speranza, 1608

CRISPOLDI, TULLIO, *Meditationi sopra il Pater noster*, Venetia, Stefano da Sabio, (Sept.) 1534

CRISPOLDI, TULLIO, *Meditationi dechiarative del Paternostro, ad esercitio di fede et di charità, massimamente circa il perdonare, et insieme alcuna cosa de l'Ave Maria, et di tutti santi, et de li morti,* Venetia, Stefano da Sabio, (Dec.) 1534

CRISPOLDI, TULLIO, *De la Ave Maria et del Credo, et dimonstrare in qual cosa debbiamo haver fede in Dio*, Venetia, Stefano da Sabio, 1535

DAVIDICO, LORENZO, *Monte d'oratione composto per il reverendo sacerdote M. Lorenzo Davidico Predicatore fidelissimo.* In Rome, per i tipografi Valerio e Luigi Dorico, l'anno del Giubileo, 1550

La devota oratione di San Francesco con una laude bellissima, s.l., s.d., s.p.

La devota orazione di Santo Antonio, s.l., s.d., s.p.

La devotissima contemplatione del peccatore al Crocifisso, in Venezia, in Frezzaria, al segno della Regina, 1586

Legenda devota del Romito et de Pulcini, cavata della vita patrum, e una Oratione del beato Simone da Trento devotissima, s.d., s.l.

FISHER, JOHN, *Assertionis Lutheranae confutatio iuxta verum ac originalem archetypum, nunc ad vnguem diligentissime recognita. Per reuerendum patrem Ioannem Roffensem episcopum, academie Canthabrigien cancellarium.* Aeditio vltima, variis annotationibus in margine locupletata, Venetiis, in aedibus Gregorii de Gregoriis, August 1526

FISHER, JOHN, *Ioannis Roffensis episcopi et S.R.E. Cardinalis, Tractatus de orando Deum, et de fructibus precum, modoque orandi*, Rome, apud Franciscum Zanettum, 1578

FISHER, JOHN, *Breue trattato di Giovanni Vescouo Roffense ... del modo di pregare Iddio, e de' frutti che si cauano dall'oratione.* Napoli, ex officina Horatii Saluiani, appresso Giovanni Giacomo Carlino & Antonio Pace, 1592

(*La*) *Forma de le orationi ecclesiastiche e il modo d'amministrare i Sacramenti, e di celebrare il santo Matrimonio, secondo che s' usa ne le buone Chiese.* Stampato da Giovanni Battista Pinerolo, 1560

FREGOSO, FEDERICO, *Pio et christianissimo trattato della oratione, il quale dimostra come si debbe orare et quali debbeno essere le nostre preci a Iddio per conseguire la eterna salute et felicità*, Venetia, Gabriel Giolito de' Ferrari, 1542

GAGLIARDI, ACHILLE, *Breve compendio intorno alla perfettione cristiana. Dove si vede una pratica mirabile per unire l'anima con Dio. Del M.R.P. Achille Gagliardi. Teologo della Compagnia di Giesù.* In Napoli, per Giovan Giacomo Carlino, 1614

GAGLIARDI, ACHILLE, *Breve compendio di perfezione cristiana. Un testo di Achille Gagliardi S.I. Introductory essay and critical edition* (M. Gioia ed.), Rome-Brescia, Gregorian University Press – Morcelliana, 1996

GAUCCI, ANGELO, *Discorsi spirituali*, in Macerata, appresso Sebastiano Martellini, 1598

Ghelfucci, Capoleone, *Il Rosario della Madonna Poema Eroico del sig. Capoleone Ghelfucci da Città di Castello, dato alle stampe dai figliuoli dopo la morte dell'Autore. A divotione dell'Illustrissimo Signor Cintio Aldobrandini Cardinale di San Giorgio. Agiuntovi* (sic) *nuovamente gli Argumenti a ciascun Canto*. Con privilegio. In Venetia, appresso Nicolò Polo, 1603

Girolamo da Molfetta, *Alcune regule de la oratione mentale con la contemplatione de la Corona del nome di Iesu, predicate da Fra Hieronymo da Molfetta* (1539), in *I Frati Cappuccini. Documenti e testimonianze del primo secolo*, C. Cargnoni (ed.), III/1, *Letteratura spirituale ascetico-mistica (1535–1628)*, pp. 429 et seqq.

Giulio da Milano, *Esortatione alli dispersi per Italia di Giulio da Milano. Vi è aggiunta una Meditatione sopra del Paternoster*, Trento, 1549

Guanzelli, Giovanni Maria da Brisighella, *Indicis librorum expurgandorum in studiosorum gratiam confecti Tomus primus. In quo quinqinginta auctorum libri prae coeteris desiderati emendatur per Fr. Jo. Mariam Brasichellen. Sacri Palatii Apostolici Magistrum in unum corpus redactus et publicae commoditati aeditus*, Romae, ex Typographia R. Cam. Apost., 1607

Historia et oratione di Santo Giorgio Cavallero, In Venetia, in Frezzaria al segno della Regina, 1586

Interpretatione della Oratione dominica, ebraica, greca et latina, cum le expositioni di santo Mattheo, & santo Luca, & di santo Hieronymo, & di Erasmo sopra li prediti, sancto Mattheo, & Luca, ad vtile & piacere di ogni persona religiosa & amatrice delle virtuti. Nouamente composta, in Venecia, per Ioanne Antonio & fradelli da Sabio, ad istantia de Lorenzo Lorio, nel 1522 dil mese de ottobrio

Lerri, Michelangelo, *Breve informatione del modo di trattare le cause del S. Officio Per li molto Reverendi vicarii della Santa Inquisitone, instituti nelle Diocesi di Modona, di Carpi, di Nonantola, e della Garfagnana, in Modona, at the printing-shop of Giulian Cassiani*, in Modona, nella stamperia di Giulian Cassiani, 1608

Libro devoto e fructuoso a ciaschaduno chiamato Giardino de Oratione, Novamente stampato. In Venetia, per Bernardino de Viano de Lexona, 1521

Lippomano, Luigi, *Espositioni volgari del Reverendo M. Luigi Lippomano vescovo di Modone, et coadiutore di Bergamo, sopra il Simbolo Apostolico cioè il Credo, sopra il Pater nostro, et sopra i due precetti della charità, nelle quali tre cose consiste ciò che si dee dal buon christiano credere, desiderare, et operare in questo mondo. Opera catholica et utilissima ad ogni Cristiano*, Venetia, apud Hieronimum Scotum, 1541

LUIS DE GRANADA, *Pie et devote orationi, raccolte da diversi e gravi autori, per il R.P.F. Luigi di Granata, dell'ordine de' Predicatori. E novamente tradotte di spagnolo in italiano da un devoto Religioso*, Vinegia, apud Gio. and Gio. Paolo Gioliti de' Ferrari, 1580

LUTHER, MARTIN, *An Exposition of the Lord's Prayer for Simple Laymen*, in Id., *Luther's Works*, American Edition, Saint Louis, Concordia Pub. House – Philadelphia, Fortress Press, 1955– , vol. 42, *Devotional Writings*, I, ed. by Martin. O. Dietrich, pp. 19–81

LUTHER, MARTIN, *Il "Padre nostro" spiegato nella lingua volgare ai semplici laici*, ID., *Scritti religiosi*, V. Vinay (ed.), Turin, Utet, 1967, pp. 205–78

LUTHER, MARTIN, *Il Padre nostro spiegato ai semplici laici*, Turin, Claudiana, 1982

MURATORI, LUDOVICO, *Della regolata devozione*, P. Stella (ed.), Rome, Edizioni Paoline, 1990

OCHINO, BERNARDINO, *Trattato dell'oratione*, Id., *Sermones Bernardini Ochini Senensis*, [Geneva] 1544, 15 March (Sermons I–XIII)

Oratione delli confitemini della Madonna, dal R. P. F. Nicolò Aurifico Carmelitano, Palermo, for Rosselli, 1630

Oratione devotissima alla Matre di Dio, trovata nel S. Sepolcro di Christo, In Barzelona, e ristampata in Venezia, con licenza de'superiori, undated

Oratione devotissima della gloriosa Santa Catherina Vergine, e Martire. Con un nuovo Sonetto in laude di quella nuovamente aggiorno, in Venetia, Frezzaria, al segno della Regina, 1584

Oratione devotissima di Santa Margarita, con i sette Gaudii di Santa Maria Maddalena, stampata in Siena nell'anno 1581

Oratione di Santa Maria de Loretto, in Siena, undated

PICO DELLA MIRANDOLA, GIOVANNI, *Breve et acuta dichiaratione sopra il Pater nostro del signor Giovanni Pico della Mirandola*, s.d., s.l.

PILI DA FANO, GIOVANNI, *Opera vtilissima uulgare contra le pernitiosissime heresie luterane per li simplici*, In Bologna, Giovan Battista Phaello, 1532

PILI DA FANO, GIOVANNI, *Operetta devotissima chiamata Arte de la Unione*, Bressa, per Damiano e Iacomo Philippo Bros., 1536

PILI DA FANO, GIOVANNI, *Arte d'unirsi con Dio, del R. P. F. Giovanni da Fano Predicator Capuccino. Ridotta in miglior forma, accresciuta, e in quattro parti divisa, cioè nella vita purgativa, nell'illuminativa, nell'unitiva e negli esercizi ...*, in Rome, per Andrea Fei, 1622

PILI DA FANO, GIOVANNI, *Regula et testamentum seraphici patris nostri s. Francisci. Compendioso discorso dil fra Giouanne da Fano, sopra il stato dell'altissima pouertà euangelica de frati minori.* Milano, per Bros. Francesco e Simone Moscheni, 1554

PORZIO, SIMONE, *Modo di orare christianamente con la espositione del Pater noster, fatta da M. Simone Portio Napoletano. Tradotto in lingua*

Fiorentina, da Giovan Batista Gelli, Firenze, apud Lorenzo Torrentino, 1551

Porzio, Simone, *Formae orandi christianae, enarratio. Eiusdem in Euangelium Diui Ioannis scholion*, Firenze, apud Laurentium Torrentinum, 1552

Riccardi, Niccolò, *La prima parte dei ragionamenti sopra le Letanie di Nostra Signora del padre Maestro Fra Nicolò Riccardi dell'ordine de' Predicatori, e Reggente della Minerva in Roma*. Genoa, per Giuseppe Pavoni. 1626.

Rocca, Angelo, *Spositione intorno all'oratione domenicale raccolta da' più famosi Scrittori antichi et moderni che in ciò hanno scritto fin'hora, da F. Angelo Rocca da Camerino, dottor' in Theologia dell'Ordine Eremitano di S. Agostino*. Roma, apud Guglielmo Facciotto, 1594

Saiglio, Tommaso, *Thesaurus litaniarum, ac orationum sacer cum suis adversus sectarios apologiis ... Novo ordine dispositus et Litaniis de Martyrologio in singulos anni dies sumptis autus*, Paris, apud Claudium Chappellet, 1599

Sandys, Edwin, *A Relation of the state of religion: and with what Hopes and Policies it hath beene framed, and is maintained in the severall states of these western parts of the world*, London, Printed for Simon Waterson dwelling in Paules Churchyard at the signe of the Crowne, 1605

Sarpi, Paolo, *Relazione dello stato della Religione, e con quali dissegni et arti ella è stata fabricata e maneggiata in diversi stati di queste occidentali parti del mondo*, 1625, in Sarpi, *Lettere a Gallicani e Protestanti, Relazione dello Stato della Religione, Trattato delle materie beneficiarie*, Gaetano and Luisa Cozzi (eds), Turin, Einaudi, 1978, pp. 51–88

Sarpi, Paolo, *Istoria del Concilio tridentino*, Corrado Vivanti (ed.), Turin, Einaudi, 1974

Sarpi, Paolo, *Opere*, Corrado Vivanti (ed.), Rome, Istituto poligrafico e Zecca dello Stato, 2000

Sauli, Filippo, *Opus Noviter editum pro sacerdotibus curam animarum habentibus*, Milan, apud Augustinum Vicomercatum, mense Maio 1521

Savonarola, Girolamo, *Operette spirituali*, M. Ferrara (ed.), Rome, Angelo Belardelli editore, 1976

Savonarola, Girolamo, *Espositione sopra il Pater noster*, Firenze, 1494

Savonarola, Girolamo, *Expositio orationis dominicae*, Firenze, Antonio Tubini, 1500

Savonarola, Girolamo, *Trattato in difensione e commendazione dell'orazione mentale*, Firenze, Miscomini, 1492

Savonarola, Girolamo, *Trattato o vero sermone dell'orazione*, Firenze, Miscomini, 20 October 1492

Scriniolum Sanctae Inquisitionis Astensis in quo quaecumque ad id muneris obeundum spedare visa sunt, vidilicet Librorum Prohibitorum Indices ..., Astae, Apud Virgilium de Zangrandis, 1610

SERAFINO DA FERMO, *Trattato utilissimo et necessario della mentale oratione, et come acquistar si possi, del Reverendo padre Don Seraphino da Fermo Can. Regulare et predicatore rarissimo.* In Venetia, Comin da Trino, 1541

SILVESTRO DA ROSSANO, *Modo di contemplare, et dire la devotione del preciosissimo sangue del nostro Signor Giesù Christo, sparso pietosamente per noi. Composto dal R.P. Fra Silvestro Rossano Cappuccino, Predicatore evangelico, et insegnato alla Compagnia dell'Oratorio di Santa Maria dell'Humiltà di Venetia. Opera molto utile all'anime che l'useranno*, In Fiorenza, appresso Giorgio Marescotti, 1573

SILVESTRO DA ROSSANO, *Modo come la persona spirituale che ora, si habbia a disporre nella Oratione verso Iddio e li suoi Santi: per tutti li giorni della Settimana tanto la mattina come la sera detta Consonantia Spirituale. Composta da Fra Silvestro da Rossano Cappuccino, mentre predicava a San Salvatore di Venetia, nell'anno MDLXXII. Divisa in due parti, nella prima si tratta di quelle cose che sono necessarie da sapere, e nella seconda il modo che si ha da tenere.* In Venetia, apud Gabriel Giolito de' Ferrari, 1574

[STANCARO, FRANCESCO], *Espositione utilima sopra il Pater noster, con duoi devotissimi trattati, uno in che modo Dio esaudisce le orationi nostre, l'altro di penitentia*, Venetia, 1539

Thesaurus sacrarum precum sive Litaniae variae ad Deum Patrem, ad Deum Filium, ad Deum Spiritum Sanctum, ad B. Virginem, ad Sanctos Angelos et ad plures Sanctos et Sanctas Dei. Una cum septem Psalmis penitentialibus ... [et aliis] devotis orationibus ..., Venetiis, apud Beretium, 1599

THIERS, JEAN BAPTISTE, *Traité des superstitions selon l'Ecriture sainte, les decrets des Conciles, et les sentiments des Saints Pères, et des Théologiens, par M. Jean-Baptiste Thiers, Docteur en Théologie, et Curé de Vibraie. Seconde edition. Revue, corrigée, augmentée*, 4 tomes, Paris, Chez Antoine Dezallier, rue S. Jacque, à la Couronne d'or. 1697

Transito di Nostra Donna, In Siena, s.d.

VERGERIO, PIER PAOLO, *Il catalogo de libri, li quali nuovamente nel mese di maggio nell'anno presente MDXLVIII sono stati condannati e scomunicati per heretici da Giovan Della Casa legato di Venetia e d'alcuni frati. É aggiunto sopra il medesimo catalogo un iudicio, et discorso del Vergerio*, Zurich, Christoph Froschauer, 1549

VERGERIO, PIER PAOLO, *A quegli Venerabili Padri Dominicani che difendono il Rosario per cosa buona*, 1550

VERGERIO, PIER PAOLO, *Operetta nuova del Vergerio, nella quale si dimostrano le vere ragioni che hanno mosso i Romani Pontefici ad instituir le belle cerimonie della Settimana Santa*, Tiguri apud Andream Gesnerum F. Rodolphum Vuissenbachium, 1552

VERGERIO, PIER PAOLO, *Della camera, et Statua della Madonna chiamata di Loretto, la quale è stata nuovamente difesa da Fra Leandro Alberti Bolognese, e da Papa Giulio III*, 1553

VERGERIO, PIER PAOLO, *Ludovico Rasoro alla Abbadessa del Monasterio di Santa Giustina di Venetia, sopra un libro intitolato Luce di Fede*, stampato nuovamente in Milano per Giovanni Antonio da Borgo in laude della Messa, 1553

VERGERIO, PIER PAOLO, *Catalogo dell'Arcimboldo arcivescovo di Melano. Con una risposta fattagli in nome d'una parte di quei valenti huomini*, Tübingen, Morhart, 1554

VERGERIO, PIER PAOLO, *Che cosa sieno le XXX Messe chiamate di San Gregorio e quando prima incominciarono ad usarsi* ..., 1555

VERGERIO, PIER PAOLO, *Discorsi sopra i Fioretti di San Francesco, ne quali della sua vita, e delle sue stigmate si ragiona*, [Basel, Giacomo Parco] s.d.

VERGERIO, PIER PAOLO (ed.), *Forma delle publiche orationi, et della confessione, et assolutione, la qual si usa nella chiesa de forestieri, che è nuovamente stata instituita in Londra (per gratia di Dio) con l'autorità et consentimento del Re*

VERGERIO, PIER PAOLO, *A gl'Inquisitori che sono per l'Italia. Del Catalogo di libri eretici, stampato in Roma nell'Anno presente*, Tübingen, eredi di Ulrich Morhart il vecchio, 1559

VERNAZZA, BATTISTA, *Della unione dell'anima con Dio sopra il Pater noster. Tratt. della Reverenda, et Devotissima Vergine di Christo, Donna Battista da Genoa, Can. Regolare Lateranense*, in *Opere spirituali della Reverenda et Devotissima Vergine di Christo, Donna Battista da Genova, Canonica Regolare Lateranense*. In tre tomi distinte, nelle quali tutta l'altezza della Christiana perfettione, et intima amorosa union con Dio (quanto sia possibile) chiaramente s'insegna. Hor prima date in luce, con tre tavole utilissime et copiosissime, Venetia, appresso gli eredi di Francesco Ziletti, 1588

(*Le*) *virtù, et le utilità che acquistano quelli che ascoltano la Santa Messa. Raccolte da diversi Santi Dottori, per il R. Don Fabio Napolitano*, in Napoli, e ristampato in Messina, per Pietro Brea, 1594

(*La*) *vita, et morte di Santa Caterina da Siena*, printed in Siena, 1580

Secondary Literature

ABBONDANZA BLASI, ROCCHINA MARIA, *Tra evangelismo e riforma cattolica. Le prediche sul Paternoster di Girolamo Seripando*, introduction by G. De Rosa, Rome, Carocci, 1999

ADORNI BRACCESI, SIMONETTA, *Una 'città infetta'. La repubblica di Lucca nella crisi religiosa del Cinquecento*, Florence, Olschki, 1994

ALBERIGO, GIUSEPPE, 'Beccadelli, Ludovico', *Dizionario Biografico degli Italiani*, vol. VII, pp. 407–13

ALBERIGO, GIUSEPPE, 'Carlo Borromeo come modello di vescovo nella Chiesa post-tridentina', *Rivista Storica Italiana*, LXXIX, 1967, pp. 1031–52

ALBERIGO, GIUSEPPE, 'Da Carlo Borromeo all'episcopato post-tridentino', *Il tipo ideale di vescovo secondo la Riforma cattolica*, Jedin, H., Alberigo, G. (eds), Brescia, Morcelliana, 1985, pp. 99–138

AMBROSINI, FEDERICA, *Storie di patrizi e di eresia nella Venezia del '500*, Milan, Franco Angeli, 1999

ANSELMI, ANSELMO, *Cenni biografici di mons. Angelo Rocca d'Arcevia: fondatore della biblioteca Angelica in Roma*, Fabriano, apud Gentile, 1881

Atti del convegno intemazionale di studi muratoriani, Modena, I–IV volumes, 1972–1975

AUBERT, ALBERTO, 'Misticismo, valdesianesimo e riforma della chiesa in Vittoria Colonna', *Rivista di Storia della Chiesa in Italia*, XLVI, 1992, pp. 143–66

BALDINI, UGO, 'Una fonte poco utilizzata per la storia intellettuale: le "censurae librorum" et "opinionum" nell'antica Compagnia di Gesù', *Annali dell'Istituto storico italo-germanico in Trento*, XI, 1985, pp. 19–50.

BALSAMO, LUIGI, 'Venezia e l'attività editoriale di Antonio Possevino (1553–1606)', *La Bibliofilia*, XCIII, 1991, pp. 53–93

BALSAMO, LUIGI, 'How to doctor a bibliography: Antonio Possevino's practice', *Church, censorship and culture in early modern Italy*, G. Fragnito (ed.), Cambridge, Cambridge University Press, 2001, pp. 50–78

BARBIERI, EDOARDO, *Tradition and change in the spiritual literature of the Cinquecento*, in *Church, Censorship and Culture in early modern Italy*, G. Fragnito (ed.), Cambridge, Cambridge University Press, 2001, pp. 111–33, published in fuller form in, *Libri, biblioteche e cultura nell'Italia del Cinque e Seicento*, Barbieri, E. and D. ZARDIN (eds), Milan, Vita e Pensiero, 2002, pp. 3–61.

BARBIERI, EDOARDO, 'Un apocrifo nell'Italia moderna: la Epistola della domenica' *Monastica et Humanistica: scritti in onore di p. Gregorio Penco*, F. Trolese (ed.), 2 vols, Cesena, Badia di Santa Maria del Monte, 2003, vol. 2, pp. 717–32

Barzazi, Antonella, *Ordini religiosi e biblioteche a Venezia tra Cinque e Seicento*, in 'Annali dell'Istituto storico italo-germanico in Trento', XXI, 1995, pp. 141–228

Bataillon, Marcel, *Erasmo y España. Estudios sobre la historia espiritual del siglo XVI*, Mexico-Buenos Aires, Fondo de cultura economica, 1966 (II edn)

Batiffol, P., *History of the Roman Breviary*, London, Longmans and Co., 1912 (I French edn 1893)

Beginnings and discoveries. Polydore Vergil's De inventoribus rerum, An unabridged translation and edition with introduction, notes and glossary by Beno Weiss and Louis C. Pérez, Nieuwkoop, De Graaf Publishers, 1997

Berengo, Marino, *Nobili e mercanti nella Lucca del Cinquecento*, Turin, Einaudi, 1974, I edn 1965

Betti, Gian Luigi, 'Alcune considerazioni riguardo all' "Incendio de zizanie lutherane" di Giovanni da Fano pubblicato a Bologna nel 1532', *L'Archiginnasio*, LXXXII, 1987, pp. 235–43

Biondi, Albano, 'Aspetti della cultura cattolica post-tridentina. Religione e controllo sociale', *Storia d'Italia*, Annali 4: Intellettuali e potere, Turin, Einaudi, 1981, pp. 255–302

Biondi, Albano, 'La Biblioteca selecta di Antonio Possevino. Un progetto di egemonia culturale', *La 'Ratio studiorum': Modelli culturali e pratiche educative dei Gesuiti in Italia tra Cinque e Seicento*, G.P. Brizzi (ed.), Rome, Bulzoni, 1981, pp. 43–75

Bogliolo, Luigi, *Battista da Crema. Nuovi studi sopra la sua vita, i suoi scritti, la sua dottrina*, Turin, Società Editrice Internazionale, 1952

Bonora, Elena, *I conflitti della Controriforma. Santità e obbedienza nell'esperienza religiosa dei primi barnabiti*, Florence, Le Lettere, 1998

Bonora, Elena, 'Nei labirinti della censura libraria cinquecentesca: Antonio Pagani (1526–1589) e le "Rime spirituali"', *Per Marino Berengo. Studi degli allievi*, L. Antonielli, C. Capra, M. Infelice (eds), Milan, Franco Angeli, 2001, pp. 114–36

Bonora, Elena, *Giudicare i vescovi. La definizione dei poteri nella Chiesa post-tridentina*, Rome-Bari, Laterza, 2007

Borromeo, Agostino, 'A proposito del Directorium Inquisitorum di Nicolas Eymerich e delle sue edizioni cinquecentesche', *Critica storica*, XX, 1983, pp. 499–547

Bossy, John, 'The Counter-Reformation and the People of Catholic Europe', *Past and Present*, XCVII, 1970, pp. 51–70 (Italian translation: 'Controriforma e popolo nell'Europa cattolica', *Le origini dell'Europa moderna*, M. Rosa (ed.), Rome-Bari, Laterza, 1977, pp. 281–308)

Bozza, Tommaso, 'Calvino in Italia', *Miscellanea in memoria di Georgio Cernetti*, Turin, Bottega d'Erasmo, 1973, pp. 409–41

BOZZA, TOMMASO, 'Italia calvinista. Il Piovano di messer Vittor de' Popoli', *L'uomo e la storia. Studi storici in onore di Massimo Petrocchi*, vol. I, Rome, Edizioni di Storia e Letteratura, 1983, pp. 267–98

BRUNELLI, GIAMPIERO, 'Fregoso, Federico', *Dizionario biografico degli italiani*, vol. L, Rome, Istituto dell'Enciclopedia Italiana, 1998, pp. 396–9

BURKE, PETER, *Popular culture in early modern Europe*, New York, Harper & Row, 1978

BUSCHBELL, GOTTFRIED, *Reformation und Inquisition in Italien um die Mitte des XVI Jahrhunderts*, Padeborn, F. Schöningh, 1910

CAMPORESI, PIERO, 'Cultura popolare e cultura d'élite tra Medioevo ed età moderna', *Storia d'Italia*, Annali 4, *Intellettuali e potere*, Turin, Einaudi, 1981, pp. 81–157

CANTIMORI, DELIO, 'Incontri italo-germanici nell'età della Riforma', '*Rivista di studi germanici*', III, 1938, pp. 63–89, now in ID., *Umanesimo e religione nel Rinascimento*, Turin, Einaudi, 1975, pp. 112–41

CARAVALE, GIORGIO, 'Censura e pauperismo tra Cinque e Seicento. Controriforma e cultura dei senza lettere', *Rivista di Storia e Letteratura Religiosa*, XXXVIII, 2002, 1, pp. 39–77

CARAVALE, GIORGIO, *Sulle tracce dell'eresia. Ambrogio Catarino Politi (1483–1553)*, Florence, Olschki, 2007

CARELLA, CANDIDA, 'Antonio Possevino e la biblioteca "selecta" del principe cristiano', *Bibliothecae selectae. Da Cusano a Leopardi*, E. Canone (ed.), Florence, Olschki, 1993, pp. 507–16

CARGNONI, COSTANZO, 'Fonti, tendenze e sviluppi della letteratura spirituale cappuccina primitiva', Collectanea *Francescana*, XLVIII, 1978, 3–4, pp. 311–98

CARGNONI, COSTANZO, 'La devozione al sangue di Cristo in un opuscolo censurato e finora ignorato di Silvestro da Rossano', *Collectanea Francescana*, LXIX, 1999, 3–4, pp. 573–628; (now also in *Clavis scientiae. Miscellanea di studi offerti a Isidoro Agudo da Villapadiema in occasione del suo 80° compleanno*, V. Criscuolo (ed.), Rome, Istituto Storico Cappuccino, 1999, pp. 315–74)

CARLINI, G., 'Silvestro Di Franco da Rossano Calabro (1530–1596), Vicario Provinciale in Toscana', *Fra Noi*, XIII, 1996, pp. 5–33

Carlo Borromeo e l'opera della grande Riforma: cultura, religione e arti del governo nella Milano del pieno Cinquecento, FRANCO BUZZI, D. ZARDIN (eds), introduction by G. Ravasi, Milan, Credito artigiano, 1997

CASSESE, MICHELE, *Girolamo Seripando e i vescovi meridionali (1535–1563)*, 2 tomes, Naples, Editoriale Scientifica, 2002

CATALANO, GIUSEPPE, *De magistro Sacri Palatii Apostolici Libri duo. Quorum alter originem, praerogativas, ac munia, alter eorum Seriem continet, qui eo munere ad hanc usque diem donati fuere*, Rome, Typis Antonii Fulgoni apud S. Eustachium, 1751

CATTO, MICHELA, *Un panopticon catechistico: l'arciconfraternita della dottrina cristiana a Roma in età moderna*, Rome, Edizioni di Storia e Letteratura, 2003

CAVARRA, ANGELA ADRIANA, 'La Biblioteca Casanatense a difesa dell'ortodossia: bibliotecari e teologi domenicani, segretari dell'Indice e Maestri del Sacro Palazzo', *Inquisizione e Indice nei secoli XVI–XVII. Controversie teologiche dalle raccolte casanatensi*, A.A. Cavarra (ed.), Vigevano, Diakronia, 1998, pp. 1–5

CAVAZZA, SILVANO, '"Luthero fidelissimo inimico de messer Iesu Christo". La polemica contro Lutero nella letteratura religiosa in volgare della prima metà del Cinquecento', Luigi Perrone (ed.), *Lutero in Italia*, Casale Monferrato, Marietti, 1983, pp. 65–94

CAVAZZA, SILVANO, 'Pier Paolo Vergerio nei Grigioni e in Valtellina (1549–1553): attività editoriale e polemica religiosa', in *Riforma e società nei Grigioni. Valtellina e Valchiavenna tra '500 e '600*, edited by A. Pastore, Milan, Franco Angeli, 1991, pp. 33–62

CESAREO, FRANCESCO C., 'Penitential Sermons in Renaissance Italy. Girolamo Seripando and the *Pater Noster*', *The Catholic Historical Review*, LXXXIII, 1997, pp. 1–19

CHARTIER, ROGER – REVEL, JACQUES, 'Le paysan, l'ours et saint Angustin', *La Découverte de la France au XVII siècle*, Cnrs, Paris, 1980, pp. 259–64

CIAN, VITTORIO, 'Un episodio della storia della censura in Italia nel secolo XVI. L'edizione spurgata del "Cortegiano"', *Archivio storico lombardo*, s. 2, XIV, 1887, pp. 661–727

CIPRIANI, GIOVANNI, *La mente di un inquisitore. Agostino Valier e l'Opusculum De cautione adhibenda in edendis libris, 1589–1604*, Firenze, Nocomp, 2008

CISTELLINI, ANTONIO, Introduction to VALIER, AGOSTINO, *Il Dialogo della Gioia cristiana*, Brescia, Editrice La Scuola, 1975, pp. XIII–LXXXI

Conciliorum Oecumenicorum Decreta, edited by G. Alberigo, G.A. Dossetti, P.-P. Joannou, C. Leonardi, and P. Prodi, Bologna, Istituto per le Scienze religiose, 1973

CORRAIN, CLETO – ZAMPINI, PIERLUIGI, *Documenti etnografici e folkloristici nei sinodi diocesani italiani*, Bologna, Forni editore, 1970

COZZI, GUSTAVO, 'Sir Edwin Sandys e la "Relazione dello Stato della Religion"', *Rivista Storica italiana*, LXXIX, 1967, pp. 1095–1121

CRISCUOLO, VINCENZO, *Girolamo Mautini da Narni (1563–1632): predicatore apostolico e vicario generale dei Cappuccini*, Rome, Istituto Storico dei Cappuccini, 1998

CUVATO, ROBERTO, *Mattia Bellintani da Salò (1534–1611). Un cappuccino tra il pulpito e la strada*, Rome, Edizioni Collegio S. Lorenzo da Brindisi, Laurentianum, 1999

D'ALENÇON, UGO, 'Le Pére Jean de Fano', *Etudes franciscaines*, XLVII, 1935, pp. 636–47

D'ASCOLI, EMIDIO, 'Cordoni, Bartolomeo', *Dictionnaire de Spiritualité, Ascétique et Mystique. Doctrine et Histoire*, IV, Paris, 1935, pp. 1266–7

DALL'OLIO, GUIDO, *Eretici e inquisitori nella Bologna del Cinquecento*, Bologna, Istituto per la storia di Bologna, 1999

DE CERTEAU, MICHEL, 'Borromeo, Carlo', *Dizionario Biografico degli Italiani*, vol. 20, pp. 260–69

DE FIORES, STEFANO, 'Il culto mariano nel contesto culturale dell'Europa nei secoli XVII–XVIII', *De cultu mariano saeculis XVII–XVIII. Acta congressus mariologici mariani internationalis in Republica Melitensi anno 1983 celebrati*, voll. 2, Rome, PAMI, 1987, pp. 1–58.

DE FIORES, STEFANO, 'Mariologia inculturata in Italia tra passato e futuro', *Theotokos*, I, 1993, pp. 19–22

DE GAETANO, ARMAND, *Giambattista Gelli and the Florentine Academy*, Florence, La Nuova Italia, 1976

DE GREGORIO, VINCENZO, *La Biblioteca Casanatense di Roma*, Naples, ESI, 1993

DE LUCA, GIUSEPPE, *Introduzione alla storia della pietà*, Rome, Edizioni di Storia e Letteratura, 1962

DE MAIO, ROMEO, *I modelli culturali della Controriforma. Le biblioteche dei conventi italiani alla fine del Cinquecento*, in ID., *Riforme e miti nella Chiesa del Cinquecento*, Naples, Guida, 1973, pp. 365–81

DE RÉCALDE, IVAN, *Les jésuites sous Aquaviva*, Paris, Librairie Moderne, 1927

Decrees of the Ecumenical Councils, Norman P. Tanner (ed.), vol. 2, *Trent to Vatican II*, Sheed and Ward, and Georgetown University Press, 1990

DEL RE, NICOLA, *La Curia romana. Lineamenti storico-giuridici*, Rome, Libreria Editrice Vaticana, 1998 (IV edn)

DEL SOLDATO, EVA, 'La preghiera di un alessandrinista: i commenti al Pater noster di Simone Porzio', *Rinascimento*, XLVI, 2006, pp. 53–71

Devozioni e pietà popolare fra Seicento e Settecento: il ruolo delle congregazioni e degli ordini religiosi, Stefania Nanni (ed.), *Dimensioni e Problemi della Ricerca Storica*, II, 1994, pp. 5–290

DI FILIPPO BAREGGI, CLAUDIA, 'Libri e letture nella Milano di San Carlo Borromeo', *Stampa, libri e letture a Milano nell'età di Carlo Borromeo*, N. RAPONI – A. TURCHINI (eds), Milan, Vita e Pensiero, 1992, pp. 39–96

DITCHFIELD, SIMON, *Liturgy, Sanctity and History in Tridentine Italy*, Cambridge, Cambridge University Press, 1995

Domenico Scandella known as Menocchio: his trials before the Inquisition (1583–1599), Andrea Del Col (ed.), translated by John and Anne C. Tedeschi Binghamton, N.Y., Medieval & Renaissance Texts & Studies, 1996 (first Italian edition: *Domenico Scandella, detto Menocchio. I processi dell'Inquisizione (1583–1599)*, Pordenone, Edizioni Biblioteca dell'Immagine, 1990)

DOMPNIER, BERNARD, 'Les hommes d'Eglise et la superstition entre XVII et XVIII siècles', ID. (ed.), *La superstition à l'âge des Lumières*, Paris, Champion, 1998, pp. 13–47

DONATI, CLAUDIO, 'A project of 'expurgation' by the Congregation of the Index: treatises on duelling', *Church, culture and censorship in early modem Italy*, pp. 134–62

DUNI, MATTEO, *Tra religione e magia. Storia del prete modenese Guglielmo Campana (1460?–1541)*, Florence, Olschki, 1999

DYKMANS, MARC, 'Les bibliothèques des religieux d'Italie en l'an 1600', *Archivum Historiae Pontificiae*, XXIV, 1986, pp. 385–404

ELIZONDO, FIDEL, 'El "Breve Discorso" de Juan de Fano sobre la pobreza franciscana', *Collectanea Francescana*, XLVIII, 1978, pp. 31–65

Elogi di Liguri illustri, second edition re-edited, corrected, and expanded by D.L. Grillo, Genoa-Turin, 1846–77, 4 vols

ERNST, GERMANA, *Il ritrovato* Apologeticum *di Campanella al Bellarmino in difesa della religione naturale*, in 'Rivista di storia della filosofia', XLVII, 1992, pp. 565–86

ERNST, GERMANA, *Tommaso Campanella. La vita, le opera*, Rome-Bari, Laterza, 2002

ERRERA, ANDREA, *Processus in causa fidei. L'evoluzione dei manuali inquisitoriali nei secoli XVI–XVIII e il manuale inedito di un inquisitore perugino*, Bologna, Monduzzi Editore, 2000

ESZER, AMBROSIUS, 'Niccolò Riccardi, O.P. – "padre Mostro" (1585–1639)', *Angelicum*, LX, 1989, pp. 458–61

EUBEL, CONRADUS – VAN GULIK, GUGLIELMUS, *Hierarchia catholica medii et recentioris aevi*, vol. III, Monasterii, sumptibus et typis Librariae Regensbergianae, 1923

FANTINI, MARIA PIA, 'La circolazione clandestina dell'orazione di Santa Marta: un episodio modenese', *Donna, disciplina, creanza cristiana dal XV al XVII secolo. Studi e testi a stampa*, G. Zarri (ed.), Rome, Edizioni di Storia e Letteratura, 1996, pp. 45–65

FANTINI, MARIA PIA, 'Saggio per un catalogo bibliografico dai processi dell'Inquisizione: orazioni, scongiuri, libri di segreti (Modena 1571–1608)', in *Annali dell'Istituto storico italo-germanico in Trento*, XXV, 1999, pp. 587–668

FANTINI, MARIA PIA, 'Censura romana e orazioni: modi, tempi, formule (1571–1620)', *L'Inquisizione e gli storici: un cantiere aperto*, Atti dei convegni Lincei, Rome, Accademia Nazionale dei Lincei, 2000, pp. 221–44

FANTINI, MARIA PIA, 'Lo Scriniolum di Fra Giovanni Battista Porcelli (1612): da un archivio di lettere alla formazione di un manuale', *L'Inquisizione romana: metodologia delle fonti e storia istituzionale*, A. Del Col and G. Paolin (eds), Trieste, Edizioni Università di Trieste, 2000, pp. 199–256

FERRARI, LUIGI, *Onomasticon. Repertorio biobibliografico degli scrittori italiani dal 1501 al 1850*, Milan, Hoepli, 1947

FERRI, PIETRO LEOPOLDO, *Biblioteca femminile italiana*, Padua, Crescini, 1842

Filosofia, filologia, biologia: itinerari dell'aristotelismo cinquecentesco, DANILO FACCA and GIANCARLO ZANIER (eds), Rome, Edizioni dell'Ateneo, 1992

FIORANI, LUIGI, 'Astrologi, superstiziosi e devoti nella società romana del Seicento', *Ricerche per la storia religiosa di Roma. Studi, documenti, inventari*, II, 1978, Rome, Edizioni di storia e letteratura, pp. 97–162

FIRPO, LUIGI, 'La Chiesa italiana di Londra nel Cinquecento e i suoi rapporti con Ginevra', in *Ginevra e l'Italia*. Raccolta di studi promossa dalla Facoltà Valdese di Teologia di Roma, ed. by D. Cantimori, L. Firpo, G. Spini, F. Venturi, V. Vinay, Florence, Sansoni, 1959, pp. 309–412, now in ID., *Scritti sulla Riforma in Italia*, Naples, Prismi, 1996, pp. 117–94

FIRPO, LUIGI, 'Il pensiero politico del Rinascimento e della Controriforma', *Grande Antologia Filosofica*, vol. X, Milan, Marzorati, 1964, pp. 179–803

FIRPO, MASSIMO, *Il problema della tolleranza religiosa nell'età moderna*, Torino, Loescher editore, 1978

FIRPO, MASSIMO, *Il processo inquisitoriale del cardinal Giovanni Morone*, vol. I, *Il Compendium*, Rome, Istituto storico italiano per l'età moderna e contemporanea, 1981

FIRPO, MASSIMO – SIMONCELLI, PAOLO, 'I processi inquisitoriali contro Savonarola (1558) e Carnesecchi (1566–67): una proposta di interpretazione', *Rivista di storia e letteratura religiosa*, XVII, 1982, pp. 200–252

FIRPO, MASSIMO – MARCATTO, DARIO, *Il processo inquisitoriale del cardinal Giovanni Morone*, vol. II, t. 1, Rome, 1984

FIRPO, MASSIMO, 'Pasquinate', *Rivista storica italiana*, XCVI, 1984, pp. 600–621

FIRPO, MASSIMO, *Tra alumbrados e 'spirituali". Studi su Juan de Valdés e il valdesianesimo nella crisi religiosa del '500 italiano*, Florence, Olschki, 1990

FIRPO, MASSIMO, *Inquisizione romana e Controriforma. Studi sul cardinal Giovanni Morone e il suo processo d'eresia*, Bologna, Il Mulino, 1992

FIRPO, MASSIMO, *Nel labirinto del mondo. Lorenzo Davidico tra santi, eretici, inquisitori*, vol. I, Florence, Olschki, 1992

FIRPO, MASSIMO, *Riforma protestante ed eresie nell'Italia del Cinquecento*, Rome-Bari, Laterza, 1993

FIRPO, MASSIMO, *Gli affreschi di Pontormo a San Lorenzo. Eresia, politica e cultura nella Firenze di Cosimo I*, Turin, Einaudi, 1997

FIRPO, MASSIMO, *Dal sacco di Roma all'Inquisizione. Studi su Juan de Valdes e la Riforma italiana*, Alessandria, edizioni dell'Orso, 1998

FIRPO, MASSIMO, ' "Boni christiani merito vocantur haeretici". Bernardino Ochino e la tolleranza', *La formazione storica della alterità. Studi di storia della tolleranza nell'età moderna offerti ad Antonio Rotondò*, promossi da H. Méchoulan, R.H. Popkin, G. Ricuperati, L. Simonutti, Firenze, Olschki (Studi e testi per la storia della tolleranza in Europa nei secoli XVT–XVIII, vol. 5), 2001, 1, pp. 161–244.

FONTANA, VINCENZO MARIA, *Syllabus magistrorum Sacri Palatii Apostolici*, Rome, ex typ. N.A. Tinassii, 1663

FRAGNITO, GIGLIOLA, 'Per lo studio dell'epistolografia volgare del Cinquecento: le lettere di Ludovico Beccadelli', *Bibliothèque d'Humanisme et Renaissance*, XLIII, 1980, pp. 61–87

FRAGNITO, GIGLIOLA, *Gasparo Contarini. Un magistrato veneziano al servizio della Cristianità*, Florence, Olschki, 1988

FRAGNITO, GIGLIOLA, *In museo e in villa. Saggi sul Rinascimento perduto*, Venice, Arsenale, 1988

FRAGNITO, GIGLIOLA, 'Evangelismo e intransigenti nei difficili equilibri del pontificato famesiano', *Rivista di storia e letteratura religiosa*, XXV, 1989, pp. 20–47

FRAGNITO, GIGLIOLA, 'Le contraddizioni di un censore: Ludovico Beccadelli di fronte al Panormita e al Boccaccio', in *Studi in memoria di Paola Medioli Masotti*, F. Magnani (ed.), Naples, Loffredo editore, 1995, pp. 153–71

FRAGNITO, GIGLIOLA, 'La censura libraria tra Congregazione dell'Indice, Congregazione dell'Inquisizione e Maestro del Sacro Palazzo (1571–1596)', *La censura libraria nell'Europa del Cinquecento*, U. Rozzo (ed.), Convegno Internazionale di Studi, Cividale del Friuli, 9–10 November 1995, Udine, Forum, 1997, pp. 163–75

FRAGNITO, GIGLIOLA, *La Bibbia al rogo. La censura ecclesiastica e i volgarizzamenti della Scrittura (1471–1605)*, Bologna, Il Mulino, 1997

FRAGNITO, GIGLIOLA, ' "Li libbri non zò rrobba da cristiano": la letteratura italiana e l'indice di Clemente VIII (1596)', *Schifanoia*, XIX, 1999, pp. 123–35

FRAGNITO, GIGLIOLA, 'La censura ecclesiastica e Girolamo Savonarola', *Rivista di Storia e Letteratura Religiosa*, XXXV, 1999, pp. 501–29

FRAGNITO, GIGLIOLA, 'Aspetti e problemi della censura espurgatoria', *L'Inquisizione e gli storici: un cantiere aperto*, Accademia Nazionale dei Lincei, Rome 24–25 June 1999, Rome, Accademia dei Lincei, 2000, pp. 161–70

FRAGNITO, GIGLIOLA, 'Dichino corone e rosari: censura ecclesiastica e libri di devozione', *Cheiron*, XVII, 2000, pp. 135–58

FRAGNITO, GIGLIOLA, 'In questo vasto mare de libri prohibiti et sospesi tra tanti scogli di varietà et controversie": la censura ecclesiastica tra la fine del Cinquecento e i primi del Seicento', *Censura ecclesiastica e cultura politica in Italia tra Cinquecento e Seicento.* Atti della VI Giornata Luigi Firpo, C. Stango (ed.), Turin, Luigi Firpo Foundation, 5 March 1999, Florence, Olschki, 2001, pp. 1–35

FRAGNITO, GIGLIOLA, *L'applicazione dell'indice dei libri proibiti di Clemente VIII*, in 'Archivio storico italiano', CLIX, 2001, pp. 107–49

FRAGNITO, GIGLIOLA, *Proibito capire. Chiesa e lingua volgare nella prima età moderna*, Bologna, Il Mulino, 2005

FRAJESE, VITTORIO, 'La revoca dell'Index sistino e la curia romana (1588–1596)', *Nouvelles de la République des Lettres*, I, 1986, pp. 15–49

FRAJESE, VITTORIO, *Il popolo fanciullo. Silvio Antoniano e il sistema disciplinare della Controriforma*, Milan, Franco Angeli, 1987

FRAJESE, VITTORIO, *Sarpi scettico. Stato e Chiesa a Venezia tra Cinque e Seicento*, Bologna, Il Mulino, 1994

FRAJESE, VITTORIO, 'La politica dell'indice dal tridentino al clementino (1571–1596)', *Archivio italiano di storia della pietà*, XI, 1998, pp. 269–356

FRAJESE, VITTORIO, *Nascita dell'Indice. La censura ecclesiastica dal Rinascimento alla Controriforma*, Brescia, Morcelliana, 2006.

FUMAGALLI BEONIO BROCCHIERI, MARIA TERESA, *Pico della Mirandola*, Milan, Piemme, 1998

GAETA, FRANCO, *Un nunzio pontificio a Venezia nel Cinquecento. Girolamo Aleandro*, Venice-Rome, Istituto per la collaborazione culturale 1960

GETTO, GIOVANNI, *Letteratura religiosa dal Duecento al Novecento*, Florence, Sansoni, 1967

GETTO, GIOVANNI, *Letteratura religiosa del Trecento*, Florence, Sansoni, 1967

GINZBURG, CARLO, 'Folklore, magia, religione', *Storia d'Italia*, 1: *I caratteri originali*, Turin, Einaudi, 1974, pp. 601–76

GINZBURG, CARLO – PROSPERI, ADRIANO, *Giochi di pazienza. Un seminario sul 'Beneficio di Cristo'*, Turin, Einaudi, 1975

GINZBURG, CARLO, *The Cheese and the Worms. The Cosmos of a Sixteenth-Century Miller*, translated by J. and A. Tedeschi, Baltimore-London, Johns Hopkins University Press, 1980 (first Italian edition: Il *formaggio e i vermi. Il cosmo di un mugnaio del '500*, Turin, Einaudi, 1976)

Girolamo Mautini da Narni e l'ordine dei Cappuccini fra '500 e '600, Vincenzo Criscuolo (ed.), Rome, Istituto Storico dei Cappuccini, 1998

Girolamo Seripando e la Chiesa del suo tempo nel V centenario della nascita (Proceedings of the Conference held in Salerno, 14–16 October 1994), A. Cestaro (ed.), Rome, Edizioni di Storia e Letteratura, 1997

GODMAN, PETER, *The Saint as Censor. Robert Bellarmin between Inquisition and Index*, Leiden, Brill, 2000

GOTOR, MIGUEL, 'La fabbrica dei santi: la riforma urbaniana e il modello tridentino', *Storia d'Italia*, Annali 16: *Roma, la città del papa. Vita civile e religiosa dal giubileo di Bonifacio VIII al giubileo di papa Wojtyla*, L. Fiorani and A. Prosperi (eds), Turin, Einaudi, 2000, pp. 679–727

GOTOR, MIGUEL, 'La riforma dei processi di canonizzazione dalle carte del Sant'Uffizio,' *L'Inquisizione e gli storici: un cantiere aperto*, Rome, Atti dei Convegni Lincei, 2000, pp. 279–88

GOTOR, MIGUEL, *I beati del papa. Santità, Inquisizione e obbedienza in età moderna*, Florence, Olschki, 2002

GRENDLER, PAUL F., *The Roman Inquisition and the Venetian Press, 1540–1605*, Princeton, Princeton University Press, 1977

GRENDLER, PAUL F., 'The "Tre Savi sopra eresia", 1547–1605: a prosopographical study', *Studi veneziani*, new series, III, 1979, pp. 283–340

GRENDLER, PAUL F., 'Index de Rome 1590, 1593, 1596. Introduction historique', *Index des livres interdits*, vol. IX

GUARNIERI, ROMANA, 'II movimento del Libero Spirito. Testi e documenti', *Archivio Italiano per la Storia della Pietà*, vol. IV, Rome, Edizioni di storia e letteratura, 1965, pp. 351–708

GUARNIERI, ROMANA, 'Prefazione storica', to Margherita Porete, *Lo specchio delle anime semplici*, Rome, Edizioni San Paolo, 1994, pp. 7–54

GUERRA, ALESSANDRO, *Un generale fra le milizie del Papa. La vita di Claudio Acquaviva scritta da Francesco Sacchini della Compagnia di Gesù*, Milan, Franco Angeli, 2001

HUBERT, FRIEDRICH, *Vergerios publizistische Tätigkeit nebst einer bibliographischen Übersicbt*, Göttingen, Vandenhoeck & Ruprecht, 1893

HUERGA, ALVARO, 'Fray Luis de Granada y san Carlos Borromeo. Una amistad al servicio de la restauracion catolica', *Hispania sacra*, XI, 1958, pp. 299–347

HUERGA, ALVARO, *Fray Luis de Granada. Una vida al servicio de la Iglesia*, Madrid, B.A.C., 1988

I Frati Cappuccini. Documenti e testimonianze del primo secolo, Costanzo Cargnoni (ed.), III/l, Letteratura spirituale ascetico-mistica (1535–1628), Perugia, EFI Edizioni Frate Indovino, 1991

I processi di Girolamo Savonarola (1498), I.G. RAO, P. VITI, R.M. ZACCARIA (eds), Florence, Edizioni del Galluzzo (Savonarola e la Toscana, 13), 2001

I Vangeli apocrifi, Marcello Craveri (ed.), Turin, Einaudi, 1969

Il grande Borromeo tra storia e fede, Cinisello Balsamo, Cassa di risparmio delle provincie lombarde, 1984

Il libro religioso, Ugo Rozzo and Rudy Gorian (eds), Milan, S. Bonnard, 2002

Index des livres interdits, directeur J.M. De Bujanda, Centre d'Études de la Renaissance, Éditions de l'Université de Sherbrooke – Libraire Droz, Sherbrooke – Genève, vols I–X, 1985–1996

Infelise, Mario, *I libri proibiti*, Rome-Bari, Laterza, 1999

Inquisicion española y mentalitad inquisitorial, Angel Alcalà (ed.), Barcelona, Ariel, 1984

Iparraguirre, Ignacio, 'Para la historia de la oraciòn en el Colegio Romano durante la segunda mitad del Siglo XVI', *Archivum Historicum Societatis Iesu*, XV, 1946, pp. 77–126

Jedin, Hubert, *Girolamo Seripando, Sein Leben und Denken im Geisteskampf des 16. Jahrhunderts*, 2 vols, Würzburg, Rita-Verlag, 1937–38

Jedin, Hubert, Storia del concilio di Trento, 4 voll., Brescia, Morcelliana, 1974–1988

Jedin, Hubert, *Riforma cattolica o Controriforma? Tentativo di chiarimento dei concetti con riflessioni sul Concilio di Trento*, Brescia, Morcelliana, 1987 (IV ed.; I ed. 1957).

Jung-Inglessis, Eva-Maria, 'Il Pianto della Marchesa di Pescara sopra la passione di Christo' [1957], *Archivio italiano per la storia della pietà*, X, 1997, pp. 115–204

Klein, Robert, *Il processo di Savonarola*, preface by A. Prosperi, Ferrara, Corbo, 1998

Laurentin, René, 'La Vierge Marie comme signe de contradiction au XVII–XVIII siècle', *De cultu mariano saeculis XVII–XVIII. Acta congressus mariologici mariani internationalis in Republica Melitensi anno 1983 celebrati*, voll. 2, Rome, PAMI, 1987, pp. 102–5

Lavenia, Vincenzo, 'Martín Azpilcueta: un profilo', *Archivio italiano per la storia della pietà*, XVI, 2003, pp. 15–144

Lazzerini, Luigi, *Nessuno è innocente. Le tre morti di Pietro Pagolo Boscoli*, Florence, Olschki, 2002

Lebreton, Maria and Fiorani, Aloisius, *Codices Vaticani Latini. Codices 11266–11326. Inventari di biblioteche religiose italiane alla fine del Cinquecento*, Rome, Biblioteca Apostolica Vaticana, 1985

Lebrun, Francois, 'Le "Traité des superstitions" de Jean-Baptiste Thiers, contribution à l'ethnographie de la France du XVII siècle', *Annales de Bretagne et des Pays de l'Ouest*, LXXXIII, 1976, pp. 443–65

Llaneza Maximino (ed.), *Bibliografia del V.P.M. Fr. Luis de Granada de la Orden de Predicatores*, Salamanca, Calatrava, 1926–28

LLORCA, BERNARDINO, *Die Spanische Inquisition und die 'Alumbrados' (1509–1667)*, Berlin-Bonn, Ferd. Dummlers Verlag, 1934

LONGHURST, JOHN E., *Erasmus and the Spanish Inquisition: The Case of Juan de Valdés*, Albuquerque, The University of New Mexico Press, 1950

LONGO, NICOLA, 'Fenomeni di censura nella letteratura italiana del Cinquecento', *Le pouvoir et la plume*, pp. 275–84

LONGO, NICOLA, 'La letteratura proibita', *Letteratura italiana*, vol. V, *Le questioni*, Turin, Einaudi, 1986, pp. 978–88

MALENA, ADELISA, 'Inquisizione, "finte sante", "nuovi mistici". Ricerche sul Seicento', *L'Inquisizione e gli storici*, pp. 289–306

MALENA, ADELISA, *L'eresia dei perfetti. Inquisizione romana ed esperienze mistiche nel Seicento italiano*, Rome, Edizioni di storia e letteratura, 2003

MARCATTO, DARIO, *Il processo inquisitoriale di Lorenzo Davidico (1555–1560). Edizione critica*, vol. II, Florence, Olschki, 1992

MARCHETTI, VALERIO, *Gruppi ereticali senesi del Cinquecento*, Florence, Nuova Italia, 1975

MARTIN, JOHN, 'Out of the Shadow: Heretical and Catholic Women in Renaissance Venice', *Journal of Family History*, X, 1985, pp. 21–33

MARTINEZ MILLÁN, JOSÉ, 'Transformacion y crisis de la Compañía de Jesús (1578–1594)', *I religiosi a corte. Teologia, politica e diplomazia in antico regime*, F. Rurale (ed.), Rome, Bulzoni, 1998, pp. 101–29

MARUCCI, VALERIO, *Pasquinate del Cinque e Seicento*, Rome, Salerno editrice, 1983

MICCOLI, GIOVANNI, 'La storia religiosa,' *Storia d'Italia, Dalla caduta dell'Impero romano al secolo XVIII*, vol. II, Turin, Einaudi, pp. 431–1079

MITTARELLI, GIOVAN BATTISTA and COSTADONI, ANSELMO, *Annales Camaldulenses Ordinis Sancti Benedicti quibus plura interseruntur tum ceteras Italico-monasticas res, tum historiam ecclesiasticam remque diplomaticam illus*, Venetiis, Pasquali Giambattista, 1755–1773

MURRAY, ROBERT H., *The political consequences of the Reformation*, New York, Roussel and Roussel, 1960 (I edn 1926)

NICCOLI, OTTAVIA, *Prophecy and People in Renaissance Italy*, Princeton, Princeton University Press, 1990; first italian edition: *Profeti e popolo nell'Italia del Rinascimento*, Rome-Bari, Laterza, 1987

NICCOLI, OTTAVIA, *La vita religiosa nell'Italia moderna*, Rome, Carocci, 1998

O'NEIL, MARY, 'Sacerdote ovvero strione: ecclesiastical and superstitious remedies in 16th century Italy', *Understanding Popular Culture. Europe from the Middle Ages to the Nineteenth Century*, S.L. Kaplan (ed.), Berlin-New York-Amsterdam, Mouton, 1984, pp. 53–83

O'Neil, Mary, 'Magical Healing, Love Magic and the Inquisition in Late Sixteenth Century Modena', *Inquisition and Society in Early Modern Europe*, S. Haliczer (ed.), London, 1987, pp. 88–114

O'Malley, John W., *Trent and all that. Renaming Catholicism in the Early Modern Era*, Cambridge, Ma., Harvard University Press, 2000.

Oberman, Heiko Augustinus, *Masters of the Reformation. The Emergence of a New Intellectual Climate in Europe*, Cambridge – New York, Cambridge University Press, 1981

Optatus a Veghel, 'Jean de Fano,' *Dictionnaire de spiritualité*, VIII, Paris, 1974, pp. 506–9

Ossola, Carlo, '"Queto travaglio" di Gabriele Fiamma', *Letteratura e critica. Studi in onore di Natalino Sapegno*, vol. III, Rome, Bulzoni editore, 1976, pp. 239–86

Overell, M. Ann, *Italian Reform and English Reformations, c.1535–c.1585*, Aldershot, Ashgate, 2008

Ozment, Steven E., *The Reformation in the Cities. The Appeal of Protestantism to Sixteenth-Century Germany and Switzerland*, New Haven-London, Yale University Press, 1975

Pagano, Sergio, 'La condanna delle opere di fra' Battista da Crema. Tre inedite Censure del Sant'Offizio e della Congregazione dell'Indice', *Barnabiti Studi*, XIV, 1997, pp. 221–310

Paschini, Pio, 'Note per una biografia del cardinale Guglielmo Sirleto', *Archivio Storico della Calabria*, V, 1917, pp. 44–104

Paschini, Pio, 'Guglielmo Sirleto prima del cardinalato', Id., *Tre ricerche sulla storia della Chiesa nel Cinquecento*, Rome, Edizioni liturgiche, 1945, pp. 155–281

Paschini, Pio, 'Il cardinale Sirleto in Calabria', *Rivista di storia della Chiesa in Italia*, I, 1947, pp. 22–67

Paschini, Pio, 'Sirleto, Guglielmo', *Enciclopedia Cattolica*, XI, Vatican City, 1953, coll. 757–8

Paschini, Pio, 'Letterati ed Indice nella Riforma cattolica in Italia', Id., *Cinquecento romano e Riforma cattolica*, Rome, Edizioni liturgiche, 1958

Petrocchi, Massimo, 'Pelagianesimo di Battista da Crema', *Rivista di storia della Chiesa in Italia*, VIII, 1954, pp. 418–22

Petrocchi, Massimo, *Storia della spiritualità italiana*, vol. I, *Il Duecento, il Trecento e il Quattrocento*, Rome, Edizioni di Storia e Letteratura, 1978.

Petrucci, Franca, 'Crispoldi, Tullio', *Dizionario Biografico degli Italiani*, vol. XXX, 1984, pp. 820–22

Peyronel Rambaldi, Susanna, 'Educazione evangelica e catechistica: da Erasmo al gesuita Antonio Possevino,' *Ragione e 'Civilitas'. Figure del *vivere associato nella cultura del '500 europeo*, D. Bigalli (ed.), Milan, Franco Angeli, 1986, pp. 73–92

PEYRONEL RAMBALDI, SUSANNA, *Dai Paesi Bassi all'Italia. 'Il sommario della Sacra Scrittura.' Un libro proibito nella società italiana del Cinquecento*, Florence, Olschki, 1997

Pier Paolo Vergerio il Giovane. Un polemista attraverso l'Europa del Cinquecento, Ugo Rozzo (ed.), Atti del Convegno Internazionale di Studi (Cividale del Friuli, 15–16 Oct. 1998), Udine, Forum, 2000

PIRRI, PIETRO, 'Il P. Achille Gagliardi, la dama milanese, la riforma dello spirito e il movimento degli zelatori', *Archivum Historicum Societatis Iesu*, XIV, 1945, pp. 1–72

PIRRI, PIETRO, 'Il breve compendio di Achille Gagliardi al vaglio dei teologi gesuiti', ibid., XX, 1951, pp. 231–53

PIRRI, PIETRO, 'Gagliardiana 1. Un nuovo importante codice del Breve compendio di perfezione cristiana,' ibid., XXIX (1960), pp. 99–129

PLAISANCE, MICHEL, 'Litérature et censure à Florence à la fin du XVI siècle', *Le pouvoir et la plume. Incitation, contrôle et répression dans l'Italie du XVI siècle*, Paris, Université de la Sorbonne Nouvelle, 1982, pp. 233–52, recently republished in PLAISANCE, MICHEL, *L'Accademia e il Principe. Cultura e politica a Firenze al tempo di Cosimo I e di Francesco de' Medici*, Manziana, Vecchiarelli, 2004

PREMOLI, ORAZIO, *Storia dei Barnabiti nel Cinquecento*, Rome, Desclée & C, 1913

PRODI, PAOLO, *Il cardinale Gabriele Paleotti (1522–1597)*, vols I–II, Rome, Edizioni di storia e letteratura, 1959–1967

PRODI, PAOLO, 'Ricerche sulla teorica delle arti figurative nella riforma cattolica', *Archivio italiano per la storia della pietà*, IV, 1965, pp. 121–212

PROSPERI, ADRIANO, *Tra evangelismo e controriforma. Giovan Matteo Giberti, 1495–1543*, Rome, Edizioni di storia e letteratura, 1969

PROSPERI, ADRIANO, 'Il monaco Teodoro: note su un processo fiorentino del 1515', *Critica storica*, XII, 1975, pp. 71–101

PROSPERI, ADRIANO, 'Intellettuali e Chiesa all'inizio dell'età moderna', *Storia d'Italia*, Annali, *Intellettuali e potere*, C. Vivanti (ed.), Turin, Einaudi, 1981, pp. 159–252

PROSPERI, ADRIANO, 'Les commentaires du Pater noster entre XV et XVI siècles', *Aux origines du catéchisme en France*, Paris, Desclée, 1989, pp. 87–105

PROSPERI, ADRIANO, 'Penitenza e Riforma', *Storia d'Europa*, vol. IV, *L'età moderna. Secoli XVI–XVIII*, M. Aymard (ed.), Turin, Einaudi, 1995, pp. 183–257

PROSPERI, ADRIANO, 'La Chiesa tridentina e il teatro: strategie di controllo del secondo '500', *I Gesuiti e i Primordi del Teatro Barocco in Europa*, Miriam Chiabò and Federico Doglio (eds), Viterbo-Rome, Centro

Studi sul Teatro Medioevale e Rinascimentale-Torre d'Orfeo Editrice, 1995, pp. 15–30

PROSPERI, ADRIANO, 'Preghiere di eretici: Stancaro, Curione e il Pater noster', *Querdenken. Dissens und Toleranz im Kandel der Geschichte.* Festschrift zum 65. Geburtstag von Hans R. Guggisberg, herausgegeben von M. Erbe, H. Fuglister, K. Furrer, A. Staehelin, R. Wecker und C. Windler, Palatium Verlag im J & J Verlag, Mannheim, 1996, pp. 203–21

PROSPERI, ADRIANO, *Tribunali della coscienza. Inquisitori, confessori e missionari*, Turin, Einaudi, 1996

PROSPERI, ADRIANO, 'Celio Secondo Curione e gli autori italiani: da Pico al "Beneficio di Cristo"', *Giovanni e Gianfrancesco Pico. L'opera e la fortuna di due studenti ferraresi*, P. Castelli (ed.), Florence, Olschki, 1998, pp. 163–85

PROSPERI, ADRIANO, '*L'eresia del Libro grande. Storia di Giorgio Siculo e della sua setta*, Milan, Feltrinelli, 2000

PROSPERI, ADRIANO, *Il Concilio di Trento: una introduzione storica*, Turin, Einaudi, 2001

Reforma española y Reforma luterana. Afinitades y diferencias a la luz de los misticos espanoles (1517–1536), Madrid, Fundacion Universitaria Española, 1975

REBELLATO, ELISA, *La fabbrica dei divieti. Gli indici dei libri proibiti da Clemente VIII a Benedetto XIV*, Milan, S. Bonnard, 2008

ROBRES LLUCH, RAMON, 'S. Carlos Borromeo y sus relaciones con el episcopado Iberico post-tridentino, especialmente a traves de fray Luis de Granata y s. Juan de Ribera', *Anthologia Annua*, VIII, 1960, pp. 83–141

RODSCHAUSSE, JEAN, *Erasmus and Fisher: their correspondence, 1511–1524*, Paris, Vrin, 1968

ROMEO, GIOVANNI, *Inquisitori, esorcisti e streghe nell'Italia della Controriforma*, Florence, Sansoni, 1990

RONSFORD, E., 'Nuove opere sconosciute di Giulio da Milano', *Bollettino della Società di Studi Valdesi*, CXXXVIII, 1975, pp. 55–8

ROSA, MARIO, 'L' "età muratoriana" nell'Italia del '700', ID., *Riformatori e ribelli nel '700 religioso italiano*, Bari, Laterza, 1969, pp. 9–47

ROSA, MARIO, 'Pietà mariana e devozione del Rosario nell'Italia del Cinque e Seicento', *Religione e società nel Mezzogiorno tra Cinque e Seicento*, Bari, De Donato, 1976, pp. 217–43

ROSA, MARIO, 'La Chiesa meridionale nell'età della Controriforma', *Storia d'Italia*, Annali 9, *La Chiesa e il potere politico*, Turin, Einaudi, 1986, pp. 291–345

ROSA, MARIO, '*"Dottore o seduttor deggio appellarte". Note erasmiane*', *Rivista di storia e letteratura religiosa*, XXVI, 1990, pp. 5–33

ROSA, MARIO, 'L'onda che ritorna: interno ed esterno sacro nella Napoli del '600', *Luoghi sacri e spazi della santità*, S. Boesch Gajano and L. Scaraffia (eds), Turin, Rosenberg & Sellier, 1990, pp. 397–417

ROSA, MARIO, *Settecento religioso. Politica della Ragione e religione del cuore*, Venice, Marsilio, 2000

ROTONDÒ, ANTONIO, 'Nuovi documenti per la storia dell'Indice dei libri proibiti (1572–1638)', *Rinascimento*, 2nd s., III, 1963, pp. 145–211

ROTONDÒ, ANTONIO, 'Atteggiamenti della vita morale italiana del Cinquecento. La pratica nicodemitica', *Rivista storica italiana*, LXXIX, 1967, pp. 991–1030

ROTONDÒ, ANTONIO, 'La censura ecclesiastica e la cultura', *Storia d'Italia*, vol. V, tome II, Turin, Einaudi, 1974, pp. 1397–492

ROTONDÒ, ANTONIO, 'Cultura umanistica e difficoltà di censori. Censura ecclesiastica e discussioni cinquecentesche sul platonismo', *Le pouvoir et la plume. Incitation, contrôle et répression dans l'Italie du XVI siècle.* Actes du Colloque international organisé par le Centre Interuniversitaire de Recherche sur la Renaissance italienne et l'Institut Culturel Italien de Marseille (Aix-en-Provence, Marseilles, 14–16 May 1981), Paris, 1982, pp. 15–50

ROZZO, UGO, 'Sugli scritti di Giulio da Milano', *Bollettino della Società di Studi Valdesi*, CXXXIV, 1973, pp. 69–85

ROZZO, UGO, 'Incontri di Giulio da Milano: Ortensio Lando', ibid., CXL, 1976, pp. 77–108

ROZZO, UGO, 'Le Prediche veneziane di Giulio da Milano (1541)', *ibid.*, n. CLII, 1983, pp. 3–30

ROZZO, UGO, 'La cultura italiana nelle edizioni lionesi di S. Gryphe (1531–1541)', *La Bibliofilia*, XC, 1988, pp. 161–95

ROZZO, UGO, 'L'Esortazione al martirio di Giulio da Milano', *Riforma e società nei Grigioni*, pp. 63–88

ROZZO, UGO, *Linee per una storia dell'editoria religiosa in Italia (1465–1600)*, Udine, Forum, 1993

ROZZO, UGO, 'Index de Parme', *Index des livres interdits*, vol. IX, pp. 17–185

ROZZO, UGO, 'L'espurgazione dei testi letterari nell'Italia del secondo Cinquecento', *La censura libraria nell'Europa del secolo XVI*, U. Rozzo (ed.), Udine, Forum, 1997, pp. 219–71

ROZZO, UGO, 'Italian literature on the index', *Church, censorship and culture in early modern Italy*, pp. 194–222

ROZZO, UGO, 'Savonarola nell'Indice dei libri proibiti', in *Girolamo Savonarola: da Ferrara all'Europa*, Proceedings of the International Conference, Ferrara, 30 March–3 April 1998, G. Fragnito and M. Miegge (eds), Florence, Sismel-Edizioni del Galluzzo (Savonarola e la Toscana, 14), 2001, pp. 239–68.

RUFFINI, FRANCESCO, *Francesco Stancaro. Contributo alla storia della Riforma in Italia*, Rome, Religio, 1935

RUSSO, CARLA, 'La religiosità popolare nell'età moderna: problemi e prospettive', *Problemi di storia della Chiesa nei secoli XVII–XVIII.*, Naples, Edizioni Dehoniane, 1982, pp. 137–90

Sacerdote Angelo M. Rocca, Turin, Ufficio delle Letture Cattoliche, 1908

SALVETTO, PAOLO, *Tullio Crispoldi nella crisi religiosa del Cinquecento. Le difficili 'pratiche del viver christiano'*, Brescia, Morcelliana, 2009

San Carlo Borromeo, Catholic Reform and Ecclesiastical politics in the second half of the Sixteenth Century, John M. Headley, John B. Tomaro (eds), Washington, The Folger Shakespeare, 1988

San Carlo e il suo tempo, Rome, Edizioni di Storia e Letteratura, 1986

SCADUTO, MARIO, *L'epoca di Giacomo Laínez 1556–1565. L'azione*, Rome, Edizioni La Civiltà Cattolica, 1974

SCARAMELLA, PIERO, *Le Madonne del Purgatorio. Iconografia e religione in Campania tra rinascimento e controriforma*, Genoa, Marietti, 1991

SCHUTTE, ANNE J., *Pier Paolo Vergerio. The Making of an Italian Reformer*, Geneva, Droz, 1977

SCHUTTE, ANNE J., *Printed Italian vernacular religious books 1465–1550. A finding list*, Geneva, Droz, 1983

SEIDEL MENCHI, SILVANA, 'Le traduzioni italiane di Lutero nella prima metà del Cinquecento', *Rinascimento*, XVII, 1977, pp. 31–108

SEIDEL MENCHI, SILVANA, *Erasmo in Italia, 1520–1580*, Turin, Bollati Boringhieri, 1987

SIGNOROTTO, GIAN VITTORIO, *Inquisitori e mistici nel Seicento italiano. L'eresia di Santa Pelagia*, Bologna, Il Mulino, 1989

SIMONCELLI, PAOLO, *Evangelismo italiano del Cinquecento. Questione religiosa e nicodemismo politico*, Rome, Istituto Storico Italiano per l'età moderna e contemporanea, 1979

SIMONCELLI, PAOLO, 'II "Dialogo dell'unione spirituale di Dio con l'anima" tra alumbradismo spagnolo e prequietismo italiano', *Annuario dell'Istituto storico italiano per l'età moderna e contemporanea*,' vols XXIX–XXX, 1977–78, Rome, Istituto storico italiano per l'età moderna e contemporanea, 1979, pp. 565–601

SIMONCELLI, PAOLO, 'Preludi e primi echi di Lutero a Firenze', *Storia e politica*, XXII, 1983, pp. 674–744

SIMONCELLI, PAOLO, 'Documenti interni alla Congregazione dell'Indice 1571–1590. Logica e ideologia dell'intervento censorio', *Annuario dell'Istituto storico italiano per l'età moderna e contemporanea*, XXXV–XXXV, 1983–84, pp. 189–215

SIMONCELLI, PAOLO, *La lingua di Adamo. Guillaume Postel tra accademici e fuoriusciti fiorentini*, Florence, Olschki, 1984

SIMONCELLI, PAOLO, 'Inquisizione romana e Riforma in Italia', *Rivista storica italiana*, C, 1988, pp. 3–125.

SOLFAROLI CAMILLOCCI, DANIELA, 'La monaca esemplare. Lettere spirituali di madre Battistina Vernazza (1497–1587)', *Per lettera. La scrittura epistolare femminile tra archivio e tipografia, secoli XV–XVII*, G. Zarri (ed.), Rome, Viella, 1999, pp. 235–61

SOMMERVOGEL, CARL, *Bibliothèque de la Compagnie de Jesus*, I, Brussels-Paris, tome. I, 1891

SOPRANI, RAFFAELLO, *Li scrittori della Liguria e particolarmente della marittima*, Genoa, P.G. Calenzani, 1667

SORRENTINO, ANDREA, *La letteratura italiana e il Sant'Uffizio*, Naples, Perrella, 1935

SPINI, GIORGIO, *Tra Rinascimento e Riforma. Antonio Brucioli*, Florence, La Nuova Italia, 1940

Stampa, libri e letture a Milano nell'età di Carlo Borromeo, Nicola Raponi – Angelo Turchini (eds), Milan, Vita e Pensiero, 1992

STANISLAO DA CAMPAGNOLA, 'Bartolomeo Cordoni da Città di Castello e le due prime edizioni del suo "Dialogo"', *Bollettino di storia patria per l'Umbria*, LXXX, 1983, pp. 89–152

STANISLAO DA CAMPAGNOLA, '"Giardino di orazione" e altri scritti di un anonimo del quattrocento. Un'errata attribuzione a Niccolò da Osimo', *Collectanea franciscana*, XLI, 1971, pp. 5–59

STEGMANN, ANDRÉ., 'Le '"De inventoribus rei christianae" de Polydor Virgil ou l'érasmisme critique', *Colloquia erasmiana turonensia*, the Centre d'études supérieures de la Renaissance de Tours (eds), De Pétrarque à Descartes, 24, vol. I, Paris, 1972, pp. 313–21

STEWART, AGNES, *The life of John Fisher cardinal Bishop of Rochester; with an appendix containing the bishop's funeral sermons, letters*, London, Burns & Oates, 1879

STROPPA, SABRINA, 'L'annichilazione e la censura: Isabella Berinzaga e Achille Gagliardi', *Rivista di storia e letteratura religiosa*, XXXII, 1996, pp. 617–25

STROPPA, SABRINA, *Sic arescit. Letteratura mistica nel Seicento italiano*, Florence, Olschki, 1998

TACCHELLA, LUIGI, *San Carlo Borromeo ed il cardinal Agostino Valier (carteggio)*, Verona, Istituto per gli studi storici veronesi, 1972

TACCHELLA, LUIGI and MARY MADELINE, *Il cardinale Agostino Valier e la riforma tridentina nella diocesi di Trieste*, Udine, Arti grafiche friulane, 1974

TEDESCHI, JOHN, 'The Question of Magic and Witchcraft in Two Inquisitorial Manuals of the Seventeenth Century', ID., *The Prosecution of Heresy. Collected Studies on the Inquisition in Early Modern Italy*,

Binghamton, New York, Medieval and Renaissance Texts and Studies, 1991, pp. 229–58

TEDESCHI, JOHN, *The Italian Reformation of the Sixteenth Century and the Diffusion of Renaissance Culture. A Bibliography of the Secondary Literature (ca. 1750–1996)*, compiled by John Tedeschi in association with James M. Lattis, *Historical Introduction* by M. Firpo, Panini, Modena, 2000

TURCHINI, ANGELO, 'Il libro delle "Rivelazioni" di Francesco Negri detto il Fabianino. Orazione mentale e dispositivi di controllo inquisitoriale nel Seicento veneto', *Annali dell'Istituto storico italo-germanico in Trento*, XVII, 1991, pp. 379–559

TURCHINI, ANGELO, *Sotto l'occhio del padre. Società confessionale e istruzione primaria nello Stato di Milano*, Bologna, Il Mulino, 1996

VASOLI, CESARE, 'Da un centenario all'altro. Bilancio degli studi savonaroliani', *Una città e il suo profeta. Firenze di fronte al Savonarola*. Proceedings of the National Convention (Florence, 10–13 December 1998), G.C. Garfagnini (ed.), Florence, Edizioni del Galluzzo (Savonarola e la Toscana, 15), 2001, pp. 3–35

VISMARA, PAOLA, 'Muratori "immoderato". Le censure romane al *De ingeniorum moderatione in religionis negotio*', *Nuova rivista storica*, LXXXIII, 1999, pp. 315–44

VENTURI, FRANCO, *Settecento riformatore. I: Da Muratori a Beccaria 1730–1764*, Turin, Einaudi, 1969

WOTSCHKE, THEODOR, 'Francesco Stancaro. Ein Beitrag zur Reformationgeschichte des Ostens', *Altpreussische Monatsschrift*, XLVII, 1910, pp. 465–98, 570–613

ZAMBELLI, PAOLA, 'Bartolomeo Cordoni', *Dizionario Biografico degli Italiani*, vol. VI, Rome, 1964, pp. 707–8

ZAMBELLI, PAOLA, 'Scienza, filosofia, religione nella Toscana di Cosimo I', *Florence and Venice: comparisons and relations. Acts of two Conferences at Villa I Tatti in 1976–1977*, organized by Sergio Bertelli, Nicolai Rubinstein, and Craig Hugh Smyth, vol. 2: *Il Cinquecento*, Florence, La Nuova Italia, 1980, pp. 1–52

ZAMBELLI, PAOLA, *L'Apprendista stregone. Astrologia, cabala e arte lulliana in Pico della Mirandola e seguaci*, Venice, Marsilio, 1995

ZAPPERI, ROBERTO, *La leggenda del papa Paolo terzo: arte e censura nella Roma pontificia*, Turin, Bollati Boringhieri, 1998

ZARDIN, DANILO, 'Mercato librario e letture devote nella svolta del Cinquecento tridentino. Note in margine ad un inventario milanese di libri di monache',*Stampa, libri e letture a Milano.*

ZARDIN, DANILO, *Carlo Borromeo. Cultura, santità, governo*, Milano, VeP, 2010

Index

0 1341 1366839 3